Character & Context in Chinese Calligraphy

The Art Museum, Princeton University

Character & Context in Chinese Calligraphy

Edited by
Cary Y. Liu, Dora C.Y. Ching, and Judith G. Smith

This volume was published on the occasion of the international symposium "Character and Context in Chinese Calligraphy," March 27, 1999, organized in conjunction with the exhibition "The Embodied Image: Chinese Calligraphy from the John B. Elliott Collection."

The Art Museum, Princeton University
March 27 – June 27, 1999

The Seattle Art Museum
February 10 – May 7, 2000

The Metropolitan Museum of Art
September 15, 2000 – January 7, 2001

The symposium and the publication of this volume of scholarly papers were made possible by Martha Sutherland Cheng, Class of 1977.

The exhibition was organized by The Art Museum, Princeton University, and made possible by the Publications Committee of the Department of Art and Archaeology, Princeton University; the National Endowment for the Arts; The Henry Luce Foundation, Inc.; The Andrew W. Mellon Foundation; the Joint Committee on Chinese Studies of the American Council of Learned Societies and the Social Science Research Council; and anonymous donors.

ISBN 0-943012-29-5

Library of Congress Catalog Card Number: 98-83210

Book design and composition by
Joseph Cho and Stefanie Lew,
Binocular, New York

Glossary typeset by
Birdtrack Press, New Haven, Connecticut

Printed and bound in Canada by
Friesens

Cover illustration
Wang Hsi-chih (303–361). Detail from *Ritual to Pray for Good Harvest* (*Hsing-jang t'ieh*), T'ang tracing copy. Letter mounted as a handscroll, ink on paper, letter, 24.4 x 8.9 cm; scroll, 30 x 372 cm. The Art Museum, Princeton University, bequest of John B. Elliott (1998-140). (photo: Bruce M. White)

To the memory of John B. Elliott, Class of 1951

A dragon leaping at the Gate of Heaven,
a tiger crouching at the Phoenix Tower.
—Emperor Wu (r. 502–49)

Contents

Peter C. Bunnell / Wen C. Fong

The Art Museum, Princeton University

Foreword

Calligraphy, "the art of writing," played a formative role in Chinese civilization, where the past is treated as a source of cultural authority and legitimacy. Because the legacy of the past is transmitted through the written character, there is a personal and public reverence for writing, which accounts for calligraphy, more than painting, sculpture, or architecture, being the most venerated art form in China.

In recent years, interest in the study and appreciation of Chinese calligraphy has led to new approaches and exhibition strategies. Beyond the histories of script styles, formal analyses, or important studies on connoisseurship, calligraphy has reached a wider audience by being viewed as performance art, in relation to painting and poetry, in comparison to Abstract Expressionism, or as texts meant to be read. Although each new perspective broadens our understanding of this unique art, it is also important to place the origins, practice, theory, and criticism of calligraphy in historical and cultural contexts. The organization of this collection of symposium papers reflects this view.

The symposium "Character and Context in Chinese Calligraphy" was organized by The Art Museum, Princeton University, in conjunction with the opening of the exhibition "The Embodied Image: Chinese Calligraphy from the John B. Elliott Collection," March 27, 1999. The symposium and the volume were made possible through the generous support of Martha Sutherland Cheng, Class of 1977. Curators of the exhibition are Cary Y. Liu, associate curator of Asian art, The Art Museum, and Robert E. Harrist, Jr., associate professor of art and archaeology, Columbia University, guest curator, with the assistance of Dora C.Y. Ching, project coordinator, The Art Museum.

A longtime benefactor of The Art Museum, John B. Elliott, Class of 1951, established one of the premier collections of Chinese calligraphy outside China. With his death on July 25, 1997, Princeton University lost a loyal alumnus and friend. While we are saddened he did not live to see the exhibition, or attend the symposium, his collection of Chinese calligraphy and painting has found a home at The Art Museum, where John Elliott envisioned it as a teaching resource for the study of Chinese art and culture. The impressive quality and scope of the Elliott Collection, with examples of major works ranging in date from the third century to the modern period, are celebrated in the exhibition and its accompanying publication, *The Embodied Image: Chinese Calligraphy from the John B. Elliott Collection* by Robert E. Harrist, Jr., and Wen C. Fong, with contributions by Qianshen Bai, Dora C.Y. Ching, Chuan-hsing Ho, Cary Y. Liu, Amy McNair, Zhixin Sun, and Jay Xu. The essays examine aspects of the culture of calligraphy from religious writing, the aesthetics of the strange or unusual, to the significance of stele, couplet, and letter formats. Introductory essays discuss the "four revolutions" in the history of calligraphy and the importance of reading calligraphy to its practice and appreciation.

The symposium volume also presents new perspectives on the study of Chinese calligraphy. Michael Nylan offers a historian's view on the origins of calligraphy as an art form and its relation to the concept of culture. Huiwen Lu and Hua Rende contribute papers with independent views on stone stele inscriptions of the Northern Wei dynasty (386–534), an area of study that may shed new light on a little understood period in calligraphy history. Eugene Y. Wang reexamines the classical Wang Hsi-chih (303–361) tradition, focusing on a relatively idiosyncratic work that has largely escaped historical interpretation. On calligraphy in the Sung dynasty (960–1279), Harold Mok investigates the little known influence of seal and clerical scripts, while Peter Sturman explores the limits of individualism in the practice of cursive script. The period of Mongol rule in China, the Yüan dynasty (1260–1368), is discussed by Uta Lauer who examines the link between the eccentric calligraphy of the Ch'an monk Chung-feng Ming-pen (1262–1323) and the rise of orthodox styles among the literati in China and Zen monks in Japan. In conclusion, Shih Shou-ch'ien considers the social role of calligraphy as exchange items in the formation of Ming dynasty (1368–1644) literati culture, focusing on the gift calligraphy of the Soochow artist Wen Cheng-ming (1470–1559).

Many people must be thanked for their help with this project. We are most indebted to Allen Rosenbaum, director emeritus, The Art Museum, whose vision and enthusiasm were the guiding forces that made the exhibition and symposium possible, and such a success. We are particularly grateful to Charles K. Steiner, associate director, The Art Museum, for his conscientious supervision, planning, and preparations throughout this project. We especially wish to acknowledge Cary Y. Liu and Dora C.Y. Ching, who were responsible for the organization of the symposium. Throughout this project, we benefited greatly from the advice and guidance of Jill Guthrie, managing editor, The Art Museum.

This volume of papers was edited by Cary Liu, Dora Ching, and Judith G. Smith. The innovative design for the book, also used for the poster and flyer, is by Joseph Cho and Stefanie Lew of Binocular. The commitment and expertise of this dedicated group have been nothing less than heroic.

We would like to thank the symposium speakers, who submitted their papers under a very tight schedule, and our chair, Robert E. Harrist, Jr., whose advice throughout this project was invaluable. Thanks also go to Angela Darling, typist, Elizabeth Powers, proofreader, and David W. Goodrich of Birdtrack Press for typesetting the Chinese glossary. Illustration photography at Princeton was provided by John Blazejewski, and printed by Alison Speckman. Photographs of works from the Elliott Collection were made by Bruce M. White and printed by Chris Schwer. We would like also to acknowledge David T. Liu, Class of 1999, who volunteered countless hours preparing the Chinese glossary and fulfilling other responsibilities for both this volume and the exhibition catalogue. Daniel M. Youd carefully translated Hua Rende's paper, presented in Chinese at the symposium. Qianshen Bai assisted with the photographs for this paper and was the liaison for Hua. Symposium arrangements were efficiently executed by Cynthia Horr, director, Visitor and Conference Services.

Other members of the staff of The Art Museum to whom we would like to express our thanks for their help with the symposium and its publication include: Calvin Brown and Gerrit Meaker, preparators; James Cryan, business manager; Dorothy Hannigan, secretary; Craig Hoppock, building superintendent; Nicola Knipe, editorial assistant; Patti Lang, coordinator of volunteers; Cheryl Marro, office assistant; Maureen McCormick, registrar; Karen Richter, assistant registrar, photo services; Ruta Smithson, public information officer; Albert Wise, security manager, and the entire security staff; and Carla Zimowsk, former office assistant. We would also like to thank the Friends of The Art Museum for their generous support of the reception and dinner celebrating the opening of the exhibition. Throughout the planning of the exhibition and symposium, we have received support from the Princeton University Development Office, and gratefully acknowledge the assistance of Sue Hartshorn, Kirsten J. Hund, Douglas C. Lovejoy, Jr., Norman H. McNatt, and Charles Rippin. We are grateful also for the encouragement of S. Georgia Nugent, associate provost of Princeton University.

A project of this magnitude would not have been possible without financial support from many sources. We are grateful to the Department of Art and Archaeology, Princeton University, for an exceptional grant through the Publications Committee in support of the exhibition catalogue. We are also indebted to The Henry Luce Foundation, Inc., for its very generous grant and to The Andrew W. Mellon Foundation for its support through an endowment established in 1985. We are also grateful to the National Endowment for the Arts both for a grant made in 1998, specifically for the exhibition, and for the Challenge Grant awarded in 1984 to support projects of the caliber of "The Embodied Image." A planning workshop-conference in 1996 for the exhibition and catalogue was supported by the Joint Committee on Chinese Studies of the American Council of Learned Societies and the Social Science Research Council.

This project is the culmination of decades of seminar and dissertation research on the Elliott Collection, conducted by students in the Program of Chinese and Japanese Art and Archaeology in the Department of Art and Archaeology, Princeton University, and numerous scholars. It was with this purpose and in this spirit that John B. Elliott devoted over thirty years to building his collection. We hope the exhibition, symposium, and their respective publications will encourage increased interest and be the impetus for further scholarship in the field of Chinese calligraphy.

Peter C. Bunnell
Acting Director

Wen C. Fong
Faculty Curator of Asian Art

Chronology

Shang Dynasty	**ca. 1600 – ca. 1100** BC
Chou Dynasty	**ca. 1100 – 256** BC
Western Chou	ca. 1100 – 771 BC
Eastern Chou	770 – 256 BC
Spring & Autumn Period	770 – ca. 470 BC
Warring States Period	ca. 470 – 221 BC
Ch'in Dynasty	**221 – 206** BC
Han Dynasty	**206** BC – AD **220**
Western (Early) Han	206 BC – AD 9
Hsin	AD 9 – 24
Eastern (Later) Han	25 – 220
Three Kingdoms	**220 – 280**
Wei	220 – 265
Shu	220 – 265
Wu	222 – 280
Six Dynasties*	**222 – 589**
Western Chin	**265 – 317**
Southern Dynasties	**317 – 589**
Eastern Chin	317 – 420
Liu Sung	420 – 479
Southern Ch'i	479 – 502
Liang	502 – 557
Ch'en	557 – 589
Northern Dynasties	**386 – 581**
Northern Wei	386 – 534
Eastern Wei	534 – 550
Western Wei	535 – 556
Northern Ch'i	550 – 577
Northern Chou	557 – 581

Sui Dynasty	**581 – 618**
T'ang Dynasty	**618 – 907**
Liao Dynasty	**907 – 1125**
Five Dynasties	**907 – 960**
Later Liang	907 – 923
Later T'ang	923 – 936
Later Chin	936 – 946
Later Han	946 – 950
Later Chou	950 – 960
Sung Dynasty	**960 – 1279**
Northern Sung	960 – 1127
Southern Sung	1127 – 1279
Chin Dynasty	**1115 – 1234**
Yüan Dynasty	**1260 – 1368**
Ming Dynasty	**1368 – 1644**
Ch'ing Dynasty	**1644 – 1912**
Republic	**1912 – 1949**
People's Republic	**1949 –**

* *Refers to the six dynasties whose capital was Nanking: Wu, Eastern Chin, Liu Sung, Southern Ch'i, Liang, and Ch'en.*

Michael Nylan

Bryn Mawr College

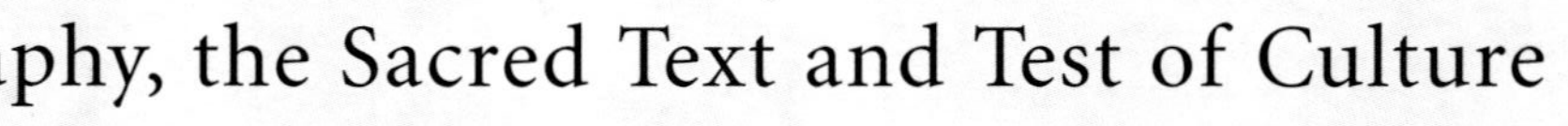

Calligraphy, the Sacred Text and Test of Culture

Few attempts have been made to explain calligraphy's place as the premier art in pre-modern China. American and Chinese scholars alike have apparently assumed that the mere fact that "a symbol system was in continuous use for more than thirty-five hundred years" or that "the two great institutions that have held the Chinese state together — the ruling elite and the writing system — have coexisted in mutual support for three thousand years"[1] was enough to insure that written forms carried a far greater aesthetic weight than in most other civilizations. Alternatively, scholars have repeatedly invoked the supposedly archaic practice of communicating with the gods via written materials as sufficient explanation for a phenomenon that manifests itself more than a millennium after the Shang oracle bones; in doing so, they have compounded an initial misunderstanding of the bones' function by wrongly presupposing an absolute continuity in the content of religious beliefs over long stretches of time and space.[2] One of the more interesting attempts to address the phenomenon, John Hay's essay "The Human Body as a Microcosmic Source of Macrocosmic Value in Calligraphy," takes a different tack, however, in drawing the reader's attention to parallels between the specific vocabulary fashioned to explain calligraphy's particular aesthetic appeal and the language of *ch'i* theory in Chinese science.[3] Still, analogies constructed between the "bones" of calligraphy and the "bones" of the body, however extensive or elegant, do not speak to the *origins* of calligraphy as fine art. They can only remind us of the inescapable *effect* of calligraphy's secure elevation to the status of art, for once calligraphy became a locus of cultural value, it was incumbent that it fit within the standard framework of cosmological discourse underlying all the discussions of science and art from the mid- to late Western Han period (206 BC–AD 8).[4]

This essay challenges the notion that calligraphy was the inevitable product or transparent reflection of certain distinctive Chinese traits or beliefs that have prevailed since time immemorial. Instead, it contends that calligraphic forms began to be regarded as the premier art in a particular time and place, the late Eastern Han (25–220), as a result of complex semantic shifts in the language accompanied by major shifts in attitudes toward texts and textualization. For well over a millennium in China, this essay shows, writing (as either "graphic form" or "literary composition")

The character *wen*

Figure 1a (left)
Seal script. Detail from a rubbing of the inscription on a bronze bell. Early Western Chou period, 9th century BC, from Ch'ang-an Chang-chia-p'o (the maker is Hsing Shu). H. 37.5 cm. From *Chung-kuo wen-wu ching-hua* 1992 (Peking: Wenwu ch'u-pan-she, 1992), pl. 107.

Figure 1b (middle)
Clerical script. Detail from *Stele for I Ying* (*I Ying pei*), 153, Temple of Confucius, Ch'ü-fu, Shantung. Rubbing. From *Shoseki meihin sōkan* (Tokyo: Nigensha, 1965), v. 2, no. 22.

Figure 1c (right)
Cursive script. Detail from Chih-yung, *The Thousand Character Essay* (*Ch'ien-tzu wen*). From *Shoseki meihin sōkan* (Tokyo: Nigensha, 1964), v. 6, no. 69.

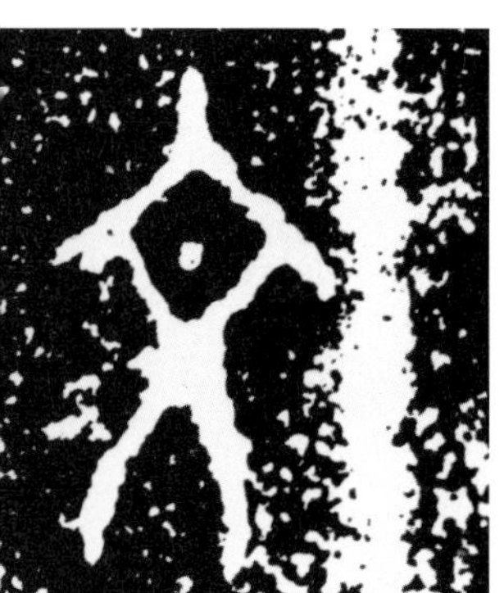

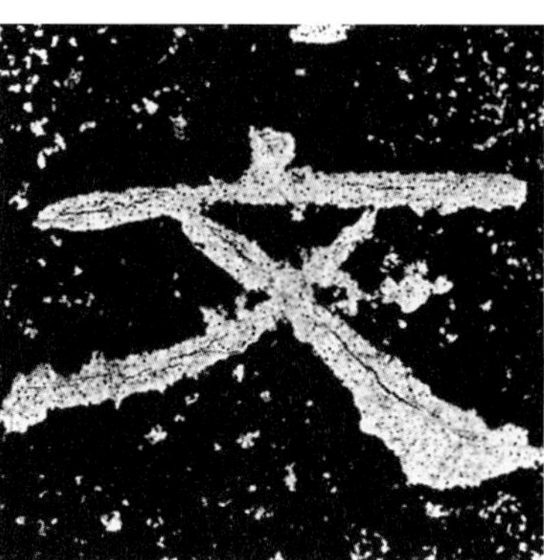

tended to be somewhat downplayed, if not positively disparaged, as a lesser technique or tool; for much of that period, the ultimate sign of gentlemanly cultivation was instead held to be the ability to quote the *Odes* or recite extemporaneous variations on them to facilitate social and diplomatic interaction. Only a fool would be blind to the undeniable beauty of many examples of writing in the bone and bronze inscriptions dating to Anyang and Western Chou (ca. 1100–771 BC)—and their beauty comes not by accident, I warrant. The refusal to attach the words "calligraphic art" to such writings therefore stems from a determination to explore the attitudes of the high culture toward the value of beautiful writing and the ability to execute it. The high culture's attitude changes so definitely in late Eastern Han that it seems meaningful to reserve the word "art" for the calligraphy produced in a setting shaped by radically new views about the function and value of fine writing.

In essence, before late Eastern Han, fine writing served to dignify the content of a text, to dignify the object the text was placed on, or both. A finely written Western Chou investiture inscription, for instance, at once declares the importance of the event it commemorates and beautifies the bronze on which it appears, so that content and ornament jointly redound to the credit of the person invested, in whose possession the vessel lies. Thus my argument that graphic forms in their earliest occurrences, as traced in the oracle bone (*chia-ku*) or the seal (*chuan*) and clerical (*li*) scripts shown in fig. 1, are meant to confer added dignity upon a precious object or an exemplary person. (This is therefore "functional beauty," which I would distinguish from "art" for the purposes of this essay.) In the late Eastern Han, by contrast, fine writing begins to be connected with the special abilities and qualities of the person who does it—no longer an anonymous artisan employed by a person of high social status but rather a person of high status himself. By the late second and early third century AD, the period that witnesses the creation of the standard (*k'ai*), running (*hsing*), and cursive (*ts'ao*; fig. 1) scripts,[5] elegant writing is thought to reveal the extraordinary dignity of the writer. It is this double change—the change of executant from anonymous servant to admired artist and the change by which fine writing no longer embellishes production but discloses the producer—that makes it useful for us to reserve the word "art" for the products of the latter.

Discussions of the origins of calligraphy have hitherto been structured largely in terms of stark dichotomies: form vs. content, decoration vs. substance, religious vs. secular, individualistic vs. public-minded impulses. Such dichotomies, usually treated as transhistorical, generally muddy rather than illuminate the problem of calligraphy's origins, first because they ignore the specific historical context prompting certain aesthetic developments, and second because such formulae are themselves at odds with the spirit of early aesthetic theory in China, which deemed a facility for precise rendering to be less admirable than the ability to intimate the inclusive, the multi-referential, and the multivalent. If they are to follow this essay's argument, readers will need to put aside these formulaic ways of thinking. Readers meanwhile will be asked to focus on three words in Chinese whose historical evolution has shaped aesthetic theory. The most important of these words, of course, is *wen*, which at first means "[exemplary] pattern" (not necessarily visual) and only much later comes to mean "written text" and even "culture." The other two key words threading through this essay are *hsiang*, defined as "images emblematic of a hidden order"; and *t'u*, defined as "charts identifying the site and distinctive configurations of power." *T'u* charts run the gamut from maps given as tokens of enfeoffment to fantastic figural representations of the local gods of the soil, such as the second-century BC example from Ma-wang-tui (fig. 2).[6]

Though evolutions in thinking are never as neat as the historian's periodization implies, extant texts reveal a lengthy progression in thinking about *wen*, which passed through no fewer than seven conceptually discrete stages. In Stage 1, from the early Chou (10th century BC) through the Spring and Autumn (770–ca. 470) period, talk of *wen* ("pattern") primarily signified exemplary behavior worthy of admiration and emulation (that is, "model behavior"). In Stage 2, roughly the Warring States period (475–221 BC), the search began for the cosmic analogues to explain, verify, and bolster theories about exemplary human behavior. At the same time, a small expansion in the semantic field of the term *wen* extended it to some few select types of exemplary "writing" designed to convey a strongly transformative message, presumably because the effectiveness of this sort of magical or quasi-magical communication depended upon profound sympathies inherent in the naturally patterned world of Heaven-and-Earth.[7] In Stage 3, during the Ch'in (221–206 BC) and the early Western Han (206 BC–AD 9), the state urged literate men to abandon cosmic and ethical speculation, which might generate a dangerous disunity, and devote their energies to devising *wen tzu* ("precise naming," a brand-new term coined to mark their greater preoccupation) in support of the imperial projects.[8] Then, in Stage 4, the leading thinkers of the second century of Western Han, in rejecting the state's wealth-and-power policies, worked hard not only to confirm but also to elaborate systematic correlations between human and cosmic patterns. But even at so late a stage in Chinese history, writing in and of itself (as one sort of *wen*) was not particularly valued by the elites who at that very moment were themselves establishing elegant touchstones for its use, since the "true classicists" (*chen Ju*) believed writing too liable to loss or abuse by careerist "clerks," the narrow-minded professionals.[9]

Figure 2
Detail from *Diagram of the Local Gods of the Soil* (*She-shen t'u*), ca. 168 BC, from tomb no. 3 at Ma-wang-tui. Silk fragment, ink and color on silk, 45 x 43.5 cm. From *Chung-kuo k'ao-ku wen-wu chih mei*, v. 8, *Hui-huang pu-hsiu Han chen shih* (Taipei: Kuang-fu shu-chü ch'i-yeh ku-fen yu-hsien kung-ssu; and Peking: Wen-wu ch'u-pan-she, 1994), pl. 8.

However, with Stage 5, in mid-Eastern Han, there came a major break in thinking about *wen*, with many *shih* openly applauding the greater value of texts in comparison with either speech or exemplary behavior. Only written texts, it was alleged, could help *shih* maximize their potential for greatness in their three most characteristic activities: preserving the classical Way of Antiquity, aligning themselves with the genuine spirit of the past through literary production, and confirming the legitimacy of the ruling house. (Leading scholar-officials nonetheless continued to fulminate against the frequent misuse of writing's potentials by government hacks.)[10] Stage 6, dating to the final decades of the Eastern Han, witnessed a second major break. Henceforth, the production of elegant literary works became less closely identified with the court bureaucracy and more with a stance of outright opposition to government abuses. Given such abuses, nostalgia for a golden age associated with good rule developed in tandem with the inclination to advertise to one's peers and ruler the purity and strength of one's commitments to the realm beyond the sullied world of politics.[11]

Until the collapse of the Han, however, *shih* were too uncertain in their attitudes about the Han state to forsake it entirely as the main source of power and authority. Political ambivalence found its aesthetic counterpart in a comparable ambivalence toward certain script styles not thought to conduce to the ultimate dignity of public office, with the result that both the bird (*niao*) and cursive styles, which offered far greater artistic scope for accomplished draftsmen, were relatively neglected by *shih* and left to craftsmen gathered at the court.[12] It was only in Stage 7, then, corresponding to the Wei-Chin period (AD 220–420), that *shih* succeeded finally in seeing their own group as a viable alternative to the throne, a rival source of authority. At that point, elites at all levels searching for ways to promote their own claims to extra-governmental authority over and against those of the state and the merely literate came to appreciate the advantages of promoting high standards in elegant calligraphic form. Insofar as both the technical and ethical demands of producing proper calligraphic form could be set far higher than those for the judicious selection of texts to be written, calligraphic forms could be—and were—employed to exclude the *hoi polloi* from real consideration in this period of rapid reinfeudation. As it happened, thanks to various technical advances in the Han, a hitherto unmatched virtuosity in calligraphic form was indeed available for the first time to the non-artisan, so that fine calligraphy—with its accrued connotations of exemplary behavior, cosmic strength, encyclopedic knowledge, adherence to the past, detachment from corruption, and arduous training in the polite arts acquired after basic literacy—became the preferred form of public expression by a certain group of elites intent upon claiming high status and authority. Therefore, it was this confluence of political and class interests, as well as of technical and literary advances, that unexpectedly propelled calligraphy—not poetry and not painting—to its high rank as the premier art in China. And it has been the continuing impact of such associations that has helped to maintain calligraphy's rank among those who would base their highly politicized stances on the claim that they have risen far above mere politics.[13]

Granted, at this stage in the level of our knowledge, no reconstruction of the distant past can reasonably avoid charges that it is overly speculative, since few relevant documents survive from early China and those that do are often ambiguous. The same binome used for cursive or "grass-style" calligraphy, *ts'ao-shu*, to give but one example, also means "to draft a document."[14] Still, even preliminary conjectures about this important topic are worth hazarding, not only because they may reopen academic debate about the origins of Chinese calligraphy, but also because they have much wider implications for the study of civilization in China. According to the tentative reconstruction offered here, literate elites in early China were by no means unified in their attitudes toward the role of texts and textualization within the political process. This suggests that scholars must rethink long-cherished notions about the centrality of writing to ancient Chinese civilization that have usually gone unquestioned.[15] Perhaps anachronistic views that are part of the larger construct of a monolithic Chinese civilization have deterred art historians from posing the very basic question, How was it that talk of calligraphy came increasingly to dominate theories about the arts from the Six Dynasties period (222–589) onward, gradually supplanting the musical recitation of the *Odes* as the quintessential marker for the cultured gentleman? Why calligraphy, we must ask, and not one of the other available alternatives?[16]

Stages 1–4: Early Attitudes Toward *Wen*

The origin of the character *wen*, which appears first in the Shang oracle bones (ca. 1300 BC), is—like that of all the other oracle-bone forms—unknown. For a long time, speculation has started from the belief that *wen* represents a crisscross pattern, with the latest analysis interpreting that pattern as a tattoo on the human body signifying high status, as indicated by precious jades found in royal tombs of the time (fig. 3).[17] Some scholars, following the lead of Arthur Waley, have assumed that the single character *wen* served to represent graphically what were, in effect, two distinct words: a stock epithet of the royal ancestors, whose exact meaning is still unknown, and the word "pattern."[18] My own impulse is to counter this assumption with the argument that the epithet always extols the dead ancestor for having "set a model pattern" of behavior for his or her descendants. One early example drawn from the *Odes* lauds, for example, the remote

Figure 3 (left)
Line drawing of a jade figure from the tomb of Fu Hao, ca. 1200 BC. From Liu Tun-yüan, *Mei-shu k'ao-ku yü ku-tai wen-ming* (Taipei: Yün-ch'en wen-hua ch'u-pan-she, 1994), 41, fig. 1.

Figure 4 (right)
Bronze bell with inscription, Late Western Chou period, 9th century BC, from Ch'ang-an Chang-chia-p'o (the maker is Hsing Shu). H. 37.5 cm. From *Chung-kuo wen-wu ching-hua 1992* (Peking: Wen-wu ch'u-pan-she, 1992), pl. 107.

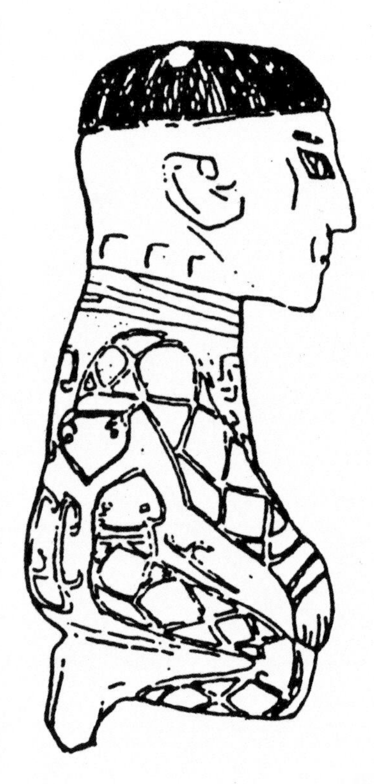

ancestor of the Chou royal house, the legendary Hou-chi, whose domestication of wheat and barley led to the creation of stable, wealthy communities organized on the basis of sedentary agriculture.[19] The earliest texts known from China, then, apply *wen* to those memorable patterns that endure in time as an ideal locus for the appreciative gaze of cultivated elites. Legitimate dynastic authority itself finally rests upon the careful emulation of such venerable models.[20] But as so much of Shang and early Western Chou history remains shrouded in mystery, it is traditions about the Master, Confucius (551–479 BC), dating to a time six centuries after the Shang-Chou transition, that would seem to offer our first opportunity to elicit reliable information regarding the possible etymology and extensions of *wen*.

In the Confucian *Analects* (compiled in the early 4th century BC?), no fewer than sixteen passages discuss *wen*, *wen hsüeh* (the study of *wen*), *wen ts'ai* (ornaments of *wen*), and *wen chang* (displays of *wen*).[21] Unfortunately, the *Analects* offers less elucidation than we might expect from such a number of passages, in part because it is a patchwork of aphorisms dating to many different eras, in part because the context for these *wen* and *wen*-compounds is often so vague as to admit of quite different constructions by successive generations of commentators.[22] Nevertheless, enough context exists to show that *wen* carries one of two meanings in the *Analects*: Either it describes the exemplary behavior ascribed to the Ancients, behavior that went beyond the basic moral obligations to kin and ruler to forge wider societal connections of benefit to all,[23] or it refers to that brilliant ornament that overlays a substance, greatly enhancing its basic value. The text establishes a strong tie between these two distinct meanings when it likens the effect of superb human refinement upon the fundamental human nature to that of fine painting laid on a plain surface.[24] By analogy, the Confucian ideal of benevolent rule through rites and music presupposed a latent harmony in life that could be brought to a still higher pitch of perfection through conscious human agency. The impression of monumental strength imparted by the Western Chou bell shown in fig. 4, cast five hundred years before Confucius in the heyday of Chou moral rule, is therefore only intensified by the considered use of fine cloud-form ornaments and intaglio writing. (Excessive decoration, in Confucius' definition, would by contrast mask or weaken the true nature of a thing rather than bring out its distinctive potential.)[25] The *Analects*, like most other early Warring States texts, presupposes a near identity between the moral and the aesthetic such that the good and the beautiful tend to be conflated, particularly when discussion turns to consider things of lasting beauty.[26] Equally to the point, only a single, very late passage in the *Analects* employs *wen* in the sense of written characters.[27]

Figure 5
Clothing box decorated with astronomical chart with the twenty-eight constellations, from the tomb of the Marquis I of Tseng, Sui-hsien, Hupei, 433 BC. Painted lacquer, l. 71 cm; w. 47 cm. From *Chung-kuo k'ao-ku wen-wu chih mei*, v. 5, *Chan-kuo ti-hsia yüeh-kung* (Taipei: Kuang-fu shu-chü ch'i-yeh ku-fen yu-hsien kung-ssu; and Peking: Wen-wu ch'u-pan-she, 1994), pl. 82.

Texts of the late Warring States period, which are both more numerous and more varied in content than those of earlier eras, allow us to sketch with greater confidence the next stage in the evolution of the semantic center for *wen*. In general, genuine Warring States texts are preoccupied with finding the ultimate sources of human behavior and social organization. Numerous incommensurate structures for political institutions had been proposed by theorists competing for political patronage, so early Chinese thinkers looked to the cosmos to verify the relative worth and applicability of such models. The consensus was that all things had evolved from an unseen unitary origin, described as *T'ien* or *Tao* and construed either as the benevolent anthropomorphic god Heaven or the phenomenal order of Heaven-and-Earth. Hence, the supreme good for humans was to be sought in a thorough grounding in the cosmic regularities. Most Warring States thinkers began to reflect upon the major patterns in the natural world (e.g., the progression of the seasons, the regular movement of constellations in the night sky, the configurations of the earth) in the light of their implications for human society, the better to support their arguments by natural and so incontestible "proofs." Literary and visual texts of the late Warring States through the early Western Han period pushed the boundaries of *wen*, always within a context of kingly rule, until it covered those larger patterns in the cosmos believed to be of supreme significance for the human order. Hence the famous injunction by the "Great Commentary" to the *Changes* (*I ching*; late 3rd century BC?) to "contemplate Heaven's patterns," even the "patterns of birds and beasts," so as to gain insight into the foreordained human task of "completing the patterns of Heaven and Earth."[28] Or the frequent visual references of the time alluding to the image of the perfect ruler who resides at the still center while the societal sectors revolve around him, in the manner of that unmoved mover, the Dipper, which presides over the major constellations of the four directions in their solemn procession through the night sky over the span of the liturgical year (fig. 5). Then, too, an equal concern with understanding the root causes for spectacular irregularities within All-under-Heaven ended in the highly detailed classifications of comets and other portents correlating form to source that are compiled from this period onward (fig. 6). At the same time, Warring States thinkers seldom troubled to distinguish between written and spoken accounts, let alone elevate the written to a special position vis-à-vis inherited culture.[29]

For roughly a century and a half following unification under the Ch'in in 221 BC, the Ch'in and Western Han states encouraged literate elites to turn away from their concern with *wen* as cosmic patterns. Strictly speaking, the study of cosmic patterns was now reserved as an imperial prerogative, and scholar-officials were to engage in it only upon the emperor's express command.[30] Instead, the newly centralized empires, anxious to suppress or co-opt all dissident voices, had their highest officials attend to *wen* in the reductionist sense of *wen tzu*, words that precisely name. On a stone stele erected at Lang-ya (fig. 7), for instance, Ch'in's First Emperor boasted of having "unified the measures of vessels and implements, and standardized the *wen tzu* in writing [*shu*]."[31] Through their standardization of bureaucratic forms recording speech, then, the Ch'in and early Han emperors, as proponents of Legalist and Huang-Lao theories of statecraft, proposed to lay claim to perfect dominion over the universe captured by that speech. Quite consistent in their beliefs and practice, the early emperors promoted those literati who composed speeches carefully, who wrote script forms accurately, and who could readily call up the political precedents contained in hallowed texts, including the corpus of the Five "Confucian" Classics.[32] Even in their occasional literature they preferred the distinctive *fu* rhyme-prose, where exhaustive catalogues of highly specialized vocabulary were skillfully fashioned into exact descriptions on set themes.[33]

Under the Han, the state's evident lack of interest in the ethical issues thrown up by the Classics drew repeated fire from many of its self-described loyal supporters. Arguing vociferously against the state's wealth-and-power agenda executed by the "vulgar classicists" (*su Ju*) in its employ were the classical Confucian masters such as Tung Chung-shu (187–104 BC), who called upon all "true classicists" to return to that earlier ideal proposed by the Sage, emulation of the exemplary behavior of the Ancients.[34] Meanwhile, classicists in either camp, the "vulgar" or the "true," knew that to further their own aims they had to display a mastery of several oral and written traditions, including those associated with the Five Classics, for emperors and kings liked their supplicants to couch requests in elegant language replete with allusions, just as they demanded proofs by historical analogy whenever major changes in public policy were under review. Regardless of their ethical orientations and academic specializations, those in government employ culled available traditions for good examples of the proper linguistic forms for courtly persuasion through indirection. Still, no particular emphasis was yet placed on the value of written forms per se, as Ssu-ma Ch'ien's (145–86 BC) *Archival Records* (*Shih chi*) (comp. ca. 100 BC) attests; quite the contrary. All those in government employ naturally relied on writing as a bureaucratic tool in the course of administering the state, as when a Han bamboo-strip document from the far-flung reaches of the empire instructs local officials to refer capital cases to the throne for final judgment (fig. 8). But those claiming to draw inspiration from Confucius specifically deplored any suggestion that mere writing (in the form of bureaucratic documents, laws, or even binding rules for behavior), rather than the propagation of ethical values through the emulation of exemplary figures in authority, might be regarded as the primary tool of governance.

Figure 6 (left)
Detail from painting of comets and explanatory text (*Hui-hsing t'u*), ca. 168 BC, from tomb no. 3 at Ma-wang-tui. Ink and color on silk. From Fu Chü-yu and Ch'en Sung-chiang, *Ma-wang-tui Han mu wen-wu* (Changsha: Hu-nan ch'u-pan-she, 1992), 129.

Figure 7 (right)
Detail from *Lang-ya Stone Stele*, 219 BC. Rubbing. From *Shoseki meihin sōkan* (Tokyo: Nigensha, 1964), v. 1.

By the end of the Western Han, the leading classical scholars at court, led by Liu Hsiang (79–8 BC) and Yang Hsiung (53 BC–AD 18), made concerted efforts to weave together all the constituent strands of meaning hitherto attached to the single expression "cultivating *wen*": conforming with the glorious deeds of the dead; attaining enduring status and value; epitomizing the cosmic regularities; and mining certain authoritative traditions—not all of them in writing—for insight into the supreme sources of order. Otherwise, they feared, the sociopolitical order would soon descend into outright opportunism and ideological chaos.[35] Since Liu Hsiang was imperial bibliographer, chief redactor of ancient texts in the imperial library, and author of many essays and treatises, including one on "reading" portents as infallible divine messages,[36] one might reasonably expect Liu to have equated the entire patrimony of inherited culture with the written word. Similar expectations might be held of Yang Hsiung, author of the first major dictionary in China, specialist in ancient script forms, and acknowledged genius in two literary forms: the epistolary and the prose poem.[37] But though the celebrated writings of both these men helped to pave the way for a much later shift in focus to the written word as an ideal repository of the past, neither thinker invested texts with the distinctive "god-like" or "divine" (*shen*) status that they would enjoy some two centuries afterward.[38] In the minds of Liu and Yang, written texts in general—even those transmitted from the sages of old—were too problematic, being liable to loss, misreadings, forgery, and falsehoods.[39]

Yang Hsiung, for instance, mindful of the proliferation of competing ethical visions propounded in a broad spectrum of written texts that purported to be authoritative, compared texts to more mundane goods whose real value would have to be "weighed in the balance" by a moral arbiter, the teacher, who would distinguish good from bad.[40] The quality of his teachers, not the number of texts at his command, would then determine a person's ethical character. While Liu and Yang in their own works both set the standards for civilized writing, both expressed their utter disdain for the mere trappings of culture, especially those literary techniques that relied upon memorization and regurgitation. To their way of thinking, their state and society all too often erroneously valued those techniques more than the single-minded self-cultivation of the sage, which schooled humans to render good judgments.[41] In consequence, their contemporaries' attention was often sadly diverted from the more remarkable insights open to them regarding human beings' inborn potential to track and inscribe mysteriously—without recourse to ordinary reading or writing—the cosmic-social harmonies in All-under-Heaven through sagely behavior. The extraordinary power of *wen* as sublime pattern surpasses the utilitarian confines of conventional writing.

Figure 8
Bamboo slips unearthed in Wu-wei, Kansu, Western Han dynasty (206 BC–AD 9). Each approx. 23.3 x 1 cm. The text puts the phrase "Sovereign Emperor, His Majesty" on its own bamboo strip to ritually indicate the extraordinary nature of the authority invested in the Son of Heaven. The next strip orders local officials to "broadly fulfill the King's Instructions" in their administration of justice. From *Chung-kuo mei-shu ch'üan-chi, Shu-fa chuan-k'o pien* (Peking: Jen-min mei-shu ch'u-pan-she, 1987), v. 1, pl. 47.

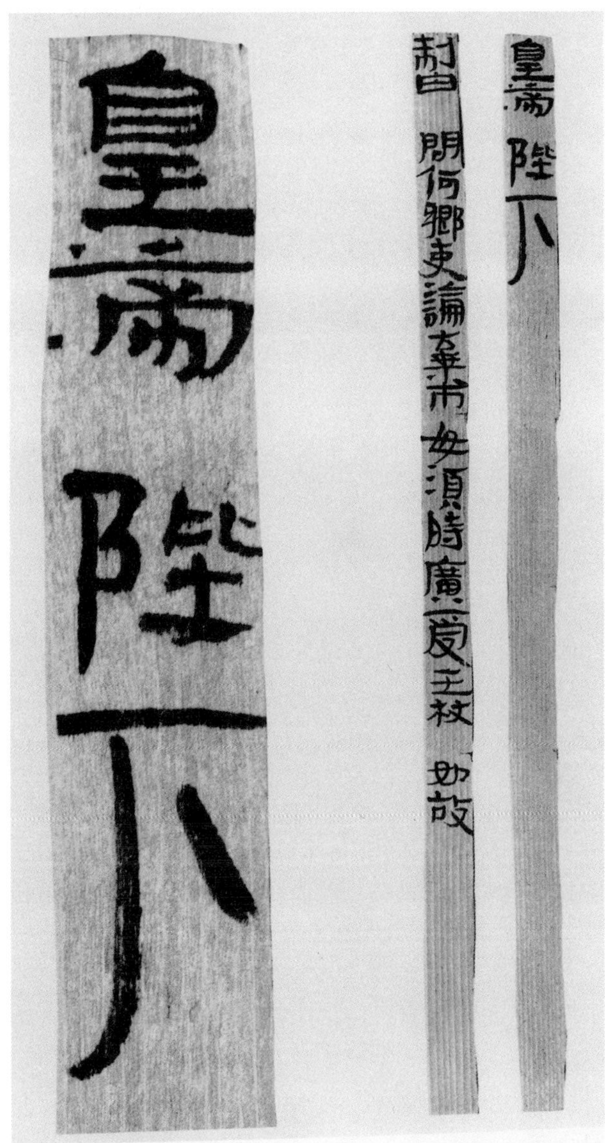

Figure 9

Nine Palaces Diagram (*Chiu-kung t'u*) and *Table of Branches and Stems* (*Kan-chih piao*), detail from the *Book of Hsing te*, version B, ca. 168 BC, from tomb no. 3 at Ma-wang-tui. Ink and color on silk, 44 x 84 cm. From Fu Chü-yu and Ch'en Sung-chiang, *Ma-wang-tui Han mu wen-wu* (Changsha: Hu-nan ch'u-pan-she, 1992), 135.

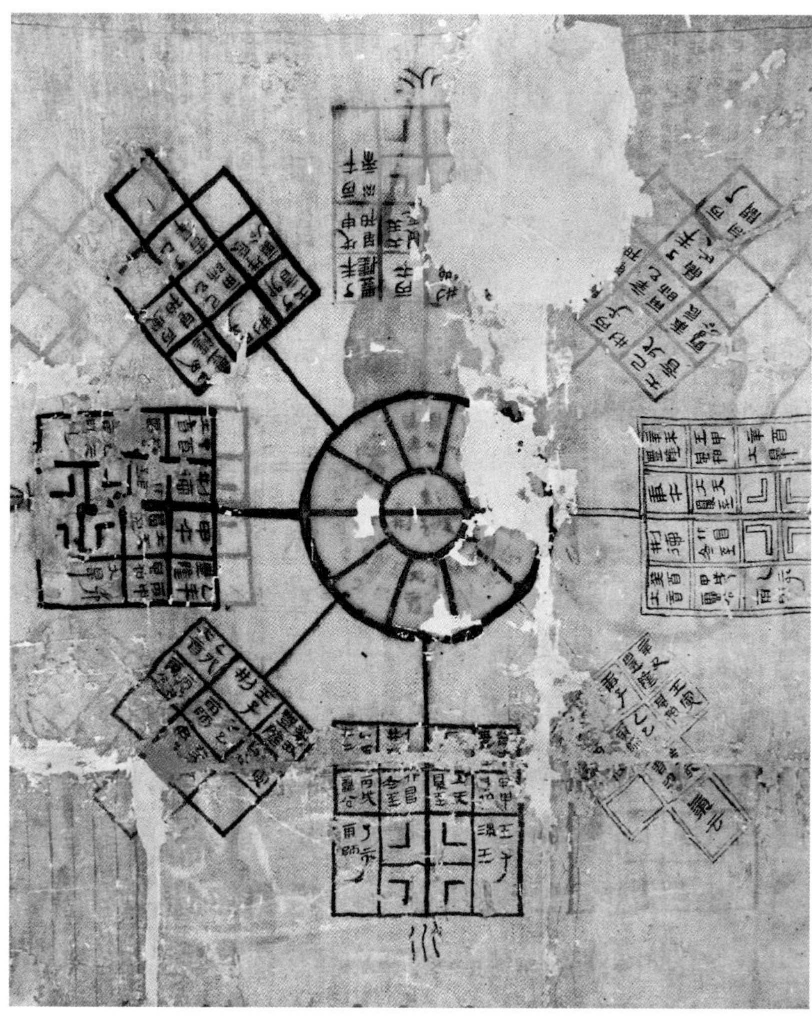

Expanding upon the work of Hsün-tzu (d. ?235 BC), Liu and Yang stressed the aesthetic dimensions of good behavior, conceived as that conjunction of the pragmatic and the moral that captures the essence of the cosmic Tao. The gentleman was himself to become an "image" or "emblem" of virtue for others; that was, in fact, his sole function.[42] Like Hsün-tzu, these classicists decried the false discrimination and over-discrimination of the sophists as much as a lack of discrimination. For in their views, human beings approached divinity to the degree that they exemplified inclusiveness, rather than "one-sidedness," partiality, or the exclusionary impulse. Believing as they did that mere writing "could not completely express words, or words, ideas,"[43] they were more interested in "schemata of recurrent patterns, ultimate origins, and numerical categories implying totality"[44]—all compact distillations of phenomenal experience which promised to order the unforeseen in human existence while avoiding the misleading demarcations and dichotomies of rhetorical language. Thus, their probable reliance on the kinds of elaborate diagrams on precious silk or lacquered wood known from Ma-wang-tui (Hunan), Ju-yang (Anhwei), and related sites, each of which graphically depicts the parallel symmetries binding the triadic realms of Heaven-Earth-Man, symmetries that allowed the good man to improve materially both his own fate and that of his compatriots by actions synchronized with the sun, moon, and stars (figs. 9, 10).

It is hardly surprising that Liu Hsiang conducted serious alchemical experiments and concerned himself with portent reading, or that Yang Hsiung pondered the subtle interrelations of the musical, numerical, and astronomical orders, since these two found ordinary language, not to mention texts, insufficient to convey the subtle mysteries of phenomenal existence. Nor is it surprising that intellectual historians hail Liu Hsiang and Yang Hsiung as the first self-conscious advocates of "the return to antiquity" (*fu-ku*) movement, for Liu and Yang intended to redirect learning back to its pre-Ch'in focus, whereby societal models would be tested in terms of their cosmic analogues. Once such a redirection had been achieved, the teachings—not the writings—of truly authoritative men (principally Confucius and his chief disciples, in which group they placed themselves) would be raised to a position commensurate with cosmic portents sent by Heaven. Taking their notion of Confucius as guide, these classical masters insisted on the unassailable propriety of the noble man's preoccupation with the full range of ideas associated with *wen*, though such a preoccupation often enough led moralists to condemn the state's concerns.[45] Only through such a holistic approach could the person of cultivation eventually develop the requisite level of taste to experience the keenest pleasure—equally moral and aesthetic in its dimensions—in immersing the self in the archaic grandeur of the classical models. Confronted with the delectable examples of the sages, whose lives combined social utility and eternal beauty in equal measure, the good man would have no trouble rejecting as second-rate the showy surface glitter found in later decorative forms.[46]

Up to the very end of Stage 4 in late Western Han, then, the extant literary record is clear on several key points. Ordinary written texts, not to mention script forms, though useful in the maintenance of empire and the furtherance of careers, were by no stretch of the imagination to be regarded as inherently "divine." Only a few revelatory messages directly inscribed in unusual written forms by the gods on rare materials (e.g., on human or animal body parts, or on precious jades) merited that adjective, for example, the mysterious River Chart and Lo Writing, magic squares miraculously traced on the backs of a turtle and a dragon.[47] Still more notably, the single-minded desire to exemplify cosmic and social principles, in perfect replication of the Ancients' humane example, was best awakened by an acquaintance with charismatic behavior, not by mere knowledge of past speeches or events written down.

Stage 5: The First Watershed with New Paradigms for *Wen*

Just at this juncture, however, the first sign appeared to herald what shortly would become a revolution in attitudes about texts and textualization. Around 5 BC, Liu Hsiang's son, Liu Hsin (53 BC–AD 23), whose fame as a classicist rivaled that of his famous father, lodged a formal letter of protest at court, complaining that the court-appointed Academicians (*po-shih*) were more anxious to protect their own professional privileges than to discover the essential ethical truths laid down by the masters of classical antiquity; as a result, the Academicians shamefully persisted in upholding their own modern-script (*chin-wen*) versions of the Five Classics, despite the undeniable superiority of recently discovered versions transcribed in archaic (that is, pre-Ch'in; *ku-wen*) script.

As one of the most important archaic-script texts had been attributed to a sage who allegedly had "himself seen the Master," Liu Hsin's main argument in support of the *ku-wen* manuscripts' superiority sharply distinguished between texts that basically transcribed "what had been passed along by hearsay" down through the ages (by which he meant the modern-script versions) and texts that transcribed "what had been personally witnessed" (the archaic-script versions). Even across the ages, one can feel the scorching anger that Liu Hsin leveled at those Academicians who had the audacity to "trust to oral transmission and turn their backs on written records transmitted [from the past]."[48] "The level of detailed knowledge could never be the same," he concludes, in the two sorts of texts.[49] To put Liu Hsin's remarks in context, we must remember that in mid- to late Western

Figure 10
Astronomical charts with drawings and transcript,.divination board and drawing from the tomb of the Marquis of Ju-yang, Anhwei, ca. 173–65 BC. Black lacquer on wood. From Toru Nakano et al., *Bronze Mirrors From Ancient China: Donald H. Graham, Jr. Collection* (Hong Kong: Techpearl Printing Ltd., 1994), 46.

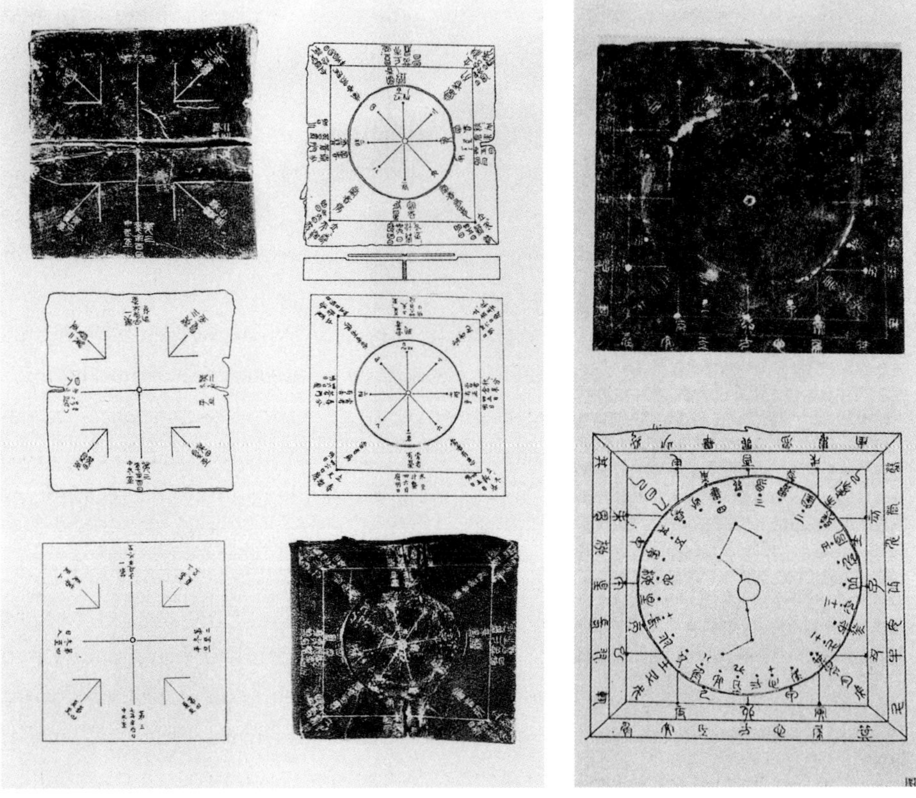

Han, occasional finds of *ku wen* characters preserved on bronze, bamboo, and silk served to remind some scholar-officials that, at least in some cases, writing had helped to preserve the genuine Way of the Ancients down through the ages.[50] Indeed, if the archaic/modern script (*chin-wen/ku-wen*) controversy had any significance for Han, it must have lain in the stark choice it presented literati on the all-important subject of their Central States' heritage, a choice between truths supposedly contained in long-standing oral traditions and truths transmitted through texts. For the modern-script side represented a host of ethical teachings embodied first in oral traditions and then transcribed at a relatively late date in the current Han script, while the archaic-script proponents claimed to have in their possession more accurate written records dating back to the Golden Ages of the distant past.

Of course, neither the sporadic "discoveries" of texts inscribed in nearly indecipherable archaic script nor Liu Hsin's excoriations could ever on their own have occasioned an entire revolution in paradigms. But some sort of quiet revolution had occurred by the second half of the first century AD; gradually, old notions of *wen* as behavioral patterns tied to the cosmic order were supplemented and then overshadowed by a newer idea of *wen* as textual production of benefit to the state. That cannot be doubted, if the literary works of Pan Piao (3–54) and his son Pan Ku (32–92) are at all representative of their era (see below). Unfortunately, the extant texts dating to the period do not satisfactorily explain this revolution. Indeed, their authors seem quite unaware that a revolution has taken place. After all, so much within the upper echelons of the court bureaucracy had remained the same. The demand for careful paperwork in a centralized bureaucratic empire was no greater than it had been in the preceding centuries—though the invention of cheap paper around the year 105, which facilitated the production of multiple copies of standard works, obviously increased the likelihood that vital records would be preserved through the physical medium of texts.[51] Nor were the desires to maintain and expand the empire especially new, even if such desires always came back to writing. From its early days, the administration of far-flung regions had meant frequent written exchanges from capital to outlying district, each of which attested to the absolute superiority of a unified written script over a jumble of local variants.

Despite such obvious continuities, it seems that a number of factors may have converged in the early first century AD, sparking an impulse to privilege state-approved literary production and thereby exempting some specific types of written text from the old charges that they were the last refuge of career functionaries willing to embrace the letter but not the spirit of the past. We can trace to this time, for instance, a self-conscious desire to separate the wordmeisters (a group once confined to legalistic jurists but now subsuming all court entertainers, with both types of servant equally liable to charges of sycophancy) from the *shih*, who have been destined for high office and great responsibility by virtue of their thorough schooling in classical traditions.[52] In consequence, the foremost literary figures of the age sought to make their rhyme-prose pieces (*fu*) much less verbal and more textual, for by that means they might not only avoid the "taint" attached to professional entertainers but also better position the men of their class to claim a kind of moral parity with the reigning emperor.[53] Yang Hsiung, far more than the poet Ssu-ma Hsiang-ju (ca. 179–117 BC) before him, had already aimed for new effects which relied to an unprecedented degree on the visual pleasures to be had from graphic complexity or graphic alliteration, and from the use of disyllabic or polysyllabic *impressifs* to suggest the sensory experiences of light and color, no less than those of sound and smell.[54] Over the generations, the *fu* poets' persistent love for exhaustive descriptions of exotic items and monumental sites portending great luxury and high status only heightened the *fu*'s imaginary visual impact, nudging educated tastes ever further away from the very different sensibility gained through sustained study of the relatively simple musical *Odes*.[55] The wildly enthusiastic reception accorded such supremely artful works, in other words, may well have weaned gentlefolk away from their older habits of oral recitation within the *Odes*' traditions, habits that had previously been the hallmark of ultimate refinement.[56] Perhaps also the introduction of Buddhist ideas into China moved men to associate sagely wisdom more often with the eye than with the ear.[57]

At any rate, during this same period, from late Western Han through the Wang Mang (r. 9–23) interregnum and the early Eastern Han periods, various court factions at predictable intervals "discovered" miraculous *t'u* (charts) and lengthier apocryphal texts testifying to the divine authority invested in one or another of the rival claimants for the throne. Despite the inevitable reactions by skeptics, this may have succeeded in reconfirming for some the sacred origin of graphic images, signifying legitimate authority.[58] At the very least, each new revelation received from Heaven or the Ancients sent conscientious scholars scurrying once more to try to render current interpretations of classical texts doubt-free, though a spate of extracanonical communications could only complicate the problem of deciphering texts of great age or dubious provenance.[59]

Still, political calculations among the *shih* are probably the major factor leading to the growing emphasis on text-based knowledge. In the wake of the invention of the first truly cheap paper in the first century AD, literacy had become much more widespread. Some hereditary elites responded to this change with considerable alarm, anxious lest the state's limited political patronage be shared with the *arrivistes*, defined as those who had merely learnt texts through texts, without spending long years practicing the classics and the allied arts under the tutelage of acknowledged masters. After all, the numbers of literate candidates for office were multiplying far too rapidly for the state apparatus to absorb them, with the result that men of privilege began to engage in sedulous self-promotion via textual genealogies and the genealogizing of their preferred texts. All of this, in turn, generated a vastly changed intellectual climate in the Eastern Han.[60] (Interestingly enough, however, none of the Eastern Han elite foresaw how much the textualization of classical traditions would itself contribute to the growing tendency to critique the literary basis for their cherished institutions; instead, in their naiveté, they thought of texts simply as a way to conserve the past.)[61]

Essentially, those in power could feel confident of their ability to retain power for themselves and their circle of relatives and friends only if they adopted one of two tactics: Either they could up the ante by insisting that only "broad learning" (*po hsüeh*) reflecting a firm grounding in the entire range of canonical and semi-canonical texts—not just one Classic—truly qualified a man for high office and good reputation.[62] Or they could argue that the skillful reproduction of texts, in their literary and also physical aspects, was the single best test of the degree to which men had fully internalized the authoritative message contained in the state-sponsored texts. With both tactics, truths once assumed to lie in consistent practice informed by reference to cosmic principles and canonical traditions now were to be had only from the kind of persistence in reading and writing that few outside the highest elite circles could ever afford.

No doubt many other factors as yet unclear to us helped to effect this first major paradigm shift.[63] What is clear enough, by contrast, is the effect that the shift had upon many Eastern Han texts from at least the year 50 onward. For instance, a memorial presented to the court around the same time by Pan Ku's father, Pan Piao, offers alongside older definitions of *wen* a brand-new definition of *wen* and *wen chang* in terms of neo-canonical writing dedicated to the Han throne by its loyal elites. According to the memorial, the current problems of the throne originated in the court's regrettable emphasis on ritual training at the expense of textual learning: "Although the August Heir Apparent and the princes [already] knot their hair [correctly] and learn to inquire, and though they nourish and practice ritual and music, their instructors are not yet equivalent to the worthy and talented, and the offices are mostly lacking the old canonical texts." The memorial then goes on to propose a suitable remedy: the corpus of ancient canonical writings must form the basis for any study of ritual and music. The memorial clearly intends a correspondent downgrading of rites and music at court.[64] Shortly afterwards, Pan Ku, in the preface to his "Two Capitals" *fu*, portrayed the steady production of fine literary pieces—not the ritual splendor associated with the Western Han or the bloody conquests of the Ch'in—as both the chief and the invariable measure of the success of the ruling house. In the same work, he then proceeded to make the astonishing assertion that present-day literary composition follows exactly the same principles as those of antiquity, thereby implicitly answering those critics of the written word who had believed that it could not capture the past in spirit.[65] Whenever the educated person frames the proper literary phrases, he is said to recreate antiquity, so long as his literary products are offered in solemn tribute to the state.

Examples of this paradigm shift are hardly confined to the literary works of the Pan family, nor are they confined to literary theory alone. The dictionary *Shuo-wen chieh-tzu*, completed in about 100 by Hsü Shen, for instance, presents the related argument that "a proper understanding of the written language" is a prerequisite for participants in successful government; hence Hsü Shen's determination to order the universe through graphic classifiers and his concomitant insistence that the graphic forms themselves conserve and convey archaic meaning beyond mere sound.[66] By implication, both the activity of writing and the written forms themselves are crucial to the preservation of the archaic past in a way that verbal speech can never be. Turning then to the realm of practical politics, another stunning indicator of this paradigm shift came with Shun-ti's decision in 132 to order candidates who had once been nominated for official posts solely on the basis of their exemplary behavior as "Filially Pious and Incorrupt" to be tested on their knowledge of the written texts of the Classics or on their "ability to draft documents."[67]

Undoubtedly, however, the single most striking illustration of this momentous paradigm shift consists of a simple comparison of parallel passages describing the activities of ardent classicists (*Ju*) in the wake of two successive dynastic crises, the first following the collapse of Ch'in in 206 BC and the second following the downfall of Wang Mang in AD 23. The *Archival Records* account of the classicists, put together around 100 BC, consistently identifies the exemplary Way of the Ancients with appropriate behavior carried out in the context of ritual and musical performance. (The sole exception to this is the case of Confucius, who reportedly compiled the *Spring and Autumn Annals* (*Ch'un ch'iu*) on the basis of ancient archives, after he had given up all hope of ever gaining a position of authority in the political arena.) The comparable *Han History* (*Han shu*) account, dating some two hundred years after the *Archival Records*, converts the *Archival Records*' preoccupation with the polite performance arts (*liu i*) to talk about "the texts of the Six Arts," a clear reference to the texts of the "Confucian" Classics. The *Han History* similarly equates the Way of the Ancients with the "canonical records" (*tien chi*) of Kingly Teaching rather than with ideal conduct.[68] Meanwhile, Confucius himself, once the compiler of a single text, has become redactor of all, a man fully conversant with all "the written records of antiquity and modern times" (*ku chin chih p'ien chi*) and a diligent reader of the *Changes* text. Emendations in the language that the dynastic histories employ in the chapters devoted to classical learning would be noteworthy even if they were not underscored by additional changes registered in the same official accounts. But there are such changes. Thus when the classicists from Confucius' home state of Lu go to offer their services to one contender for the throne during the civil wars that followed despotic Ch'in, the histories say that "they carried the K'ung family ritual vessels in their arms in order to express their allegiance"; by this gesture, the classicists signaled their readiness to place their highly ritualized way of life at the service of the contender.[69] (A second version of the same story found in the same account has these candidates for public office "carrying on their backs" Confucius' *own* ritual vessels as they go to profess their allegiance.) But a mere two hundred years later, during the civil wars that rocked the empire after Wang Mang's fall, the dynastic histories relate that the Eastern Han *Ju* "carried off on their backs their charts and written texts" (*t'u shu*) when they decided to defect to the camp of the Eastern Han founder.[70]

Figure 11
Unidentified artist (9th century?); attributed to Wang Wei (699?–761?). Detail from *Portrait of the Scholar Fu Sheng.* Handscroll, ink and color on silk. Osaka Municipal Museum. From James Cahill, *Chinese Painting* (Geneva: Skira, 1960), 18. For the evolving iconographic representations of Fu Sheng, see Kaizuka Shigeki, *Kaizuka Shigeki chosatsu shū* (Tokyo: Chūō Kōronsha, 1976–78), v. 6, 303–12.

In light of this dramatic shift from ritual practice to text-based knowledge as the basis for classical learning, refinements in the textual tradition —rather than appropriately modeled social interactions—were increasingly viewed as the primary avenue by which to approach the past. In effect, the sacred past had become largely synonymous with the literary past, its culture heroes recast as literary creators. Take the case of the Ch'in and early Western Han *Documents* (*Shu ching*) master, Fu Sheng, for example, who was originally honored for his faithful oral transmission of the prescribed classical teachings to the state's minions. By mid-Eastern Han, Fu Sheng begins to appear in stone carvings in the new iconographic guise that he will have in later paintings: as devoted teacher at death's door making every effort to pass along to the next generation of students the handscroll on which he has painstakingly transcribed the text of the classic (fig. 11). Notwithstanding the more favorable climate for texts and textualization among classicists in the early second century AD, most of the conceptual strands required for the final elevation of calligraphy to premier art were still missing. Pan Piao and Pan Ku were certain that the rubric of celebrated *wen* (now largely synonymous with *wen chang*, texts of "literary splendor") should be limited to written texts (a) concerned with public affairs and (b) drawing inspiration from classical texts of great antiquity. Their emphasis on literary splendor, in other words, still did not entail a corresponding stress on the beauty of the graphic forms. Apparently, calligraphy's claims to art could not easily be lodged until the topic of *wen* in all its complexity was at least partly divorced from the topic of public office holding.[71]

Stages 6 and 7: Empire's Fall and Calligraphy's Rise

It was Pan Piao's student, Wang Ch'ung (27–100)—a thinker far more representative of his age than most modern scholars care to admit —whose work substantially weakened the previously close links forged between the favored textual traditions and government service, though Wang's work was nearly unknown until almost a century after his death.[72] Wang Ch'ung weakened these links in two ways. First, he redefined the essential project of the classicists, seeing it neither in terms of Western Han ideals, which presupposed a single-minded desire to realize the twin goals of self-cultivation and benevolent government through ritual practice, nor in terms of the Eastern Han ideals espoused by the Pans, which held literary splendor to be a kind of tribute offered up for the glory of the ruling house. Wang preferred to see the classical project in terms of the solitary scholar's ability to attain consistent mastery over the literary forms required in formal public disputations. If the court failed to conduct such disputations regularly, Wang continued, the court of history would itself decide a man's worth on the basis of his literary production.[73] Literary performance, not ethical praxis or faithful service to the authorities, had become in Wang's mind the most reliable test of a man's inner worth—and that, rather than the state's benefit, is Wang's chief concern. (In a perfunctory nod to convention, Wang asserted that such refinements in the individual personality will assuredly, if only gradually, conduce to the greater public good.)[74] Second, Wang ostensibly continued the celebration of *wen chang* (literary splendor) that Pan Piao and Pan Ku had undertaken before him. But while citing the usual roster of famous men (e.g., Lu Chia [ca. 228–140 BC], Ssu-ma Ch'ien, Liu Hsiang, and Yang Hsiung) as models, Wang cast the outstanding contributions of these men in an entirely new light. Although all wrote in their capacity as public servants, a fact that qualified them for true "greatness" in the Pans' calculations,[75] in Wang's mind these men were chiefly to be praised for their brave oppositional stance to the conventional political discourse bandied about by the "vulgar classicists." For Wang Ch'ung, consumed with rage at the powers-that-be who had overlooked his obvious merit, the force of elegant writing had always to stem from the power of righteous protest—protest denouncing the government's persistent failure to recognize talent.[76] Grave yet self-interested dissatisfaction with the status quo *is* the constant Way of the Ancients, according to Wang, rather than an occasional necessity when the times are badly out of joint.[77]

In one essay, therefore, Wang Ch'ung specifically rejects the old-fashioned *Ju* contention that one should "measure talent and ability only in terms of behavioral outcome." Such an idea, he writes, reflects a failure to appreciate the special character of literary works, the production of which ought to be the ultimate goal of all textual learning. At the same time, they also fail who do not see that writing by mere clerks (a term meant to dismiss careerists) differs in quality from the supremely valuable writing by true classicists (defined as those with broad learning). Mere talent or the ability to wield a brush, physically and rhetorically, have little or no inherent value, being the skills of contemptible craftsmen, Wang contends.[78] "The means by which the classicists surpass the literate clerks" is that their knowledge of texts "refines their characters and ornaments their talents," so that they can "develop more completely in virtue" (a term that Wang consistently equates with literary virtuosity) due to their greater command of proper models. Wang Ch'ung then concludes his essay with the declaration that when it comes to producing works of high literary merit, the skills (that is, the physical ability to produce script forms as well as the ability to produce rhetorically powerful phrases) always count for less than a profound understanding of culture.[79] Petty skills are no substitute for real art, which relies on knowing the Great Way. By this line of reasoning, writing by mere clerks, whether it benefits the court or not, is by its very nature a poor and paltry thing (*p'in*). But by contrast, the literary works of those who are truly well-versed in the classics carries a unique flavor, being spare rather than florid; truthful rather than exaggerated; forceful rather than pusillanimous; vibrant with passion rather than dead to the world. Such art, being divine and eternal, is justifiably termed *wen*, for *wen*'s exemplary patterns are by definition supremely important, sublimely beautiful, and notably constant.[80]

Note that Wang attributes to strongly oppositional writing informed by classical values the very same qualities that will a century later be ascribed to calligraphy: the spareness offset by the contained passion, the directness informed by cultivation, the maturity and "surplus" (*yu i*) capacity that so perfectly mirror the fundamental order of Heaven-and-Earth that they are rightly deemed divine.[81] Through arguments such as these Wang successfully managed to devalue many of the old moralizing texts known from antiquity without ever succeeding in promoting his own literary efforts. Quite significantly, however, Wang's long-winded *Discourses Weighed* (*Lun heng*) offers no sign that he saw any connection between the literary and the calligraphic arts, though candidates for public office would all have practiced writing in a neat hand.[82] Ignoring the possibilities now open to men of his class, thanks to better writing instruments and cheaper paper, Wang undoubtedly would have viewed the skillfully modulated cursive script on a wooden label for a documents case (fig. 12) simply as yet another source of factual information. Setting down the correct forms was no more than "elementary learning," *hsiao hsüeh*, for Wang and his contemporaries.[83] Spurred by bitter disappointment, Wang's contributions lay elsewhere. He was one of the first in the Eastern Han, for example, who felt compelled to broach the tricky topic of the complex relation between talent, learning, opportunity, and literary production—a topic that would be taken up over and over again by succeeding generations.[84] However, what concerns us here is the overall tone of Wang's work, which perfectly reflected the curious ambivalence that Wang and his contemporaries felt toward the royal house and the court. For while Wang refused to regard them as the final arbiters of literary taste, he was nonetheless willing to defer to them, on the off chance that his public protestations of loyalty might yet win him fame and fortune. As we will see, the same ambivalence toward the royal house marks the entire corpus of writings in the late second century.

Wang had composed his bitter *Discourses* in old age—when he had nearly lost hope that he, in the absence of great wealth and influential sponsors, would ever be recognized by the court.[85] But most members of the educated elite, young or old, who came after him in the final decades of the Eastern Han felt equally uncertain where to place their allegiance, if only because there remained the possibility that yet another mid-dynastic restoration might mean court patronage for their own factions. Notwithstanding their considerable disorientation, they could not afford to stand quietly to the side as the empire's administration slipped steadily from their hands into those of the parvenus: the maternal relatives of the emperors (*wai ch'i*), the military strongmen, and the eunuchs who increasingly made puppets of the reigning emperors. Inevitably divided among themselves with respect to their career prospects and goals, the classicizing elites were still publicly united in their opposition to the venality and debauchery of the court and its hangers-on. Sick of the effete scions of the Liu house, who now ruled mainly by proxy, the *shih* in the late second century could not but be irked by their present situation, which left them largely without the secure group status that they had come to expect the throne to ensure. Hence the constant stream of memorials, remonstrances, petitions, and critical essays from such literary giants as Chu Mu (100–163) and Wang Fu (95–165), Chao I (ca. 130–185), Ts'ai Yung (132–192), and Ying Shao (d. 203?). Tireless in their fulminations against favoritism by the court, all these scholar-officials of late Eastern Han loudly proclaimed in their writings their consummate loyalty to the throne even as they questioned its ability to attract really good men like themselves to state service.

Faced with uncertainty but unwilling to break with the throne, the *shih* expressed their anxieties in a number of distinctive ways that influenced public discourse under Ling-ti (r. 168–88) and Hsien-ti (r. 189–220). Three sorts of characteristic expression seem especially germane to any discussion about the origins of calligraphy. First, in an age of rapid social change, the *shih* expressed mounting desire for greater permanence through public writings on stone, despite stone's older—and quite unsavory—associations with the megalomaniacal "no-death" impulses of the First Emperor of Ch'in. It was not only that stone was thought to be a more permanent and more prominent medium of communication than bamboo, silk, or paper. The use of stone bespoke as well a desire to have later generations judge the merits of a case now presumably fixed forever (be it an individual life recorded on a stone stele or the state-sponsored versions of the "Confucian" Classics), since those currently in authority could not be trusted to display the requisite discrimination. Second, given the Han court's steady loss of moral credibility, members of the *shih* turned increasingly to their peers when they sought to determine the locus of moral authority in this life and beyond. Thus, memorials and remonstrances might flood into court, but it was the letters to peers (*shu*), often filled with seemingly innocuous accounts of everyday activities, the short but incisive character sketches of famous men circulating as "criticism by the pure" (*ch'ing i*), and the memorial inscriptions for the dead (*pei wen*) that the *shih* most avidly perused,

Figure 12
Wooden label for a documents case, after AD 25. The label identifies its contents as a register of arms and their conditions, "complete, serviceable, broken, or damaged," issued to Ta-chien command, Yü-men Pass, for the year AD 14. From *Shoseki meihin sōkan* (Tokyo: Nigensha, 1965), v. 4, no. 35, 12.

looking for signs of the times and deliberations by the just.[86] Newcomers to the field may marvel at the literary and artistic energy expended in the production of such projects, as demonstrated in the superbly engraved *Stele for Ts'ao Ch'üan* (*Ts'ao Ch'üan pei*; fig. 13), but the demand for more telling "images" of the leading figures in society arose naturally enough at a time when allegiances too hastily given spelt proscription, destruction, or death to individual *shih*.[87] Not one whit less public than the materials sent to the court for its approval, this sort of less official—and thus less formulaic—material promised to yield greater insights into the characters of important persons. Third, as the *shih* based their claims to superiority at this time on their position as supposedly "pure" and "plain" public servants (in contradistinction to the "impure" and "frivolous" denizens of the *fin de siècle* Han court), they were apt to despise anything that smacked of the purely decorative or the unserious. Leading *shih* accordingly showed surprisingly little interest in exploring the artistic potential of certain styles of writing that were not emblematic of the serious business of governing (for example, the cursive "grass style" and the intricate bird style), though such styles, in the wake of continuing improvements in the various tools for writing, surely allowed a far wider range of articulation to their users.[88] The image of the recording clerk (fig. 14), dated to 176, attests to the strange blend of conservatism and innovation that runs through the period, for the image we see presents a study in contrasts. Obviously a man who likes his comforts, the subject has a keen eye as well, and though he poses—in standard fashion— in his official robes and hat in an obvious bid to impress all viewers, he also has his large inkstone and water jar near to hand, as if to indicate his readiness to further the public weal. Faced with such unsettled and unsettling circumstances, the most responsible of the *shih* tried to ascertain not *why* but *when* the dynasty would be in final crisis.[89] And once they had accepted the inevitability of decline, howsoever reluctantly, nostalgia for the not-necessarily-so-distant past, when good order, right hierarchy, and *shih* predominance prevailed, just as inevitably pervaded the works of the opinion makers.[90]

These four tropes of ambivalence—writing to secure lasting fame, writing to gain the admiration of one's peers, writing to maintain one's public dignity, and writing to establish unbreakable affinities with the past—come together in the life of Ts'ai Yung, who was not only one of the first figures to come close to qualifying for the title of "calligrapher" by this essay's definition but also the very man to rescue Wang Ch'ung's writings from oblivion.[91] In late Eastern Han, when for the first time the quality of a man's brushwork could contribute to his reputation, Ts'ai had mastered in addition to calligraphy no fewer than three of the six aristocratic arts associated with the old Chou empire: poetry, music, and literary composition

Figure 13 (left)
Stele for Ts'ao Ch'üan (*Ts'ao Ch'üan pei*), 185. Rubbing. From *Shoseki meihin sōkan* (Tokyo: Nigensha, 1964), v. 3, no. 31.

Figure 14 (right)
Image of the clerk in charge of records keeping. Detail of a wall painting from tomb no. 1 in Wang-tu, Hopei. Eastern Han (25–220), 176. From *Han T'ang pi-hua* (Peking: Wen-wu ch'u-pan-she, 1974), pl. 8.

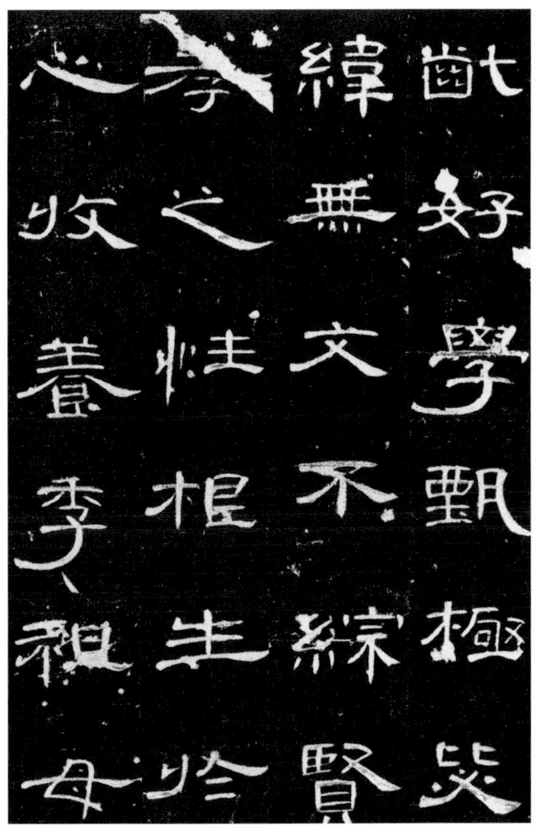

(*shu*). Ts'ai could compose and chant poetry in all styles, though he tended to favor the new; he was an excellent musician (on the *ch'in*); and he composed elegant essays presumably set down in his own elegant script. But while such arts in aristocratic Chou, in theory at least, were to be employed in government service, Ts'ai resented the throne's assumption that he would trade art for patronage. Ts'ai's official biography tells us, for example, that because of his skill in playing the *ch'in*, he was invited to court shortly after a coup in 159. Doubting that those in charge (the eunuchs and their associates) were capable of appreciating him as anything more than an entertainer, he stayed home, pleading grave illness. There, "at his leisure," he "played with antiquity," avoiding all contact with the prominent men of his own age.[92] Believing that the moral man must advertise his oppositional stance, Ts'ai's writings proclaimed his steadfast resolve to forego conventional success as a career bureaucrat, even if this meant "turning his back on the ruler." The truly great, a group in which Ts'ai included himself, preferred to "make friends with" the great men of the past through their literary endeavors, for only in that way could they actually "roam free and easily" in this troubled world.[93]

Despite his air of lofty detachment, Ts'ai continually offered his opinions on court matters in lengthy memorials bound to offend. He argued for major ritual reforms, and he was obviously ambitious for the advancement of his own faction.[94] Put in charge of collating texts in the Eastern Palace imperial library in 171, within two years Ts'ai Yung was spearheading the drive to fix forever in stone the authoritative versions of the Five Confucian Classics.[95] As Ts'ai Yung told it, the main canonical works should be inscribed on stone tablets in the capital, so as to prevent the "vulgar classicists" from exploiting for their own selfish purposes the confusion engendered by the many mistakes in the multiple editions then in circulation. Having secured the emperor's assent for the project, Ts'ai Yung personally

Figure 15
Fragment from *Hsi-p'ing Stone Classic*, Eastern Han period, 175–83. Rubbing. From Jessica Rawson, ed., *Mysteries of Ancient China: New Discoveries from the Early Dynasties* (London: The British Museum Press, 1996), 215, fig. 117.2.

supervised the preparation of authoritative editions, and with his own hand he brushed the red characters (to be afterwards cut into the stone by lesser men) on the Stone Classics steles, erected outside the Imperial Academy, several fragments of which survive (fig. 15).[96] Of course, Ts'ai's inscriptions on stone sent conflicting messages. On the one hand, they professed the state's commitment to honor the antique Way of the sages; on the other, they alluded to the uncomfortable fact that empires might rise and fall, while the monumental works inspired by the classical vision of the Ancients endured forever. No court could ever "own" men of true worth or their worthy writings; the court must therefore acknowledge its subservience to the moral Word—that was the implicit message sent by Ts'ai's vermilion characters,[97] just as the final execution of the written forms was of less moment than the initial conjunction of inspired soul and divine content.

No less ambivalent was Ts'ai's attitude toward certain script forms, despite—or because of—his own fame with the brush. As the story goes, Ts'ai believed the emperor to be too indiscriminate in both his love of learning and his choice of advisors. So when Ling-ti granted special favors to men who showed special talent in forming the technically demanding designs of the bird script (*kung shu niao chuan*), Ts'ai was quick to denounce the court's preference for technical virtuosity with the brush over genius of the heart/mind, with its mental and moral dimensions. According to Ts'ai, the "twenty or thirty people" summoned to court under Ling-ti, many of whom had been registered at the Vast Capital Gate Academy (*Hung-tu-men hsüeh*) under imperial sponsorship, were men of "bad conduct, disciples of those who rush to grab power."[98] Ts'ai Yung memorialized the emperor that he would do well to attend to the basics of good government—maintaining a complex ritual schedule superintended by the classicists and advancing men like Ts'ai—instead of offering his precious support to "those who can write or paint and make *fu*," men whose talents did not necessarily extend to formulating good government policy.[99] For Ts'ai, the political struggle could not be kept separate from an aesthetic struggle, for fine materials exquisitely worked either added to the effete airs besetting the court or they facilitated another mid-dynastic renewal of the throne. The choice was clear enough. For could not every person of sufficient refinement sense the very different implications for human morality that two powerfully beautiful objects might hold? Looking back at the kinds of objects that Ts'ai would have known from court, one imagines that Ts'ai's objections would have singled out for censure those relaying a feeble decadence in high culture, the bronze *hu* from Man-ch'eng, for instance, with its highly stylized but essentially vapid decorations composed of repeated bands of vaguely auspicious slogans set in "bird-and-insect script" and

Figure 16 (left)
Hu vessel with bird script, Western Han (206 BC–AD 9), from the tomb of Tou Wan, Man-ch'eng County, Hopei. Bronze with gold and silver inlay, h. 44.2 cm. Hopei Provincial Museum. From China Cultural Relics Promotion Center, ed., *Treasures: 300 Best Excavated Antiques from China* (Peking: New World Press, 1992), 206.

Figure 17 (right)
Liu-po game board, Warring States Period (ca. 470–221 BC), from the tomb of a royal attendant to the Prince of Chung-shan, P'ing-shan County, Hopei. Stone, 44.9 x 40 cm. Hopei Provincial Museum. From China Cultural Relics Promotion Center, ed., *Treasures: 300 Best Excavated Antiques from China* (Peking: New World Press, 1992), 40.

inlaid in gold and silver thread (fig. 16). Good men, in Ts'ai's characterization, "Contained the purity of the numinous empyrean/ Like lofty peaks [in their monumental greatness]/ It was they who issued auspicious omens and sent down spirits."[100] In the perfection of their persons, then, noble *shih* represented sites where the magical properties of the revelatory *t'u*, no longer strictly the preserve of the holders of Heaven's Mandate, were conjoined with the solemn dignity imparted by *wen*. Given Ts'ai's faith in the classically trained person as the epitome of permanent value, it is tempting to relate his ideals to items like the massive stone board of fig. 17, whose visual allusions, no less intricate in form than those of the bronze *hu*, artfully lend impressive vigor and vitality to the complex of classical notions that Ts'ai espoused. (The TLV groundwork of the stone board maintains the orderliness of the cosmos; the ornate box at center celebrates the centered self as focus of the trained human energies; the coiled serpent and tiger in bas-relief affirms the subtle symmetry threading through the triadic realms of Heaven-Earth-Man; the earthen colors detail the sacred division of the universe into five directions; and so on.) In any case, we know that Ling-ti, as a sign that he accepted some small part of Ts'ai's criticisms, in 178 commissioned the portraits of Confucius and seventy-two disciples to be painted on the walls of the Hung tu men Academy—where the likenesses of the *shih*'s patron saints, no doubt, were meant to serve as visual reminders of the inherent superiority of the *shih*'s way of life over their rivals' irresponsibility.[101]

At the same time that he was roundly condemning others for writing script in decorative styles, Ts'ai Yung in three separate pieces praised the sacred origins and pragmatic powers of the two script styles—the clerical and seal script—most closely identified with the heyday of the Central States' rule in Western Chou and Han.[102] His "*Fu* on the Brush" began quite typically,

Long ago, Ts'ang Chieh started the business
    [when he invented writing].
Quill and ink were then created,
And texts and contracts begun by this.
Now, given its institution by a top sage
and [its utility] in setting up norms,
No thing is more noble than the brush.
In tracing its ultimate origin,
In looking to its achievements,
Its brilliance is such
That no thing can surpass it!...
It records the Three Kings in their good fights,
It duly notes their aides' diligence
    [in the sacred line of duty],

By it is transmitted the Six Classics, and
By it put together the Hundred Thinkers,
So as to establish the supreme sovereign
And put in order the constant relations.[103]

Thus Ts'ai, the most famous writer of his age (in both the senses of literary production and aesthetic production of written forms), strongly asserted that the value of writing must reside in its association with vigorous empire. By this, he implicitly decried the notion that the ultimate value of writing lay in the sheer beauty of its external forms, though legend credits him with the invention of the exquisite "flying white" (*fei-pai*) technique.[104]

Ts'ai's writings elevated the notion of *ku*, "solitariness" or the will to stand apart from the crowd, to a high virtue, while insisting that such integrity be somehow employed in the cause of fuller integration in the whole society and state. Such fine distinctions were lost on the court powers. Eventually the sheer contrariness of Ts'ai's political purity, a purity that informed both his official communications with the throne and other ostensibly unofficial but highly public venues (e.g., Ts'ai's acclaimed stele inscription for a leader of student protests), so infuriated the Han court that he was twice sent to jail, where he finally fell ill and died.[105] Ironically, Ts'ai's tragic death—occurring as it did just when the vogue for elegant script forms was gaining a wider currency among the *shih*—may have lent his favorite script forms an enviable air of noble failure. Such an association would, in turn, have helped to remove calligraphy further from the old taint of craft and so qualify it for a higher place as the supreme art of gentlefolk.[106] Possibly for the first time after Ts'ai Yung's death, then, the careful execution of certain script forms identified with moral—rather than actual—rule was enough to advertise to all the world that a person's fund of taste and moral discrimination went far beyond that available to mere careerists, qualifying him for the lasting fame and divine status once reserved for emperors.[107] Still, in Ts'ai's own lifetime, his ability to write aesthetically pleasing forms, like his abilities to make music and poetry, had been regarded as a polite accomplishment only, if the official records are to be trusted.

By his death in 192, many of the elements required for the eventual elevation of calligraphy to the ranks of premier art in China were already in place. At least two script forms (the formal seal and clerical script) had attained some status with the *shih*, in view of their unassailable association with kingly rule. Also, in the absence of real leadership by the throne, leading *shih* saw themselves as loci of the divine powers once believed to be the sole prerogative of the Sons of Heaven. By this point in time, too, as noted above, *shih* as educated men of good birth were intent upon finding new ways out of their present predicament, for the customary pursuits of their estate, government service and the study of moralizing texts, were increasingly closed to them. There were too many literate people for the court to hire; court appointments were too liable to political corruption; and the official proscriptions in effect for much of the second half of the second century had excluded many potential candidates among the *shih* from office holding.[108]

Nonetheless, even in the closing days of the Han dynasty, some key elements required for calligraphy's elevation to art were missing still, chiefly a more pervasive belief among the *shih* in the magical property of calligraphic forms to disclose that divine spark believed to reside in superior humans; also a decided preference for the unofficial in both written content and script style. For when the less modulated seal script and clerical script gave way to the regular, running, and cursive scripts, with each giving greater play to brushes deftly wielded, scripts more easily assumed the nuanced forms of inspired revelations. And once the rhythmic calligraphic forms balanced firm precision with insouciant grace, great value could be attached to them, naturally enough, value that was eventually translated into a thriving art market. For the first time, we see an unprecedented celebration of the sheer physicality of the act, now thought to impart bodily health and sociable pleasures in equal measure to the calligrapher.[109] Only with the final coming together of these disparate elements was calligraphy no longer to be counted as one among many minor polite arts, as it had been in Ts'ai Yung's time. Rather, it had become a symbol saturated with fabulous associations, through whose medium could be glimpsed the sublime perfection of the calligrapher's soul.

The sudden conjuncture of the aforementioned elements is traceable, at least in part, to sweeping changes in the political circumstances of the Chien-an (196–220) and Wei-Chin eras, whose dramatic events, in the words of one great scholar of the period, "transformed China from a powerful empire into a vast cemetery."[110] As soon as most of the empire came under the control not of the patrician Yüan Shao (d. 202) but of Ts'ao Ts'ao (155–220), the parvenu grandson (by adoption) of a palace eunuch, widespread disaffection among many *shih* turned instead to outright disgust. Besides, there was no time for indecision and ambivalence now, for office holding had become a positive liability. Aside from the attendant physical dangers, it was quite unclear whether great success in conventional career terms might not earn one eternal condemnation by history as a sycophant or scoundrel among slaves. Obviously, under such unhappy circumstances, when most men could no longer hope to improve their fates very much by accommodations with present realities, many grew intrigued by the idea of acquiring secret powers, no less than by the prospect of a return to fair antiquity through mind travel.[111]

As a result, all over the empire the finest silk was "cut into ribbons onto which magic words and incantations were painted."[112] Moreover, the self-referential yet refined public "play with antiquity" performed by *shih* in their artistic pursuits — liable to be condemned as selfish and anti-social in better days when a legitimate dynasty was in charge — now seemed to offer the solace and detachment that one needed first to confront the world in all its confusion and then to advertise one's nobility to one's peers and betters in or out of state service. After all, when no firm answers were likely to be gained from the state-sponsored version of the Way of the Ancients, the turn to calligraphy's "play" with antique forms nicely conveyed both a proper acquaintance with the official past and a considered rejection of it, coupled with a fine disdain for the "ordinary run of people who clung to the ancient books [such as the Five Classics], being entangled in the past."[113] And if the powers-that-be remained suspicious, what better testimony to the disinterested purity of one's motives could there be than short snatches of occasional writing spontaneously set down in the careless cursive script?[114] Furthermore, because the allied arts of literary composition and calligraphy had the twin virtues of being at once distinctive yet capable of indirection, there was a strong chance that their writers — like the worthy *Odes*-makers of old — might be better known to the ages through their works in circulation than through the usual commemorative modes considered reliable enough in times of peace: the lengthy genealogies piously promoted by one's descendants over the generations, the official accounts making up the dynastic histories, and even the physical monuments marking ancestral temples and graves.[115]

With any luck, in other words, clear and vigorous writing might yet triumph over time's ruin. Failing that, long life — and a bit of cash, too — would do in these uncertain times, when man-made disasters often left petty officials and students so poor that they had to eke out their livings as artisans or farmers. So inasmuch as it was the practice of calligraphy that could provide scholar-officials with greater wealth, better physical and psychic health, or simply a convenient excuse for sociable gatherings, it was calligraphy that eventually would become synonymous with scholarly life. No less importantly, to some elite *shih* in this period of rapid reinfeudation, the long hours spent practicing calligraphy while committing the whole of classical literature to memory were exercises to be applauded, insofar as they worked to demarcate those of "good birth" from the merely literate.

It was only with the fall of the Han empire, then, that all conditions for the elevation of the calligraphic form to the status of art were met. That commingling of personal feelings and sociopolitical protest which had begun with Wang Ch'ung a century earlier had evidently needed to acquire an added intensity before it could be transmuted into that "transparent" acceptance of fate and change required to produce the perfect conflation of form and content in calligraphic script—or so they presumed at the time. "Only somebody who cared no more for [the usual notions of] honour or disgrace" could produce calligraphy whose "square and round spills forth/ in compositions rejecting every [old] standard."[116]

That fine calligraphic writing could now in the post-Han period epitomize the noble spirit is what we learn from the stories told of Wang Hsi-chih (303–361) and his son Wang Hsien-chih (344–388).[117] When contemporaries described Wang Hsi-chih's calligraphy as "Now drifting like a floating cloud, now rearing up like a startled dragon," they were ascribing divine powers to Wang himself, as the stories show.[118] Transparency offset by limpid subtlety, a readiness to embody change while keeping to the still center, and a capacity to exult in one's commitment to beauty—such qualities were admired in the character no less than in the script.[119] In such a context was the famous *Preface to the Orchid Pavilion* (*Lan-t'ing hsü*) composed: "On this day, the sky was bright and the air was clear and mild; a breeze was gently blowing. Feasting our eyes and giving rein to our feelings—how utterly enjoyable! And even though we lacked any accompaniment of silk or bamboo, of pipes or stringed instruments, for every cup there was a chanted poem—quite enough to express the hidden feelings of our hearts!" The same air of easy, effortless grace, I would argue, lingers still about the tracing copy attributed to Wang Hsi-chih entitled *Ritual to Pray for Good Harvest* (*Hsing-jang t'ieh*; fig. 18).

Paradoxically, it was not long before the freedom occasioned by a partial rejection of failed empire and the old canons generated a host of invented traditions lauding calligraphy's new conceptual empire, all of them signaling calligraphy's belated rise to the dizzy heights attained earlier by oral and then written traditions attached to the Classics. There soon arose, for instance, a vast theoretical literature on the subject of calligraphy, much of it positing the old potential identity between beauty and the new morality, suitably framed in a new medium.[120] Testifying to calligraphy's sacred origins, legends were spun out and elaborate genealogies drawn up to establish authoritative lines of transmission for masters and products, often with a view to facilitating insertion of the self in a pivotal role in the propagation of a living tradition.[121] Script styles proliferated, so much so that as many as 120 different styles had been recorded by the early sixth century.[122] And once a distinctive method of critical evaluation for connoisseurs had been set up, and a flourishing art market spawned, it was only a matter of time before the first copies designed to promote faithful emulation of the masters followed, along with outright forgeries of the more powerful examples of calligraphic art.[123]

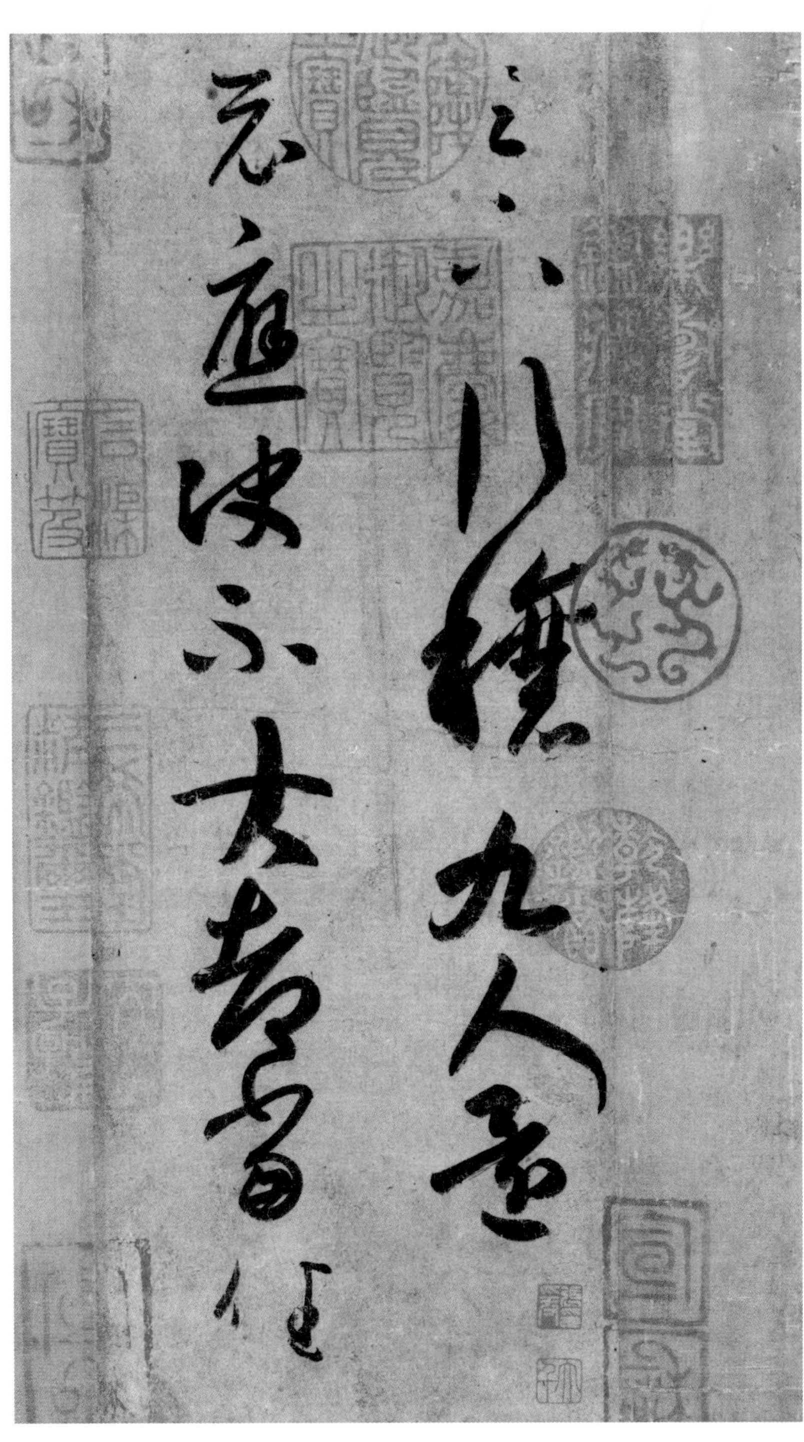

Figure 18
Wang Hsi-chih (303–361). Detail from *Ritual to Pray for Good Harvest* (*Hsing-jang t'ieh*), T'ang tracing copy. Letter mounted as a handscroll, ink on paper, letter, 24.4 x 8.9 cm; scroll, 30 x 372 cm. The Art Museum, Princeton University, bequest of John. B. Elliott (1998–140).

* * *

Martin Kern has rightly spoken of the "inexhaustible efficacy" of the word *wen*, which led it to absorb and reflect a wide range of different meanings in different circumstances.[124] Over time, *wen* became the most powerful medium available to men of culture wishing to articulate their ideals and promote that process whereby humans through exemplary practice attain the level of divine insight and efficacy formerly attributed to the gods. In early China, nobility of character often presupposed the flexibility to respond appropriately to change. The art of the moral life by definition therefore contained sufficient depth, complexity, variety, and richness to render it a source of perennial delight to the viewer's eye. Discourse about marvelous "patterns" in Chinese culture apparently superseded discourse about logical discrimination for the very reason that pattern was perceived as infinitely inclusive and potentially integrative, in the very likeness of the Great Way, unlike the powers of discrimination, which were necessarily more limited and limiting. As the *Analects* says, a man is "broadened" (*po*) by *wen*.[125]

Nonetheless, long centuries of change were required before one category of significant pattern, the written script forms, would be regarded as a sufficient repository of extraordinary human value in and of itself, rather than the tool of bureaucrats or the specialty of craftsmen. Though much of the picture remains to be pieced together, the common assumption that China has from time immemorial been preeminently an "empire of texts" is demonstrably false. It is the invention of later scholars who have sought to prove by the undeniable fact of a writing system continuously employed within China's borders the more dubious proposition that an essentially unified China has enjoyed for millennia "the longest, continuous civilization" in the world.

1 Special thanks go to Robert W. Bagley, Martin Kern, Michael Loewe, Virginia Bower, and Gerry Boswell for their generous help in the preparation of this manuscript. The citations are from Arthur F. Wright, "Chinese Civilization," in Harold D. Lasswell, Daniel Lerner, and Hans Speier, eds., *Propaganda and Communication in World History*, v. 3, *The Symbolic Instrument in Early Times* (Honolulu: University Press of Hawaii, 1979), 222; John King Fairbank, *The Great Chinese Revolution: 1800–1985* (New York: Harper & Row, 1986), 3.

2 The classic works discussing writing as communication with the gods are Kristofer Schipper, "The Written Memorial in Taoist Ceremonies," in Arthur Wolf, ed., *Religion and Ritual* (Stanford: Stanford University Press, 1974), 309–24; Jonathan Chaves, "The Legacy of Ts'ang Chieh: The Written Word as Magic," *Oriental Art* 23, no. 2 (Summer 1977), 200–215; Emily Ahern, *Chinese Ritual and Politics* (Cambridge:

Cambridge University Press, 1981); a newer work is Robert Chard, "Rituals and Scriptures of the Stove Court," in David Johnson, ed., *Ritual and Scripture in Chinese Popular Religion: Five Studies* (Berkeley: University of California, 1995), 3–54. Note the many fine works on the history of calligraphy begin with oracle-bone inscriptions, for example that by Tseng Yuho, *A History of Chinese Calligraphy* (Hong Kong: The Chinese University Press, 1993).

I would like readers to register two important points here. First, in popular literature, the Shang oracle-bone inscriptions (OBI) have been characterized as "messages communicated to the spirits." Nonetheless, the OBI must have been made after the ritual application to the gods had been performed; the OBI represent, then, a record of such invocations made to the gods and sometimes — not always — the responses received from the gods. It is important to remember, then, that ritual communication between the spirit and human worlds did not take written form in Shang, so far as we know. Only later do we find written communications as the primary mode of communication with the gods. Second, if the Chinese method of communicating with their gods via written documents were a sufficient explanation of calligraphy's elevated status as premier art, there should have been signs of such high status long before the late Eastern Han. For another view, see Wang Ning-sheng, "Ts'ung Yüan shih chi shih tao wen tzu fa ming," *K'ao-ku hsüeh-pao*, no. 1 (1981), 1–44.

3 John Hay, "The Human Body as a Microcosmic Source of Macrocosmic Value in Calligraphy," in Susan Bush and Christian Murck, eds., *Theories of the Arts in China* (Princeton: Princeton University Press, 1983), 74–104. Lothar Ledderose, "Chinese Calligraphy: Its Aesthetic Dimension and Social Function," *Orientations* 17, no. 10 (October 1986), 35–50, points to three features of Chinese calligraphy which are "unique to this art form": (1) the direct rapport between viewer and artist, made possible through the factors of time and movement; (2) the unparalleled tightness in the artistic tradition, technically, and stylistically, and (3) the peculiar mode of handing down works of calligraphy through the ages, letting them grow continuously and making art history part of the aesthetic experience. None of the three features are unique to calligraphy, however. Theories about the *Odes*, for example, are predicated upon the direct rapport between odes-maker and odes-reciter or odes-reader, and painting scrolls were handed down in much the same way as pieces of calligraphy. More informative is Lothar Ledderose, "Some Taoist Elements in the Calligraphy of the Six Dynasties," *T'oung Pao* 70 (1984), 246–78, on early Taoist strains in the history of calligraphy.

4 Yin/yang theory (but not Five Phases theory) dominated technical discussions from the late Chou period. A good introduction to this topic is Li Han-san, *Hsien Ch'in Liang Han chih yin-yang wu-hsing hsüeh shuo* (Taipei: Wei-hsin Books, 1984); and A.C. Graham, *Disputers of the Tao: Philosophical Argument in Ancient China* (La Salle: Open Court, 1989), 313–69.

5 Note that "writing" as an important, let alone preeminent, meaning for *wen* cannot be attested prior to the Eastern Chou period. Martin

Kern, "Ritual, Music, and the Written Text: Historical Transitions of *wen* in Early China," ms. under review for publication, shows that "writing" was one aspect of *wen* by Eastern Chou, but "certainly not a central one" (p. 3). Kern's hypothesis is confirmed by remarks in Li Tse-hou with Liu Kang-chi, *Liang Han mei hsüeh shih* (Taipei: Chin-feng, 1987), 198. Undoubtedly, the largest conceptual block to understanding aesthetic notions in early China, then, remains our mistaken belief that writing and written forms are what the early Chinese meant by *wen*. For the definition of *hsiang* as emblematic image, see *Han fei tzu chi chieh*, comp. by Wang Hsien-shen (Taipei: World Press, n.d.), 6.20.108.

Regarding the significance of the revelatory *t'u* (see below), we mistake their purpose if we assume that an interest in them coincides with a desire for the general "dissemination of knowledge." Emperor Wu and his successors had established a policy of storing writings and setting up officials to copy them, but "they were all stored in the secret archives." See Pan Ku, *Han shu* [hereafter HS] (Peking: Chung-hua shu-chu, 1962), 30:1701. Such secret caches supposedly contained the materials the dynasty would need to maintain its power by ritual, magical, and political means. Lothar Ledderose, "Taoist Elemements," 27, suggests the secrecy with which later calligraphic masterpieces were kept.

6 As far back as the Wu-ting Shang oracle-bone inscriptions, some inscriptions were written in black and red ink and some were carved in inlaid pigment. At least one inscription (not an oracle bone) was inlaid with turquoise, and there were also jades that show writing in vermilion ink. See Tseng Yuho, *A History of Chinese Calligraphy*, figs. 2.5–2.7, citing materials from the Academia Sinica, Taipei and the Palace Museum, Peking; and Robert Bagley, *Shang Ritual Bronzes in the Arthur M. Sackler Collections* (Cambridge: The Arthur M. Sackler Foundation, 1987), fig. 103.4. It is tempting to regard red ink and precious inlays as "ornament" (what lends dignity to the content of the message), though we know too little of Shang customs to speak with assurance. The OBI are not really historical records (chronicles), as Bagley reminds us; they often record only the texts of invocations, and not the replies from the ancestors or the historical outcomes. Note that I reserve the term "calligraphy" for a specific art whose particular aims lie beyond mere decoration. In general, it seems that the place of the "polite arts" in pre-Ch'in times was quite different from that in the Wei-Ch'in period, though the continuous use of key vocabulary masks this lack of continuity.

7 In no fewer than four out of seven occurrences of *wen* as "writing" in the fourth-century BC *Tso chuan*, for instance, the character refers to messages inscribed on a newborn's hand at birth that signify that person's future. See *Tso chuan*, Duke Yin 1 (*fu* 1); Duke Min 2 (*fu* 1); Duke Chao 1 (*fu* 7); Duke Chao 32 (6 *Tso*). The three other uses (in Duke Hsüan 12 (3 *Tso*); Duke Hsüan 15 (3 *Tso*); and in Duke Chao 1 (*fu* 8) use *wen* to refer to the specific written forms that a word takes in signifying the inner workings of the cosmos. *Wen* there refers, in consequence, not primarily to writing per se (for which the terms *shu* or *tien* are used), but to writing as divine

portent. Such written forms must be analyzed in the same way as the graphic forms of the *I ching* hexagrams, so as to reveal the future. This may explain why the later *Shuo-wen chieh-tzu* (comp. ca. AD 100) reserves the term *wen* for single graphic elements. See William Boltz, *The Origin and Early Development of the Chinese Writing System* (New Haven: American Oriental Society, 1994), 141–42.

8 According to extant materials, both the Ch'in and the early Western Han rulers selected for high office those who favored precise methods of bureaucratic naming, although the dynastic histories emphasize the repressive nature of the wealth-and-power discourse of Ch'in imperialism so as to contrast it with the relatively *laissez-faire* Huang-Lao theories adopted by the early Western Han state under emperors Kao-tsu through Wen. Examples of bureaucratic precision under Ch'in have been provided by the nearly thirty statutes and legal catechisms on procedures found in the 1975 excavations at Shui-hu-ti, Yün-meng, Hupei (*terminus ad quem* 217 BC), no less than by the military manuals found at Yin-ch'üeh-shan, Lin-yi, Shantung (excavation first reported 1974), dated to the years 140–118 BC. The need for such precise and uniform application of the laws is explained in a letter dated to 227 BC: "Anciently, the people everywhere had their own local customs. They differed in what they found beneficial and in their likes and dislikes.... This is why the sage-kings created laws [*fa*] and regulations [*tu*], with which to straighten and correct the hearts of the people." See Denis Twitchett and Michael Loewe, eds., *Cambridge History of China, Vol. 1, The Ch'in and Han Empires* (Cambridge: Cambridge University Press, 1986), 75; *Shui-hu-ti* (1978); and "Chiang-ling Chang-chia-shan Han chien kai shu," *Wen-wu*, no. 1 (1985), 9–15, which reports on early Western Han legal documents in 500 strips from tomb M247, Chiang-chia-shan, Chiang-ling, Hupei.

9 For the argument that *Ju* means "classicist," only a small sub-group of which are true "Confucians" in the sense of ethical followers of the Sage, see Michael Nylan, "Rethinking Han Classicism," in Kai-wing Chow, On-cho Ng, and John B. Henderson, eds., *Imagining Boundaries: Changing Confucian Doctrines, Texts, and Hermeneutics* (Albany: SUNY Press, 1999). The sharp distinction between "true *Ju*" and "vulgar *Ju*," which can be traced back to the writings of Hsün-tzu, is an important one in Han times. While cynics may suspect that the Han classicists were wont simply to label all their opponents as "vulgar," the "true *Ju*" were said to have continued Confucius' preoccupation with moral empire, in contrast to the "vulgar *Ju*," who were more intent upon getting ahead in conventional terms. Note the parallel distinction between the "technician" skilled in only one specific art and the "true *Ju*" who can lay claim to an integrated vision of the universe, which is also relevant to this discussion. For Hsün-tzu's dictums on the subject, see his ch. 8 devoted to "Ju Teachings," in *Hsün-tzu yin te* (Peking: Harvard-Yenching Institute, 1950) (Sinological Index Series no. 22) 23/8/87; 24/8/90–94; 24/8/100; cf. *chüan* 41 of the *Li chi*, devoted to the "Conduct of the [Ideal] Ju." For the "technicians," see Yang Hsiung, *Fa yen*, in (*Hsin pien*) *Chu-tzu chi cheng* (Shanghai: World Books, 1935; rpt., Taipei, 1978), II, 12:39.

10 In their fulminations, they were wont to quote *Analects* 14/25: "The Master said, 'In the old days, men studied for the sake of self-improvement, but nowadays men study in order to impress other people'" (trans. after Waley, 187). On the term *shih*: The word does not correspond to "gentry" since the ultimate basis of *shih* power was not land, but continued access to office. This essay uses the term "scholar-officials" to refer both to scholars and to officials, to potential candidates for office as well as to actual office holders.

11 To a degree, all classicists presume and exploit an "experience of deficiency" in the present vis-à-vis the past (to borrow the Egyptologist Jan Assmann's term, *Defizienzerfahrung*). But in late Eastern Han, that "experience of deficiency" greatly intensifies, producing an overwhelming sense of nostalgia for the past.

12 This argument directly contradicts Lao Kan's (1960; see n. 14 below) theory, which posits the existence of the calligraphic arts, principally expressed in cursive writing, throughout the Han.

13 Richard Curt Kraus, *Brushes with Power: Modern Politics and the Chinese Art of Calligraphy* (Berkeley: University of California Press, 1991).

14 For example, both Lao Kan, "Han tai ti shih shu yu ch'ih tu," *Ta-lu tsa-chih* 21.1/2 (July 15, 1960), 69, and Lothar Ledderose, "Chinese Calligraphy," 36–37, cite an anecdote included in Fan Yeh, *Hou Han shu* [hereafter HHS] (Peking: Chung-hua shu-chü, 1965) 14.557. The anecdote says of Liu Mu, cousin and contemporary of Emperor Ming of Eastern Han (r. 58–75), that he *shan shih shu* and *tso ts'ao shu ch'ih tu*. As both statements relate to Liu Mu's fame as author of prose and poetry, the first is more likely to mean that he was "good at composing in the [particular formal] archival style" conventionally used for court documents; and the second, that he composed ten pieces in draft. It is doubtful, in other words, whether either statement refers to fine calligraphic style. Cf. the biography of Huang-fu Kuei's wife, included in HHS 84.2798, where context shows that the phrase *neng ts'ao shu* is more likely to mean "was capable of drafting [official] documents," rather than was "capable of writing calligraphically in cursive style." My supposition is confirmed by the glosses of Ying Shao and Yen Shih-ku, which refer to writing in large seal script, the script style required for formal bureaucratic documents.

15 This essay disputes the notion that there was one culturally unified elite in early China. It assumes instead many competing court and extra-court groups in operation throughout the period under review. Some of these groups tended to value writing as decoration (e.g., Emperor Ling and his trainees at the Hung-tu-men Academy) and some as bureaucratic tool (e.g., those derided as "vulgar *Ju*" by moralizing classicists like Yang Hsiung). Other groups were apt to see writing and reading texts as an integral, if elementary, step in the preparation required for true ethical insight.

16 Below, I suggest that painting lost out because of its preoccupation with exact or precise representation (mimesis), which many classicizing thinkers rejected as less inclusive—and therefore less inherently powerful—than *wen* as distilled but immeasurably rich pattern.

17 For *wen* as a crisscross pattern, see

Hsü Shen, *Shuo-wen chieh-tzu fu chien tzu* [hereafter SW] (Hong Kong: Taiping Books, 1966), 9A/185. According to that text, "*wen* is an image [*hsiang*] of *wen* [crisscross patterns] that meet [or interact with] one another." (Note that it is rare for the SW to define a character in terms of itself.) As Lothar von Falkenhausen (1996), "The Concept of *wen* in the Ancient Chinese Ancestral Cult," *Chinese Literature: Essays, Articles, Reviews* (CLEAR) 18 (1996), 1–22, points out, all modern amplifications of this statement try "to account for the appearance of the actual archaic graphs, which Hsü [Shen, author of the *Shuo-wen*] and his contemporaries had misread." For the theory that *wen* is a tattoo, see Chou Fa-kao et al., *Chin wen ku lin* (Hong Kong: The Chinese University, 1974), XI, 5533–5535 (entry 1199); Liu Tun-yüan, "Shuo-wen yü wen tzu," *Mei-shu k'ao-ku yü ku-tai wen-ming* (Taipei, Yün-ch'en wen-hua, 1994), 40–45. (Mei-shu k'ao-ku ts'ung-k'an series no. 2). Numerous objections may be leveled at this identification of *wen* as tattoo, for example: (1) There is no reason to assume that the persons represented with tattoos were of high status; and (2) Nor would it be safe to assume that those who made and used the Anyang-period bronzes showing tattooed men also used the same language as Anyang — and so the same word *wen*.

18 Arthur Waley, trans., *The Book of Songs* (London: George Allen & Unwin, 1938; rpt., New York: Grove Press, 1996), with additional trans. by Joseph R. Allen, 346. Herrlee G. Creel, *The Origins of Statecraft in China, Vol. 1: The Western Chou Empire* (Chicago: University of Chicago Press, 1970), 67, believed that *wen* referred to "accomplishments," and even "civilization" from earliest times. No good evidence, however, supports the early abstract use of the character *wen* meaning "civilization" or "culture." I accept the scholarly consensus that *wen* was first applied to noble ancestors as a pious epithet and that only much later, in late Eastern Chou, it was used in posthumous names for dead rulers to reflect history's unbiased judgment.

19 Ode 275, "Ssu wen" (Contemplating *wen*). For translations, see James Legge, trans., *The Shiking* (Oxford, Oxford University Press, 1935), 580–81; Arthur Waley, *The Book of Songs*, 160; and Bernard Karlgren, trans., *The Book of Odes* (Stockholm: BMFEA, 1950), 243–44.

20 Lothar von Falkenhausen, "The Concept of *Wen*," 3, translates *wen* as "accomplished." I suspect *wen* refers to those patterns that are pleasing to regard, while *wu* refers to those that are fearsome to regard, as in Ode 285. After all, *wen* frequently appears in the compound *lieh wen* ("resplendent and *wen*"), and it is used of pennons and chariot equipment. Cf. *Analects* 3/14, where *wen* is associated with the *yu yu* ("ornamental") behavior of the Chou dynasty. That would account for two later inscriptions dating to the middle Spring and Autumn period where the compound *wen wu* seems to refer to more abstract aspects of governance, the "civil" and the "martial" (ibid., 5).

21 Note that the term *wen chang* in modern Chinese refers to "writing" (specifically, "essays"), but it clearly cannot bear that meaning in early extant texts. Martin Kern, "Ritual, Music, and the Written Text," 6ff., argues persuasively that *wen chang* in early texts such as the *Analects* refers primarily to a "well-figured

and clear appearance" or "refined forms" (i.e., an impressive appearance that holds the gaze). Given the importance of the term to later Chinese moral and aesthetic theory, it is interesting that the term does not appear in the canonical *Documents* or *Odes*. Even in Warring States texts, there is no single instance in which *wen chang* refers unambiguously to "literary composition" (ibid., 11). In Western Han texts, the term *wen chang* refers to normative ritual, ritual insignia, or textile patterns (what Kern calls "crafted form"). In Eastern Han, however, the term increasingly refers to "normative texts." See below.

22 For example, *Analects* 7/25 describes *wen* only as one of the four teachings of the Master Confucius. And *Analects* 7/33 has Confucius saying that he surpasses other men in *wen*.

23 See, e.g., *Analects* 1/6. Admittedly, many scholars have assumed that *wen* refers in such passages to the "polite arts" of the Chou aristocracy, defined in most accounts as six in number: rites, music, archery, charioteering, writing (*shu*), and mathematics. But that analysis is far from certain. Two examples in the *Analects* seem relevant here: In the first passage, *Analects* 5/15 (Waley, 110), Confucius responds to a query about the meaning of *wen* in the proper name K'ung Wen-tzu by saying: "He was diligent and fond of study. He was not afraid to inquire of [social] inferiors. That is why he was called 'Wen.'" In the second, *Analects* 12/24, Tseng-tzu says that the "noble man uses *wen* to meet with (*hui*) friends—as friends are needed to support *jen* (humane) behavior." Note that *Analects* 14/18 (Waley, 185) seems to associate condescension and kindness to inferiors with *wen*. Such passages clearly refer to *wen* as exemplary behavior, though Confucius intends to take a hand in redefining such behavior, so that nobility of character will count for more than aristocratic birth or elite fashion. It seems doubtful that the *Analects*' definition of *wen* as exemplary behavior is an accurate definition of *wen* for the Ancients; it is only the meaning that the *Analects*' Confucius means to attribute to the Ancients.

24 *Analects* 6/18 (Waley, 119). *Analects* 12/8 suggests that it is the patterns in the fur (i.e., what overlays the skin) that make the hides of tigers and panthers far more valuable than the hides of dogs and sheep, which are otherwise similar. Human "ornament" or "refinement" consists of "rites and music," according to *Analects* 14/12.

25 This essay, following Confucius, distinguishes appropriate *wen* from the excessive; the former is something like (noble) "ornamentation," and the second (mere) "decoration," two acceptable translations for *wen*. See *Analects* 6/18; 19/8. It is *wen*'s tendency to lapse into mere decoration that is denounced by Han Fei (d. 233 BC) and Mo-tzu (d. 390 BC). The early *Ju* classicists, in denying that all patternization is harmful, would have patternization be divided into appropriate and inappropriate sorts, depending on whether it takes or "does not take its model from antiquity" (HS 25B.1256).

26 Shih Ch'ang-tung, *Hsien Ch'in chu tzu mei-hsüeh ssu-hsiang shu-p'ing* (Peking: Chung-hua shu-chü, 1976; 2nd. ed., 1979), 1–26. Shih points out that *mei o* (beautiful and ugly) is interchangeable with *shan o* (good and evil). The *Li sao*, of course, is one of many literary works to play up this identity between the moral and the aesthetic, for there the

beautiful and fragrant flower is metaphor for the noble protagonist: "Having from birth this inward beauty,/ I added to it fair outward adornment:/ I dressed in selinea and shady angelica,/ and twined autumn orchids to make a garland..." (lines 9–12).

27 *Analects* 15/26 (Waley trans., 198, renumbered 15/25). I follow the standard analyses for the dating of the *Analects.*

28 See *Chou i yin te* (Peking: Harvard-Yenching Institute, 1935) (Sinological Index Series supplement no. 10), 40/Hsi A/3; 45/Hsi B/2; 43/Hsi A/9. Given the constraints of space, there is little time to delve into the intricacies of the Hsi-tz'u's arguments. The best guide to them remains Willard Peterson, "Making Connections: 'Commentary on the Attached Verbalizations' of the *Book of Change,*" *Harvard Journal of Asiatic Studies* 42, no. 1 (June, 1982), 67–116.

29 See Jane Geaney, "Language and Sense Discrimination in Ancient China" (Ph.D. diss., University of Chicago, 1996). *Wen* is still not even the principal word assigned to written texts; *shu* (texts), *tien* (canons), or *tz'u* (phrases) are used more often.

30 The *Shih chi,* for example, speaks of the fear with which rulers regarded Tsou Yen, who elaborated a cosmological theory; the *Shih chi* leaves readers to draw the conclusion that Lü Pu-wei and Liu An, Prince of Huai-nan, may have lost their lives in part because the texts which they sponsored encroached upon imperial prerogatives in explicating cosmic patterns. See Ssu-ma Ch'ien, *Shih chi* [hereafter SC] (Peking: Chung-hua shu-chü, 1959), 74.2344; 85.2510; 118.3082. HHS 82A.2716 suggests that the state-appointed "aide in the study of patterns" in early Eastern Han still bore an official responsibility to interpret unexpected changes in the cosmic patterns.

31 It is no coincidence that the expression *wen tzu,* where *tzu* refers to *ming,* "naming," appears first on the Ch'in stele at Lang-ya. See SC 6.245. The Ch'in invention of the compound *wen tzu* seems to signify the desire to strip significant pattern — at least as it is used by Ch'in subjects — of most of its religious associations. Certainly, it represents a push to greater clarity, when *wen* had always stood for greater inclusivity, being both the sign and what it signifies. *Wen tzu,* in other words, implies the search for exact representation, rather than symbolic expression; a bureaucratic tool rather than the omen requiring interpretation. Ultimately, state control would derive largely from the control over naming displayed in bureaucratic functions.

32 For the state's preference for career professionals who composed careful speeches and wrote script forms accurately, see SC 121.3118-20. I put "Confucian" in quotation marks because the Five Classics were not inherently Confucian. See Michael Nylan, *The Five "Confucian Classics"* (ms. under review), ch. 1. In early Western Han, these Classics were prized because they contain "old patterns" — the transcription of cultural traditions transmitted down through the ages. By the Eastern Han, the texts were valued increasingly because they contain "old characters" (*wen*) in antique form, according to Eastern Han scholars like Hsü Shen (active ca. AD 100) and Pan Ku (32–92). See below for the modern/archaic script controversy.

33 For the *fu,* see David Knechtges' masterful translations of the *Wen hsüan, or, Selections of Refined*

Literature, by Xiao Tong (Princeton: Princeton University Press, 1982), 3 volumes to date; and Mark Edward Lewis, *Writing and Authority in Early China* (Albany: SUNY Press, 1999), ch. 5.

34 Mark Csikszentmihalyi and Michael Nylan, "Constructing Lineages and Inventing Traditions in the *Shij*" (forthcoming). *Analects* 2/12, of course, had decried the notion that the gentleman could be a mere "tool" in the hands of his ruler.

35 The term *hsiu wen* is the title for *chüan* 19 in Liu Hsiang's *Shuo yüan*.

36 Martin Kern, "Ritual, Music, and the Written Text," 26, reminds us that it was Liu Hsiang who "identified individual works, fixed their titles, ordered and named the chapters, and hence divided and arrested the stream of writings into distinctive and self-contained entities," thereby working against the "fluid" nature of most pre-imperial texts. As Kern notes, "The bare fact that many of the excavated pre-imperial and early Han manuscripts do not bear a title or even chapter designations is most telling in this respect."

37 Allegedly, there were earlier examples of dictionaries in China (e.g., that by Ssu-ma Hsiang-ju), but these are no longer extant. The *Erh ya* (comp. 3rd century BC?) is often called the earliest Chinese dictionary, but in fact it represents a kind of thesaurus or compendium of glosses that were probably in origin annotations to passages in early texts. See ECT, 94–99.

38 However, Liu Hsiang and Yang Hsiung, following the *Tso chuan* and Hsün-tzu, did assume that both speech and writing constituted "portents" or "portraits" of the inner intentions. Speech and writing are "golden" when "they help us see the men who know [the sages]." See THC 61/A, 3 (Nylan trans., 357). For the later divine status of the written word, see the works of Ts'ai Yung and Huan Wen (with the latter attributed to Ts'ui Yüan), recorded in *Ch'üan Hou Han wen* [hereafter CHHW], v. 2, in Yen K'o-chun, comp., *Ch'üan Shang-ku San-tai Ch'in Han San-kuo Liu-ch'ao wen* (Hupei, 1894; rpt., Taipei: World Books, 1964), 45/7a and 69/6a–6b, 80/1a–b. Ts'ai says, for instance, that the six seal forms *ju-shen* ("approach divine status"), as they are emblematic of marvelous transformation.

39 Therefore, both writers are careful to distinguish, as Ssu-ma Ch'ien had been before them, between authoritative figures who left writings behind and writings that tended to lack "true" authority, either because they are only of superficial attraction or because they are lost, fragmented, or liable to misconstruction. In this they followed the tradition attributed to Confucius in *Analects* 12/3: "The Master said, 'Seeing that the doing of it [humane behavior] is so difficult, how can one be otherwise than chary of speaking about it?'" Hence, Yang Hsiung's propensity to talk in terms of a divine Mystery which can be intuited but never adequately verbalized. Cf. *Analects* 13/3. See FY 5.13 on the unreliability of most of the "Confucian" Classics.

40 FY 1.2. Though *wen* in mid-Han times comes increasingly to refer to the Classics thought to contain the ritual, political, and legal precedents provided by the Ancients in their conduct, as well as to information demonstrating the close links between Heaven-sent portents and kingly behavior, fierce debates among the literati raged over the primary content of the word *wen*:

Are texts *wen* only insofar they convey the correct moral messages? And must men study texts in order to be called "learned"? Was it not the case that professional bureaucrats were well-versed in the Five "Confucian" Classics and yet demonstrably ignorant of ethical patterns in their behavior? The men who saw themselves as "true *Ju*" or "classicists" were far less concerned with the faithful transmission of doctrinal statements than with the emulation of appropriate patterns of conduct (a term that included both speech and actions).

41 For Yang Hsiung's famous statement on the relation of single-minded study to real understanding, see Huan T'an, cited in TPYL 739.2a, as translated by Timoteus Pokora in *Hsin-lun* (*New Treatise*) *and Other Writings by Huan T'an* (*43 BC–28 AD*) (Ann Arbor: Center for Chinese studies, University of Michigan, 1975), 73.

42 SY 19.655–56.

43 CYYT 44/Hsi A/12. Note that while "words do not fully express ideas," the *Odes* "fully express [their authors'] commitments [*shih yen chih*]." See CCYT 318/Hsiang 27/5 *Tso*. The two statements are not in direct contradiction since the *Odes* communicates by its musical rhythms as much as by its lyrics. Similarly, *t'u* are said to communicate more fully than mere *yen*.

44 Mark Lewis (1999), 459 in ms.

45 An awareness of this lies behind Yang Hsiung's refusal to submit to the share his notes for the *Fang yen*. This is certainly what Yang refers to in his prose poem when he says that he fears the court's propensity to "redden his clan" (i.e., massacre it). These late Western Han classical masters were far more reliant upon state sponsorship than their early Western Han predecessors. Liu Hsiang, a member of the royal family, was commanded by the ruling house to undertake various important commissions, for example, and Yang Hsiung's works, unlike those of Ssu-ma Hsiang-ju before him, were nearly all commissioned by the Han court. Note that one meaning of the word *fu* is to "present as tribute" to the throne. For more on this, see David Knechtges, *The Han Rhapsody: A Study of the Fu of Yang Hsiung* (Cambridge: Cambridge University Press, 1976).

46 Yang Hsiung therefore prefers the "offerings of the [sagely] Odes-makers" to "offerings of the phrase makers with [their merely] beautiful styles" (HS 30:1746). Yang and Liu mean thereby to assert the superiority of a flexible, generalized intellect (such as might be claimed by the man of letters) over specific skills employed in limited domains (such as might be claimed by the professional artist or bureaucrat). (Note that this turn of phrase may also imply the superiority of the centralized Chou state encapsulated in the *Odes* tradition over and against the southern traditions, as Martin Kern suggests.) In his mature writings, Yang roundly rejects the conventional notion of art, which aims to appeal to as many men as possible through sheer beauty. According to Yang, true connoisseurs prefer the ultimate challenge of apprehending the formless and the soundless (HS 87B.3576–78). See Li Tse-hou, *Liang Han mei-hsüeh shih*, 198, and Chang Yung-hsin, *Han yüeh-fu yen-chiu* (Nanking: Chiang-su ku-chi, 1992), 139–40. Both confirm Yang's contention that the composition of *fu* poetry was driven by the desire to make *fu* language as gorgeous as possible.

47 Both the Lo shu and Ho t'u were magic squares, but we do not know the exact form that these sacred diagrams took in early times. For further information, see Schuyler Cammann, "Old Chinese Magic Squares," *Sinologica* 7 (1962), 14–53.

48 See Liu Hsin's formal letter of protest recorded in HS 36.1969–70.

49 HS 36.1967. Liu Hsin, of course, adapts familiar arguments from Warring States' thought (that seeing is believing; that it is better to witness an event than to rely on hearsay; that the senses are generally trustworthy) to a brand-new use. In particular, Liu aims to establish the superiority of one text, the *Tso chuan*, over the *Kung-yang* and *Ku-liang* commentaries on the grounds that the *Tso*'s author knew Confucius himself.

50 For example, a bronze tripod was unearthed at Feng-yin in the autumn of 113 BC, prompting Emperor Wu to initiate new cult activities.

51 The invention of cheap paper also made it easier to be literate, since the young no longer needed to study with a master in order to learn a text. Literacy increased in consequence, and this, too, made it more likely that texts would be associated with preservation of past.

52 Numerous examples of this separation could be cited. For four, see Huan T'an, cited in *I lin* (SPPY) 3/7b (trans. in Pokora, 15–16) and Yen 15/9a (trans. in Pokora, 168); Pan Ku's "Two Capitals" *fu* (trans. in Knechtges, 95, lines 9–16); and HS 87B.3575, lumping together the jesters Shun-yü K'un and Meng with the poet Ssu-ma Hsiang-ju as those who "encourage, rather than restrain" bad behavior by the emperor. Note that while Pan Ku's *fu* distinguishes but does not condemn the wordmeisters, Pan's other writings openly condemn the wordmeisters, as Li Tse-hou, *Liang Han mei-hsüeh shih, chüan* 7, shows. Many were still convinced that writing was all too likely to appear as the tyrant's writ. This is no doubt the origin of the myth of Ts'ang Chieh, which says that ghosts cried on behalf of the common people when writing was invented. See the trans. in A. Forke, *Lun heng: Wang Ch'ung's Essays* (n.p., 1907; rpt., New York: Paragon, 1962), II, 184.

Certainly, from the point of view of some *shih*, the *fu*'s performance was tied too closely to immortality cults, to the military, and to the local magnates' excessive delight in luxury. See Chang Yung-hsin, *Han yüeh-fu yen-chiu*, 94–95.

53 For the early history of the *fu* and *yüeh-fu* in connection with court entertainers, see ibid., ch. 4. Han Wu-ti was apparently the first ruler to hire *wen jen* ("men of cultivation") to compose lyrics for his court. The *shih*'s growing desire to distinguish their group from that of mere entertainers began then, as is evident from the biographies of Ssu-ma Ch'ien, Ssu-ma Hsiang-ju, Tung-fang Shuo, and Yang Hsiung (SC 121; HS 57, 65, 87). Hence Yang Hsiung's insistence that those who are mere "artisans cannot surpass those who are connoisseurs [of their art]." See Li Tse-hou, *Liang Han mei-hsüeh shih*, 203. Note that we are told in SC 117:2053 that Ssu-ma Hsiang-ju "never ventured to discuss affairs of state with the high ministers," while Yang Hsiung felt supremely qualified, despite some justifiable fears for his life, to pronounce verdicts on public policies and a host of historical figures in his two prose masterpieces, the *Fa yen* and the *T'ai hsüan ching*. Note also the slim possibility that Yang

Hsiung's speech impediment played a role in this change also, though the poet Ssu-ma Hsiang-ju earlier suffered from the same malady.

54 Martin Kern (private communication) suggests that the *fu* of Ssu-ma Hsiang-ju are "entirely different" from those of Yang Hsiung. Ssu-ma's are "mainly oral texts" in contrast to Yang's, which are mainly "written texts" (though still made to be recited). The fact that the three different versions of Ssu-ma's pieces found in the *Shih chi*, *Han shu*, and *Wen hsüan* often use different graphical components suggests that Ssu-ma Hsiang-ju's piece was known mainly as oral recitation, rather than as fixed text.

55 A decrease in oral performance may have sent *shih* scurrying in their search for another performance art that would publicly identify them as "gentlemen." It may be the *Odes*, which had served well as diplomatic language prior to unification in 221 BC, found no comparable niche in the unified empires of Ch'in and Han.

56 See Chang Yung-hsin, *Han yüeh-fu yen-chiu*. Remonstrance of all sorts was seen as more problematic in Eastern Han, as is clear from the gingerly treatment accorded the topic in the *Po hu t'ung*, in *Kuo-hsüeh chi-pen ts'ung-shu* (Taipei: Commercial Press, 1968), v. 68, 2B/1a–5b, and in Ying Shao, *Feng su t'ung i fu t'ung-chien* (Peking: Centre franco-chinois d'études sinologiques, 1943), 5.27. The foregoing remarks represent only the first highly speculative attempt to account for a strong impression gained from the official dynastic histories: that there was a marked decline in interest in the *Odes* traditions after early Western Han. Compare SC 121 (the "Forest of *Ju*"), where stories of the *Odes* masters predominate, with its counterpart HS 88, where much less attention goes to the *Odes*, aside from repeating the old tales found in SC 121. HHS 79B suggests that there were few acknowledged masters of the *Odes* in the Eastern Han, and the Stone Classics inexplicably omit the *Odes* altogether from its roster of Five Classics, substituting for it the *Analects*. Consider also the disparaging remarks made about Confucius' (reputed) compilation of the *Odes* vs. the fulsome praise accorded Confucius' compilation of the *Ch'un Ch'iu* (Spring and Autumn Annals), in Liu P'an-sui, comp., *Lun heng chi chieh* [hereafter LH] (n.p., 1932; rpt., Peking: World Books, 1967), ch. 27, "On pre-eminence" (Forke, II, 295ff.). According to *Po hu t'ung* 4A/9a, following *Li chi* ch. 26, Eastern Han thinkers had the *Ch'un Ch'iu* teaching what the *Odes* was said to have taught in the pre-Ch'in period: "appropriateness of expression and the proper comparison of things." The *Odes* merely teach "affability and liberality."

57 Kenneth DeWoskin, *A Song for One or Two: Music and the Concept of Art in Early China* (Ann Arbor: University of Michigan, 1982) shows how much early images of sageliness spoke of the ear, in contrast to later Buddhist imagery that focused on the eye.

58 Both Wang Mang and Kuang-wu ti (r. 25–57) were widely known to be "true believers" in the political prophecies recorded in the apocryphal texts (*ch'en wei*). For evidence of longstanding traditions requiring the sanction of graphic images for the transfer of legitimate authority, see Toyota Hisashi, "Shū Tenshi to bumbu no so no shiyo ni tsuite," *Shikan* 127 (1992), 2–17.

59 Roy Andrew Miller, "The *Wu ching i-i* of Hsü Shen," *Monumenta Serica* 33 (1977), 1–21; William Boltz, *The Origin and Early Development*, 151ff. Hence, the repeated necessity to resort to scholastic conferences and polemical literature in the attempt to resolve the numerous textual controversies that had arisen in connection with the various editions of the Classics.

60 Note that the early Western Han texts, including the *Shih chi*, stress how few and how faulty were the textual traditions that remained from the pre-imperial period. By contrast, Eastern Han scholiasts, living at a time more distant from the past, tended to claim that a number of canonical texts still existed to offer more secure avenues of immersion into the past. Most scholars have thought that the extensive genealogizing of texts was one principal mode of scholarship that had gone on since time immemorial in China, but evidence drawn from the *Han shu* (comp. ca. AD 100), itself a genealogizing text, suggests otherwise. The specifics of this argument are to be found in Mark Csikszentmihalyi and Michael Nylan, "Constructing Lineages and Inventing Traditions."

61 Here I register my disagreement with the dominant Eastern Han views on textualization, which were often rather naive. Setting oral traditions down on paper made them more much liable to critical scrutiny (and potential rejection) by the literate; also, more liable to loss during times of great turmoil. For once great numbers of traditions are written on paper, a corresponding number may not also be committed to memory. In that case, when important libraries are ruined, the loss is irreparable.

62 Many scholars, including P'i Hsi-jui, *Ching hsüeh li shih*, ed. by Chou Yü-t'ung (Peking: Chung-hua, 1959), ch. 3–4, have noted the gap between Western Han academic ideals, which assumed a focus on a very few texts, and the repeated Eastern Han calls for "broad learning."

63 The enormity of the shift, I suggest, is comparable to that of the shift between Roman Catholicism (which accepts that God operates through an evolving tradition) and Protestantism (which puts first priority on belief in the textual traditions recorded in the Bible).

64 I am indebted to Martin Kern, "Ritual, Music, and the Written Text," for drawing my attention to this memorial, for translating it, and for analyzing the memorial in terms of "the instrumentalization of the Confucian canon" (ms., 21–22). Most of this paragraph summarizes Kern's excellent work. The phrase "learning to inquire" is a possible allusion to *Analects* 3/15 and 16/10, which describe the habits and concerns of the truly noble educated man.

65 See Martin Kern, "Ritual, Music, and the Written Text," 26ff. (esp. 30). At that point, codifying and expounding the appropriate written texts could become the "great undertaking in organizing the state" because by then a special sympathy, at least in theory, had been established between old and new, between seen and unseen, between thought and deed; again, in theory, this sympathy would lead the empire in the single-minded pursuit of correct goals, so that it could reflect and draw strength from the combined insights of both the Ancients and the new men of Han.
Many other pieces of evidence, including the Mao Preface to the

Odes, attest to this change, but the limitations of this essay format preclude any attempt to fully review the relevant materials here.

66 William Boltz, *The Origin and Early Development*, 151ff. Cf. Wang Ch'ung's arguments on the archaic meanings imbedded in graphic forms, as recorded in LH 3.15.76 (Forke, I, 322) and LH 16.49.337 (Forke, II, 364).

67 Hans Bielenstein, *The Bureaucracy of Han Times* (Cambridge: Cambridge University Press, 1980), 136. I say "solely on the basis of their exemplary behavior" because that was nominal qualification for such candidates, though many candidates were undoubtedly nominated because of the excellence of their connections.

68 HS 88.3589.

69 SC 121.3115–16. The classicists of Lu are closely identified with the ethical teachings attributed to Confucius, given the strength of local traditions at that time. And K'ung is the family name of Confucius himself. As neither the Ch'in nor Wang Mang probably deserved their reputations for despotism, my characterization of them simply follows historical convention.

70 HHS 79A.2515. Pan Ku's HS does not treat this incident, as it lies outside his purview. The relevant HHS passage surely draws upon Eastern Han traditions, however, as can be seen by (a) clear parallels elsewhere with material in HS 88, Pan Ku's treatise on the classicists; and by (b) clear parallels with another late Eastern Han record, the *Ching-chou wen-hsüeh chih-kuan chih* (Official Record of the College in Ching-chou), by Wang Ts'an (177–217). According to Wang's *Record*, Lord Liu, regional governor of Ching-chou "under Han," ordered Sung Chung, a renowned classical scholar, to establish an academy in Ching-chou to which his colleagues would be invited. Reportedly, "those who came from afar carrying texts on their backs and ritual implements on their shoulders numbered over 300, including Ch'i-wu K'ai." For more information, see Mark Csikszentmihalyi and Michael Nylan, "Constructing Lineages and Inventing Traditions."

71 The cumulative literary achievements of Yang Hsiung, Liu Hsiang, and the Pan family proved so compelling that later men in Eastern Han times took *wen* (expanded now to include "literary texts" composed in faultless form) as the proper focus of cultural accomplishments, even after the central government, and by extension the monumental works that it had sponsored, had fallen into decay or disrepute. Ironically, many wished to emulate Yang Hsiung's genius in writing, while they ignored Yang's strictures against an undue focus on literary activity.

72 I do not mean to imply here that Wang Ch'ung was the only person to begin to sever the conceptual links between literary works and state service. Had I more time and space, Chang Heng's (78–138) "*Fu* on the Two Capitals" would also serve nicely for the purposes of comparison, for the *fu* reflects Chang's awareness of the power of language not only to display, enchant, and persuade, but also to reveal the poet's own sensibility toward his subject. Note the reemergence of the ostensibly unofficial voice, which yet remains highly public in its functions.

73 LH 28.192 states, for example, "I have never yet understood what was the idea behind Confucius' making rit-

ual." LH 38.272–274 meanwhile debates the commonplace notion that the *Ju* should devote themselves to moral learning. For Wang's views of the importance of writing, see LH 82, *passim*. For Wang, winning rhetorical arguments is the final and most obvious test of the sage. For further information, see Michael Nylan, "Han Classicists Writing in Dialogue about their own Tradition," *Philosophy East and West* 47, no. 1 (1997), 133–88.

74 LH 12.35.252. Based on context, I take Wang's phrase "the Way of the Former Kings" to refer to the "good of the state." Reasoning that all truth and authority derives from a remote origin that has been lost or forgotten and that the moral degeneration of the present age is a direct consequence of losing those primal truths, two main solutions presented themselves to Wang. The first was to re-assess all subsequent literary accounts so as to privilege the main line of transmission of unitary truth from its origin, thereby excluding partial, secondary, or faulty versions of the truth that do not fully reflect the past. The second was to engage in the exact same type of literary activity as men of the distant past, the better to fully "immerse" oneself in their spirit. (In the second point, Wang of course follows Pan Ku's lead.)

Both impulses are familiar to us from Wang Ch'ung's writings, which make twin claims: both that Wang has the requisite familiarity with old books to discern the ultimate past; and that he has the requisite talent to tread the same path as the great literary luminaries of the past. For Wang Ch'ung, the ability to direct one's response to the political scene to the act of literary composition "proves" one's "natural" fitness for high office. For the literary basis for this belief, see HSWC 7.15b (Hightower, 248).

75 Of course it was the Pans who created the Table of Great Men, Ancient and Modern.

76 Not surprisingly, by mid- to late Eastern Han, there is far more interest in the notion of Confucius composing counter-cultural works unaided by the state apparatus than there had been at any time since Ssu-ma Ch'ien, who had himself suffered castration by the state. Note that Martin Powers, *Art and Political Expression in Early China* (New Haven: Yale University Press, 1991) tried to draw our attention to a related shift in the terms of discourse for the visual arts.

77 Wang occasionally contradicts himself, of course, as I have argued in "Han Classicists Writing in Dialogue." Wang is therefore not above composing formal paeans of praise for the Han ruling house. But such paeans are anomalies best explained by his craven desire for public recognition; they do not tally with his main arguments. In his justly famous letter to Jen An, Ssu-ma Ch'ien had made the argument that the great works of canonical literature had all been composed by men of great moral learning who had suffered grave injustices: King Wen of Chou, Confucius, and Ssu-ma Ch'ien himself. Wang Ch'ung is quite uninterested in morality, by contrast, and far more interested in the link between literature and a lack of public recognition.

78 See LH 12.35.252, for the denunciation of clerkly writing; see ibid., 256, for the comparison of clerks to mere craftsmen. In this, Wang appears to gain support from Yang Hsiung's pronouncements, but Wang has twisted them to serve new ends.

79 For the identification of the classical meaning (*ching i*) as basic (*pen*) and the writing (*pi mo*) as secondary (*mo*), see LH 12.35.256.

80 Real art, insofar as it epitomizes a Great Way rather than a mere concern for profit, is divine and eternal. See LH 12.35.252–53. On the constancy of *wen*, the *Han shih wai chuan* (*Ssu-pu ts'ung-k'an so-pen*), 3/19 remarks: "Heaven does not change its course/ Earth does not alter its form./ Sun and moon shine bright,/ The ranked stars are constant." The translation follows James Robert Hightower, trans., *Han shih wai chuan: Han Ying's Illustrations of the Didactic Application of the Classic of Songs* (Cambridge, 1952). Thus the greatness of *wen* lies in the fact that it endures. Compare the claims for writing made in Ts'ao P'i's *Lun wen*.

81 LH 12.35.255.

82 Wang, in fact, seems to have lacked any aesthetic appreciation. For the six forms of script learned by apprentice clerks, see HS 30.1722. For writing texts as merely a way to save oneself future bureaucratic trouble, see Huan T'an, cited in Li Fang, comp., *T'ai-p'ing yü-lan* (Shanghai: Commercial Press, 1935; rpt. Taipei: Hsin-hsing, 1959), 614/4a (trans. after Pokora, 171).

83 See LH 13.38.278 (trans. Forke, I, 106).

84 A century later, Ts'ai Yung's (132–192) writings, possibly under the influence of Wang Ch'ung, also include one of the key early texts proposing to assess the relative merits of talent (most often equated with literary talent), of ethical reclusion, and of state service — the merits of which would be debated by almost all important authors of the early Six Dynasties period. For other authors preoccupied with this topic, see Étienne Balazs, *Chinese Civilization and Bureaucracy: variations on a theme* (New Haven: Yale University Press, 1964), ch. 13; Mark Asselin, "'A Significant Season': Literature in a Time of Endings, Cai Yong and a Few Contemporaries" (Ph.D diss., University of Washington, 1997).

85 LH 85, Wang's autobiography, has Wang writing the text in his sixties, after he has nearly given up hope of official advancement.

86 Ts'ai Yung's "*Fu* Recounting a Journey" has its counterpart in Chao I's "*Fu* Satirizing the Age, Detesting Iniquity," insofar as both prose poems share a pronounced political bent. See footnote 102 below, and Mark Asselin, "A Significant Season," ch. 2. Pan Ku had written earlier that "One strives that after death his name shall not perish/ This is the standard of the ancients." See *Wen hsüan* 14.645 (trans. after Knechtges, III, p. 101, lines 129–32).

87 Mark Asselin, "A Significant Season," introduction (second of the unnumbered pages), writes of "a shift in the center of clerisy-written literature from the court" to "public" exchange, i.e., circulation of works among members of the clerisy class. Numerous other examples could be adduced. These include Chao I, also a famous calligrapher by avocation, who along with Ts'ai Yung wrote the earliest essays on calligraphy. For Han letters, consult also Eva Yueh-wah Chung, "A Study of the *shu* (letters) of the Han Dynasty" (Ph.D. diss., University of Washington, 1982). It is important to note that letters were generally written in the cursive styles (running or grass).

88 See below for the condemnation of certain script styles by Ts'ai Yung and others. On the technical improvements in the tools for writing script forms, see Tseng Yuho, *A History of Calligraphy*, Appendix C; Tsien Tsuen-hsuin, "Paper and Paper-Making in Han," in Joseph Needham, ed., *Science and Civilisation in China* (Cambridge: Cambridge University Press, 1985), V (1), 380–442. As was the case with Islamic calligraphy, "more rounded, cursive scripts had been used since early times for personal correspondence, and to meet the needs of commerce and administration within the rapidly expanding ... empire." See Albertine Gaur, *A History of Calligraphy* (London: The British Library, 1994), 90. A comparison can also be made with Egyptian hieroglyphs, a formal script usually employed only for monumental purposes, since there was a perfectly serviceable cursive script from very early on in the history of writing in Egypt.

89 From 132 to 193, no fewer than fourteen rival emperors proclaimed themselves in the provinces, where insurgent religious sects were employing mystical symbols to herald the end of the dynasty. In addition to the four major external plots against the throne (in 147, 161, 178, 188), there were also a number of failed palace coups against the emperor (in 107, 127 (?), 147, and 188), which had no goal but to replace the reigning emperor with another member of the Liu ruling house.

90 Mark Asselin, "A Significant Season," 4, dubs the works of these men *kairotic* literature (from the Greek *kairos*), in that their structure and themes reflect an unprecedented nostalgia for the past.

91 For Ts'ai's biography, see HHS 60B. Throughout his career, Ts'ai Yung was a study in ambivalence. He pronounced himself too good for the likes of the court, yet he could not refrain from advising it. The other Han dynasty men whose brushwriting was praised by posterity were Ts'ui Yüan (active 100); Chang Chih (active 190); Chung Yu (151–230) and Chao I (see above). For the questionable attribution of a work praising "cursive-style writing" to Ts'ui Yüan in CHHW 45/7a, see Li Tse-hou, *Liang Han mei-hsüeh shih*, 242. In any event, this piece seems more to praise the convenience of using *ts'ao shu* than its inherent expressiveness as an art form. See also Lothar Ledderose, "Some Taoist Elements," 267.

92 HHS 60B.1980, which applauds Ts'ai's decision not to consort with the (corrupt) men of his own age. Such a decision would have been unthinkable to classical masters two centuries earlier, who had emphasized that the distinctive way of humans was "to make contact."

93 The idea of "making friends" with like-minded people of the past occurs first in *Mencius* 5B/8. The reference to "roaming free and easily" is, of course, to the first chapter title of the *Chuang-tzu*.

94 See Okamura Shigeru, "Sai Yu o meguru Go Kan makki no bungaku no susei," *Nihon Chūgoku Gakkai hō* 28 (1976), 61–78. Mark Asselin, "A Significant Season," ch. 2, shows that Ts'ai Yung was one of many *shih* who were torn between their desire to "clean up corruption in government affairs" and to withdraw from society.

95 Hans Bielenstein, "Loyang in Later Han Times," *Bulletin of the Museum of Far Eastern Antiquities* 48 (1976), 70, supplies a list of the classics inscribed on the Stone Classics. Curiously, the *Odes* were omitted while the *Analects* was included. The selection of texts is nowhere explained, according to Bielenstein.

The Eastern Lodge (*Tung-kuan*) was the most famous of the imperial libraries, where the official dynastic histories were composed in installments. See ibid., 29–30.

96 The tablets were regarded as great curiosities at the time. Many came to copy the texts and later *Ju* consulted them, until they were destroyed, possibly in the Yung-chia crisis of 312. See HHS 60B.1990.

97 When we come to vermilion characters written directly on stone, both the technical requirements and the degree of possible virtuosity of stroke are quite different from those of characters written directly on paper, silk, wood, or bamboo. Lao Kan (1960) therefore wisely suggests that stele inscriptions and formal inscriptions in general should be treated quite separately from documents on more perishable materials. Certainly, the stone-stele style of late Eastern Han is more formal and less "calligraphic" than writings inscribed on other materials. But unfortunately, too few examples remain from this period to explore the implications of such differences in detail.

98 HHS 60B.1992. For information on the Hung-tu-men Academy within the southern palace complex, see Hans Bielenstein, "Loyang in Later Han Times," 27–28. This school was personally established by Emperor Ling on March 15, 178, acting upon a eunuch proposal which sought to establish an institution that would provide a counterweight to the Imperial Academy filled with *shih.* Its stated purpose was to train young men to write government documents on tablets, to compose *fu* poetry, and to improve their calligraphy, especially in a then-popular kind of script known as bird-style. Upon graduation, some of those who attended the school were immediately appointed to high office as provincial governors or inspectors, as members of the palace Secretariat, or as courtiers; some were even granted noble rank. Ts'ai Yung, like many others, regarded the students at this school as mere "utensils" or "tools" liable to sycophancy. Ts'ai was one of many to urge that the entire school be abolished, but such remonstrances were ignored.

99 HHS 60B.1996.

100 Citing a stele inscription written for Ch'en Shih and attributed to Ts'ai Yung (trans. slightly modified from Asselin, 353).

101 See HHS 8.340, 60B.1996; *chih* 13.3272; 14.3294.

102 For Ts'ai Yung's "Power of the Seal Script" and "Power of the Clerical Script," see CHHW 80/1a–b; cf. Chao I's "Contra the Grass-style" (*Fei ts'ao shu*), in ibid., 82/9b–11a. Of course, Ts'ai did not favor the decorative bird script derived from the "barbarian" states of Ch'u and Shu, which would imply approval of disunity and regional power. For a prose "Discourse on Calligraphy" attributed to Ts'ai Yung, see Tseng Yuho, *A History of Chinese Calligraphy*, 227.

103 *Ch'o* (put together) can mean "to stop," "to attach together," or "to compile."

104 See Khoo Seow Hwa and Nancy L. Penrose, *Behind the Brushstrokes: Tales from Chinese Calligraphy* (Singapore: Graham Brash, 1993), 28.

105 Ts'ai Yung was considered the best composer of stele inscriptions in Han. The most famous of his stele inscriptions (composed in 169) recounted the life of Kuo T'ai, the student protest leader during the famous proscriptions at the end of the Eastern Han. The stele inscription was reportedly written to apprise others of the fact that Kuo T'ai's "deeds will not perish." Ts'ai Yung is also supposedly the author of the important "Stele Inscription for [the immortal] Wang Tzu-ch'iao" (dated to 165), which expressed his dual longings for immortal fame and for another, better way of life.

106 For political reasons also, Ts'ai's death ensured his reputation. Ts'ao Ts'ao and his sons were all most anxious to demonstrate the utter depravity of Hsien-ti, the last emperor of Han, so that they could force Hsien-ti to abdicate in their favor. The Ts'aos found useful rhetorical capital in the fact that Hsien-ti had allowed Ts'ai to languish in jail without a hope of pardon. It is not for no reason, then, that Ts'ao Ts'ao acted as faithful patron to Lady Ts'ai Wen-chi, Ts'ai Yung's daughter.

107 One is tempted to relate this to the idea, first propounded in late Eastern times by a member of the prominent Hsün family, that any text of sufficient value may qualify as "classic" — not just those products attributed to the ancient sage-kings. See Michael Nylan, *The Five "Confucian" Classics*, ch. 1.

108 At the time of Ch'eng-ti (r. 32–7 BC), there were reportedly 3,000 students enrolled in the Imperial Academy; by the mid-second century AD, there were reportedly over 30,000 students. See Hans Bielenstein, *The Bureaucracy of Han Times*, 68–71; also CHC, p. 465, citing HHS 67.2186. Mark Asselin, 27, also speaks of the dearth of employment opportunities, disenchantment with government corruption, and the court's failure to recognize"worthy" ministers. Chao I's "*Fu* Satirizing the Age, Detesting Iniquity," lines 19–20, summarizes the current situation in this way: "Those bowing and bending become the famous and powerful,/ Those petting and patting, the puissant and brutal."

109 On the greater attention to the extra-mundane: Lothar Ledderose, "Some Taoist Elements," shows that famous calligraphers such as Wang Hsien-chih "developed a cursive style for secular calligraphy under the influence of manuscripts that had been written in religious inspiration" (269); to the calligraphic qualities familiar from writing in trance were added various refinements by masters of the brush. On the general turn to "unofficial styles": it is surely significant that Wang Hsi-chih and Wang Hsien-chih were known for their running, cursive, and standard (*k'ai*) scripts, and not for their use of clerical script. But note that Wang Hsi-chih still tended to favor the more formal *chin-li* or *k'ai* script. On the cursive scripts as intimations of inspired revelations: Even in the fifth century AD, T'ao Hung-ching (456–536) remarked of the mystic Yang Hsi that his "writing was hurried and abbreviated," in *ts'ao-shu* and *hsing-shu*, "when he received the revelation." Fair copies, however, were executed in a formal script style (*chin-li*, or "modern clerical," a proto-*k'ai shu*) that was "neat and carefully written." See Lothar Ledderose, "Some Taoist Elements," 257. For the expansion of script styles by AD 252, see Tseng Yuho, *A History of Chinese Calligraphy*, 149. On the healthy pleasures of calligraphy: Writing was seen as a way to nourish the vital spirit in at least two ways. First, it allowed spirit-contact with other great men through history whose gaze is sympathetic; and second, it taught the person that to live well is to "trust to one's emotions and one's nature." For further information, see Jean François Billeter, *The Chinese Art of Writing* (New York: Skira, 1990), esp. ch. 6–7, on the "body senses" and the "active body"; and Li Tse-hou, *Liang Han mei-hsüeh shih*, ch. 9.

110 Étienne Balazs, *Chinese Civilization and Bureaucracy*, 194.

111 Étienne Balazs, *Chinese Civilization and Bureaucracy*, writes perceptively, "During the long and comparatively peaceful reign of the Han, there was no need for any of the extremist systems of antiquity. [Most] minds did not seek to inquire beyond the limits of Confucian pragmatism" (195). On the desire to return to the past: Social memory had invested the past with greater clarity, meaning, and legitimacy than the present. Hence Ts'ai Yung's *fu*, which says: "I researched into tales of old,/ These affairs were clearly set forth." Thus contemplation of the past was a form of historical retrospection, as well as a way to mitigate one's own sense of alienation from present politics.

112 See Wang Fu's chapter "On Excessive Luxury," *Ch'ien fu lun* (SPPY) 3/6b.

113 See Ts'ui Shih, *Cheng lun*, cited in Étienne Balazs, *Chinese Civilization and Bureaucracy*, 208.

114 In other words, in my view, it took the series of crises that occurred in the years 159–220 (including proscriptions of many scholarly factions from public office; massive student protests, a still more massive religious uprising, the massacre of the palace eunuchs, several military takeovers, and the utter destruction of the capital city) for most *shih* to realize that the empire was truly gone and public service either useless or dangerous, that just as the "[Chou] empire, long divided, had had to unite [so the Han] empire, long united, had to divide." Epigraph drawn from the *Three Kingdoms* (*San-kuo yen-yi*), after the trans. by Moss Roberts (Berkeley: University of California Press, 1991), 5. See CHC, 360–65, for the strong presumption that Heaven singularly favored the Liu ruling house, as it had granted them a mid-dynastic restoration.

This sort of writing has often been erroneously described as "private" and "individualistic," but as Barbara Herrnstein-Smith, *Poetic Closure: A Study of How Poems Work* (Chicago: University of Chicago Press, 1968), 16–17, shows, to read such lyrical works is never to read a "private meditation"; it is to read a piece produced for public consumption. Note also that an admirable adaptability and flexibility was admired when it was thought to be rather in the spirit of the past, not a slavish imitation of the past.

115 Already the occasional *fu* had taken over some of the *Odes*' functions. (This may account for the relative lack of attention to *Odes* traditions in Eastern Han. The Stone Classics did not even contain a text of the *Odes*.) For example, in a counterpart to *shih yen chih* ("The *Odes* express the inner commitments"), Ts'ai Yung's "*Fu* Recounting a Journey" states outright that he writes "these words revealing my hidden feelings." Note that the feelings may be hidden inside the poet, but the feelings are still about public issues. This very *fu*, for example, openly criticizes court politics.

Regarding the unreliability of conventional modes of commemoration: Ts'ai Yung himself in 191 proposed the removal of the spirit tablets of Emperors Ho, An, Shun, and Huan from the Han ancestral temple (HHS, *chih* 9.3197), on the grounds that these rulers lacked merit.

116 Tung Ch'i-ch'ang's (1555–1636) colophon, assessing a work attributed to Wang Hsi-chih. See Lothar Ledderose, "Some Taoist Elements," 263.

117 The best stories are found in Liu I-ch'ing's *Shih-shuo hsin-yü* [hereafter SSHY], which has been beautifully translated and annotated by Richard Mather in Richard B. Mather, trans., *Shih-shuo hsin-yü, A New Account of Tales of the World, by Liu I-ch'ing* (Minneapolis: University of Minnesota, 1976). Another work full of pertinent information is *Chung-kuo shu-fa ch'üan-chi*, ed. by Liu T'ao [Liu Chen-ch'eng] (Peking: Jung-pao-chai, 1991), v. 19.

118 See SSHY 14, entry 29 (Mather trans., 315).

119 See, e.g., SSHY 8, entry 133 (Mather, 241); SSHY 6, entry 34 (Mather, 192); SSHY 8, entry 144 (Mather, 243).

120 One of the earliest extant critical pieces is *Ku-lai neng-shu jen-ming* (Calligraphers since ancient times), by Yang Hsin (370–442), which is still available in *Fa-shu yao-lu* 1/7a–7b. The *Chen kao* has a whole theory of script, whereby three scripts are said to exist: (1) the highest, which exists only on a timeless, primordial level, and can be used only by celestial beings; (2) the second, "cloud-seal script," which is used for writing talismans, and is not readily intelligible to mortals; and (3) ordinary script, which has been "coerced" into conforming to definite shapes, so that while it is essentially materialized and falsified, it is at least intelligible to ordinary folk. See *Chen kao*, esp. 1/7b–10a.

121 The elaboration of legends continued right through the Ch'ing period (1644–1912), when Lu I-chen and Chang T'ing-hsiang, in their book *Yü Yen lou shu-fa*, had the primeval culture-hero Fu Hsi creating a divine "dragon script"; Shen Nung, the Divine Farmer, a sacred "grain script"; and the Yellow Emperor, the mysterious "cloud script" used up to their day in sacred Taoist talismans.

122 Yü Yüan-wei (502–557), *Liang Yü Yüan-wei lun-shu*, in Chang Yen-yüan, *Fa-shu yao-lu* (*Ts'ung-shu chi-ch'eng* edition), ch. 2, 25–26.

123 T'ao Hung-ching in a postscript (ch. 19–20) to the *Chen kao* (ca. 500) describes "the efforts of connoisseurs and historians, confronted with problems of authenticity, to establish a canon of genuine scriptures." T'ao prescribes standards of connoisseurship; he also describes the efforts of earlier connoisseurs (some working singly and some by committee) to decide questions of authenticity and thereby establish "correct" models for emulation.

124 Martin Kern, "Ritual, Music, and the Written Text," 1–2, contributes an important observation: the specific content attributed to *wen* as adjective or noun changed repeatedly in early Chinese history so as to reflect the dominant cultural discourse(s) of the time.

125 *Analects* 9/11.

Huiwen Lu
Princeton University

Calligraphy of Stone Engravings in Northern Wei Loyang

With the relocation of the capital of the Northern Wei dynasty (386–534) from P'ing-ch'eng (modern Ta-t'ung, Shansi) to Loyang, Honan, in the late fifth century, a new distinctive style of calligraphy appeared on stone engravings in the Loyang area. This style, executed in regular (*chen* or *cheng*) script[1] and featuring slanted character compositions and angular strokes with crisp edges (see fig. 1), was markedly different from the calligraphic style of the preceding Northern Wei P'ing-ch'eng period as well as the contemporaneous Southern Ch'i dynasty (479–502). Through its use mainly in dedicatory inscriptions of Buddhist sculptures at the Lung-men Caves and on stone epitaphs in the Northern Wei royal tombs in the Mang Mountains, this type of calligraphy reflected the social and cultural changes brought about by the move of the Northern Wei capital to central China. In addition, it incorporated new stylistic elements of the calligraphic tradition in southern China, and, most importantly, revived the earlier Eastern Han (25–220) and Western Chin (265–317) tradition of stone engraving preserved at Loyang. This essay analyzes the formation of the Northern Wei Loyang calligraphic style, emphasizing the role of stone engravings in Northern Wei culture and their stylistic sources. It attempts to dispel the notion that the Northern Wei Loyang style was developed with no stylistic precedents, and posits that the revival of the practice of engraving calligraphy on stone can be seen as an embodiment of the Northern Wei emperors' political ambitions.

Ramifications of the Relocation from P'ing-ch'eng to Loyang

Emperor Hsiao-wen's (r. 471–99) decision in 493 to relocate the Northern Wei capital to Loyang — the former capital of the Eastern Han, Wei (220–265), and Western Chin dynasties[2] — represents the culmination of a series of cultural changes. In the 480s Hsiao-wen had embarked upon an ambitious reform program to transform the nomadic heritage and steppe culture of his people, the Hsien-pei, into an aristocratic society organized according to Chinese bureaucratic and Confucian ideals.[3] In 493, having symbolically chosen to occupy what was conceived of as the geographic and cultural center of China,[4] the emperor led his army and officials south across the Yellow River with the dream of "making a brilliant home on the Central Plain."[5]

Through a series of further imperial decrees enacted over a period of several years following the move to Loyang, Emperor Hsiao-wen attempted to change fundamentally the culture and customs of the Hsien-pei people. In 494 traditional Hsien-pei dress was banned in favor of Chinese dress,[6] and in 495 the Hsien-pei language of the north was similarly banned and replaced by Chinese as the official court language.[7] The Hsien-pei émigrés were also forced to register as permanent residents of Loyang, and after death were to be buried south of the Yellow River.[8] In 496, the royal family's surname, T'o-pa, was changed to the Chinese surname Yüan,[9] and other Hsien-pei surnames were likewise assigned single-syllable Han Chinese equivalents.[10] As a result of this conscious policy of sinification, the lives and identity of the Hsien-pei people were completely reshaped.

Emperor Hsiao-wen's reforms also contributed to the creation of a new attitude toward stone engravings, many examples of which are preserved today at the Lung-men Buddhist Caves and the Mang royal tombs built by the Hsien-pei émigrés. Commemorative stone inscriptions are found in large quantities at Lung-men and in the Mang royal tombs, whereas such inscriptions were rare at P'ing-ch'eng. The erection of commemorative stone engravings had been an important political and mortuary practice since the Eastern Han period. The sudden increase in the production of stone engravings in Northern Wei Loyang was directly related to Emperor Hsiao-wen's relocation of the capital to Loyang, where there remained a large number of stone engravings of the highest quality from previous dynasties.

As part of his campaign to emulate the political life and cultural splendor of Loyang during the Eastern Han, Wei, and Western Chin dynasties, Emperor Hsiao-wen set about preserving the cultural legacies of the earlier periods in and around the capital city, ordering that important monuments and old tombs be protected and maintained. He personally surveyed many sites, and in 493 visited the old site of the Imperial Academy in the city to view the Confucian classics engraved on stone stelae.[11] In 495 he issued a decree that farming could not occur near any of the tombs or tomb stelae belonging to high officials of previous dynasties.[12] Many stone stelae in Loyang were thus preserved and came to serve as artistic models for the production of commemorative stone engravings in the Northern Wei.

The dedicatory inscriptions of Buddhist sculptures at Lung-men reflect the influence of the practice of erecting stelae. Shortly after their arrival in Loyang, the Hsien-pei began construction of the Lung-men Caves along the Yi River just southwest of the city, following the model of the Yün-kang Caves near P'ing-ch'eng. As at Yün-kang, sculptures were commissioned by devotees in order to acquire merit for their deceased family members, for themselves, for the emperor, or for the state. In terms of sculptural style and Buddhist iconography, however, the caves at Lung-men differ from their

Figure 1
Detail of *Dedicatory Inscription by Madam Ch'iu-mu for Her Deceased Son Niu-chüeh* (*Ch'iu-mu fu-jen wei wang-hsi Niu-chüeh tsao-hsiang*), Northern Wei dynasty (386–534), 495. Rubbing of stone engraving at Lung-men Caves, Loyang, Honan, original stone, 65 x 33 cm. Shodō Hakubutsukan. From *Shodō zenshū* (Tokyo: Heibonsha, 1966), v. 6, pl. 38.

Figure 2
Dedicatory Inscription by Sun Ch'iu-sheng and Others (*Sun Ch'iu-sheng teng tsao-hsiang-chi*), Northern Wei dynasty (386–534), 502. Rubbing of stone engraving in Ku-yang-tung, Lung-men Caves, Loyang, Honan, 162 x 48 cm. Peking Library. From *Pei-ching t'u-shu-kuan ts'ang Chung-kuo li-tai t'o-p'ien hui-pien* (Collection of Rubbings in the Peking Library) (Cheng-chou: Chung-chou ku-chi ch'u-pan-she, 1989), v. 3, 54.

northern model. One of the most remarkable differences is the sheer number of inscriptions with lengthy texts, many of which record the reasons for the donation or commission, the wishes of the patrons, and the date. Sometimes a complete list of donors' names is also included. The idea of including so much information in the inscriptions may have been inspired by local stelae, such as the Western Chin *Stele for the Three Visits of the Emperor to the Imperial Academy* (*Huang-ti san-lin p'i-yung pei*; see fig. 4), dated 278, erected in front of the Imperial Academy in Loyang, which records the names of the faculty members and students at the Imperial Academy who donated the stele. A Northern Wei example of 502 from the Ku-yang cave at Lung-men, *Dedicatory Inscription by Sun Ch'iu-sheng and Others* (*Sun Ch'iu-sheng teng tsao-hsiang-chi*; fig. 2), records the date, the patrons' wishes, and the names of the author and calligrapher (in the upper section) as well as the donors' names (in the lower section). In contrast, the few inscriptions found at the Yün-kang Caves are mostly limited to the identification of the Buddha or bodhisattvas depicted in the sculptures. Only in several rare instances is a longer inscription found at Yün-kang, including one on a horizontal rectangular panel located beneath the sculptures.[13]

At Lung-men, the arrangement of inscriptions within cave niches and the format of the inscriptions incorporate not only the earlier Northern Wei practices at Yün-kang, but also local influences. For example, a sculpture niche in the Ku-yang cave (fig. 3), the oldest cave at Lung-men, has two long inscriptions, each in a different format. One inscription is carved on a polished square-shaped panel placed below the main sculpture niche, continuing a rare practice at Yün-kang. The other inscription is carved on a polished vertical rectangular-shaped panel on the cave wall to the left of the sculpture niche. Notably, the latter panel resembles the shape of a freestanding stele composed of a title piece at the top and a text panel below. Swirling dragons carved at the top of the title piece are a stylistic feature characteristic of stelae dating from the Western Chin period. The same decorative motif is found, for example, in the *Stele for the Three Visits of the Emperor to the Imperial Academy.* Clearly, the Northern Wei adapted the traditional stele format for their dedicatory inscriptions in the Buddhist caves at Lung-men.

The Northern Wei aristocracy's increased interest in making commemorative stone engravings also contributed to the growth in the production of stone epitaphs (*mu-chih-ming*). Hundreds of stone epitaphs belonging to the Northern Wei royal family and high-ranking officials have been unearthed at tomb sites in the Mang Mountains to the north and northwest of Loyang.[14] The epitaphs, most of which are square or rectangular in shape, are inscribed with the name, titles, brief genealogy, and biography of the deceased as well as the eulogy for the deceased. The earliest of these

Figure 3
Niche dedicated by Monk Fa-sheng at Ku-yang-tung (south wall, niche no. 3, layer 3), Lung-men Caves, Loyang, Honan. From the Depository for Cultural Relics of Lung-men and the Archaeology Department, Peking University, eds., *The Grotto Art of China, The Lung-men Grottoes* (Tokyo: Heibonsha, 1987), v. 1, pl. 140.

Figure 4
Detail of *Stele for the Three Visits of the Emperor to the Imperial Academy* (*Huang-ti san-lin p'i-yung pei*), Western Chin dynasty (265–317), 278. Rubbing of stone stele from Yen-shih, Honan, 274 x 109 cm. Institute of Study of Humanities, Kyoto University. From *Shodō zenshū* (Tokyo: Heibonsha, 1965), v. 3, pl. 89.

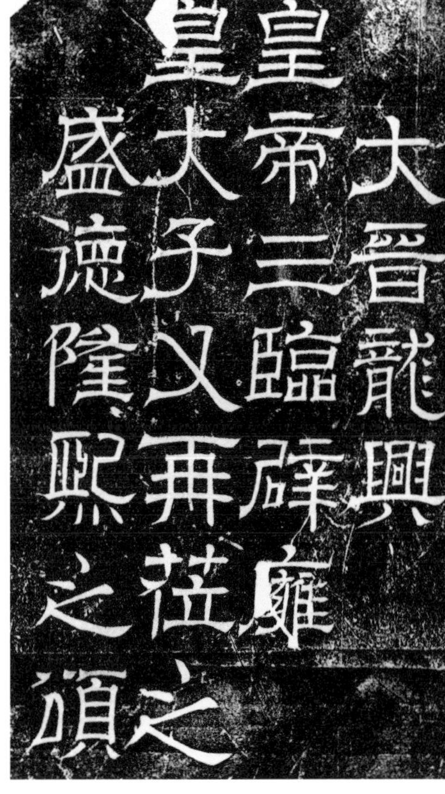

Figure 5 (left)
Epitaph of Yüan Chen, Northern Wei dynasty (386–534), 496. Rubbing of stone epitaph unearthed from Loyang, Honan, 66 x 66 cm. Peking Library. From *Pei-ching t'u-shu-kuan ts'ang Chung-kuo li-tai t'o-p'ien hui-pien* (Collection of Rubbings in the Peking Library) (Cheng-chou: Chung-chou ku-chi ch'u-pan-she, 1989), v. 3, 30.

Figure 6 (right)
Epitaph of Yüan Ssu, Northern Wei dynasty (386–534), 507. Rubbing of stone epitaph unearthed from Loyang, Honan, 59 x 62 cm. Peking Library. From *Pei-ching t'u-shu-kuan ts'ang Chung-kuo li-tai t'o-p'ien hui-pien* (Collection of Rubbings in the Peking Library) (Cheng-chou: Chung-chou ku-chi ch'u-pan-she, 1989), v. 3, 99.

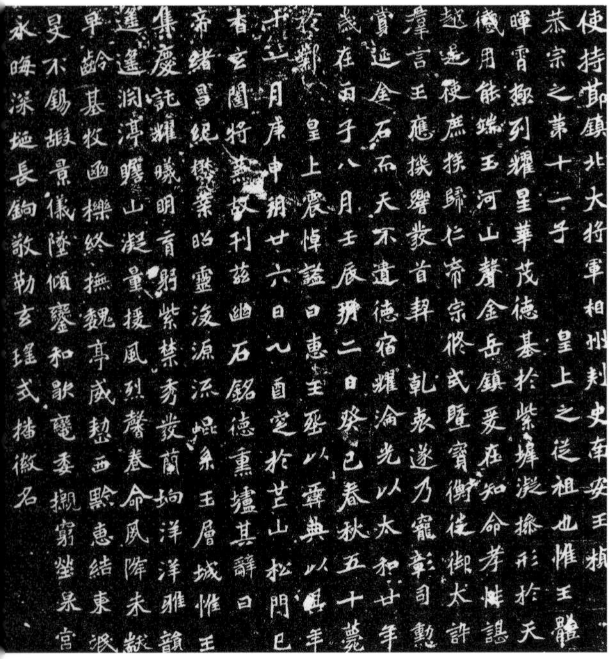

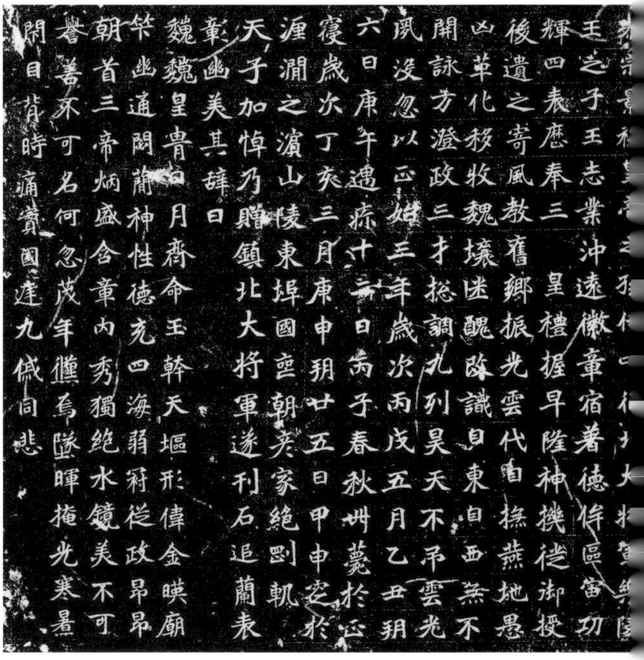

epitaphs is the *Epitaph of Yüan Chen* (fig. 5), dated 496. Yüan Chen (447–496), the great uncle and a confidant of Emperor Hsiao-wen who strongly supported the relocation of the capital, died in the north at Yeh (Lin-chang, Honan) in the eighth month of 496. Because of his close relationship with the emperor, he was buried three months later in the Mang Mountains near the new capital. Other epitaphs, such as that for Yüan Ssu (468–507; fig. 6), are evidence that Hsiao-wen's decrees requiring the adoption of Chinese names and residency and burial in Loyang were indeed executed.

The form of stone epitaphs produced under the Northern Wei at Loyang was quite different from that of the earlier P'ing-ch'eng period. The Northern Wei tomb of Ssu-ma Yüeh (462–508), near Loyang, yielded a stone epitaph composed of two rectangular slabs found lying one on top of the other in the southeast corner of the rectangular tomb chamber.[15] The lower slab bears the epitaph inscription while the upper piece functions as a protective cover. Northern Wei epitaphs discovered in the Loyang area are often in this form. Most are square in shape, measuring about fifty to seventy centimeters, and may or may not have the upper cover.

Inscribed stone epitaphs found inside tomb chambers probably derived from tomb stele that were originally erected near or in front of the tomb. The origin of such epitaphs can be traced to the third century when extravagant funerary stone sculptures and stelae were banned by the governments of both the Wei and the Western Chin in the wake of an economic recession that followed a period of prolonged warfare. Freestanding tomb stelae were subsequently placed in the tomb chamber, as seen in Western Chin examples.[16] During the Southern Dynasties period (317–589), beginning in the Sung dynasty (420–479), standing stelae continued to be used, but in some cases they were replaced by rectangular or square stone epitaph slabs placed flat on the floor of the tomb chamber. The inscriptions on these types of epitaphs are longer, and include the deceased's name, titles, and biography, and the eulogy. Square-shaped stone epitaphs placed inside the tomb chamber became prevalent in Northern Wei Loyang and are so similar in shape and size that they appear to have been standardized. The Northern Wei examples in turn served as models for epitaphs in later generations.[17]

The Northern Wei epitaph format was possibly derived from epitaphs produced in southern China during the Southern Dynasties period. Very few epitaphs have been found in Northern Wei tombs at P'ing-ch'eng. The large, richly furnished tomb of Ssu-ma Chin-lung (d. 484), a descendant of the Western Chin royal family and a high-ranking official at the P'ing-ch'eng court, is an example of a Northern Wei tomb of that period. The tomb contained three freestanding rectangular stone panels which functioned as epitaphs: the first panel, recording Ssu-ma Chin-lung's name, titles, and the date the panel was erected, was placed above the entrance to

Figure 7
Engraved Inscription from Ssu-ma Chin-lung's Tomb, Northern Wei dynasty (386–534), 484. Rubbing of stone panel unearthed from Ta-t'ung, Shansi, 64.2 x 45.7 x 10.5 cm. Original stone in Museum of Ta-t'ung, Shan-si. From *Wen-wu*, no. 3 (1972), 27.

the tomb chamber (fig. 7); the second, bearing the same inscription, was installed in the hallway leading to the main burial chamber; and the third, which belonged to Ssu-ma Chin-lung's wife, was located in the same hallway. The form of these stone panels is similar to Western Chin epitaphs dating to the third century.[18] The inscriptions, which provide only the date, name, and title of the deceased, are also shorter in length than those of the later Northern Wei Loyang period. From this evidence, it seems likely that the flat square-shaped epitaphs with long inscriptions that are characteristic of Northern Wei Loyang were indeed influenced by changes in the epitaph form in the Southern Dynasties.

The establishment of the Northern Wei capital at Loyang brought the Hsien-pei in close contact with practices in Loyang and in southern China. This collision of cultures not only led to the creation of new formats for stone engravings, but also stimulated the development of a new calligraphic style.

The Appearance of a New Calligraphic Style

The earliest stone engraving from Northern Wei Loyang is an inscription at the Lung-men Caves — *Dedicatory Inscription by Madam Ch'iu-mu for Her Deceased Son Niu-chüeh* (*Ch'iu-mu fu-jen wei wang-hsi Niu-chüeh tsao-hsiang*; fig. 1) — dated 495, shortly after the relocation of the capital to Loyang. The earliest known Northern Wei tomb in the Mang Mountains dates to 496. Construction of the Lung-men Caves and the Mang tombs continued up until the end of the Northern Wei dynasty in 534. The stone engravings from these sites, spanning a period of four decades, comprise a rich, comprehensive, and well-documented body of visual material.

As early as the eighteenth century, original stone epitaphs and rubbings of stone engravings from the Northern Wei Loyang period were sold on the art market. With the growing interest among Chinese scholars in the eighteenth and nineteenth centuries in the study of bronze and stone inscriptions — a movement known as *chin-shih-hsüeh* — the demand for early examples of engraved or carved calligraphy increased. In the early twentieth century, Westerners and Chinese uncovered large quantities of epitaphs from tombs. Most of these epitaphs and their rubbings are in the collections of museums and libraries in China, Japan, and the United States. The Peking Library's publication of its extensive collection of stone rubbings includes three volumes of Northern Wei stone engravings, which encompass most of the major examples of Lung-men inscriptions and Mang tomb epitaphs.[19] The *Catalogue of Epitaphs from the Han, Wei, and Northern and Southern Dynasties* (*Han Wei Nan-pei-ch'ao mu-chih chi-shih*), compiled by Chao Wan-li, is another valuable resource.[20] In the 1950s Chao researched the collections of rubbings and original engraved stones in China dating from the late Eastern Han through the Sui (581–618) dynasty. He documented 609 stone epitaphs — recording the measurements of the stones, the sites where they were found, and previous scholarship — and reproduced in his catalogue a rubbing of each epitaph. Over half the epitaphs are Northern Wei examples found in the Loyang area.[21] The analysis of the calligraphic style of Northern Wei stone engravings presented here draws extensively upon the material published in these two comprehensive catalogues.

The style of calligraphy in Northern Wei Loyang stone engravings varies and also changes over time. Most of the engravings, however, were executed in the newly developed *chen* (regular) script and are distinguished by slanted compositions and crisp, angular strokes. The calligraphy of the Lung-men inscriptions and the Mang tomb epitaphs share these stylistic features. The following examination of the formation of this style focuses on early examples from the Northern Wei Loyang period, from the 490s to before 510.

The *Dedicatory Inscription by Madam Ch'iu-mu for Her Deceased Son Niu-chüeh* of 495, the earliest inscription at Lung-men, features long horizontal and vertical strokes that often begin with a sharp triangular-shaped head and end in the same manner. The small dots have an irregular triangular shape. Structurally, there is little evidence of a continuous flow between two adjacent strokes: single strokes and dots are arranged together yet retain a discrete and distinctive shape. The *Dedicatory Inscription by Sun Ch'iu-sheng and Others* (fig. 8), written several years later, in 502, has thicker strokes and more squared-off edges. Although apparently by a different hand, the two inscriptions share the same basic stylistic features.

Scholars have pointed out that the calligraphy on the Mang tomb epitaphs was executed with greater care than that in the Lung-men inscriptions. Evidence of this can be seen in Yüan Chen's and Yüan Ssu's epitaphs (figs. 5, 6), which show more subtle changes in the thickness of the strokes and greater variety in the shapes of the strokes. (It should also be noted that the tomb epitaphs are smaller in scale than the Lung-men stone engravings, and thus were easier to carve.) Despite these differences in the quality of the calligraphy, however, the epitaphs and the inscriptions display the same stylistic features of slanted compositions and angular, sharp-edged strokes.

This calligraphic style differs greatly from that of stone engravings produced in the P'ing-ch'eng period. The most significant difference between the two styles is the type of script employed. In Loyang, calligraphers adopted the regular script form for stone engravings in place of the older, more formal clerical (*li*) script, which had been in common use since the Han dynasty (206 BC–AD 220). Clerical-script characters are basically made up of horizontal and vertical strokes, with each stroke added onto another stroke. While the push and pull of the brush alters the thickness of the

Figure 8
Detail of figure 2, *Dedicatory Inscription by Sun Ch'iu-sheng and Others* (*Sun Ch'iu-sheng teng tsao-hsiang-chi*), Northern Wei dynasty (386–534), 502.

Figure 9
Detail of *Stele for the Temple of the Mountain Spirit of Mt. Sung* (*Sung-kao-ling-miao pei*), Northern Wei dynasty (386–534), 456. Rubbing of stone stele from Honan, 204 x 97 cm. Palace Museum, Peking. From *Chung-kuo mei-shu ch'üan-chi, Shu-fa chuan-k'o pien* (Peking: Jen-min-mei-shu ch'u-pan-she, 1986), v. 2, pl. 86.

Figure 10
Detail of *Epitaph of Liu Tai*, Southern Dynasties period (317–589), 487. Rubbing of stone epitaph unearthed from Cheng-chiang, Kiangsu, 65 x 55 cm. Original stone in Museum of Cheng-chiang, Kiangsu. From *Chung-kuo mei-shu ch'üan-chi, Shu-fa chuan-k'o pien* (Peking: Jen-min-mei-shu ch'u-pan-she, 1986), v. 2, pl. 79.

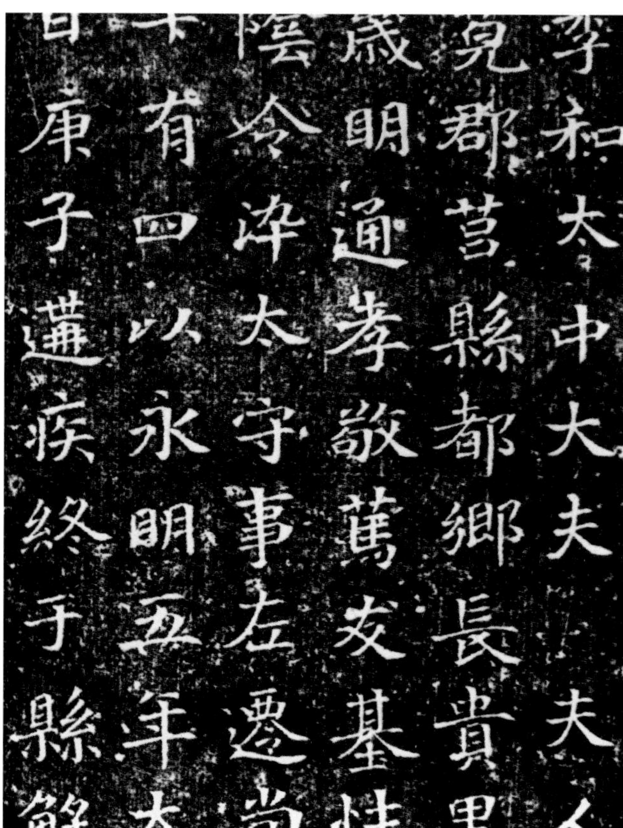

strokes, the movement of the brush is in one direction. The character composition is symmetrical and stable. Regular script was developed from clerical script after the fall of the Han dynasty, in the third century. In contrast to the earlier clerical-script form, regular script is characterized by freer brush movement and a more complex, less rigid character composition. Individual strokes may contain brush movements in more than one direction, and joints appear where the brush turns.

The stone panel from Ssu-ma Chin-lung's tomb (fig. 7), dated 484, is representative of the style of calligraphy on stone engravings from the late P'ing-ch'eng period. Unlike the regular script used in the Loyang examples, the calligraphy on this panel is executed in the older clerical-script form. Composed of even horizontal and vertical strokes, the characters are symmetrical and balanced. Although some of the brush movements resemble the brush turnings of regular script, most are additive and one-directional. Of the few extant examples of stone engravings from the P'ing-ch'eng period, the earliest is *Stele to Commemorate the Emperor's Eastern Tour* (*Huang-ti tung-hsün pei*), dated 437.[22] The same stylistic characteristics are seen in the *Stele for the Temple of the Mountain Spirit of Mt. Sung* (*Sung-kao-ling-miao pei*; fig. 9), erected two decades later, in 456.

In the late fifth century, regular script was written by brush on paper or silk and employed for daily use in the Northern Wei as well as the Southern Dynasties. The appropriation of regular script for stone engravings in Loyang represents a new invention in Northern Wei calligraphy, one most likely inspired by examples from the Southern Dynasties, such as the epitaphs of Liu Tai (d. 487; fig. 10) and Lü Ch'ao (d. 489),[23] both of which were excavated from tomb sites near Chien-k'ang (modern Nanking), the capital of the Southern Dynasties. Although the adoption of regular script for stone engravings may have been influenced by practices in the Southern Dynasties, the Northern Wei attitude toward the medium of stone and the style of calligraphy appropriate for stone engravings was quite different. Liu Tai's epitaph engraving, which recalls the regular-script style of the Southern Dynasties Monk Chih-yung (ca. 514–604) in his transcription of *The Thousand Character Essay* (*Ch'ien-tzu wen*; fig. 11), carefully reproduces the subtle changes in the thickness of the strokes and the minute movements of the brush in the fluid character composition of the original handwritten text. Judging from the Liu Tai epitaph and similar examples, Southern Dynasties carvers attempted to reproduce in the stone engravings the calligraphic style produced by the movements of brush on paper or silk.

Northern Wei Loyang engravings, in contrast, bear less resemblance to handwritten manuscripts. The *Avatamsaka Sutra* (*Hua-yen ching*; fig. 12), produced by the government-sponsored workshop at Tun-huang, in 513,[24] can be taken as a representative example of Northern Wei brush-written

Figure 11
Monk Chih-yung (ca. 514–604). Detail of *The Thousand Character Essay* (*Ch'ien-tzu wen*), Southern Dynasties period (317–589), 6th century. Ink on paper. Private Collection, Japan. From *Shoseki meihin sōkan* (Tokyo: Nigensha, 1964), v. 6, no. 69.

Figure 12
Detail of *Avatamsaka Sutra* (*Hua-yen ching*), Northern Wei dynasty (386–534), 513. Handscroll. Otani University, Kyoto. From Fujieda Akira, "Hokugi shahon kegonkyō," *Bokubi* 120 (1962), 16.

calligraphy during the late fifth and early sixth centuries. The slanted character composition in examples of engraved calligraphy from the same period—the *Dedicatory Inscription for Niu-chüeh* (fig. 1), *Dedicatory Inscription by Sun Ch'iu-sheng and Others* (figs. 2, 8), *Epitaph of Yüan Chen* (fig. 5), and *Epitaph of Yüan Ssu* (fig. 6)—reflect to some extent the style of the Tun-huang sutra scroll, but the engravings exaggerate the geometric shapes of the strokes. Angular, sharp edges are predominant, and the character composition is more restricted and regimented.

What is striking about the calligraphy of Northern Wei Loyang engravings is its close resemblance to graphic design. A comparison between the character *tien* in fig. 12 (third character) and the character *yüan* in fig. 1 (last character in the third column) is illuminating in this regard. The two characters have almost identical components, with similarly slanted angles and arrangements of strokes. Yet in the engraving (fig. 1), the individual strokes are more geometric in shape, with pronounced angular edges. Each stands alone as a discrete element instead of being smoothly connected to the next stroke as in the handwritten manuscript (fig. 12). Many scholars attribute this difference in calligraphic style to the skills of the stone carvers, their tools, and the limitations of the stone as a medium. However, I believe that the crisp, angular edges of the strokes and the reduction of three-dimensional turns into flat shapes are effects that were deliberately pursued by the Northern Wei Loyang calligraphers. Instead of mimicking the brushwork and character compositions of handwritten calligraphy, they chose to treat stone as a special medium for calligraphy distinct from silk or paper. The style of calligraphy in stone engravings arose from a collaborative effort between the calligrapher and the carver, in which the calligrapher took into account the nature of the medium and the carver's tools and turned to his advantage the special effects that could be realized in the working of a chisel on a stone surface.

Revival of the Tradition of Stone-Engraving Calligraphy in Loyang

While the use of regular script for stone engravings was derived from the Southern Dynasties, the actual style of calligraphy in Northern Wei Loyang was a revival of an earlier stone-engraving tradition from the late Eastern Han, Wei, and Western Chin periods. A rubbing of a fragment of the *Stone Classics* (fig. 13) erected at the Imperial Academy in Loyang during the Eastern Han dynasty, between 175 and 184, is evidence of this stylistic legacy. The square character composition and the shape of the carved strokes are more like graphic designs than forms written in ink with a flexible brush. The stiff turnings and sharp triangular-shaped endings of the strokes have the appearance of outlines that have been drawn and then filled in. Set alongside an example of calligraphy written with brush and ink on a bamboo slip (fig. 14), the schematic turnings and shapes of the strokes in the engraved characters appear to be reduced versions of the more complicated brush movements in the handwritten characters. Compare, for example, the character *yüan* in the bamboo slip (the first character in the first column) with the same character in the *Stone Classics* (the third character in the third column). The engraved character outlines the general shape of the right diagonal stroke of the brush-written character, dismissing the traces of the brush and further emphasizing the geometric quality of the stroke. The triangular-shaped ending of the left diagonal stroke shows the same process of reduction. The generalization of brush movements and stroke shapes in the *Stone Classics* is deliberate, not the result of poor execution. Each character has become an image or a symbol, and the movement of the calligrapher's hand has been erased. This style, which emphasized the emblematic quality of characters, was well suited for public and monumental stone stelae designed to promote the state-supported philosophy of Confucianism.

After the collapse of the Han empire, this calligraphic style continued to develop in the Three Kingdoms (220–280) and Western Chin periods. In the Western Chin *Stele for the Three Visits* (fig. 15), the triangular-shaped endings of the strokes seen in the earlier *Stone Classics* are further exaggerated with even sharper edges. Sometimes one stroke was written as two, the first resembling a dot, as in the vertical stroke in the center of the character *tung* (the last character in the third column) and sometimes an extra stroke was added, as in the radical *hsin* of the character *en* (the fourth character in the third column). The square composition and angular strokes of the characters displayed in the *Stele for Good Omens from Heaven* (*T'ien-fa shen-ch'en pei*; fig. 16) of the Wu kingdom (222–280), erected in 276, echo the style of the previous examples. This interest in creating highly ornamental effects in calligraphy for stone engravings is especially evident in works of the late third century. It is likely that the Northern Wei adopted the idea of emphasizing the display quality of characters from Eastern Han and, in particular, Western Chin practices.

A vast number of stone stelae from the late Eastern Han, Wei, and Western Chin provided Northern Wei calligraphers and craftsmen with a repertoire of stylistic sources for new artistic creation. One of the most important sources of stone engravings in Loyang was the stone stelae erected in front of the Imperial Academy, including the Eastern Han and Wei *Stone Classics* and the Western Chin *Stele for the Three Visits.* The *Stone Classics* were still partly intact despite the damage inflicted by wars and fire in the final years of the Eastern Han and Western Chin.[25] Before the relocation of the Northern Wei capital to Loyang, the *Stone Classics* had been cut down at the order of the governors of Lo-chou, including Feng Hsi (act. ca. 5th

Figure 13 (left)
Fragment of Stone Classics, Eastern Han dynasty (25–220), 175–84. Rubbing of stone engraving. Palace Museum, Peking. From *Chung-kuo mei-shu ch'üan-chi, Shu-fa chuan-k'o pien* (Peking: Jen-min-mei-shu ch'u-pan-she, 1987), v. 1, pl. 161.

Figure 14 (right)
Detail of *Memorial Written on a Bamboo Slip*, Eastern Han dynasty (25–220), 158–59. Ink on bamboo, 23 x 2.6 x 0.3 cm. Institute of Archaeology, Kansu. From *Chung-kuo mei-shu ch'üan-chi, Shu-fa chuan-k'o pien* (Peking: Jen-min-mei-shu ch'u-pan-she, 1987), v. 1, pl. 82.

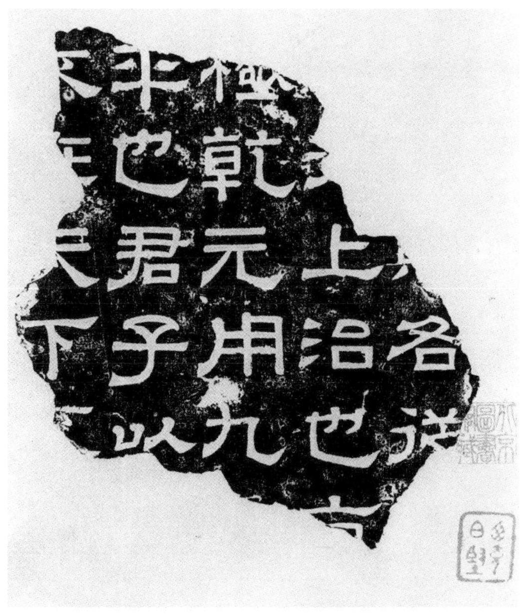

century) and Ch'ang Po-fu (act. ca. 5th century), to be used in the construction of Buddhist temples and pagodas.[26] Archaeological excavations have confirmed that many of the fragments of the Eastern Han *Stone Classics* discovered at the site of the Imperial Academy had been chipped, an indication that the stelae were cut down and reused as building materials.[27] Some of the fragments are in odd geometric shapes,[28] further evidence that the stones were cut down for this purpose. Fragments of Eastern Han tomb stelae have even been found in Northern Wei tombs where they were used as pillars to support gates.[29] Drawing upon this evidence, I propose that these stone stelae were more readily available to Northern Wei calligraphers and craftsmen than has previously been thought.

The calligraphic style of stone stelae inherited by Northern Wei calligraphers from the late Eastern Han, the Three Kingdoms, and the Western Chin held an important place in the history of calligraphy from the second to the fourth century. This style was categorized as stone-engraving script (*ming-shih shu*) in *The Collection of Capable Calligraphers from Ancient Times* (*Ts'ai ku-lai neng-shu jen-ming*), written in the fifth century by Yang Hsin (370–442). In this literary record, the famous third-century calligrapher Chung Yu (151–230) was noted for his mastery of three different script forms: stone-engraving script, singled out as his greatest specialty; manuscript script (*chang-ch'eng shu*), used in memorials and official documents on paper or silk; and free-running script (*hsing-ya shu*), used in correspondence with friends.[30] As attested by this record and other documentary sources, calligraphy was categorized according to function and media in the second and third centuries. Specific scripts were used for specific purposes, and clear distinctions were made between calligraphy for public use and calligraphy for private use. Distinctions were also made between calligraphy for stone engravings and calligraphy on paper or silk. Commemorative writings on stone, usually undertaken by the state for purposes of propaganda, were important and valued during this time.

Stone was prized for its durability, and, like bronze, had long been used by the Chinese for commemorative writings that were intended to last forever. Large stone stelae or slabs could be erected anywhere, for a multitude of purposes and for a large public audience, present and later generations included. The history of carving commemorative inscriptions on stone can be traced back to the fifth century BC or earlier,[31] and extends through modern times. Chinese commemorative stone engravings never took the form of figural representations; inscriptions served as the principal means of conveying messages. Stone engravings were used primarily for three purposes: to confirm or even foster the memory of a righteous ruler for the public; to mark the location of a tomb and commemorate the deceased; and to dedicate sculptures or temples. The state played a leading role in

Figure 15
Detail of *Stele for the Three Visits of the Emperor to the Imperial Academy* (*Huang-ti san-lin p'i-yung pei*), Western Chin dynasty (265–317), 278. Rubbing of stone stele from Yen-shih, Honan, 264 x 104 cm. Palace Museum, Peking. From *Chung-kuo mei-shu ch'üan-chi, Shu-fa chuan-k'o pien* (Peking: Jen-min-mei-shu ch'u-pan-she, 1986), v. 2, pl. 20.

Figure 16
Detail of *Stele for Good Omens from Heaven* (*T'ien-fa shen-ch'en pei*), Wu kingdom (222–280), 276. Rubbing of stone stele. Ninraku Museum, Nara. From *Shodō zenshū* (Tokyo: Heibonsha, 1965), v. 3, pl. 80.

sponsoring the production and installation of large inscribed stone stelae, which served effectively to broadcast a political program—an emperor's claim over certain territory, the heavenly mandate for his rule, the establishment of a set of norms for his people to follow, and so forth. It is no accident that the first large projects to set up stone markers, carried out at the order of the First Emperor of Ch'in (r. 221–205 BC) on his journeys to eastern China, were undertaken for political reasons.[32]

Stelae continued to be used for such purposes in later generations. In the Eastern Han dynasty, central and local governments erected stelae of the highest quality to propagate the state philosophy of Confucianism. The erection of stone stelae at the temple of Confucius in Ch'ü-fu, Shan-tung, and the *Stone Classics* at the Imperial Academy in Loyang, for example, were state-sponsored projects.[33] After the fall of the Eastern Han, the rulers of the rival Three Kingdoms made use of stone stelae to help establish their mandate to rule. Emperor Wen (r. 220–26) of Wei had erected a stele inscribed with a memorial from his officials exhorting him to take the throne and another stele inscribed with his acceptance in order to justify his having usurped the throne from the Han.[34] Emperor Kuei-ming (r. 264–84) of Wu established the *Stele for Good Omens from Heaven* to legitimize his claim of the heavenly mandate for his kingdom.[35] This tradition was continued in the Western Chin dynasty, as seen in the *Stele for the Three Visits* erected at the Imperial Academy in Loyang by faculty members and students to commemorate the visits of Emperor Wu (r. 265–89) and the heir-apparent.

Commentaries on calligraphy compiled in the fourth and fifth centuries describe the stone-engraving script as a form derived from *pa-fen*, a script used for inscriptions on precious vessels for the court and on stone stelae and large tablets for palaces, temples, and city gates. Many of the famous masters of the *pa-fen* script were civil officials in the central government who received their commissions from the emperor or the court. For instance, Ts'ai Yung (133–192), Court Gentlemen for Consultation (*I-lang*) during the Eastern Han, was the calligrapher of the *Stone Classics* that were erected at the Imperial Academy between 175 and 184.[36] After the Han empire collapsed, well-known masters of the *pa-fen* script, such as Shih I-kuan (act. ca. late 2nd–early 3rd century) and Liang Ku (act. ca. late 2nd–early 3rd century), were summoned by the generals of the rival military powers to write stelae, hanging scrolls, and palace tablets.[37] In the Western Chin dynasty, Ch'en Ch'ang (act. ca. 4th century), who served as Director of the Palace Library and was known for his *pa-fen* script, wrote the inscriptions for all the Western Chin palaces.[38]

Stone-engraving script apparently fell out of use after the collapse of the Western Chin, in 317. From that time until the reunification of the country under the Sui dynasty, in 589, China was divided among many short-lived dynasties and kingdoms. In the south, large commemorative stelae, especially those with political purposes, were rare. Most of the stone engravings dating from the Eastern Chin were intended for funerary purposes, and some were used as temporary tomb markers.[39] The earlier ornamental and emblematic stone-engraving script, such as that found in the Western Chin, was rarely employed in stone stelae in the Southern Dynasties.[40] Instead, a less formal and elaborate form of the clerical script was used in stone engravings.[41] After the Eastern Chin period, calligraphy on stone engravings in the Southern Dynasties tended to imitate the effect of handwriting, as seen in the *Epitaph of Liu Tai* (fig. 10) of 487.

The stone-engraving tradition that flourished under the Western Chin was forgotten — or perhaps intentionally disregarded — during the Southern Dynasties period. Calligraphy written with a brush on paper or silk, a form of writing that allowed more freedom of self-expression, began to attract the attention of calligraphers as well as critics. With the formation of imperial collections of works of famous calligraphers on paper and silk, critical commentaries on these works also flourished.[42] In his *Gradings of Calligraphers* (*Shu-p'in*), Yü Chien-wu (487–551) ranked 123 calligraphers from the second to the sixth century based on their writings in cursive and regular script on paper and silk. Although he acknowledged the different script types used for monumental inscriptions and the skills required to execute such calligraphy, Yü revealed his dislike of these script forms by excluding from his grading system calligraphers who practiced them.[43]

The Northern Wei revival of the stone-engraving style of calligraphy in Loyang during the late fifth and sixth centuries is notable in this historical context. Since the Eastern Han dynasty, the tradition of stone stelae and the special calligraphic style employed in stelae engravings — a form of writing that served to underscore the public, emblematic, and monumental features of the stone medium — had come to signify a strong and unified empire. The eagerness with which the Northern Wei court adopted and revived the stone-engraving tradition after the relocation of its capital to Loyang clearly reveals the desire of the court to associate itself with the lineage of the great empires of the Eastern Han and Western Chin.

1 *Chen* or *cheng* is usually referred to as *k'ai* (standard script) in modern scholarship. Further study is needed to clarify when the term *k'ai* in traditional texts on calligraphy was used to mean the type of script that will be discussed in this essay. It was probably not earlier than the late Northern Sung when Mi Fu (1052–1107) used the combined term *chen-k'ai* in his *Hai-yüeh ming-yen*; see Mi Fu, *Hai-yüeh ming-yen*, in Huang Chien, ed., *Li-tai shu-fa lun-wen-hsüan* (Selection of texts on calligraphy) (Shanghai: Shang-hai shu-hua ch'u-pan-she, 1979), v. 1, 361. *K'ai* was perhaps gradually accepted as the name for the script after that time. In most of the traditional texts on calligraphy, however, *chen* or *cheng* are the most commonly used terms. From the third to the sixth century, *k'ai* referred exclusively to the *pa-fen* script, a standardized form of *li* (clerical script) used mostly for monumental inscriptions in the second century. During this period, the new script *chen* or *cheng* was also called *li* or *chin-li* (modern *li*), since it derived from clerical script (which was supposedly invented by Chung Yu [151–230] in the third century). To avoid confusion in this essay, I use *chen*, *cheng*, or regular script to describe the script type of Northern Wei Loyang calligraphy instead of *k'ai*, *li*, or modern *li*. *Li* will refer exclusively to the old clerical script.

2 Archaeological finds show that the city walls of Northern Wei Loyang actually followed those of ancient Loyang. The remains of the city are located approximately 15 km east of the modern city of Loyang, which is bordered on the north and northwest by the Mang Mountains and overlooks the Lo River to the south. See Wang Chung-shu, *Han Civilization*, trans. K.C. Chang et al. (New Haven and London: Yale University Press, 1982), 36–41. Archaeological reports include "Han Wei Loyang ch'eng ch'u-pu k'an-ch'a" (Preliminary surveys of the Han and Wei cities of Loyang), *K'ao-ku*, no. 4 (1973), 198–203; "Han Wei Loyang ch'eng i-hao fang-tzu ho ch'u-t'u te wa-wen" (House floor no. 1 and unearthed tile inscriptions in the city of Loyang of the Han and Wei dynasties), *K'ao-ku*, no. 4 (1973), 209–14; Su Pai, "Pei Wei Loyang ch'eng ho Pei Mang ling-mu" (The city of Loyang of the Northern Wei and imperial tombs of the northern Mang), *Wen-wu*, no. 7 (1978), 42–52. Written sources include the descriptions of the city of Loyang in the official histories of Northern Wei and Yang Hsüan-chih's *Loyang ch'ieh-lan chi*, (Records of the monasteries of Loyang), written about 550.

3 The program included land and tax reforms, changes in the local government and the bureaucracy, and revisions in the genealogical classification of the aristocracy. See W.J.F. Jenner, *Memories of Loyang: Yang Hsüan-chih and the Lost Capital (493–534)* (Oxford: Clarendon Press, 1981), 28–29.

4 On the decision to relocate and the process of relocating, see ibid., 38–62.

5 For Emperor Hsiao-wen's conversation with one of his confidants about the relocation of the capital, see Wei Shou, *Wei shu* (Wei History) (Peking: Chung-hua shu-chü, 1974), v. 2:19, 464–65.

6 Ibid., v. 1:7, part 2, 176–77.

7 Anyone under the age of thirty who violated this decree could suffer dismissal from the court. See ibid., v. 2:21, part 1, 536.

8 Ibid., v. 1:7, part 2, 178.

9 Ibid., v. 1:7, part 2, 179.

10 Ssu-ma Kuang, *Tzu-chih-t'ung-chien* (Peking: Chung-hua-shu-chü, 1956), v. 10:140, 4393.

11 Wei Shou, *Wei shu*, v. 1:7, part 2, 173.

12 Ibid., v. 1:7, part 2, 178.

13 The earliest and longest inscription at Yün-kang is dated 483. Carved on a horizontal rectangular stone panel placed beneath three seated bodhisattvas, it dedicates the sculptures to Emperor Hsiao-wen and his grandmother, the dowager empress Feng. See *Chung-kuo mei-shu ch'üan-chi, Tiao-su pien* (The complete works of Chinese art: sculpture) (Peking: Wen-wu ch'u-pan-she, 1988), v. 10, 124.

14 The Mang tombs have been extensively plundered and damaged over time. Using the few existing records and based on evidence from several archaeological excavations since 1949, scholars have been trying to locate the Northern Wei tombs in this area. See Kuo Yü-t'ang, *Lo-yang ch'u-t'u shih-k'o shih-ti chi* (A record of the times and locations of the unearthed stone engravings in Loyang) (Loyang: Lo-yang ta-hua shu-pao kung-ying-she, 1941). For archaeological reports, see "Lo-yang Yüan Shao mu" (Yüan Shao's tomb in Loyang), *K'ao-ku*, no. 4 (1973), 218–24; "Ho-nan Lo-yang Pei-Wei Yüan I mu tiao-ch'a" (Survey of the Northern Wei tomb of Yüan I in Loyang), *Wen-wu*, no. 12 (1974), 53–55. No imperial tomb has been officially excavated. Scholars and archaeologists have tentatively identified several large mounds on the west bank of the Ch'an River, which runs north to south through the Mang Mountains, as the mausoleums of the emperors Hsiao-wen, Hsüan-wu (r. 500–27), and Hsiao-chuang (r. 527–28). Most of the other royal tombs are located on the east side of the Ch'an River. See "Lo-yang Pei-Wei Ch'ang-ling i-chih tiao-ch'a" (Survey of the Ch'ang mausoleum of the Northern Wei in Loyang), *K'ao-ku*, no. 3 (1966), 155–58; "Lo-yang Pei-Wei Ching-ling wei-chih te ch'üeh-ting ho Ching-ling wei-chih te t'ui-ts'e" (Confirmation of the location of the Ching mausoleum and speculation about the location of the Ching mausoleum in Loyang), *Wen-wu*, no. 7 (1978), 36–41.

15 "Meng-hsien ch'u-t'u Pei-Wei Ssu-ma Yüeh mu-chih" (The Northern Wei stone epitaphs of Ssu-ma Yüeh unearthed in Meng county), *Wen-wu*, no. 12 (1982), 44–46; "Ho-nan sheng Meng-hsien ch'u-t'u Pei-Wei Ssu-ma Yüeh mu-chih" (The Northern Wei stone epitaphs of Ssu-ma Yüeh unearthed in Meng county, Honan), *K'ao-ku*, no. 3 (1983), 279–81.

16 See, for example, *Epitaph of Liu Tao*, in *Chung-kuo mei-shu ch'üan-chi, Shu-fa chuan-k'o pien* (Complete works of Chinese art: calligraphy and seal-carving) (Peking: Jen-min-mei-shu ch'u-pan-she, 1986), v. 2, pl. 25.

17 For further discussion of this topic, see Hua Jen-te, "Wei Chin Nan-pei-ch'ao mu-chih kai-lun" (A general survey of epitaphs from the period of disunity), in Liu Cheng-ch'eng, ed., *Chung-kuo shu-fa ch'üan-chi* (Peking: Jung-pao-chai, 1995), v. 13, 1–17.

18 "Shan-si Ta-t'ung Shih-chia-chai Pei-Wei Ssu-ma Chin-lung mu" (Ssu-ma Chin-lung's tomb in Shih-chia-chai, Ta-t'ung, Shan-si), *Wen-wu*, no. 3 (1972), 26–27.

19 *Pei-ching t'u-shu-kuan ts'ang Chung-kuo li-tai t'o-p'ien hui-pien* (The collection of rubbings in the Peking Library) (Cheng-chou: Chung-chou ku-chi ch'u-pan-she, 1989), v. 3–5.

20 Chao Wan-li, *Han Wei Nan-pei-ch'ao mu-chih chi-shih* (Catalogue of epitaphs from the Han, Wei, and Northern and Southern Dynasties), in *Shih-k'o shih-liao hsin-pien, ti-san-pien* (Historical materials of stone engravings, third compilation) (Taipei: Hsin-wen-feng ch'u-pan kung-ssu, 1986), v. 3, 4.

21 Chao arranged the epitaphs by the genealogy of the owners of the tomb instead of the dates in order to facilitate the use of the texts as a source of information on the history of the Northern Wei dynasty.

22 The stele records Emperor T'ai-wu's (r. 424–51) patrol to Mt. Heng (in modern Hopei) and his demonstration of riding and shooting in front of officials on his way back to P'ing-ch'eng. See *Chung-kuo mei-shu ch'üan-chi, Shu-fa chuan-k'o pien* (1986), v. 2, 154–55.

23 For Lü Ch'ao's epitaph, see *Shodō zenshū* (Tokyo: Heibonsha, 1966), v. 5, pl. 21.

24 For a study of the sutra copying office in Tun-huang during the Northern Wei, see Fujieda Akira, "The Tunhuang Manuscripts: A General Description (Part II)," *Zinbun* 10 (1969), 17–22; and "Hokugi shahon kegonkyō," *Bokubi* 120, 1–40.

25 Wei Shuo, *Wei shu*, v. 5:83, part 1, 1819; and v. 1:7, part 2, 173.

26 See Feng Hsi's biography in Wei Shuo, *Wei shu*, v. 5: 83, part 1, 1819; and Ts'ui Kuang's biography in ibid., v. 4:67, 1494.

27 "Lo-yang ku-ch'eng t'ai-hsüeh i-chih hsin ch'u-t'u te Han shih-ching ts'an-shih" (The fragments of Han stone classics unearthed at the site of the Imperial Academy in Lo-yang), *K'ao-ku*, no. 4 (1982), 386–87.

28 See *Chung-kuo mei-shu ch'üan-chi, Shu-fa chuan-k'o pien* (Peking: Jen-min mei-shu ch'u-pan-she, 1987), v. 1, 162–63.

29 Ibid., v. 1, 90; pl. 112.

30 Huang Chien, ed., *Li-tai shu-fa lun-wen-hsüan* (Shanghai: Shang-hai-shu-hua ch'u-pan-she, 1979), v. 1, 46.

31 The earliest example of engraved inscriptions on stone is probably the *Stone Drums* (*Shih-ku*), ten round stones engraved with poetry. See *Chung-kuo mei-shu ch'üan-chi, Shu-fa chuan-k'o pien* (1987), v. 1, pl. 24.

32 The First Emperor of Ch'in set up stone markers on the mountains he ascended and had inscribed on the markers texts praising the virtue of the Ch'in state. The inscriptions describe the emperor's great accomplishments in unifying the world, subjugating all, adjusting laws and regulations, clarifying human concerns, and bringing peace and happiness to all. The purpose of setting up inscribed stone markers was to claim his authority over the territory and to ensure that the virtue and achievements of the Ch'in would never be forgotten. Six stone markers were set up on Mount I, Mount T'ai, Mount Lang-yeh, and Mount Chih-fu, in modern Shan-tung; Mount Kuei-chi, in modern Chekiang, and Mount Chieh-shih, in modern Hopei. Fragments of the stone markers on Mount T'ai and Mount Lang-yeh still survive today. See Ssu-ma Ch'ien, *Shih chi* (Records of the Grand Historian) (Peking: Chung-hua shu-chü, 1959), v. 1, 242–52. For stone markers on Mount T'ai and Mount Lang-yeh, see *Shodō zenshū* (Tokyo: Heibonsha, 1965), v. 1, pls. 135, 136.

33 For the study of the *Stone Classics*, see Chang Kuo-kan, *Li-tai shih-ching k'ao* (An examination of stone classics in successive generations) (Taipei: Ting-wen shu-chü, 1972). For archaelogical reports, see "Han-Wei Loyang ku-ch'eng t'ai-hsüeh i-chih hsin-ch'u-t'u te Han shih

ching ts'an-shih" (The fragments of Han stone classics in the remains of the Imperial Academy in Loyang), *K'ao-ku*, no. 4 (1982), 381–89.

34 For a general description of the background and texts of these two stelae, see *Shodō zenshū* (Tokyo: Heibonsha, 1965), v. 1, 164–66. For illustrations of the stelae, see ibid., pls. 55–58. Emperor Wen of Wei also erected a stele at the Temple of Confucius in Ch'ü-fu, Shantung, to praise his act of bestowing titles of honor on Confucius' descendants and restoring the Temple of Confucius. This was part of his program to justify his assumption of the throne. See ibid., v. 1, 166; pls. 59–60.

35 See *Shodō zenshū* (Tokyo: Heibonsha, 1965), v. 1, 172–73; pls. 77–82.

36 Fan Yeh, *Hou Han shu* (Eastern Han History) (Peking: Chung-hua shu-chü, 1973), v. 7:60, part 2, 1990. Chiang Shih, *Lun-shu piao* (Memorial on calligraphy), in Huang Chien, ed., *Li-tai shu-fa lun-wen hsüan*, v. 1, 65.

37 Wei Heng, *Ssu-t'i shu-shih* (Forces of the four scripts), in Huang Chien, ed., *Li-tai shu-fa lun-wen hsüan*, v. 1, 15.

38 Yang Hsin, *Ts'ai ku-lai neng-shu jen-ming* (Collection of capable calligraphers from ancient times), in Huang Chien, ed., *Li-tai shu-fa lun-wen hsüan*, v. 1, 46.

39 Hua Jen-te argues that most of the Eastern Chin epitaphs were temporary tomb markers of aristocrats transferred from the north. See Hua Jen-te, "Lun Tung-chin mu-chih chian-chi lan-t'ing lun-pien" (On the epitaphs from Eastern Chin and the debates on Lan-t'ing), *Ku-kung hsüeh-shu chi-k'an* 13, no. 1 (Autumn 1995), 27–62.

40 The *Epitaph of Hsieh-k'un* (dated 323), for example, is evidently a continuation of the Western Chin stone-engraving tradition. See *Chung-kuo mei-shu ch'üan-chi, Shu-fa chuan-k'o pien* (1986), v. 2, pl. 68. The pointed, sharp strokes of the characters in *Stele for Ts'uan Pao-tzu* (dated 405), in the Yün-nan area, also share the same ornamental features of the examples in the Western Chin. See *Chung-kuo mei-shu ch'üan-chi, Shu-fa chuan-k'o pien* (1986), v. 2, pl. 71.

41 For example, *Epitaphs of Wang Hsing-chih and His Wife*. See *Chung-kuo mei-shu ch'üan-chi, Shu-fa chuan-k'o pien* (1986), v. 2, pl. 69.

42 On imperial collections of calligraphic works, see Yü Ho's (act. ca. 5th century) account of remounting and cataloguing the calligraphy collections of Emperor Ming (r. 465–72) of Sung. Yü Ho, *Lun-shu piao* (Memorial on calligraphy), in Huang Chien, ed., *Li-tai shu-fa lun-wen hsüan*, v. 1, 49–55.

43 Yü Chien-wu, *Shu-p'in* (Gradings of calligraphers), in Huang Chien, ed., *Li-tai shu-fa lun-wen hsüan*, v. 1, 86.

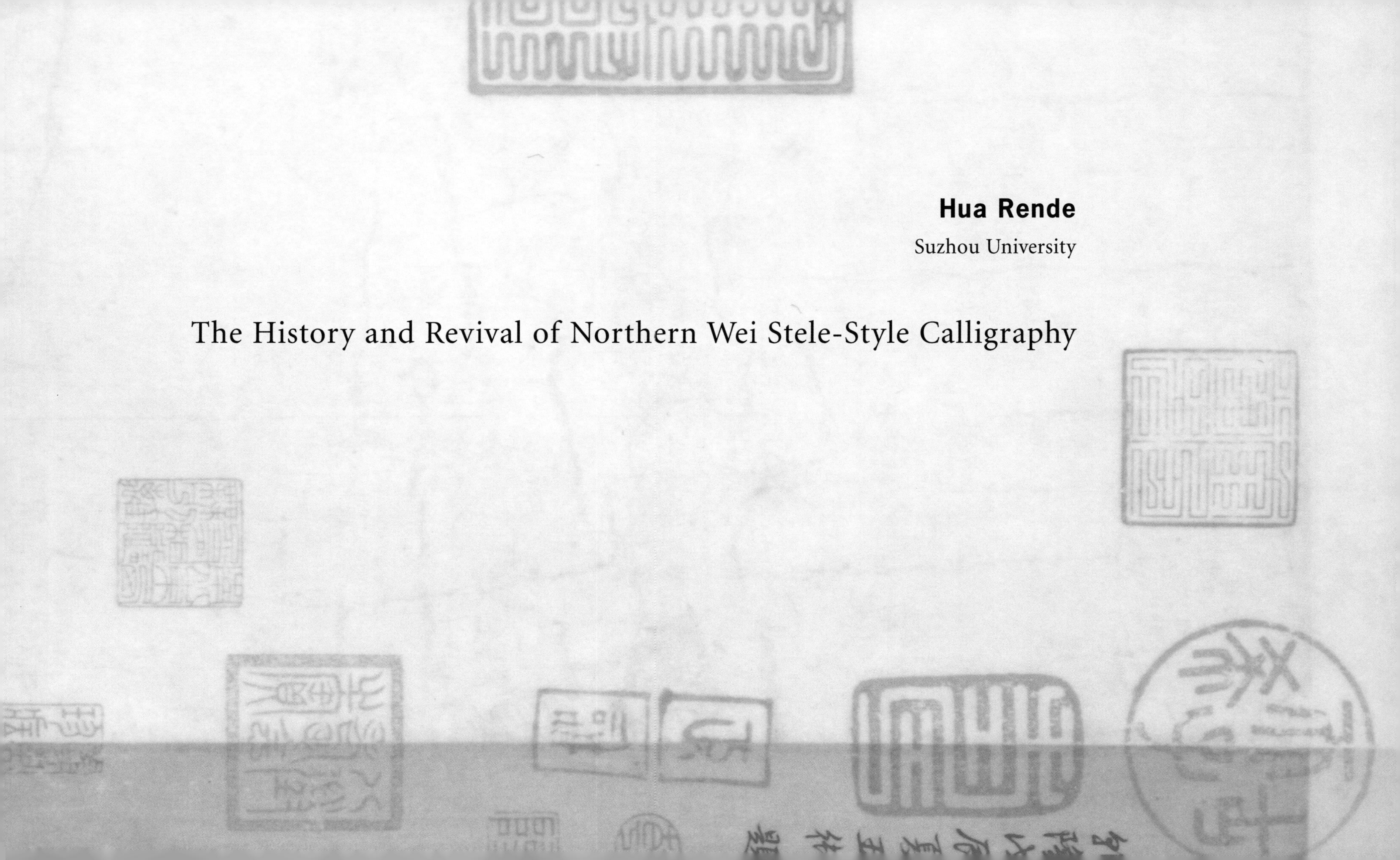

Hua Rende

Suzhou University

The History and Revival of Northern Wei Stele-Style Calligraphy

The term "Wei stele style" (*Wei pei t'i*) was first used by scholars in the late Ch'ing dynasty (1644–1911) to describe the type of calligraphy engraved on Northern Wei (386–534) stelae in the area of Loyang, Honan. This style, characterized by a compact structure, slanting strokes, and prominent angular dots, is an early variation of standard script (*k'ai-shu*). The period in which the style flourished corresponds to the years following Emperor Hsiao-wen's (r. 471–99) relocation of the Northern Wei capital to Loyang in 494 and up to the collapse of the dynasty in 534. Representative works from this period include *Twenty Inscriptions from Lung-men* (*Lung-men erh-shih p'in*), inscriptions on tomb epitaphs from the T'ai-ho (477–99), Ching-ming (500–503), and Cheng-shih (504–508) reign periods, and commemorative stelae such as those for Chia Ssu-po (*Chia Ssu-po pei*), Chang Meng-lung (*Chang Meng-lung pei*), and Monk Ken of Ma-ming Temple (*Ma-ming-ssu Ken fa-shih pei*).

Northern Wei Stele Style and the Calligraphic Tradition of the Ts'ui and Lu Families

During the Han and Wei dynasties, among scholarly families special aptitudes in classical scholarship and the art of calligraphy were passed down from generation to generation. The Ts'ui and Lu families of Shansi produced a number of accomplished calligraphers. According to documentary sources of the period, the calligraphic styles practiced by these two families were highly influential in the early years of the Northern Wei. Ts'ui Hung's (d. 418) biography in the *Wei History* (*Wei shu*) describes his place in the family lineage and goes on to discuss the transmission of calligraphic styles within the Ts'ui and Lu families:

> Hsüan-po [Ts'ui Hung] did not write court proclamations and official documents. He especially excelled at informal writing in cursive [*ts'ao*] and clerical [*li*] scripts, and his calligraphy was used as a model by many. Ts'ui Yüeh, Hsüan-po's grandfather, and Lu Shen [284–350] of Fan-yang were well known for their wide-ranging accomplishments in the art of calligraphy. Lu Shen modeled his style on that of Chung Yu [151–230], while Ts'ui Yüeh worked in the tradition of Wei Kuan [220–291]. For cursive script, however, both Ts'ui Yüeh and Lu Shen studied

> the calligraphy of So Ching [239–303], whose genius each was able to capture. Lu Shen transmitted his art to his son Lu Yen; and Lu Yen transmitted his art to his son Lu Miao.[1] Ts'ui Yüeh transmitted his art to his son Ts'ui Ch'ien, and Ts'ui Ch'ien transmitted his art to his son Ts'ui Hsüan-po. In this way, calligraphic traditions were passed on within these families for generations without interruption. As a result, at the beginning of the Northern Wei, the two most highly valued calligraphic styles were those of the Ts'ui and Lu families. Hsüan-po's free-running (*hsing-ya*) script was especially deft, though there are few surviving examples.[2]

From this we learn that the clerical and standard script styles of the Ts'ui and Lu families were based respectively on those of Wei Kuan and Chung Yu. These traditions that were inherited by the two families were relatively conservative, and the standard script must have been like that of the Wei-Chin period (3rd–5th century), with strong traces of clerical script.

Ts'ui Hung's son Ts'ui Hao (d. 450) was, like his father, a highly regarded calligrapher. According to the biography of the Secretarial Court Gentleman Li Ching-hsi in the official history of the Northern Chou (557–581) dynasty (*Chou shu*), Li Ching-hsi "liked to study antiquity. Once he studied calligraphy with Minister of Personnel Ts'ui Hsüan-po. He also learned standard and seal scripts from Minister of Education Ts'ui Hao, as these calligraphic traditions were transmitted in the Ts'ui family."[3] Ts'ui Hao's biography in the *Wei History* states that "Hao was a skilled calligrapher. People often requested copies of the *Model Essay on Draft Cursive* [*Chi-chiu-chang*] from him."[4] Ts'ui Hao made several hundred copies of this work during his lifetime. While his calligraphy was as forceful as that of his ancestors, in terms of technical skill it was not as deftly executed. Praised by his contemporaries, Ts'ui Hao's calligraphy in standard, seal (*chuan*), and draft-cursive (*chang-ts'ao*) was assembled in various combinations for use in model-books.[5] In 450 Ts'ui Hao was executed by the Northern Wei Emperor T'ai-wu (r. 424–52). In fact, the entire Ts'ui family of Ch'ing-ho was put to death, along with the Lu family of Fan-yang, the Kuo family of T'ai-yüan, and the Liu family of Ho-tung, all of whom were related by marriage to the Ts'ui clan.

Since the Ts'ui and Lu families enjoyed great reputations, it is not surprising that their calligraphic styles were highly valued. Nor is it surprising that inscriptions on stelae erected by the state during the early Northern Wei period show the influence of their styles. Before the relocation of the Northern Wei capital to Loyang in the late fifth century, stelae inscriptions were executed in a calligraphic style that incorporated many of the features of clerical script. Examples include *Stele for the Temple of Mt. Hua* (*Ta-tai*

Figure 1 (left)
Detail of *Stele for the Temple of the Mountain Spirit of Mt. Sung* (*Sung-kao-ling-miao pei*), Northern Wei dynasty (386–534), 456. Rubbing. From *Chung-kuo mei-shu ch'üan-chi, Shu-fa chuan-k'o pien* (Peking: Jen-min mei-shu ch'u-pan-she, 1986), v. 2, 157.

Figure 2 (right)
Detail of *Stele to Commemorate the Emperor's Eastern Tour* (*Huang-ti tung-hsün chih pei*), Northern Wei dynasty (386–534). Rubbing. From *Chung-kuo mei-shu ch'üan-chi, Shu-fa chuan-k'o pien*, v. 2, 155.

Figure 3
Detail of *Buddhasamghati Sutra* (*Chu Fo yao chi ching*), Western Chin dynasty (265–317). *Chung-kuo mei-shu ch'üan-chi, Shu-fa chuan-k'o pien*, v. 2, 57.

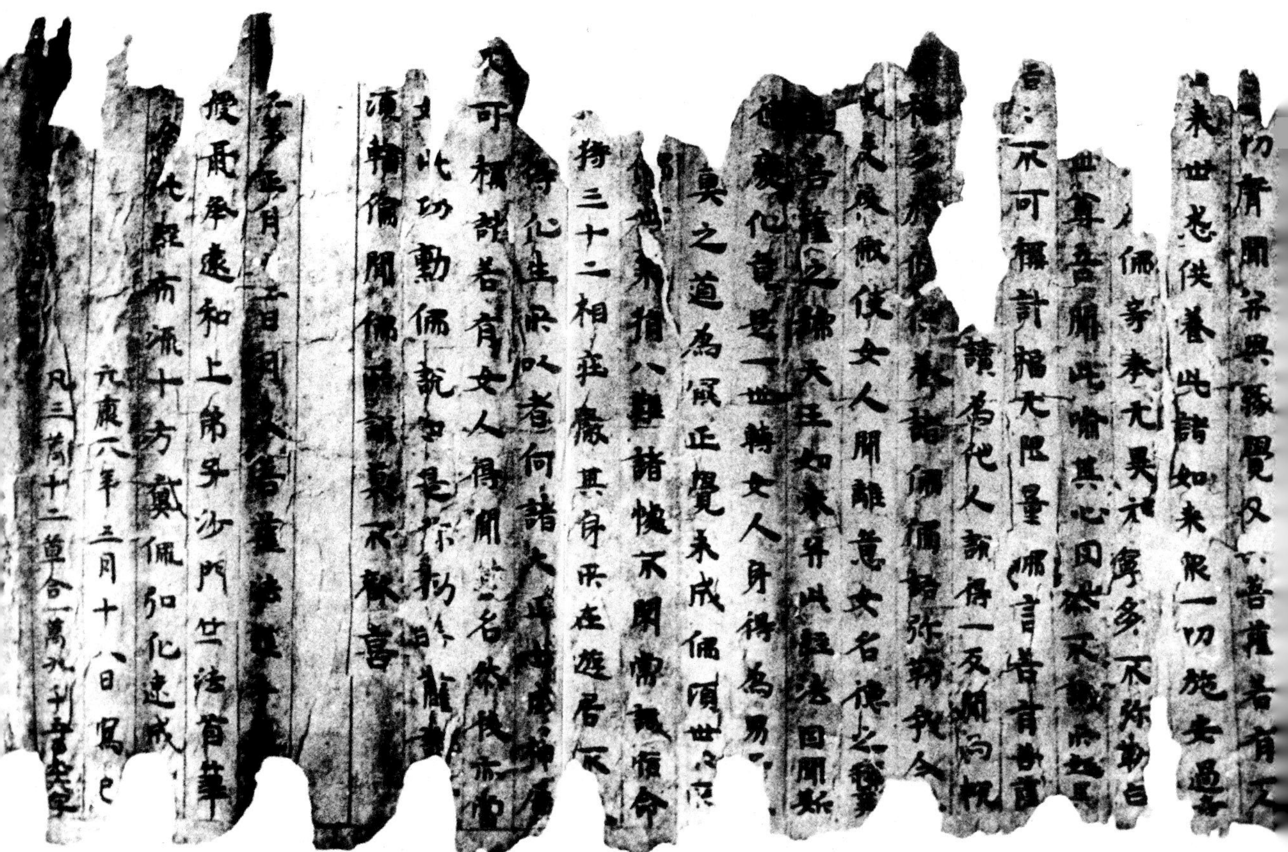

Hua-yüeh miao pei); *Stele for the Temple of the Mountain Spirit of Mt. Sung* (*Sung-kao-ling-miao pei*; fig. 1), dated 456;[6] and *Stele Commemorating Pi-kan* (*Tiao Pi-kan wen*).

Other works such as *Stele to Commemorate the Emperor's Eastern Tour* (*Huang-ti tung-hsün chih pei*; fig. 2) and *Hymn in Praise of the Emperor's Southern Tour* (*Huang-ti nan-hsün chih sung*) still have many characteristics in common with clerical script, but the characters are more slanted and their structure is more compact. However, as we will see in the discussion that follows, true Northern Wei stele-style calligraphy was not part of the Ts'ui-Lu calligraphic tradition.

Northern Wei Stele-Style Calligraphy and Sutra-Writing Style

At the end of the Western Chin dynasty (265–317), the various ethnic groups of northern China formed independent political units, which vied with each other to rule central China. With the fall of the Western Chin capital Loyang in 311, large numbers of aristocratic families emigrated south. In 317 Ssu-ma Jui, Prince of Lang-yeh, founded the Eastern Chin (317–420), establishing his capital at Chien-k'ang (modern Nanking). For the next 270 years—a period marked by political disunity and military rivalry—north and south China were cut off from each other, and cultural exchange was all but impossible.[7]

In the south, the calligraphy of Wang Hsi-chih (303–361) and his son Wang Hsien-chih (344–386) was very popular. The southern calligraphic style, however, did not make a mark in north China until Yü Chin-teng conquered Chiang-ling in 554. After Wang Pao, a famous scholar at the court of the southern Liang dynasty (502–557), traveled to Ch'ang-an (modern Sian), aristocrats of the Northern Chou (557–581) began to study his calligraphy. Wang Pao's calligraphy, which exemplified the southern style, was deeply indebted to that of his maternal uncle Hsiao Tzu-yün, who earned fame as an innovative calligrapher in the southern tradition of Chung Yu and the Two Wangs. The introduction of the southern calligraphic style into north China was a momentous development, resulting in a significant change in the calligraphic style of the Northern Dynasties. Prior to this development, the calligraphic styles of north and south China were completely different, a reflection of the long years of political disunity and lack of cultural interchange.

During the period of the Northern and Southern Dynasties (317–589) Buddhist monks traveled freely between the north and the south.[8] The discovery of the Library Cave at the Mo-kao caves in Tun-huang, in 1900, brought to light thousands of examples of calligraphy from the Eastern Chin, the Sixteen Kingdoms (301–439), and even the Northern Sung (960–1127). Most of these works are copies of Buddhist sutras. Other sutras from

Figure 4 (left)
Fragment of *Upasakashila Sutra* (*Yu-p'o-sai chieh ching*), Northern Liang (397–439). From *Chung-kuo mei-shu ch'üan-chi, Shu-fa chuan-k'o pien*, v. 2, 64.

Figure 5 (right)
Detail of *Avatamsaka Sutra* (*Hua-yen ching*), Northern Wei dynasty (386–534). From *Chung-kuo mei-shu ch'üan-chi, Shu-fa chuan-k'o pien*, v. 2, 203.

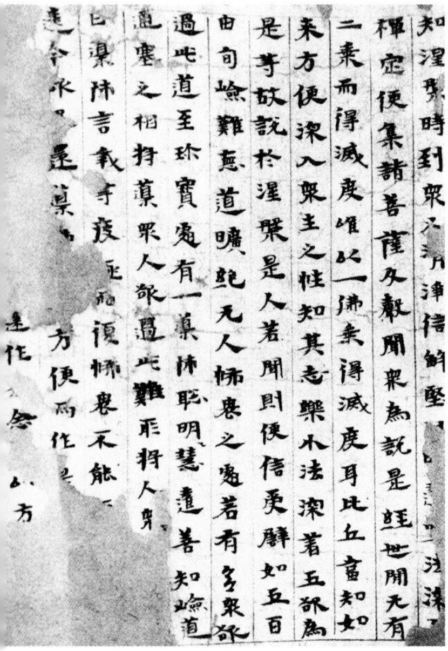

these periods have also been recovered from sites in Sinkiang, including Kucha and Shan-shan.[9]

Buddhism was introduced to China from India in the Eastern Han dynasty (25–220). The first sutra translated in China was the *Sutra in Forty-two Sections* (*Ssu-shih-erh-chang ching*). During the years that he lived and worked in China, in the mid-second century, the Central Asian monk An Shih-kao translated more than thirty Buddhist sutras; Chih Ch'ien, another foreign monk, translated more than ten sutras. Other Central Asian as well as Chinese monks also took part in sutra translation projects. During the Wei and the Chin dynasties, the pace of activity increased, with hundreds of sutras translated and circulated in manuscript copies. Aside from Loyang, translations were carried out in Tun-huang, T'ien-shui, Ch'ang-an, Sung-shan, Ch'en-liu, Huai-yang, and Kuang-chou, among other places.

The calligraphy of the majority of sutras copied during the Wei and Chin periods reflects certain stylistic changes that first appear at the end of the Han dynasty (206 BC–AD 220), when clerical script began to give way to standard and running script. In the sutra-style calligraphy of this period, the horizontal and right diagonal strokes resemble the rhythmic and plump strokes of clerical script, but the left diagonal strokes (*p'ieh*) and hooks (*kou*) that are characteristic of standard script begin to appear. In the split-stroke, or *pa-fen*, style of Eastern Han stele inscriptions, the *p'ieh* and *kou* strokes are almost nonexistent. These types of strokes first occurred with the rapid execution of clerical script, which required a reduction in the number of strokes, and thereafter became a basic feature of standard-script calligraphy.

In copying sutras, characters could not be written cursorily, as this would demonstrate a lack of reverence. Nevertheless, sutras had to be produced with maximum efficiency. For this reason, the beginning of a stroke was made with the tip of the brush, with no attempt to round it out; strokes were finished by pressing the brush down hard. Changes in brush direction were executed by stopping the brush momentarily but without lifting the brush completely off the paper, which imparted a feeling of strength and vigor to the characters (fig. 3). Moreover, a grid was employed in the copying of sutras, with the number of lines per page and the number of characters per line (usually 17) following certain rules. An earlier copy of the same sutra was used as a model. Those who copied sutras were usually monks and nuns or professional sutra-copiers. They seldom had the opportunity to see examples of calligraphy by famous masters, and learned their calligraphic style from the sutra manuscripts, using the manuscripts as their models and refraining from making their own innovations. Thus the sutra-writing style changed little as it was transmitted during the Wei and Chin dynasties, and most of the sutras translated during the

Northern and Southern Dynasties were copied in this style. Although the calligraphic style of sutras became less like clerical script in the latter half of the Northern and Southern Dynasties, it remained distinct from other styles of calligraphy (figs. 4, 5). Known in later times as "Six Dynasties sutra-writing style" (*Liu-ch'ao hsieh-ching-t'i*), this type of calligraphy was employed in both north and south China.

Early Northern Wei Stele-Style Calligraphy: Dedicatory Inscriptions at the Lung-men Caves

Calligraphy employed in dedicatory inscriptions (*tsao-hsiang chi*) of Buddhist images differs greatly from that in Buddhist sutras. In ancient times, when believers in the religion sought benefit for themselves or others, they often had images of Buddhas erected in temples or carved in caves. Occasionally these images were cast in gold. (Taoists also produced images, but in far fewer numbers.) Dedicatory inscriptions recorded the name of the Buddha, a prayer, and perhaps the name of the donor. Although the carving of such inscriptions reached the height of popularity during the late Northern Dynasties period, the practice continued into the Ming dynasty (1368–1644).

After the Northern Wei capital was moved to Loyang in 494, work was begun on the Lung-men Caves, in I-ch'üeh, southwest of the city. Caves and niches were constructed at Lung-men from this time forward. At Lung-men, there are more than 2,100 caves, 10,000 Buddhist images, and 3,600 inscriptions carved in niches or on stelae, most of which date to the Northern Wei, T'ang (618–907), and Ming periods. In the Ku-yang cave, the oldest at Lung-men, there are twenty relatively long dedicatory inscriptions, in addition to shorter ones. Most of the Ku-yang cave inscriptions were carved between 495 and 507 (from the nineteenth year of the T'ai-ho reign period to the fourth year of the Cheng-shih reign period). In the Ch'ing dynasty, these inscriptions became known as the *Twenty Inscriptions from Lung-men.*

During the Han and the Wei, engraved stelae and epitaphs were produced in great quantities in the Loyang area. Although stelae production was periodically prohibited and the stelae often destroyed, the tradition of stone engravings was better preserved in Loyang than elsewhere. The hard, gray limestone cliffs of the I-ch'üeh mountains was well suited to the detailed carving of characters, a factor that contributed to the proliferation of Buddhist images and inscriptions at Lung-men. Moreover, the quality of the rock assured that the inscriptions would endure over time.

During the Northern Dynasties period (386–581), the carving of dedicatory inscriptions to accompany Buddhist images was a common practice in Shensi, Honan, Hopei, and Shantung. While the construction of caves and the sculpting of Buddhist images occurred in northwest China during this period, the practice of carving inscriptions was rare. For example, there is only one inscription from this period in the Yün-kang Caves, *Dedicatory Inscription by Monk Fa-tsung and Others* (*I-shih Fa-tsung teng wu-shih-ssu jen tsao-hsiang-chi*; fig. 6), dated 483. The paucity of inscriptions at Yün-kang may be attributed to the fact that the coarse sandstone of the caves proved unsuitable for the carving of characters.

The practice of carving such inscriptions began with the creation of the Lung-men Caves. The Ch'ing scholar K'ang Yu-wei (1858–1927) stated in the *Kuang i-chou shuang-chi* that the "Buddha image inscriptions at Lung-men belong to one style. Among the earliest examples of the angular brush style, they convey a sense of grandeur and strength." Representative works from Lung-men include:

1. *Dedicatory Inscription by Madam Ch'iu-mu for Her Deceased Son Niu-Chüeh* (*Ch'iu-mu Ling-liang fu-jen yu ch'ih tsao-hsiang-chi*), dated 495
2. *Dedicatory Inscription by I-fu* (*I-fu tsao-hsiang-chi*), dated 496
3. *Dedicatory Inscription by Monk Hui-ch'eng* (*Pi-ch'iu Hui-ch'eng tsao-hsiang-chi*; fig. 7), dated 498

Figure 6
Dedicatory Inscription by Monk Fa-tsung and Others (*I-shih Fa-tsung teng wu-shih-ssu jen tsao-hsiang-chi*), Northern Wei dynasty (386–534), 483. From *Chung-kuo mei-shu ch'üan-chi, Tiao-su pien*, v. 10, 124.

Figure 7 (left)
Dedicatory Inscription by Monk Hui-Ch'eng (*Pi-ch'iu Hui-ch'eng tsao-hsiang-chi*), Northern Wei dynasty (386–534), 498. Rubbing. From *Chung-kuo mei-shu ch'üan-chi, Shu-fa chuan-k'o pien,* v. 2, 162.

Figure 8 (right)
Detail of *Dedicatory Inscription by Sun Ch'iu-sheng, Liu Ch'i-tsu, and Others* (*Sun Ch'iu-sheng, Liu Ch'i-tsu erh-pai jen teng tsao-hsiang-chi*), Northern Wei dynasty (386–534), 502. Rubbing. From *Chung-kuo shu-fa Lung-men erh-shih p'in* (Peking: Wen-wu ch'u-pan-she, 1980), 75.

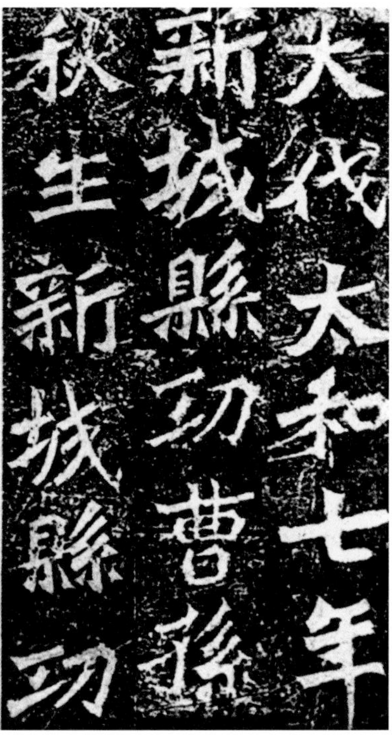

4 *Dedicatory Inscription by Sun Ch'iu-sheng, Liu Ch'i-tsu, and Others* (*Sun Ch'iu-sheng, Liu Ch'i-tsu erh-pai jen teng tsao-hsiang-chi*; fig. 8), dated 502
5 *Dedicatory Inscription by Kao Shu, Hsieh Po-tu, and Others* (*Kao Shu, Hsieh Po-tu san-shih-erh jen teng tsao-hsiang-chi*), dated 502.
6 *Dedicatory Inscription by Monk Hui-kan* (*Pi-ch'iu Hui-kan tsao-hsiang-chi*), dated 502
7 *Dedicatory Inscription by Dowager Hou* [grandmother of Prince Kuang-ch'uan] *for Emperor Ho-lan Han* (*Kuang-ch'uan Wang tsu-mu t'ai-fei Hou wei wang-fu Ho-lan Han tsao-hsiang-chi*), dated 502
8 *Dedicatory Inscription by Dowager Hou* (*Kuang-ch'uan Wang tsu-mu t'ai-fei Hou tsao-hsiang-chi*), dated 502
9 *Dedicatory Inscription by Yang Ta-yen* (*Yang Ta-yen tsao-hsiang-chi*; fig. 9)
10 *Dedicatory Inscription by Monk Tao-chiang* (*Pi-ch'iu Tao-chiang tsao-hsiang-chi*)
11 *Dedicatory Inscription by Wei Ling-ts'ang and Hsüeh Fa-shao* (*Wei Ling-ts'ang Hsüeh Fa-shao tsao-hsiang-chi*; fig. 10).

In some of these inscriptions both the author of the text and the calligrapher are identified. In others, the style of the writing provides clues about the identity of the calligrapher.[10]

Development of Northern Wei Stele-Style Calligraphy

Although individual calligraphers imparted their own unique style of writing to the inscriptions in the Lung-men caves,[11] there are at least two basic characteristics of the Northern Wei stele style. The first is the slanted and compact structure of the characters. Vertical strokes tend to slant down toward the right while horizontal strokes tend to tilt upward. Brushstrokes are arranged so that the main stroke is elongated, creating a compact structure. Since the dedicatory inscriptions at Lung-men were all written on vertical cave walls and written with the brush in the right hand, it was only natural for horizontal strokes to be lower on the left and tilted upward on the right and for vertical strokes to slant down toward the right.[12] This tendency became even more pronounced when standard-script characters were carved onto cliff faces and stelae.[13]

During the early Northern Wei period, dedicatory inscriptions in Shansi were carved onto stelae measuring approximately one meter in height. The carved characters, which tend to be irregular and unsophisticated, are noticeably different from those on later Northern Wei stelae found in the Loyang area. This can be seen, for example, in the *Dedicatory Inscription by Yao Po-to* (*Yao Po-to tsao-hsiang-pei*; fig. 11). Since the inscription was carved

Figure 9 (left)
Detail of *Dedicatory Inscription by Yang Ta-yen* (*Yang Ta-yen tsao-hsiang-chi*), Northern Wei dynasty (386–534). Rubbing. From *Chung-kuo shu-fa Lung-men erh-shih p'in*, 142.

Figure 10 (right)
Dedicatory Inscription by Wei Ling-ts'ang and Hsüeh Fa-shao (*Wei Ling-ts'ang, Hsüeh Fa-shao tsao-hsiang-chi*), Northern Wei dynasty (386–534). Rubbing. From *Chung-kuo shu-fa Lung-men erh-shih p'in*, 181.

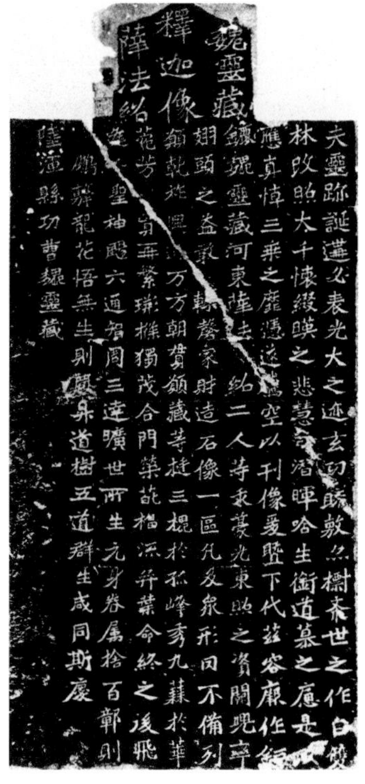

onto the stele before it was erected, the characters are not slanted as they are in the Lung-men Cave inscriptions.

The second characteristic concerns the method by which the inscriptions were carved. There was no attempt to capture the subtle effects of the calligrapher's brushwork. Rather, the carver used his chisel to make straight, deep incisions on either side of the stroke, creating simple grooves to indicate the shape of the stroke. Horizontal strokes were often carved as straight rectangles, and dots and hooks as triangles. Horizontal strokes were joined to vertical strokes with slanted incisions, which indicate a change in the direction of the brush. Instead of carving the characters in the sequence in which they were written, the carver first executed all the strokes that went in one direction and then the strokes that went in another direction. In consequence, within a single character, there is very little variation in strokes of the same type, such as a horizontal, vertical, or oblique stroke, or a dot or hook. Since the carver generally did not know how to read the characters, this method of carving was both convenient and efficient. If he were not careful, the carver could easily overlook the red outline of the character written by the calligrapher and make mistakes in the carving, which would remain undetected if the inscription was not checked after the work was completed.[14] This method of carving helps to explain the somewhat rigid and even monotonous calligraphic style of the Lung-men inscriptions. Although the Ch'ing scholar K'ang Yu-wei considered the Lung-men inscriptions to be "some of the earliest examples of the angular brush style," this style was mainly the creation of the stone carvers.

The stiffness of Northern Wei stele-style calligraphy is undoubtedly related to the decline of the stone carvers' art during the years of incessant warfare that beset the area around Loyang at the end of the Western Chin dynasty. During this period, few stelae were engraved, and the technical skills of carving were lost. Moreover, during the Northern Wei, patrons who commissioned the production of Buddhist images were primarily concerned that their names and prayers be recorded in the inscriptions, and were often less concerned about the artistic quality of the calligraphy. This was also the case with many patrons who made donations to temples in later periods. The names of the patrons and the amounts of their donations were recorded in a ledger of merit. As this was sufficient to demonstrate their good intentions, patrons paid no attention to the calligraphic quality of the writing in the ledger. Furthermore, the style and content of the inscriptions were of little concern to the temple monks, who cared mostly about the grandeur of the images.

Because most of the early Buddhist caves and sculpture niches were commissioned and paid for by wealthy aristocrats and high government officials, inscriptions were engraved in the format of stelae, placed in prominent positions, and executed with a certain degree of care. Most of the *Twenty Inscriptions from Lung-men* are of this kind. However, inscriptions like *Dedicatory Inscription by Cheng Ch'ang-yu* (*Yün-yang po Cheng Ch'ang-yu tsao-hsiang-chi*; fig. 12) from the Ku-yang cave are coarse, with characters and sentences repeated and some characters miscarved, attesting to the fact that little attention was given to the execution of the inscriptions and that they were not checked after they were carved. Some of the later short dedicatory inscriptions were carved haphazardly in the open spaces around the sculptures. On the whole, then, dedicatory inscriptions were carved with less care than inscriptions on stelae or stone epitaphs.

Calligraphic Style of Engraved Epitaphs from Northern Wei Loyang

In conjunction with the relocation of the Northern Wei capital to Loyang, Emperor Hsiao-wen enacted a series of reforms designed to change the traditional customs of the Hsien-pei people to conform with Han Chinese practices. For example, the emperor proclaimed that "when those who had emigrated to Loyang died, they must be buried in Honan and their bodies shall not be permitted to be moved to the north for burial."[15] Since such regulations were forcibly imposed, many Hsien-pei aristocrats felt that they could do nothing more than set up tomb epitaphs and inscribed markers with the hope that their sons or grandsons would later move their remains to final resting places in their native home in the north. Emperor Hsiao-wen also advocated the erection of engraved stelae. The original purpose of the construction of stelae was to ensure that ancestral tombs would remain identifiable despite the ravages of time. Thus officials and aristocrats began to erect stelae both to mark their tombs and to provide a record of their ancestors' accomplishments. In the years following the relocation of the capital, the erection of stone epitaphs and stelae came into fashion among the aristocracy. Although prevalent in the area around the new capital city, this practice did not spread to the border regions. Because they were placed above ground, stelae were easily destroyed. Stone epitaphs that were buried in tombs, however, have survived in greater number. In later periods, especially during the Ch'ing dynasty when the study of bronze and stone inscriptions flourished, many Loyang epitaphs were excavated and preserved.

The engraved epitaphs produced in the Loyang area during the forty-year period from the establishment of the capital to the end of the dynasty can be divided into three distinctive styles. The early examples, dating from 496 to 507, exhibit slanted strokes and prominent angular chisel cuts. The brushstrokes are vigorous and sharp, similar to the commemorative inscriptions of the *Twenty Inscriptions from Lung-men*. Examples include:

1. *Epitaph of Yüan Chen* (*Yüan Chen mu-chih*; fig. 13), dated 496
2. *Epitaph of Yüan Yen* (*Yüan Yen mu-chih*), dated 498

Figure 11 (left)
Detail from *Dedicatory Inscription by Yao Po-to* (*Yao Po-to tsao-hsiang-chi*), Northern Wei dynasty (386–534). Rubbing. From *Chung-kuo mei-shu ch'üan-chi, Shu-fa chuan-k'o pien*, v. 2, 170.

Figure 12 (right)
Dedicatory Inscription by Cheng Ch'ang-yu (*Yün-yang po Cheng Ch'ang-yu tsao-hsiang-chi*), Northern Wei dynasty (386–534). Rubbing. From *Chung-kuo mei-shu Lung-men erh-shih p'in*, 63.

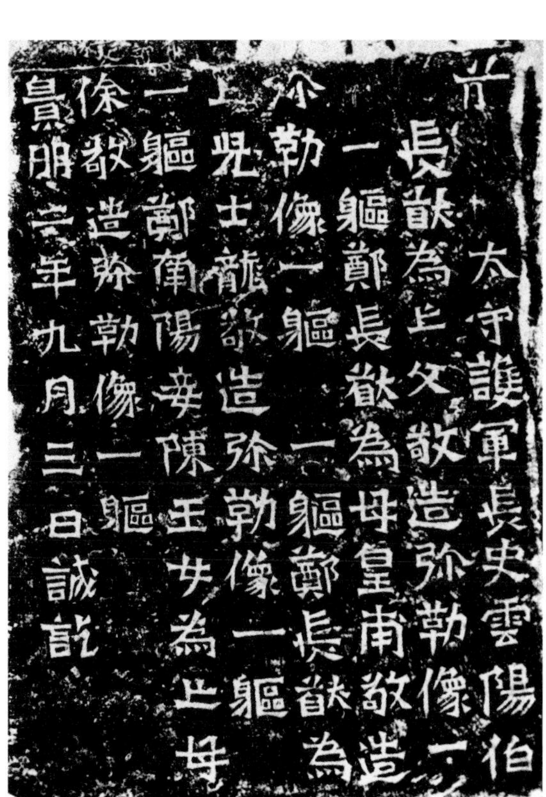

Figure 13 (left)
Detail of *Epitaph of Yüan Chen* (*Yüan Chen mu-chih*), Northern Wei dynasty (386–534), 496. Rubbing. From *Chung-kuo shu-fa ch'üan-chi* (Peking: Jung-pao-chai, 1995), v. 13, 44.

Figure 14 (right)
Detail of *Epitaph of Ch'ang Chi-fan* (*Ch'ang Chi-fan mu-chih*), Northern Wei dynasty (386–534). Rubbing. From *Chung-kuo mei-shu ch'üan-chi, Shu-fa pien*, v. 2, 202.

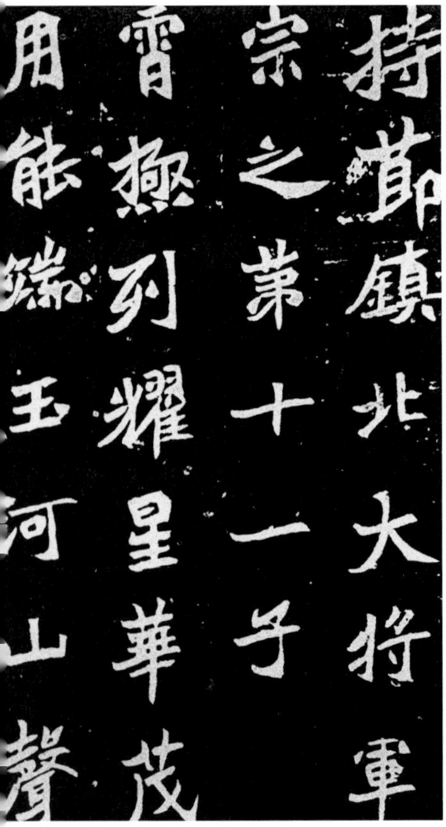

3 *Epitaph of Yüan Chien* (*Yüan Chien mu-chih*), dated 499
4 *Epitaph of Yüan Pin* (*Yüan Pin mu-chih*), dated 499
5 *Epitaph of Han Hsien-tsung* (*Han Hsien-tsung mu-chih*), dated 499
6 *Epitaph of Yüan Ting* (*Yüan Ting mu-chih*), dated 500
7 *Epitaph of Yüan Yü* (*Yüan Yü mu-chih*), dated 501
8 *Epitaph of Madam Li, Consort of Yüan Ch'eng* (*Yüan Ch'eng chi Li shih mu-chih*), dated 501
9 *Epitaph of Mu Liang* (*Mu Liang mu-chih*), dated 502
10 *Epitaph of Madame Hou-ku, Consort of my Grandfather* (*Hsien-tsu pin Hou-ku shih mu-chih*), dated 503
11 *Epitaph of Chang Cheng* (*Chang Cheng mu-chih*), dated 503
12 *Epitaph of Yüan Shih-ho* (*Yüan Shih-ho mu-chih*), dated 505
13 *Epitaph of Li Sheng* (*Li Sheng mu-chih*), dated 505
14 *Epitaph of K'ou Chen* (*K'ou Chen mu-chih*), dated 506
15 *Epitaph of Hsi Chih* (*Hsi Chih mu-chih*), dated 507
16 *Epitaph of Yüan Chien* (*Yüan Chien mu-chih*), dated 507
17 *Epitaph of Yüan Hsü* (*Yüan Hsü mu-chih*), dated 507.

All these works are typical of Northern Wei stele-style calligraphy, and they clearly reflect the influence of the dedicatory inscriptions from Lung-men. It is possible that the carvers of the Lung-men inscriptions were also responsible for these epitaphs.

During the second period, from 508 to 519, inscriptions on stone epitaphs become more refined and gentle, and stylistic variations proliferate. A number of epitaphs engraved in the same calligraphic style appear to come from the same hand, suggesting that professional epitaph writers may have emerged during this period. Since the stone carvers had had time to practice and perfect their craft, the calligraphic style of the inscriptions are more harmonious and flowing. As they developed more sophisticated techniques, the carvers were able to express more effectively the subtle qualities of brush-written characters. Nonetheless, many of the engraved stone epitaphs carved at this time continued the vigorous style of the earlier period. Among the representative works of the period are:

1 *Epitaph of Madam Keng, Concubine of Kao-tsung* (*Kao-tsung pin Keng shih mu-chih*)
2 *Epitaph of Madam Chao, Concubine of Kao-tsung* (*Kao-tsung ch'ung hua Chao shih mu-chih*)
3 *Epitaph of Yüan Ch'üan* (*Yüan Ch'üan mu-chih*)
4 *Epitaph of Consort Wei, wife of Mu Liang* (*Mu Liang ch'i Wei t'ai-fei*)
5 *Epitaph of Feng Hsi* (*Feng Hsi mu-chih*)

Figure 15 (left)
Detail of *Stele for Chang Meng-lung* (*Chang Meng-lung pei*), Northern Wei dynasty (386–534). Rubbing. From *Chung-kuo mei-shu ch'üan-chi, Shu-fa chuan-k'o pien*, v. 2, 182.

Figure 16 (right)
Detail of *Epitaph of Hou Hai* (*Hou Hai mu-chih*), Eastern Wei dynasty (534–550). Rubbing. From *Liu-ch'ao mu-chih ching-hua* (Shanghai: Yu-cheng shu-chü, n.d.).

6 *Epitaph of K'ou P'ing* (*K'ou P'ing mu-chih*)
7 *Epitaph of K'ou Yen* (*K'ou Yen mu-chih*).

Also noteworthy are *Epitaph of Ssu-ma Shao* (*Ssu-ma Shao mu-chih*), from Meng-hsien, Honan, and *Epitaph of Yang Fan* (*Yang Fan mu-chih*), from Hua-ying, Shensi.

The final period in the stylistic evolution of Northern Wei stele-style calligraphy lasted for just over ten years, from 520 to the end of the dynasty in 534. The number of stone epitaphs that survive from this period is far larger than that from the previous twenty years. On the whole, the style of writing tends to be more elegant and graceful, and the carving technique more refined. A rubbing of one of these inscriptions resembles the original handwritten calligraphy. Representative works from this period include *Epitaph of Ch'ang Chi-fan* (*Ch'ang Chi-fan mu-chih*; fig. 14); *Epitaph of Chang Hsüan* (*Chang Hsüan mu-chih*), from Yung-chi, Shansi; and stelae inscriptions from Shantung such as *Stele for Chang Meng-lung* (*Chang Meng-lung pei*; fig. 15), from Ch'ü-fu; *Stele for Monk Ken of Ma-ming Temple*, from Lo-an; *Stele for Kao Chen* (*Kao Chen pei*), from Te-chou; and *Stele for Kao Ch'ing* (*Kao Ch'ing pei*), from Te-chou.

Although the calligraphy of stelae inscriptions dating to the final years of the Northern Wei is less angular and strong than that in the earlier periods, the characters remain compact and slanted. Even the cliff inscriptions with large-sized characters — such as the *Stone Gate Inscription* (*Shih-men ming*) in Pao-ch'eng, Shensi, and cliff inscriptions in Lai-chou, Shantung, at Yün-feng in P'ing-tu, and in the T'ien-chu mountains — retain this stylistic feature.[16]

Decline of Northern Wei Stele-Style Calligraphy

At the beginning of the Eastern Chin, engraved stone epitaphs were produced largely in the area around Yeh (southwest of modern Lin-chang, Hopei). Almost no epitaphs from this period can be found in the Loyang area. Western Chin stone epitaphs are rare, although some have been excavated in areas around the capital city Ch'ang-an (modern Sian, Shensi). Northern Chou aristocrats also erected stone epitaphs.[17]

Eastern Wei (534–550) and Northern Ch'i (550–577) engraved stone epitaphs excavated from tomb sites along the banks of the Chang-shui, Honan, bear little resemblance in their calligraphic style to those from Loyang. The characters are upright and loosely structured; dots are weak and unsteady (fig. 16). While clerical script is predominant in these epitaphs, standard script is also used, which contributes to the unstructured appearance of the characters (fig. 17). Western Wei (535–556) epitaphs are extremely rare, but the calligraphy of those that have survived is similarly insubstantial

Figure 17
Detail of *Epitaph of Lou Hei-nü* (*Lou Hei-nü mu-chih*), Northern Ch'i dynasty (550–577). Rubbing. From *Liu-ch'ao mu-chih ching-hua*.

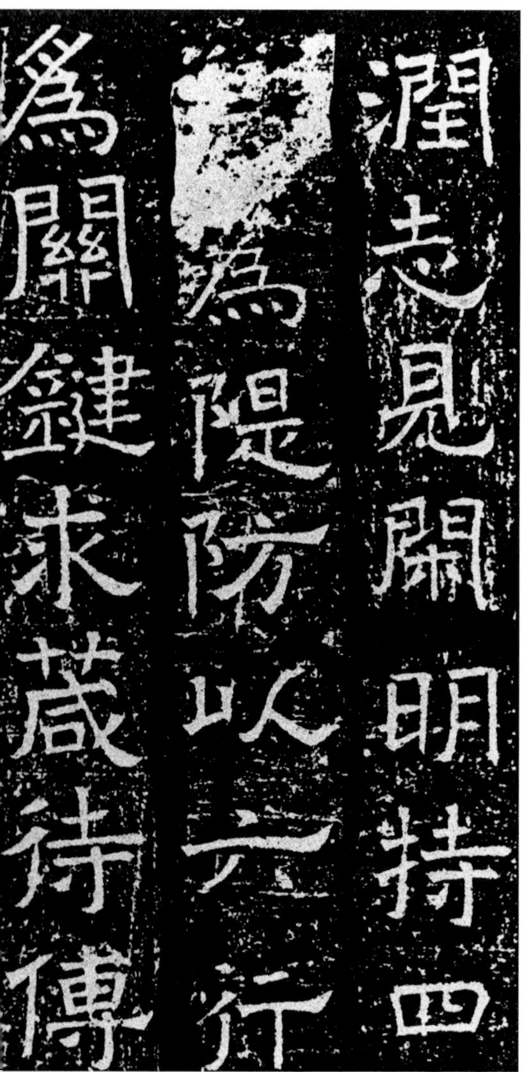

Figure 18
Detail of *Epitaph of Ts'ui Ching-yung* (*Ts'ui Ching-yung mu-chih*), Northern Wei dynasty (386–534). From *Chung-kuo mei-shu ch'üan-chi, Shu-fa chuan-k'o pian*, v. 2, 199.

and weak. The few extant epitaphs from the Northern Chou are similar in style to those of the Northern Ch'i.

As noted above, southern-style calligraphy began to attract attention in north China in the mid-sixth century with the study of Wang Pao's works. After the reunification of China under the Sui dynasty, in 589, the taste for refined and elegant calligraphy became even more pronounced in the epitaphs of the aristocracy. Works such as *Stele for the Ch'i-fa Temple* (*Ch'i-fa-ssu pei*) and *Stele for the Lung-ts'ang Temple* (*Lung-ts'ang-ssu pei*), for example, clearly show the influence of the southern calligraphic tradition.

Emperor T'ai-tsung (r. 627–49) of the T'ang dynasty promoted the calligraphy of Wang Hsi-chih, and the calligraphic style of the Northern Dynasties was soon forgotten. In 641, T'ai-tsung's son Li T'ai, the Prince of Wei, began the construction of Buddhist monuments for his mother, empress Ch'ang-sun, at the Lung-men Caves.[18] During the reigns of Kao-tsung (r. 650–83) and the empress Wu Tze-t'ien (r. 684–704), the eastern capital was rebuilt, and the construction of caves and niches was once again undertaken on a large scale at Lung-men. The slanted, angular style of the Northern Wei style of calligraphy—as seen, for example, in the Ku-yang cave—did not accord with the T'ang predilection for balance, harmony, and elegance, and inscriptions in this style were ignored.

In the T'ang, the history of calligraphy began to revolve around the work of individual renowned calligraphers and the transmission of personal styles. Critical writings on calligraphy by T'ang scholars, including Li Ssu-chen (d. 696), Chang Huai-kuan, and Chia Meng, do not mention calligraphy of the Northern Wei period, nor do they make note of masters of the Northern Dynasties, such as Ts'ui Hung, Ts'ui Hao, Lu Po-yüan, Cheng Tao-chao (d. 515), and Chiang Shih.[19] During the Sung dynasty (960–1279), the study of standard script was based on stelae from the T'ang period, while model-books were used for the study of running and cursive scripts. Only works by famous calligraphers were considered worthy of study. The Northern Sung master Mi Fu (1052–1107) wrote: "Stone carvings should not be studied as they are not the works of the original calligraphers. Rather, one must look at the original ink traces to understand the essence."[20] Despite the interest in the study of bronze and stone inscriptions in the Sung period, the angular and rather crude style of Northern Wei stele calligraphy had no appeal. Such scholars as Ou-yang Hsiu (1007–1072) and Chao Ming-ch'eng (1081–1129) recorded many inscriptions on ancient stelae, but did not include in their own collections Northern Wei dedicatory inscriptions from Lung-men. In a colophon to *Record of Stelae and Dedicatory Inscriptions of the Shen-kuei Period* (*Hou Wei Shen-kuei tsao-pei-hsiang chi*), Ou-yang Hsiu wrote:

Among all the stele inscriptions that I have collected, I never casually discarded inscriptions from before the Sui. I may learn something from them now and then. It is a shame, of course, that they often touch on Buddhist subjects and have little literary merit. Their sole redeeming feature, however, is the beauty of their calligraphy. Only the calligraphy of the Northern Wei and the Northern Ch'i is inferior. Characters in inscriptions from these dynasties are often incorrect, and I do not know how they came into being. The characters they wrote are completely different from those of other major calligraphers. This, I believe, was the result of the barbarian's ignorance of scholarship."[21]

Ou-yang Hsiu did not reject the Lung-men inscriptions solely for their textual content, but also because he believed that they were without artistic merit. In his view, the characters were overly robust, too showy, and lacked any of the modulation of the brushwork of the original calligraphy.

Rediscovery of the Northern Wei Stele Style

The early Ch'ing scholar Ku Yen-wu (1613–1682), author of *Record of Bronze and Stone Inscriptions* (*Chin-shih wen-tzu chi*), devoted himself to the study of stone and bronze inscriptions: "Night and day he gathered material far and wide from the histories and the classics."[22] Ku's contemporary Huang Tsung-hsi (1610–1695), another influential scholar, pursued literary and historical scholarship based on stele inscriptions and wrote *Essential Examples of Bronze and Stone Inscriptions* (*Chin-shih yao-li*). Once scholars such as Ku and Huang began to collect stele inscriptions as historical material, the calligraphy of these inscriptions gradually attracted their attention. Northern Dynasties stelae were at first considered rather crude, and discarded as soon as they were discovered. In 1629, however, the discovery of the Northern Wei *Epitaph of Ts'ui Ching-yung* (*Ts'ui Ching-yung mu-chih*; fig. 18) in An-p'ing, Honan, created a sensation. The epitaph soon became highly esteemed for its calligraphy. As Ho Chao, a scholar of the period, wrote:

When one first sees it, it appears ugly and crude, but when one disregards its outward appearance, its intention seems grand. Masters of the T'ang were never able to achieve such boundless expression. One should not look down upon Northern style calligraphy. The good features of Six Dynasties calligraphy stem from its internal sense of freedom, unrestrained by rules and methods.[23]

Another writer commented upon the strong interest in the calligraphic style of the *Epitaph of Ts'ui Ching-yung*:

Scholars from the court competed to view [the epitaph]. People were constantly making rubbings of it so that within twenty years the inscription was polished away and the stone was completed cracked.... Critics maintained that it was superior to the stelae for Chang Meng-lung and Chia Shih-chün. Ch'ien-fu wrote a hymn in praise of it, while Chih-shan and Kang-nan, among others, devoted themselves to copying its style. Only Chih-shan, however, succeeded in combining the distinctive features of the calligraphy engraved on the epitaph with that of Ch'u Sui-liang [596–658] to create his own distinctive style.[24]

The collecting of Northern Wei stelae epitaphs and dedicatory inscriptions gradually grew in popularity among scholars studying bronze and stone inscriptions. What became known in the Ch'ing dynasty as the *Twenty Inscriptions from Lung-men* were recorded and commented upon in various works in the eighteenth and early nineteenth centuries. These include Pi Yüan's (1730–1797) *Record of Bronze and Stone Inscriptions from Chung-chou* (*Chung-chou chin-shih chi*), Wu I's (1745–1799) *Colophons on Bronze and Stone Inscriptions in the Shou Studio* (*Shou-t'ang chin-shih pa*), Wang Ch'ang's (1724–1806) *A Collection of Bronze and Stone Inscriptions* (*Chin-shih ts'ui-pien*), and Ch'ien Ta-hsin's (1728–1804) *Colophons on Bronze and Stone Inscriptions in the Ch'ien-yen Studio* (*Ch'ien-yen-t'ang chin-shih-wen pa-wei*). Studies of bronze and stone inscriptions were even more commonplace in the following decades. Not a single rubbing or stone engraving was overlooked.

The eminent scholar Juan Yüan (1764–1849), who was well-versed in the study of bronze and stone inscriptions, published *Treatise on the Northern and Southern Schools of Calligraphy* (*Nan Pei shu-p'ai lun*) and *Treatise on Northern Stelae and Southern Model-Books* (*Pei pei Nan t'ieh lun*). Based on evidence from official histories and the inscriptions themselves, Juan established that there was a true tradition of Northern Dynasty calligraphy and that this style of writing therefore could not simply be dismissed as poor in quality. Pao Shih-ch'en (1775–1855) praised and promoted the Northern stele style from a different perspective, incorporating this style into his own theory of calligraphy. He stated that his brushwork was indebted to the antique style of the Six Dynasties and his character structures to the Northern stele style. He also demonstrated how the Northern stele style was exemplary in the positioning of brushstrokes and in the structure and composition of characters. Moreover, Pao Shih-ch'en, Yao Yüan-chih, and others studied the strokes in stone inscriptions from the pre-T'ang period and imitated them in brush and ink, developing their own brush method known as "starting with *ken* and ending with *ch'ien*" (*shih ken chung ch'ien*). This technique required the calligrapher to sit facing south and to start and finish a stroke according to positions that corresponded to the eight trigrams of the *Book of Changes* (*I ching*).[25] This method of handling the brush was well suited to the reproduction of the angular, robust calligraphy of Northern Wei dedicatory inscriptions dating from 496 to 507. Pao Shih-ch'en and Yao Yüan-chih both attempted to emulate ancient engraved calligraphy in brush and ink, a method later calligraphers called "infusing the force of bronze and stone" in calligraphy.

Pao Shih-ch'en had a profound influence on his contemporaries in the Chiang-nan region, where those who studied and followed his style formed a school.[26] K'ang-Yu Wei pointed out that the study of stelae inscriptions flourished in the late Ch'ing dynasty with Pao Shih-ch'en's support:

> Pao used the materials he collected and passed on the method of Teng Shih-ju [1743–1805]. He was the only one to understand the deep complexities. He composed his *Discourse on Calligraphy* (*An wu lun shu*), mounted rubbings of newly discovered stelae, and promoted the brush method. The study of bronze and stone inscriptions thus reached an apogee. During the late Ch'ing, especially in the Hsien-feng and T'ung-chih reign periods [1850–74], the study of stelae was widespread. Among children and adults everywhere, there was no one who did not talk about Northern Wei stelae or did not write Northern Wei stele-style calligraphy. Studying and writing Northern Wei stele-style calligraphy thus became customary."[27]

The study of calligraphy model-books, which had flourished since the Sung dynasty, declined in the Ch'ing. In his *On the Study of Calligraphy* (*Shu-hsüeh erh-yen*), Yang Shou-ching (1839–1915) wrote, "Of the thousands of dedicatory inscriptions made in the Northern Wei, the best are *Dedicatory Inscription by Duke Shih-p'ing*, *Dedicatory Inscription by Sun Ch'iu-sheng*, *Dedicatory Inscription by Yang Ta-yen*, and *Dedicatory Inscription by Wei Ling-ts'ang*, often called *the Four Inscriptions of Lung-men* (*Lung-men ssu-p'in*), to which more inscriptions were added to form the *Twenty Inscriptions from Lung-men*. Masters of the Northern Wei stele style mostly took these works as their standard models. Mo Yu-chih [1811–1871] and T'ao Chün-hsüan were the best."[28] Other calligraphers who excelled in Northern Wei stele-style calligraphy include Chang Yü-chao (1823–1894), Chao Chih-ch'ien (1829–1884), Li Wen-t'ien (1834–1895), Tseng Hsi (1861–1930), and Li Jui-ch'ing (1867–1920).

One of the most ardent proponents of the Northern Wei stele style was K'ang Yu-wei. In his impassioned treatise *Kuang i-chou shuang-chi*, completed in 1889, K'ang argues that engraved calligraphy of the Northern Wei is superior to that of the Southern Dynasties, Northern Ch'i, Northern Chou, and Sui. "Among Wei stelae there is not a single example that is not beautiful. Even if it is a dedicatory inscription for a child from a poor village, its structure is magnificent. Striking originality of form lies beyond a superficial crudeness. Character structure is especially compact.... For this reason we should study Wei dedicatory inscriptions and emulate their style." Abandoning a strictly evidentiary method, he offers his subjective opinions on the historical origins and influence of the Northern Wei style. He then provides a detailed critique of stelae from the Northern and Southern Dynasties, using as a model Yü Chien-wu's (487–551) *Gradings of Calligraphers* (*Shu-p'in*) and Yüan Ang's *Evaluation of Calligraphy through the Ages* (*Ku-chin shu-p'ing*).

Although *Kuang i-chou shuang-chi* omits much, is filled with contradictions, and presents subjective judgments and biased exaggerations, it nevertheless offers many original insights. For example, K'ang points out the negative effects of model-book study, and champions the principle of "transformation" (*pien*) in calligraphy. His advocacy of Northern Wei over T'ang stele-style calligraphy and the study of stelae inscriptions over model-books had a great influence on succeeding generations. After its initial publication in 1891, the treatise was reprinted eighteen times within seven years, and it has been reprinted repeatedly since 1911. As a result of K'ang Yu-wei's efforts to promote the study of stele-style calligraphy, calligraphers and connoisseurs alike have been influenced by the Northern Wei style.

Several decades ago a revised style of Northern Wei stele calligraphy emerged in China. Known as the "new Wei style" (*hsin Wei t'i*), it exaggerates certain stylized characteristics of the older Northern Wei style. With its vigorous and prominent brushstrokes, the new Wei style is lively and strong. During the Cultural Revolution, this style was frequently used to write slogans on large posters and to create the stencils used in the production of propaganda leaflets and small newspapers. Nowadays the new Wei script, along with clerical and standard scripts, is one of the basic fonts in Chinese language computer software.

Northern Wei stele-style calligraphy did not arise naturally in the development of standard script from clerical script. Rather, it appeared after the relocation of the Northern Wei capital to Loyang and then disappeared at the end of the dynasty, forty years later. It was an isolated historical and regional phenomena, and, unlike seal, clerical, and draft cursive script, did not continue to be used. The style remained unknown until the late seventeenth and early eighteenth centuries when it was rediscovered by Ch'ing scholars. Northern Wei stele-style calligraphy was subsequently praised and promoted as a means to develop a new brush method and to create a new spirit and aesthetic sensibility in the art of calligraphy.

Translated from the Chinese by Daniel M. Youd

1 Lu Shen's sixth-generation grandson, Lu Po-yüan, also excelled in calligraphy. He wrote all of the inscriptions on the signboards (*t'i-pang*) that hung over the entrances to the palace halls at the capital in P'ing-ch'eng (modern Ta-t'ung, Shansi).
2 Wei Shou, *Wei shu* (Wei History) (Peking: Chung-hua shu-chü, 1974), *chüan* 24.
3 Ling-hu Te-fen, *Chou shu* (Chou History) (Peking: Chung-hua shu-chü, 1974), *chüan* 47.
4 During and after the Wei-Chin period, *Chi-chiu-chang* was the common name for *Chi-chiu-p'ien.* Because calligraphers often used old-style cursive script to write *Chi-chiu-chang*, this script became known as *Chi-chiu-chang* cursive, or *chang-ts'ao* (draft cursive), which is different from *chin-ts'ao*, modern cursive. See Hua Rende, "Chang-ts'ao pien" in *Shu-fa yen-chiu* 5 (1995).
5 *Wei shu, chüan* 35.
6 Since Ts'ui Hao was a Taoist and had connections with K'ou Ch'ien, it is likely that the calligraphers of the *Stele for the Temple of Mt. Hua* and the *Stele for the Temple of the Mountain Spirit of Mt. Sung* also studied the Ts'ui style.
7 Emperor Hsiao-wen of the Northern Wei exchanged ambassadors with the Southern Ch'i court many times. On one occasion he asked if the court would lend him some books. Southern Ch'i officials ultimately refused his request despite the fact that Wang Jung submitted a memorial arguing that "sending the classics abroad, transmitting the *Odes* and the *Histories*" might be helpful in pacifying the northern barbarians and would have no harmful effects on the court. Emperor Wu of the Southern Ch'i agreed with Wang Jung, but the books were never lent to Hsiao-wen. See Hsiao Tzu-hsien, *Nan Ch'i shu* (Southern Ch'i History) (Peking: Chung-hua shu-chü, 1972), *chüan* 47.
8 *Wei shu*, 3029.
9 For example, an inscription to a copy of *The Vasudharasūtra* (*Ch'ih-shih ching*), from Shan-shan, dating to the seventh year (449) of the Ch'eng-p'ing reign period of the Later Liang (386–403), reads: "Copied by Chang Chieh-tzu of Wu-k'o tan-yang chün, 26 sheets of paper used." There are also examples of sutras copied during the T'ien-chien (502–19), P'u-t'ung (520–27), and Ta-t'ung (535–46) reign periods of the Liang dynasty. See Tz'u Hsi, "Yu Wei Chin Nan Pei Ch'ao ti hsieh-ching k'an tang-shih te shu-fa," *Wen-wu*, no. 4 (1963), 30–31, 33–34.
10 Among these examples, the *Dedicatory Inscription by Monk Hui-ch'eng* concludes with the phrase, "Calligraphy by Chu I-chang, composed by Meng Ta." At the end of the prayer in *Dedicatory Inscription by Sun Ch'iu-Sheng, Liu Ch'i-tsu, and Others*, the author and the calligrapher are identified: "Composed by Meng Kuang-ta, calligraphy by Hsiao Hsien-ch'ing." The character composition in this work and in the *Dedicatory Inscription by Kao Shu, Hsieh Po-tu, and Others*, both dated to same year, is very similar, suggesting that the two inscriptions were carved by the same person. The other inscriptions, such as that by Monk Hui-ch'eng and by Wei Ling-ts'ang and Hsüeh Fa-shao do not name the calligrapher but are probably by the same hand.
11 For example, the little-known calligraphers Chu I-chang and Hsiao Hsien-ch'ing.

12 Seal and clerical scripts are oriented horizontally and have a square-shaped structure. Standard script, however, is a regularized form of running script and thus slants naturally. Running script came into existence during the mid-Han period. Standard script first appeared at the end of the Han and the beginning of the Wei.

13 Northern Wei stelae with slanting characters — such as *Stele to Commemorate the Emperor's Eastern Tour* (*Huang-ti tung-hsün chih pei*) and *Hymn in Praise of the Emperor's Southern Tour* (*Huang-ti nan-hsün chih sung*) — pre-date the Lung-men inscriptions. The latter work is especially large; based on the excavated fragments, the stele was originally 137 cm wide and 29 cm thick. If the ratio of width to height was 1:3, then the stele must have been at least 4 meters tall. See "Shansi Ling-ch'iu pei Wei Wen-ch'eng te nan-hsün pei," *Wen-wu*, no. 12 (1997), 17. Stelae of this size were usually carved after they were erected.

14 In early times, characters were written directly onto the stele in red ink and then carved. During the T'ang and Sung periods, a different method was adapted: the outline (*shuang-kou*) of the original calligraphy was traced onto a semi-translucent piece of paper, the outline was filled in with red ink, and the paper then pressed against the stone stele to create a copy of the characters to be carved.

15 *Wei shu, chüan* 7, part b.

16 Clerical script, which features more upright and open structures, was not used for stelae inscriptions after the Northern Wei capital was moved to Loyang.

17 Although the *Collected Works of Yü Tzu-shan* includes nineteen engraved stone epitaphs, most of them are from Northern Ch'i rather than Northern Chou. Furthermore, Northern Chou inscriptions are not as concentrated in a single geographic area.

18 On this occasion, Ch'u Sui-liang (596–658) wrote the calligraphy for the *Stele for the I-ch'üeh Buddha Niche* (*I-ch'üeh Fo-k'an pei*).

19 In the *Rhapsody on Explaining Calligraphy* (*Shu shu fu*), only Liu Min of the Northern Ch'i and Chao Wen-yüan and Chao Hsiao-wen of the Northern Chou are mentioned. All three studied the calligraphy of Wang Hsi-chih and Wang Hsien-chih.

20 Mi Fu, "Hai-yüeh ming-yen," in *Li-tai shu-fa lun-wen hsüan* (Shanghai: Shang-hai shu-hua ch'u-pan-she, 1979).

21 Ou-yang Hsiu, *Chi-ku lü pa-wei* (revised edition by Huang Pen-chi, Ch'ing dynasty), *chüan* 4.

22 Ku Yen-wu, *Chin shih wen-tzu chi*, in *Ku T'ing-lin hsien-sheng i-shu shih chung* (revised edition by P'eng Ying-ko, Ch'ing dynasty).

23 Ho Chao, "Pei Wei Ying-chou ts'e-shih Ts'ui Ching-yung chih pa," in *I-men hsien-sheng chi, chüan* 8 (Kuang-chou edition, 1909).

24 See P'an Ning's colophon to the 1735 rubbing of *Ts'ui Ching-yung mu-chih*, in the Nanking Museum.

25 See Hua Rende, "Shih shih ken chung ch'ien," *Shu-fa yen-chiu* 1 (1986).

26 See Ho Shao-chi's colophon to "Pao Shih-ch'en pa 'Chang Hei-nü mu-chih,'" early Republic of China collotype by I-yüan chen-shang-she.

27 K'ang Yu-wei, "Tsun pei ti erh," in *Kuang i-chou shuang-chi, chüan* 1 (Wan-pen ts'ao-t'ang edition, 1891).

28 See Ts'ui Erh-p'ing, ed., *Li-tai shu-fa lun-wen hsüan* (Shanghai: Shang-hai shu-hua ch'u-pan-she, 1993), 716.

Eugene Y. Wang
Harvard University

The Taming of the Shrew: Wang Hsi-chih (303–361) and Calligraphic Gentrification in the Seventh Century

No other calligrapher has cast as profound and enduring a spell over the Chinese imagination as Wang Hsi-chih (303–361). This is explained, in part, by the fact that Wang's calligraphy formally condenses, or stylistically sublimates, a deep-seated Chinese moral sensibility schooled in a Confucian culture. The moral profile of a Confucian gentleman as "a well-balanced admixture of native substance and acquired refinement"[1] has traditionally been used to characterize Wang Hsi-chih's calligraphic style.[2] The calligraphy attributed to Wang in the final years of his life is said to embody a "tranquil disposition" that is "neither extreme nor fierce" (*pu chi pu li*) and possess an "unassertive and graceful appearance concealing a strong and solid inside."[3] No other work better exemplifies these qualities than *Preface to the Orchid Pavilion* (*Lan-t'ing hsü*; fig. 1), dated 353, in which Wang records the changing sentiment from elation to a delicious melancholy on an outing with a group of noble scholars and officials amid the idyllic landscape of southeast China. In keeping with the mellow mood, the calligraphy itself imparts a measured ease and grace, thereby betraying "a tranquil disposition." Through the calligraphy, Wang projects a persona of refined and gentlemanly self-control.

The *Preface to the Orchid Pavilion* has come to epitomize the entire Wang Hsi-chih canon.[4] The canon, however, is largely an artifice. No single original work of calligraphy in Wang Hsi-chih's own hand has survived. The extant works said to be by him are either tracing copies or ink rubbings from the original carvings or from later carved recensions several times removed from the original.[5] The canonization of Wang Hsi-chih, which has had a lasting effect on the history of Chinese calligraphy, did not occur until the seventh century, nearly three hundred years after Wang's death. These circumstances, combined with the long process of perpetuating Wang's legacy through repeated copying and reproductions, has resulted in an image of Wang Hsi-chih that bears the indelible mark of willful selections and layered reinterpretations and reconfigurations.[6] Wang Hsi-chih has become what we now believe him to be: an author with a quiescent sensibility and a calligrapher with a graceful style, as represented by the *Orchid Pavilion.* The name Wang Hsi-chih signifies not so much a historical presence as an understated calligraphic mood and a placid disposition.

The *Letter on the Disturbances* (*Sang-luan t'ieh*) as an Art-Historical Embarrassment

The image of Wang Hsi-chih and his calligraphy, however, may need to be revised once we consider a work by him that was spared the excessive paring and pruning that befell the majority of the calligraphy associated with his name. A tracing copy of a letter written by Wang late in his life and now known as the *Letter on the Disturbances* (*Sang-luan t'ieh*; fig. 2) was taken to Japan in the eighth century or earlier.[7] None of the known Chinese catalogues produced before the nineteenth century, beginning with the first official one compiled by Ch'u Sui-liang (596–658), mentions this letter, which remained unknown in China until as late as 1892 when Yang Shou-ching (1839–1915) published it in the form of an ink rubbing in *Model Calligraphies from the Lin-su Garden* (*Lin-su-yüan fa-t'ieh*).[8]

Wang Hsi-chih wrote the letter in response to the news that his ancestral tombs in northern China had been devastated by natural catastrophies:

> I, Hsi-chih, am writing with reverence. Amidst the extremity of the chaos, my ancestral tombs have once again been ravaged. My heart goes out toward them, and I wail, rant, and choke to death. I am filled with pain, my heart is broken. Tormented as I am, what can I do? What can I do? Though they were repaired in no time, I have not had the chance to rush there [to attend to them]. The grief gnaws deeply into me. What can I do? What can I do? Faced with the paper, choking with tears, I do not know what to say. Yours sincerely, Hsi-chih.[9]

The tombs were part of the Western Chin (265–317) imperial burials. Wang Hsi-chih's forebears had served as high-ranking court officials in the capital, Loyang. Wang Hsiang (d. 265), the brother of Wang Hsi-chih's great-grandfather, was Grand Guardian (*T'ai-pao*), one of the Three Dukes (*san-kung*). Upon his death in 265, he was buried in an attendant tomb in the Ch'ung-yang Mausoleum at Mount Mang, northeast of Loyang.[10] Wang Lan (206–278), Wang Hsi-chi's great-grandfather, served as Grand Master for Splendid Happiness (*Kuang-lu ta-fu*), an intimate imperial aide and adviser residing in the palace. He died in 278 and must have been buried close to his brother in the same mausoleum.[11] Wang Cheng, Wang Hsi-chih's grandfather, who served as Secretarial Court Gentleman (*Shang-shu-lang*), also was probably buried in the Ch'ung-yang Mausoleum, close to his father, Wang Lan. The *Chin History* (*Chin shu*) does not specify the location of the Western Chin imperial tombs. For reasons of frugality and security, the Chin studiously avoided ostentation in their imperial burials. Located on mountains, the tombs often were unmarked by either tumuli or above-ground memorials,[12] which has made it difficult for modern archaeologists to identify the location of the tombs. The epitaphs of Hsün Yüeh (246–

Figure 1
Wang Hsi-chih (303–361). *Preface to the Orchid Pavilion* (*Lan-t'ing hsü*), T'ang dynasty (618–907) copy (Shen-lung version). Ink on paper, 24.5 x 69.9 cm. Palace Museum, Peking. From *Chung-kuo mei-shu ch'üan-chi, Shu-fa chuan-k'o pien* (Peking: Jen-min mei-shu ch'u-pan-she, 1986), v. 2, pl. 54.

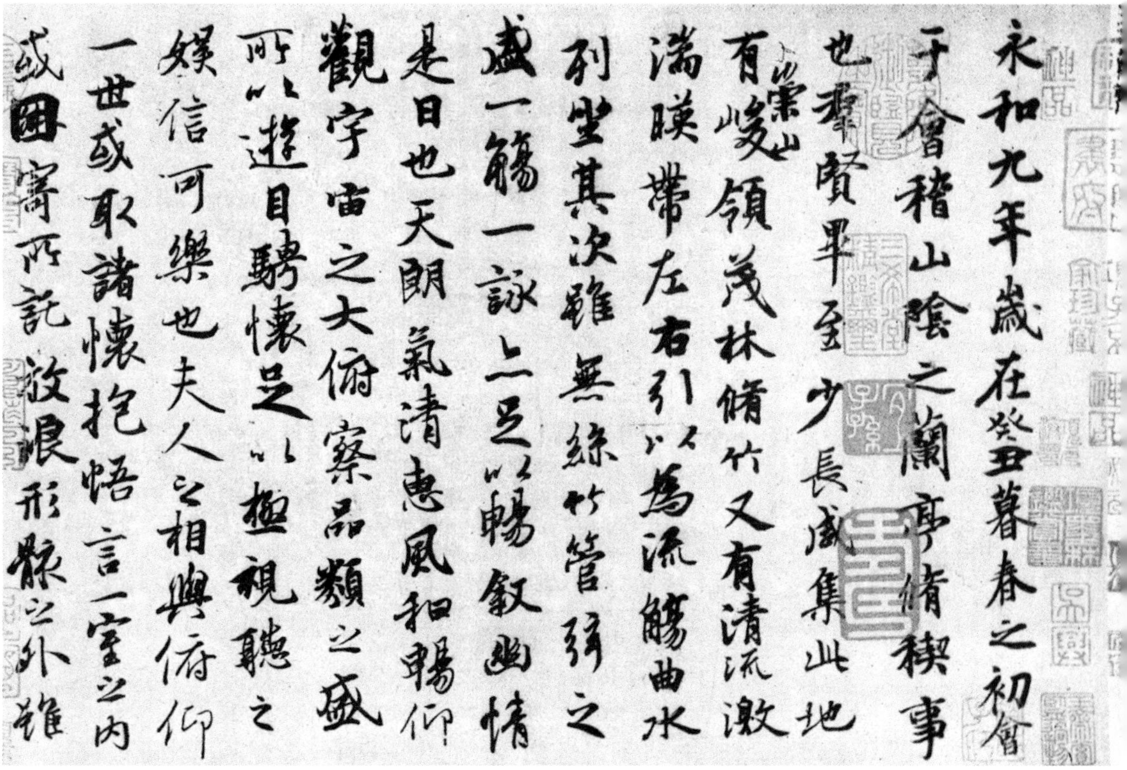

295), the Inner Court Gentleman,[13] and Tso Fen (d. 300), one of the Honored Concubines of Emperor Wu (r. 265–90), unearthed in 1918 and 1930, indicate their corresponding tomb occupants' burials to be part of the Western Chin imperial tomb complex.[14] Since both epitaphs were uncovered north of Ts'ai village, southwest of Yen-shih, their location can thus be established as the site of the Ch'ung-yang Mausoleum referenced in the *Chin History* as the imperial burial ground[15] and, by extension, the site of Wang Hsi-chih's ancestral tombs. These tombs were devastated twice, the first time by human desecration, and the second time by natural disasters. In 311 an insurgent army led by Liu Yao (d. 329) of the state of Chao (304–329), in Shansi, sacked Western Chin's capital Loyang, massacred more than 20,000 people, burned down palaces and temples, and plundered mausoleums and tombs.[16] In the following decades, the mausoleums fell into decay, as natural forces, such as heavy rains, began to take their toll.[17] In 351, as recorded in the *Chin History*, two imperial mausoleums "collapsed" (*peng*). The following year, another two, including the Ch'ung-yang Mausoleum, also "crumbled" (*peng*).[18] Wang Hsi-chih's writing of the *Letter on the Disturbances* was likely occasioned by the last two incidents.

The text of the letter is an unrestrained outpouring of anguish and pathos, and these feelings appear to be echoed in the style of the calligraphy as well. Starting with an emotionally charged staccato, the austere, crisp strokes seem to register a mounting pain. In this opening section, the brush tip is reined in forcefully at the end of each closing stroke, suggesting the calligrapher's self-control and firm hand while coping with intense emotional stress. As the letter proceeds, however, stoic restraint gives way to the onset of grief and anguish which results in the release of pent-up emotion reflected in the impulsive closing strokes. By the end of the letter, the characters no longer maintain a distinct running-script form but instead are jumbled one-stroke arabesques of cursive script, as if calligraphically acting out the "choking" grief and registering the presence of the writer at a moment of tearful agony.

The *Letter on the Disturbances* stands in sharp contrast to the *Orchid Pavilion*. The former unleashes a distraught response to a personal disaster, while the latter evokes calm thoughts and a sense of melancholy occasioned by the gathering of friends in a serene setting. One is grief incarnate, the other composed restraint. According to the modern scholar Han Yü-t'ao, the wailing and excessive mourning in the *Letter on the Disturbances* makes the received notion of Wang Hsi-chih highly suspect. Where in the letter do we find, asks Han, the "tranquil disposition" that is "neither extreme nor fierce"?[19] The significance of the letter, once it is fully considered, may prove to be iconoclastic. It does not add to the Wang Hsi-chih canon, but challenges it. It is not just another "Wang Hsi-chih"; it may well be the

Figure 2
Wang Hsi-chih (303–361). *Letter on the Disturbances* (*Sang-luan t'ieh*), 351 or 356. T'ang dynasty (618–907) copy. Ink on paper, 28.7 x 63 cm. Collection of the Japanese Imperial Household. From Nakata Yūjirō, ed., *Chinese Calligraphy* (New York and Tokyo: Weatherhill/Tankosha, 1983), pl. 16.

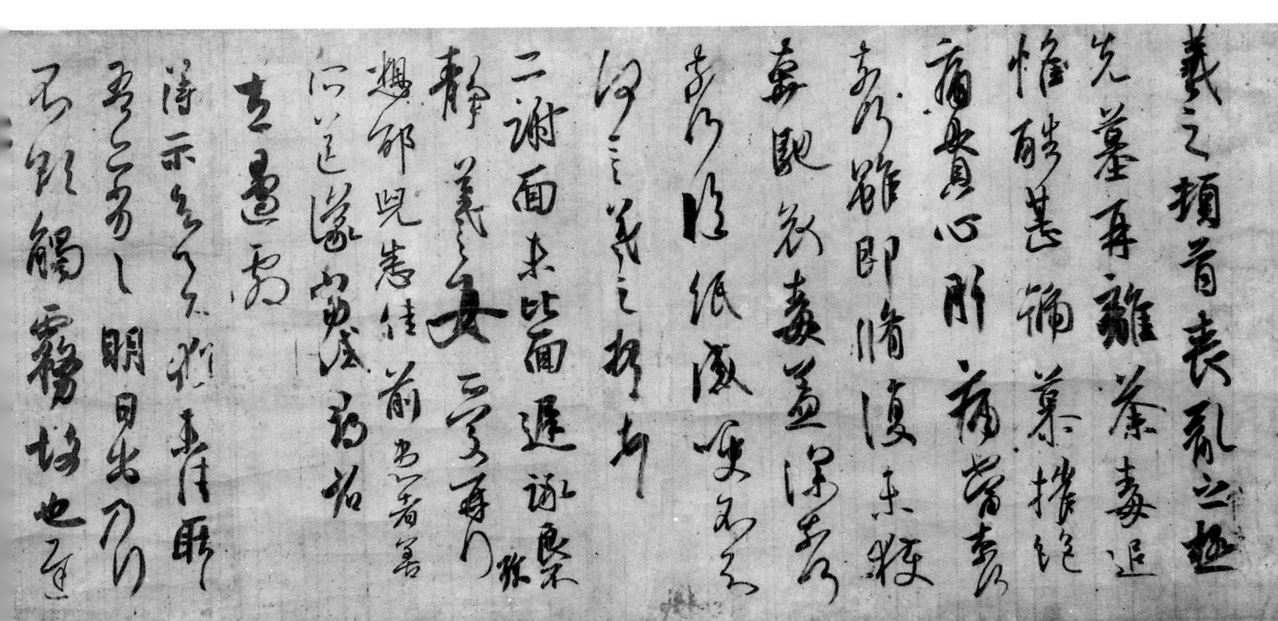

Figure 3
Wang Hsi-chih (303–361). *Old Capital Letter* (*Chiu-ching t'ieh*). Ink rubbing. From *Pao-Chin-chai fa-t'ieh hsüan* (Shanghai: Shang-hai ku-chi shu-tien, 1979), 7–8.

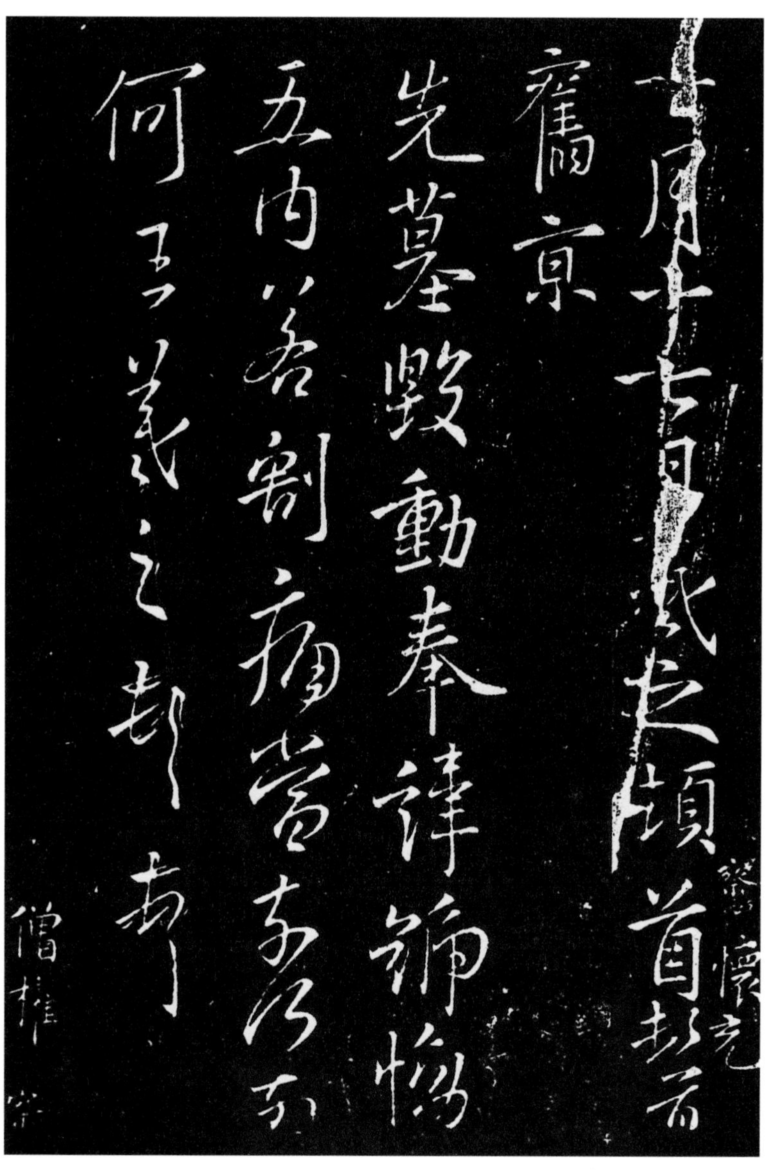

"Other Wang Hsi-chih." The notion of Wang as the calligraphic embodiment of the Confucian ideal of temperateness may well turn out to be historically untenable.

We must proceed cautiously, however, before reaching such a radical conclusion. We are likely, if not careful, to be ensnared by a pitfall peculiar to the art of calligraphy. In inferring behavioral resonances from calligraphic forms — the dispositions of brushstrokes, the overtones of gestural manners, and so forth — we must be aware that the discursive content can color our perception of the calligraphic forms. As a letter expressing sorrow, the *Letter on the Disturbances* may predispose us to see correspondences between its textual content and visual texture. For example, knowing that the character *t'ung* (see fig. 5) denotes "pain," we are likely to read that understanding into the written character and see the thrusting angularity of the strokes as enacting a figure writhing in agony. Here perception is colored by cognition; in other words, *seeing* how characters behave may be inseparable from *knowing* what they mean. If, on the other hand, we bracket the discursive content and try to describe the calligraphic strokes in purely objective stylistic terms and then measure them against the epistolary content, we might reach other conclusions. The reined-in stroke endings may just as well suggest the Confucian ideal of restraint and composure, despite the calligrapher's inner turmoil. However, this perception is also not free from underlying assumptions; it is already preconditioned by the conventional characterization of Wang Hsi-chih's calligraphy as that which displays a "tranquil disposition."

Unmoored to a historical context, neither of these two perceptual approaches — the content-laden or the content-free — stands well on its own. The art-historical interest in calligraphy rests largely in the interaction between a calligraphic form and a period perception generated by and attached to it. Historically speaking, calligraphy is no more than an "interpretive grid," to borrow a term from Yve-Alain Bois — a physical and formal structure suggesting and corresponding to a mental construct onto which one can map out a field of "semantic registers."[20]

To infer how the stylistic quality of Wang Hsi-chih's *Letter on the Disturbances* may have been perceived, articulated, and consequently moralized, we should compare it with the *Old Capital Letter* (*Chiu-ching t'ieh*; fig. 3), another work attributed to Wang, which has an almost identical semantic content and circumstantial reference. This work is listed in the Northern Sung imperial calligraphy catalogue, *Hsüan-ho shu-p'u*,[21] and appears in *Model Calligraphies from the Precious Chin Studio* (*Pao-Chin-chai fa-t'ieh*), a thirteenth-century model-book compendium of calligraphic rubbings. It reads:

> On the seventeenth day of the tenth month, I, Hsi-chih, am writing with reverence. The ancestral tombs at the old capital have been destroyed. I think of my ancestors and cry my heart out. For five days, I have been feeling piercing pains. What can I do? What can I do? Yours most sincerely, Wang Hsi-chih.[22]

The *Model Calligraphies from the Precious Chin Studio* takes its name from Mi Fu's (1052–1107) collection of art from the Eastern Chin period (317–420).[23] By the late Southern Sung (1127–1279), only two engraved stones from Mi's collection had survived, both badly damaged. During the Hsien-ch'un period (1265–74), a scholar named Ts'ao Chih-ko appropriated the name of Mi Fu's collection and made a new model-book compendium, based mostly on the highly reputable *Model Calligraphies from the Hsing-feng Hall* (*Hsing-feng-lou t'ieh*), now lost, that was compiled by his uncle Ts'ao Shih-mien, an eminent collector.[24] This compendium in turn became a major source for recarved calligraphies in model-books of the Ming dynasty (1368–1644). Despite his reservations about the quality of the carving, the Yüan scholar Ch'en I-tseng (1286–1345) allowed that "good compendia are so hard to find nowadays, scholars might as well get a taste of the semblance of the Chin and T'ang writers through this edition."[25] The *Old Capital Letter* survives in *chüan* six of this compendium.

Several of the same characters appear in both the *Letter on the Disturbances* and the *Old Capital Letter*, which allows us to compare their different stylistic incarnations in the two texts. For example, in both letters the character *mu* (tomb; fig. 4) is structurally identical and shows a slanting orientation. However, in the *Letter on the Disturbances* the character displays a more resolute brushwork, while in the *Old Capital Letter* it appears smooth and elegant. In the former work, the leftward-slanting stroke of the character ends with a blunt stop; in the latter, it finishes with a small upturned hook. The same distinction can be seen in the character *t'ung* (pain; fig. 5), which occurs several times in both letters. The *Letter on the Disturbances* characters show an unfaltering abruptness, while their counterparts in the *Old Capital Letter* exhibit in their slender strokes an ethereal grace. The vertical *p'ieh*-stroke of the same character in the *Letter on the Disturbances* descends forcefully; even when linked to another stroke, its resolute descent is uncompromising. In comparison, its counterpart in the *Old Capital Letter* glides gracefully into a curved, tapering finish.

While there seems to be little justification for the arbitrary imposition of our perceptual impressions on works rooted in historical and emotional circumstances, there is much to be said for remarks made by past observers. They were more accustomed to transposing and reducing calligraphic forms to metaphors and verbal characterizations, and using the latter as

Figure 4
The characters *hsien mu* (ancestral tombs) in Wang Hsi-chih (303–361), *Letter on the Disturbances* (*Sang-luan t'ieh*) and *Old Capital Letter* (*Chiu-ching t'ieh*). Ink rubbing. Adapted from Iijima Tachio, ed., *Ō Gishi daijiten* (Tokyo: Bijutsu seisaku, 1980), 578.

Figure 5
The character *t'ung* (pain) in Wang Hsi-chih (303–361), *Letter on the Disturbances* (*Sang-luan t'ieh*) and *Old Capital Letter* (*Chiu-ching t'ieh*). Ink rubbing. Adapted from Iijima Tachio, ed. *Ō Gishi daijiten* (Tokyo: Bijutsu seisaku, 1980), 472.

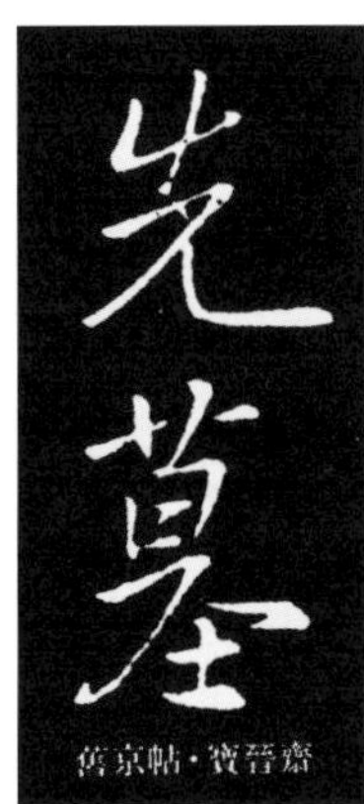

pointers and bridges to realms of experiences beyond art. Fleeting impressions, vague feelings, and intuitive percepts of formal properties, once verbalized, are reduced to categorical traits. In their new incarnation as linguistic properties, they are in turn susceptible to internal shifts within the same word of senses or references. Words used to describe brushstrokes such as "forceful" and "unswerving" were likely to find easy correspondences with human traits. Or qualities identified in a calligraphic texture like "ethereal" and "graceful" would soon be transposed to the author behind the calligraphy. Identical verbal characterizations served to bridge the gap between the calligraphic character and the calligrapher's character by virtue of being equally applicable to both. This is precisely the way Sun Kuo-t'ing (648?–703?), in his *Treatise on Calligraphy* (*Shu-p'u*), reads Wang Hsi-chih's calligraphy: "In writing about the happy gathering at the Orchid Pavilion, his thoughts roamed and his spirit soared ... his personality was controlled and far-reaching."[26] Sun Kuo-t'ing wrote these comments three centuries after Wang Hsi-chih's time, and his knowledge of Wang was not much better than ours. His recourse was an easy one: transferring the characterization of calligraphy to the calligrapher—what the Ming dynasty critic Wang Shih-chen (1526–1590), in commenting on this passage by Sun, calls "reversing the process."[27] The *Old Capital Letter* lends itself to the kind of vocabulary that Sun and his T'ang dynasty contemporaries used in describing Wang Hsi-chih and that is still with us today. The *Letter on the Disturbances*, in contrast, is an art-historical embarrassment. The tailor-made lexicon perpetuated by traditional calligraphic criticism concerning Wang Hsi-chih has not adequately prepared us to describe its formal traits.

The difference between the *Letter on the Disturbances* and the *Old Capital Letter* parallels the opposition between the *Letter on the Disturbances* and the *Orchid Pavilion* often pitched in the debate about the authenticity of the latter.[28] Taking his cue from archaeological discoveries of Eastern Chin tomb tiles with inscriptions, in particular those from the tombs of Wang Hsi-chih's relatives, in the 1960s Kuo Mo-jo declared the *Orchid Pavilion*—both the calligraphy and part of the text—to be a seventh-century fabrication. He was supported in his views by a number of well-established scholars, but also met with vehement objections from loyal Wang Hsi-chih apologists.[29] The *Letter on the Disturbances* was cited in the debate as a more credible T'ang copy, one closer to the "true" Wang Hsi-chih than the *Orchid Pavilion*.[30] In this ongoing discussion, scholars who disagree with Kuo attack his evidence,[31] but few can now assume that the *Orchid Pavilion* is a close copy of a Wang Hsi-chih original without some kind of qualification. With the authenticity of the work under question, the received characterization of Wang Hsi-chih based on the observation and description of stylistic traits of the *Orchid Pavilion* also becomes suspect.

Yet the authority of the *Orchid Pavilion* is not easily shaken. Epitomizing the entire Wang canon, the *Orchid Pavilion* has always been a yardstick with which to measure other works rather than a work to be measured. Furthermore, the *Orchid Pavilion* has an empire of words to its credit, having over time inspired a lineal textual conglomerate of verbal descriptions that overlays its calligraphic forms. Its slippery formal qualities are reduced to a standard vocabulary, a fixed set of categories and formulae, which predisposes us to see not only the *Orchid Pavilion* itself but the entire Wang Hsi-chih oeuvre in a certain way. What is vexing is that consequently, even when viewing a work like the *Letter on the Disturbances*, we find it difficult to free ourselves from the hardened categorical prism through which we habitually see a Wang Hsi-chih. In order to appreciate the *Letter on the Disturbances* we must first unlearn the inherited rhetoric of tranquility and gentility inspired by the *Orchid Pavilion.* These genteel calligraphic moods typically associated with Wang Hsi-chih, this essay shows, may well have been largely a product of the seventh-century Chinese culture that was bent on gentrifying itself. This cultural aspiration molded Wang Hsi-chih after its own desire. Various historical sources already point to the T'ang's and subsequent cultural authorities' heavy mediation and reconfiguration of Wang Hsi-chih. What is needed for us to fathom and gauge the extent to which Wang Hsi-chih may have been reconstituted is some corroborating material testimony and a stylistic frame of reference. To be sure, the existing Wang Hsi-chih canon absent the *Letter on the Disturbances* already betrays some incongruities; one need only compare Wang's *Letter to an Aunt* (*I-mu t'ieh*), in the Liaoning Provincial Museum, with the *Orchid Pavilion* to see the gap between the two. For reasons of credibility compromised through generations of recopying and recarving, works like *Letter to an Aunt* are themselves not convincing and compelling enough to hint at the "primordial" or "pristine" Wang Hsi-chih. Having the rugged *Letter on the Disturbances* thrust onto our horizon from its millennium-long hiding in Japan and considering the curious oblivion it suffered in T'ang China, we can now better sense the parochial taste governing the T'ang canonization of Wang Hsi-chih. With the *Letter on the Disturbances* as an intimation of the pristine Wang Hsi-chih, we are now in a better position to trace the trajectory whereby the rugged and spirited calligraphic quality displayed in a work like the *Letter on the Disturbances* was pruned and tamed into the mellow calligraphic disposition represented by the *Orchid Pavilion.*

Conflicting Characterizations: Gentleman or Warrior?

The body of descriptive text inspired by Wang Hsi-chih's calligraphy — in the form of quotations, stylized observations, memorable one-liners, and flights of rhetoric — has not always been a harmonious chorus of praise. It contains fragmented verbal relics that register the tortuous process in which Wang Hsi-chih was canonized, and jarring notes occasionally leap out. They add credence to the perceived difference between the *Orchid Pavilion* and the *Letter on the Disturbances*—the smooth refinement of the former versus the raw energy or archaic plainness of the latter—that is often cited in the modern debate over the authenticity of the *Orchid Pavilion*.[32] While the "tranquil disposition of a gentleman" has become the standard profile of Wang Hsi-chih's calligraphy, an alternative characterization built upon the trope of a "brave warrior" was once in use but has gradually lost its currency. In the medieval rhetorical scheme of binary oppositions, the "brave warrior" is often juxtaposed with the "gentleman":

> They surge with fury, are roused to passion—
> Oh, how like the brave warrior [*chuang-shih*]
> But in their dignified gentility, and gentle amiability
> They also resemble the gentleman [*chün-tzu*].[33]

It is precisely this complementary opposition between the brave warrior and the amiable gentleman that constitutes the dual strands in the description of Wang Hsi-chih's calligraphy. One T'ang critic describes Wang's calligraphy in this way:

> Hsi-chih's calligraphy is like a brave warrior unsheathing his sword to dam the waters and stem their flow. A dot he placed at the top is like a rock falling down from a high precipice. A horizontal stroke he made is like a cloud sweeping across a thousand miles. A slanting *na*-stroke he dashed is like the roar of wind and thunder. A vertical stroke he wrote is like a ten-thousand-year-old withered vine ... and tigers crouching across the phoenix's gateway ... like dragons leaping through Heaven's door.[34]

In the context of T'ang calligraphic discourse that tends to cast Wang's calligraphy in a graceful disposition, this view of his writing strikes one as refreshingly perverse in its characterization of Wang's calligraphy in terms of the "warrior" trope. The description draws upon two different sources. One is the Liang emperor Wu-ti's (r. 502–49) observation that "the propensity of his [Wang's] characters is sturdy and muscular, like dragons leaping through Heaven's door and tigers crouching across the phoenix's gateway."[35] The other source is a colophon, allegedly written by Wang Hsi-chih, to the "Battle Formation of the Brush," an apocryphal text attributed in T'ang times to Madam Wei (Wei fu-jen; 272–349), Wang's reputed teacher in his later hagiographies.[36] The colophon, which was also attributed to Wang in the T'ang period,[37] emphasizes the analogy between the arts of calligraphy and war: "Brush is knife; ink, armature; water and inkstone, fortresses.... The holding of the brush forebodes the auspicious and ominous.... The twists and turns of the brush are killings and slayings."[38] Even if we dismiss the attribution, we nonetheless can regard the colophon as part of the discursive formation associated with the image of Wang Hsi-chih in the T'ang period.

The strong, forceful personality of Wang Hsi-chih as projected in such early sources reinforces the rather militaristic view of calligraphy associated with him. In a chapter on personality traits in Liu I-ch'ing's (403–444) *A New Account of Tales of the World* (*Shih-shuo hsin-yü*), Wang Hsi-chih is listed under the category "backbone" (*ku-ch'i*), not the category "gentility" (*shao-jun*).[39] Similarly, in another description, Wang is "celebrated for having backbone and intestinal fortitude" (*i ku keng ch'eng*).[40] He was said to have had the audacity to point his finger at the back of the emperor and call him a "snob," a dauntless act that caused the emperor to turn around and comment: "There is no lack of sharp-tongued people in the world after all."[41] Wang Hsi-chih's official biography in the *Chin History*, allegedly written by the T'ang emperor T'ai-tsung (r. 626–49), betrays an unwitting inconsistent use of the sources despite the emperor's wish to cast the calligrapher in a certain light. Wang's political career is documented through his letters, which reveal an outspoken and spirited individual. This image of Wang contradicts that of the refined artistic persona constructed from various anecdotes. Not that the character of the historical Wang Hsi-chih has to fit the artistic persona reflected in his calligraphy, but we should be aware that the image of the historical figure as it has come down to us today is itself a textual entity and part of the general discourse surrounding Wang Hsi-chih. Its distinction from the moral persona derived from Wang Hsi-chih's calligraphic style is itself an eloquent testimony to the arbitrariness of the constructed artistic persona attached to the name of Wang Hsi-chih.

The metaphor of bone structure has long been part of the critical vocabulary of Chinese calligraphic discourse, in which "to have purely bone lacks charm, to have all flesh is deficient in strength. A dearth of ink appears drab; excess of ink leads to clumsy bluntness."[42] We should not indiscriminately transpose tropes from biographic accounts to calligraphic discourse, but it is interesting to follow their use over time in the traditional descriptions of Wang Hsi-chih's calligraphy. The critic Yang Hsin (370–442), who was a generation younger than Wang Hsi-chih, noted that the calligraphy by Wang's son, Wang Hsien-chih, "does not match his father in the force of bone, but surpasses him in coquettish charm."[43] By the seventh century, Wang Hsi-chih was perceived as having achieved in his calligraphy a perfect balance between bone and flesh, based on a changed premise that while a deficiency of bone is not acceptable, neither is an excess of bone desirable;[44] in other words, "bones" are desirable, but only to a limited degree.

Furthermore, the calligraphic ideal became that of a "placid and graceful appearance concealing inner sinew and bone," a quality that has since become typically associated with Wang Hsi-chih.[45] That the characteristic of "bone" should be *concealed* is something quite at odds with the earlier image of Wang Hsi-chih, who in the early literature had been celebrated primarily for displaying "backbone" or "bone-spirit." The appearance of this modified view in the seventh century presages a shift in the perceptual characterization of Wang Hsi-chih that would take place in subsequent centuries.

Although the textual description of Wang Hsi-chih as a historical figure known for his "backbone and intestinal fortitude" still circulated in T'ang times, there emerged a gentler calligraphic persona that increasingly departed from the historical one. People of the T'ang, having been exposed to a reinvented interpretation of Wang Hsi-chih's calligraphy, began to see his style as graceful and genteel. The descriptive vocabulary still reflected the earlier opposition between militant muscularity and refined fragility, but the persona of Wang Hsi-chih that was now projected stressed the fragile side. The critic Chang Huai-kuan, writing in 758, took Wang Hsi-chih's cursive-script calligraphy to task:

> The degree of cultivation of I-shao's [Wang Hsi-chih] calligraphy is not very high; nor does the calligraphy display a longtime honing of skills. Though it is suave and graceful, it lacks spirit. There is no weaponlike sharpness to inspire awe, no image-inducing efficacy to make one marvel. It is therefore inferior to other masters' works.[46]

Chang also notes that Wang's cursive-script calligraphy has "a feminine quality and is deficient in masculinity; it is not to be prized,"[47] a perception that was shared by Han Yü (768–824) who dismissed Wang Hsi-chih's "vulgar calligraphy" as "flaunting a bewitching coquetry."[48] Chang also mentions a calligrapher named Kao Cheng-ch'en who "has studied Yu-chün's [Wang Hsi-chih] method. His calligraphy is long on fat and flesh, and short on bone-spirit. Well-pruned and smart in dress, it has a dandyish quality."[49] According to Chang, good cursive-script calligraphy should have the "intimidating power of dragons and tigers," precisely the quality that Emperor Wu-ti of the Liang saw in Wang Hsi-chih's calligraphy[50] and, as Chang's criticism of Wang's calligraphy suggests, was now thought to be lacking.

Civility over Militarism

The opposition in calligraphic discourse between figurative descriptions of genteel moderation and muscular swaggering parallels the tension between civility (*wen*) and militarism (*wu*) during the reign of Emperor T'ai-tsung of the T'ang who came to the throne in 626 as a young military general.

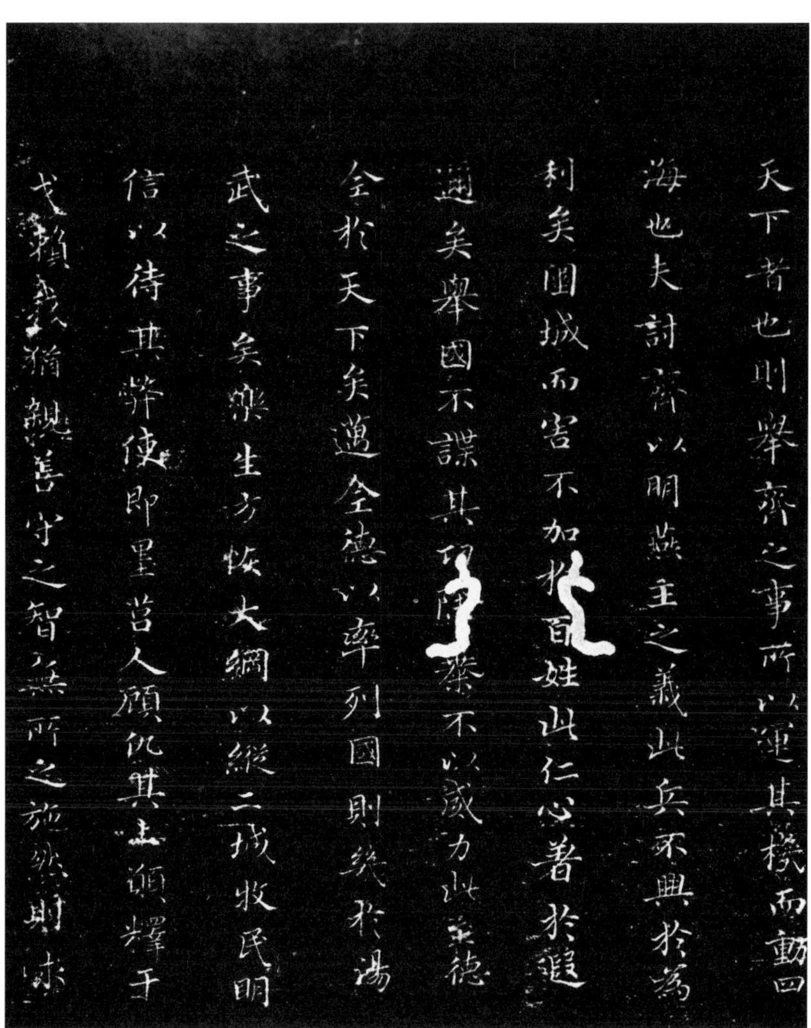

Figure 6
Wang Hsi-chih (303–361). Detail of copy of Hsia-hou Hsüan's (209–254) *Essay on Yüeh I* (*Yüeh I lun*), 348. Ink rubbing in the *Yü-ch'ing-chai t'ieh* (Model-writing compendium from the Yü-ch'ing-chai studio). From Inoue Yasushi et al., *Shodō geijutsu* (Tokyo: Chūō Kōronsha, 1971), v. 1, pl. 4.

With the consolidation of the new dynasty, the emperor became acutely aware of the need to rule by civil order rather than by military might and draconian regimentation.[51] He regretted his blind "faith in military power in [his] youth and his ignorance in learning" the Way of the ancient sages.[52] Heeding his courtier Wang Kuei's criticism of the new regime's "primacy of militarism over learning,"[53] T'ai-tsung willingly embraced the proposal of his counselor Wei Cheng to "terminate militarism [in order] to cultivate civility."[54] "I have indeed conquered the world with military prowess," the emperor confessed, "but it takes civil virtues to pacify the universe."[55] Instead of keeping the company of valiant generals from the northwest, as he had in his early military career, the emperor now spent long hours with scholars from the southeast.

The T'ai-tsung court assiduously promoted the acculturation of Confucianism throughout the country.[56] "My only liking is for the Way of Yao, Shun, Chou, and Confucius," the emperor professed. "It is what wings are to a bird and water is to fish, the loss of which means death. There is not one moment when one can go without it."[57] Confucian temples were built in every prefecture and county. Distinguished Confucian scholars were actively courted and recruited to serve in various eminent posts in the imperial court. Special literary institutes, such as the Institute for the Advancement of Literature (*Hung-wen-kuan*), were established to host literary talents. The imperial collection and collation of classical texts took on an urgency unprecedented since Han times. Standard exegetical commentaries on canonical Confucian classics were carried out at the emperor's decree. Ritual protocols were carefully designed, and a standardized educational system consisting of the National University (*t'ai-hsüeh*) and schools at the prefecture and county levels was established with a curriculum focused on the Nine Classics of the Confucian canon.

Against this backdrop, it is easy to appreciate why the *Essay on Yüeh I* (*Yüeh I lun*; fig. 6) and the *Orchid Pavilion*, with their genteel and mellow content and style, appealed to Emperor T'ai-tsung. The textual content of the *Essay on Yüeh I* in many ways speaks directly to the early-T'ang situation. Composed by Hsia-hou Hsüan (209–254),[58] the essay quotes and comments on a letter by Yüeh I, a rhetorician and military strategist of the Warring States period (ca. 470–221 BC) who served as a top advisor to King Hui of the state of Yen, to whom Yüeh I's letter is addressed.[59] It extols the renunciation of violence as a more virtuous way to govern, and advises the king, who was pondering whether to sack two cities, to overcome the enemy by exerting moral authority and influence rather than relying on sheer military aggression. The essay articulates T'ai-tsung's policy of "terminating militarism to cultivate civility." Its tone of pacifism is also relevant. In the early years of his reign, T'ai-tsung pursued a policy of détente with China's neighbors and used military force sparingly, though he gradually reversed that trend as his expansionist ambitions grew.[60] While the pacifist message would have struck a sympathetic chord with those ministers, especially Ch'u Sui-liang, who were opposed to excessive expansions of the T'ang empire, it was increasingly irrelevant to T'ai-tsung who must have been drawn instead to another message conveyed in the text. Between 630 and 645, the T'ang had defeated the Turks and made deep forays into Central Asia, and embassies and tributes flowed in from distant foreign countries. The *Essay on Yüeh I*'s portrayal of an exalted ruler "earning the admiration of neighboring states and awe of all among the Four Seas"[61] must have appealed to and flattered T'ai-tsung who saw his image reflected in that of King Hui. In 639, at the emperor's decree, the essay was taken out of the imperial collection, and Feng Ch'eng-su, one of the professional copyists at the Institute for the Advancement of Literature, was instructed to make copies of it, which the emperor in turn presented to six prominent court officials. These copies are said to "capture all the rules of standard-script calligraphy."[62]

The Early-T'ang Masters Ou-yang Hsün, Yü Shih-nan, and Ch'u Sui-liang

Three towering public figures of the T'ang dynasty—Ou-yang Hsün (557–641), Yü Shih-nan (558–638), and Ch'u Sui-liang (596–658)—were instrumental in shaping an orthodox calligraphic model under the name of Wang Hsi-chih.[63] They were not only prominent statesmen, but also celebrated calligraphers in their own right. What is significant is that their calligraphy continued to be framed as the opposition between martial masculinity and genteel femininity in descriptive tropes. Seen through the prism of the T'ang period, Ou-yang Hsün and Yü Shih-nan occupy two opposite poles of a stylistic spectrum. To the seventh-century critic Li Ssu-chen (d. 696), Ou-yang's lofty characters (fig. 7) are like "lances and halberds from weapon stocks and masculine swords about to thrust forth."[64] Similarly, the eighth-century critic Chang Huai-kuan notes that Ou-yang's calligraphy is "intimidating like lances and halberds from weapon stocks," capable of "driving forth fiercely," and his characters are like "alarmed leaping horses oblivious of danger."[65] Other T'ang commentators compared Ou-yang's characters to "thunderbolt-holding guardians glaring and scowling, and warriors clenching their fists."[66] Yü Shih-nan's calligraphy (fig. 8), in contrast, was perceived in terms of ease (*i*)[67] or charm (*mei*),[68] provoking the observation that it was like "[dames] in silk and damask languishing in spring."[69] The two calligraphers were often measured against each other:

> Ou[-yang] and Yü match each other with their respective prowess and wit.... With regard to overall formation, Yü is inferior. Ou[-yang] is

Figure 7 (left)
Ou-yang Hsün (557–641). Detail from *Huang-fu Tan pei*, 632–43. Ink rubbing, 240 x 96 cm. Rubel Collection, Harvard University. Courtesy of the Rubel Collection of Asian Art, Harvard University (C-87).

Figure 8 (right)
Yü Shih-nan (558–638). Detail from *K'ung-tzu miao-t'ang pei*, 626. Ink rubbing from Sung dynasty (960–1279) replica stele, 280 x 110 cm. Rubel Collection, Harvard University. Courtesy of the Rubel Collection of Asian Art, Harvard University (C-75).

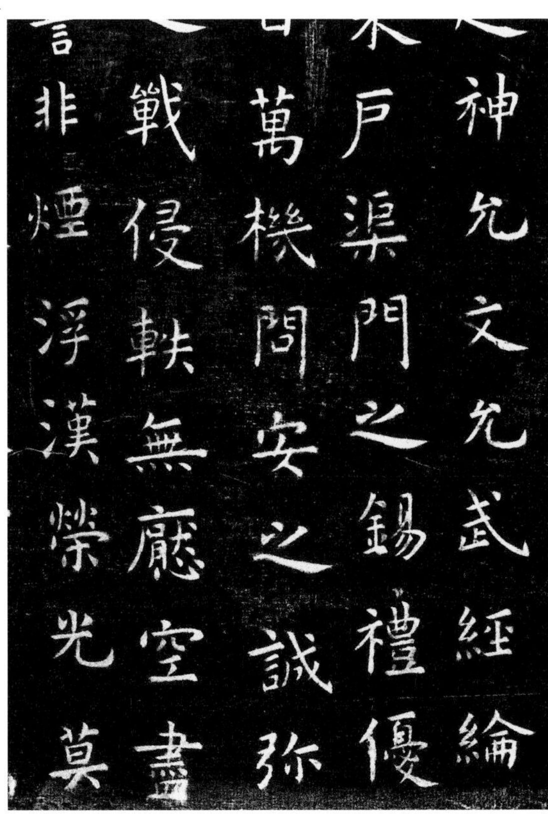

like a fearless general driving deep into [enemy lines], susceptible to occasional lapses; Yü is like a well-chosen messenger who is rarely fallible. Yü conceals the steeliness and suppleness inside, while Ou[-yang] flaunts the sinews and bones. A gentleman hides his sharp edges, and this is best embodied in Yü's [calligraphy].[70]

This polarity echoes the seventh-century critic Sun Kuo-t'ing's observation that "at times calligraphy is gentle and mild while concealing the sinews and bones inside; at other times it twists and breaks while the outside is angular and showy."[71] Sun's contemporaries would have had no difficulty in assigning these characteristics respectively to Yü and Ou-yang, and they have since become critical wisdom.[72]

Ou-yang Hsün and Yü Shih-nan both were from prominent southern families, although Ou-yang's early life was marred by the stigma of his father being an insurgent general. They served as officials under the southern Ch'en (557–589) dynasty; after the Sui dynasty (581–618) unified north and south China, both men moved to the capital city, Ch'ang-an, where Yü became a celebrity in scholarly circles and Ou-yang served in the court as an official of ritual ceremonies and established his reputation as a calligrapher. In 621, when they were in their mid-sixties, Yü and Ou-yang were retained by the T'ang court despite the fact that they had at one time been followers of the subjugated rebel Tou Chien-te (573–621). In 627, at T'ai-tsung's decree, they were appointed as the first two masters in the Institute for the Advancement of Literature to teach the method of standard-script calligraphy to junior members of the imperial family and sons of court officials.[73]

Ou-yang and Yü spent most of their formative years under the Sui dynasty. The Sui unification of China brought together the Northern and Southern calligraphic traditions, combining the expansive composition of characters found in Northern Chou (557–581) stele writing and the sleekness of characters typical of the southern Ch'en dynasty. This accounts for the similarity between the writing styles of Ou-yang and Yü. In their formative years, the Wang Hsien-chih style was in still vogue,[74] but it meant different things to each of them. For Ou-yang, it was Wang Hsien-chih's angularity and calculation in the configuration of characters that had appeal,[75] while for Yü it was the sleek and genteel aspect of Wang's calligraphy.

There are other factors that set Ou-yang Hsün and Yü Shih-nan apart. Ou-yang's sober and saturnine style owes more to the crisp and angular style of stele writing of the Northern dynasties.[76] The frequent demands placed upon him to write texts for memorial tablets, which required a structural clarity achieved by a fully stretched character composition, may have caused him to adopt this writing style.[77] Behind Ou-yang's robust and

Figure 9
Emperor T'ai-tsung (r. 626–49). *Inscription for the Hot Spring* (*Wen-ch'üan ming*), 628. T'ang dynasty (618–907) ink rubbing. Bibliothèque Nationale, Paris. From Yang Jen-kai, ed., *Chung-kuo mei-shu ch'üan-chi, Shu-fa chuan-k'o pien* (Peking: Jen-min mei-shu ch'u-pan-she, 1989), v. 3, pl. 34.

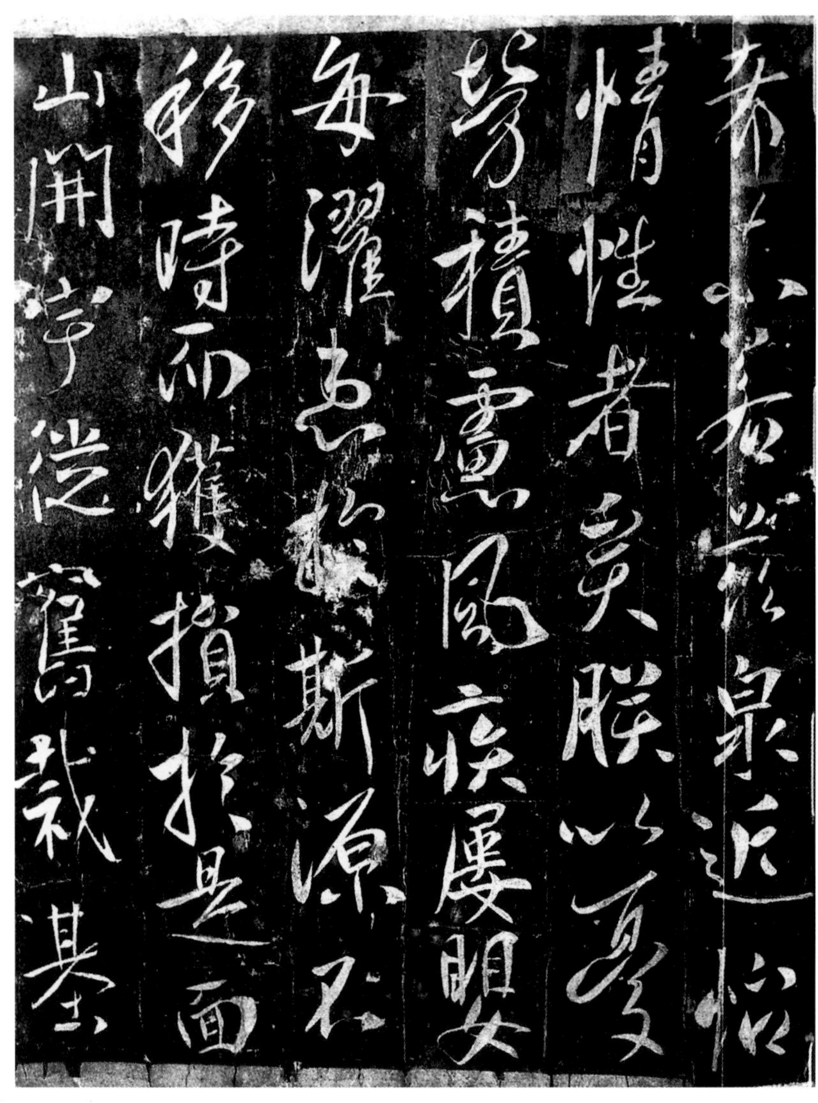

lofty calligraphy also lurk psychological factors that may have influenced his calligraphic disposition. In his adolescence he was forced to go into hiding when his father was executed in the capital after his failed insurgence.[78] In addition, he endured ridicule and humiliation because of his "extreme ugliness," which must have engendered in him a sense of defensiveness and reserve.[79] There also appears to be a correlation between Ou-yang's stoic calligraphic style and his career as a court official in charge of rituals and ceremonies, in which he applied and upheld rigorous administrative and editorial standards. As a compiler of the *I-wen lei-chü* encyclopedia, he suffered no "superficial incongruities" and ruthlessly excised excess "verbiage."[80] He also chose not to include in the compilation a dubious version of the *Orchid Pavilion* that was favored by Emperor T'ai-tsung.[81] While these factors do not immediately translate into calligraphic properties, they may have led Ou-yang to prefer certain stylistic options over others.

In contrast to Ou-yang Hsün, Yü Shih-nan's reputation initially did not rest on his calligraphy. He established himself primarily as an erudite scholar and rose in quick succession from an Adjutant to a scholar in the Institute for the Advancement of Literature, Editorial Director, Secretary to the Heir Apparent, and finally the prominent position of Director of the Palace Library. He became the emperor's mentor on matters of history, classical learning, and calligraphy. T'ai-tsung's preference for Wang Hsi-chih's calligraphy was in fact due to his apprenticeship with Yü Shih-nan,[82] and is evidenced in his *Chin-tz'u Inscription* (*Chin-tz'u ming*) and *Inscription for the Hot Spring* (*Wen-ch'üan ming*; fig. 9).

Much attention has been given to Yü Shih-nan's calligraphic schooling under the tutelage of the monk Chih-yung (active late 6th–early 7th century), Wang Hsi-chih's seventh-generation descendent, which legitimized Yü's standing as an heir to the orthodox Wang Hsi-chih tradition.[83] What is less well known is that Chih-yung's rendition of Wang Hsi-chih's calligraphy is itself problematic. He was chided by his contemporaries as having only "acquired Yu-chün's [Wang Hsi-chih] flesh" and not his "bones."[84] As modern scholars have observed, Chih-yung's elongated character composition clearly comes from Wang Hsien-chih (344–388) rather than his father, Wang Hsi-chih.[85] The Wang Hsi-chih legacy passed on to Yü, as mediated by Chih-yung, was therefore heavily influenced by the calligraphy of Wang Hsien-chih, with its untrammeled fluidity and outstretched ornateness. Parallel to this stylistic influence, Yü's literary sensibility, shaped during the Ch'en dynasty when palace poetry of erotic trivia was still in vogue, displayed a penchant for feminine sensitivity, refined ornamentation, and exquisite structural perfection.[86] It was Yü Shih-nan who in turn shaped Emperor T'ai-tsung's calligraphic taste. Ultimately, it was to Yü Shih-nan, and later Ch'u Sui-liang, that T'ai-tsung entrusted the task of authenticating

Figure 10
Ch'u Sui-liang (596–658). Detail from *Inscription on the Buddhist Grotto at I-ch'üeh* (*I-ch'üeh fo-k'an ming*), 641. Cliff carving in the shape of a stele at Pin-yang Cave, Lung-men, Loyang. Ink rubbing, 252 x 154 cm. Collection of Peking Library. From Mao Tzu-liang, ed., *Chung-kuo li-tai i-shu shu-fa chuan-k'o pien* (Shanghai: Shang-hai shu-hua ch'u-pan-she, 1994), pl. 90.

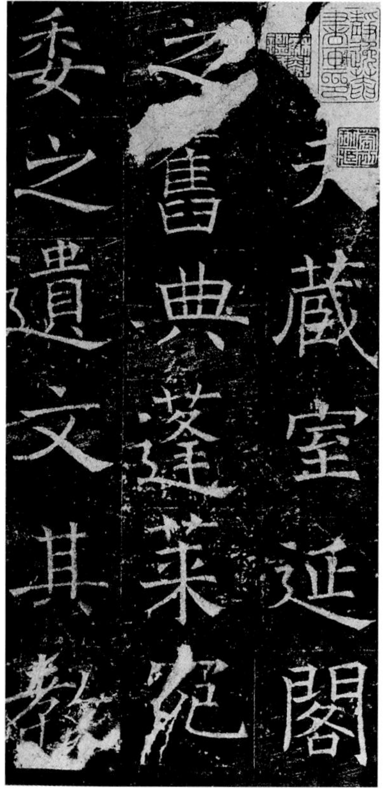

Figure 11
Ch'u Sui-liang (596–658). Detail from *Stele for Master Meng* (*Meng fa-shih pei*), 642. T'ang dynasty (618–907) ink rubbing. Mitsui Chōkōri Collection. From Inoue Yasushi et al., *Shodō geijutsu* (Tokyo: Chūō Kōronsha, 1971), v. 3, pl. 107.

and collating Wang Hsi-chih's surviving works, an indication of the kind of Wang Hsi-chih calligraphy that was perpetuated in the early T'ang. Yü Shih-nan's eminent status as an artist and an official thus should come as no surprise; he was even accorded the honor of having his portrait painted as one of the eminent Eighteen Scholars.[87]

It was in the hands of Ch'u Sui-liang, who was one generation younger than Ou-yang Hsün and Yü Shih-nan, that the taming of Wang Hsi-chih ran its full course. Yü Shih-nan's death was deeply felt by Emperor T'ai-tsung, who lamented that "from now on there will be no one to discuss calligraphy with." Ch'u Sui-liang, at the time already a consummate calligrapher, was recommended soon thereafter to fill the vacancy left by Yü Shih-nan. He was entrusted with authenticating Wang Hsi-chih's calligraphic legacy and proved to be "unerring" in his connoisseurship.[88] Ch'u soon won the emperor's trust and rose to a position at the court higher than that achieved by either Ou-yang Hsün or Yü Shih-nan.[89]

Ou-yang Hsün, a friend of Ch'u Sui-liang's father, had long recognized Ch'u's calligraphic talent. Ch'u's early work shows a distinct stylistic affinity with Ou-yang Hsün, as evidenced in his *Inscription on the Buddhist Grotto at I-ch'üeh* (*I-ch'üeh fo-k'an ming*; fig. 10), dated 641. The characters are rectangular in shape and the brushstrokes display a crisp angularity—what in the T'ang might be described as "full of sinews and bones." Another well-known work by Ch'u Sui-liang is the *Stele for Master Meng* (*Meng Fa-shih pei*; fig. 11). Executed in 642, only one year after the *I-ch'üeh Inscription*, it signals a marked change in style. The formal resemblance to Ou-yang Hsün seen in the *I-ch'üeh Inscription* now gives way to an indebtedness to both Ou-yang's angularity and Yü Shih-nan's elegance. In other words, Ch'u Sui-liang was gravitating toward Yü Shih-nan, the supposed heir to the Wang Hsi-chih tradition. For Ch'u, to follow Yü Shih-nan's style was to inherit the Wang legacy and measure up to T'ai-tsung's expectations. By 653, when Ch'u copied the *Preface to the Sacred Teaching* (*San-tsang sheng-chiao hsü*; fig. 12) for the Great Goose Pagoda, in Ch'ang-an, this shift in stylistic allegiance had been completed. Although the angularity of the brushstrokes evident in his earlier work is still present, Ch'u's characters are now softened by curves and a linear elasticity that results from swifter brush movement and flexible manipulation of the brush tip. The stately and expansive composition, which he also inherited from Yü Shih-nan, is softened in the relaxed strokes suggestive of clerical script and imparts a sense of feminine languor.[90] This style of writing is, in effect, Ch'u Sui-liang's calligraphic inheritance of the Wang Hsi-chih style as interpreted by Yü Shih-nan. The subtle stylistic change in Ch'u's writing did not escape the attention of the T'ang critic Chang Huai-kuan: "The short side of Ch'u's calligraphy is its allegiance to Yü Shih-nan; the long side is its explication of Yu-chün [Wang Hsi-chih], whose coquettish charm [*mei-ch'ü*] is not lost on Ch'u." In the eyes of Chang, Ch'u Sui-liang's characters are like delicate "female beauties and dames unable to bear [the weight of] silk; their makeup and slender figures are unmatched by Ou[-yang] and Yü."[91] In the Sui dynasty, it was Chih-yung, Yü Shih-nan's mentor, who was mocked for having only "acquired Wang Hsi-chih's flesh"; now, in the T'ang, it is Ch'u Sui-liang who, in pushing Yü's stylistic propensity to its logical conclusion, was seen by Hsü Hao (703–782) as having only "obtained [Wang Hsi-chih's] flesh."[92]

The increasingly genteel and moderate tendencies in Ch'u's calligraphic style may reflect his disposition as a statesman. In his advice to the throne, Ch'u consistently advocated moderation. He objected to the extravagance of the *feng-shan* ritual on Mount T'ai on the grounds that it placed an undue tax burden on the people. He also urged the emperor to adopt a diplomatic approach in foreign affairs, counseling him to refrain from excessive use of military force against Karakhoja (Turfan) in Central Asia[93] and vehemently protesting the emperor's decision to order a punitive expedition against the Korean kingdom of Koguryŏ.[94] As the most influential calligraphy expert at T'ai-tsung's court and the acknowledged connoisseur of Wang Hsi-chih's oeuvre, Ch'u Sui-liang placed the *Essay on Yüeh I* first among Wang's works in T'ai-tsung's collection, proclaiming it the best example of his standard-script calligraphy.[95] The authenticity of the work was not undisputed even at that time; a century earlier, the Liang emperor Wu-ti had cast serious doubts about its authorship: "Extremely slender brushstrokes are rarely found in I-shao's [Wang Hsi-chih] works. [Those in] the *Essay on Yüeh I* [are] slightly thicker. [Nevertheless] it is unlikely to have come from [Wang's hand]."[96] The liberty Ch'u took with what was at best a controversial, if not dubious, work was consistent with the early-T'ang interest in seeking classical examples from the past that could serve as analogies with contemporary situations.[97] More significantly, the *Essay on Yüeh I*'s pacifist tone and advocacy of diplomacy in place of military force accorded with Ch'u Sui-liang's own political views.

Ch'u's moderate political stance may not have had an immediate bearing on his calligraphic style. Nonetheless, it is interesting to note the subtle rapport, however implicit and tenuous, between the modes of political and calligraphic discourse. At least it asks us to consider a cultural context in which the perception of calligraphy was deeply caught up in the shrill rhetoric of martial masculinity and peaceful femininity. It explains in part Emperor T'ai-tsung's inconsistency in his calligraphic preference for different constructs of Wang Hsi-chih's calligraphy as moderate or bold, the latter of which harkened back to his former career as a military leader. There is also a contradiction in T'ai-tsung's discrimination between Wang Hsi-chih and his son Wang Hsien-chih. The emperor regarded Wang Hsi-chih's calligraphy as the perfect embodiment of virtue and beauty. Elsewhere, in harsh and scathing language he dismissed as incompetent those whom he considered lesser calligraphers — including Wang Hsien-chih — pronouncing their brushwork "inhibited" or "frigid and anemic, without abandon," and their writing lacking "even half the bones" necessary for good calligraphy and "wanting in manly spirit."[98] However, as noted by the Ch'ing dynasty (1644–1912) critic Liu Hsi-tsai, these comments more fittingly describe the received image of Wang Hsi-chih's calligraphy and, if framed in positive terms, delineate precisely those characteristics that make his style appealing.[99] Wang Hsien-chih's calligraphy, if anything, is usually criticized for being long on abandonment and ostentation and short on subtlety. T'ai-tsung's own calligraphy, especially his *Inscription for the Hot Spring* (see fig. 9), shows more affinity with Wang Hsien-chih than Wang Hsi-chih. The gap between the emperor's avowed preference for Wang Hsi-chih and his unacknowledged calligraphic affinity with Wang Hsien-chih betrayed in his *Inscription for the Hot Spring* has baffled both past and present critics.[100] It may simply reflect a complex psychological situation. For a northern warlord who found himself ruling a newly consolidated empire, the refined culture of the south, epitomized by a calligraphy tradition associated with Wang Hsi-chih, came to symbolize a level of sophistication that had yet to be scaled. For the war-weary emperor who sought moments of peace and serenity, the southern calligraphic tradition represented the stability, harmony, and civil order needed in an empire still beset by unrest: "The long hours of administration leave me with intermittent leisure hours. With the Four Seas pacified, I would like to share with my ministers some learning, and to put a peaceful face to our administration."[101] For T'ai-tsung, a more militant calligraphic style — which he probably wrongly identified with Wang Hsien-chih but which was also demonstrated by Wang Hsi-chih in the *Letter on the Disturbances* — came dangerously close to symbolizing social recalcitrance and dynastic disorder. It may also have brought to mind his former days as a soldier and his lack of cultural refinement. Even when praising Wang Hsi-chih's calligraphy, he could only frame his ideas abstractly and was unable to articulate specific qualities. He had yet to master a vocabulary that could render in positive terms the feminine civility of Wang Hsi-chih's calligraphy while dismissing its masculine militarism. This reversal of values from the exclusive affirmation of martial qualities to the appreciation of genteel grace in calligraphic style and the corresponding minting of new terms with which to praise the latter had to wait for Sun Kuo-t'ing in the late seventh century, but the initial impetus was provided by Emperor T'ai-tsung.

Calligraphy and Mourning

The revival of Confucianism in the early T'ang galvanized the question of the calligraphic representation of mourning, as expressions of joy and sorrow were at the heart of the theory of representation in Confucian thought. Emotional stirrings often lead to symbolic expressions, as in music. Traditional Confucians regard such expressions as a measurement of the success or failure of a government. Thus we read in the *Book of Rites* (*Li Chi*):

> Hence, the airs of an age of good order indicate composure and enjoyment. The airs of an age of disorder indicate dissatisfaction and anger, and its government is perversely bad. The airs of a state going to ruin are expressive of sorrow and [troubled] thought. There is an interaction between the words and the airs [of the people] and the character of their government.[102]

In the *Book of Rites* rulers are urged to regulate society through ceremonies and music — and, by extension, the arts. Human nature is understood to be essentially still, yet has the propensity to be stirred by external things. According to traditional Confucian teaching: "But for their [affections of] grief, pleasure, joy, and anger there are no invariable rules."[103] Therefore, it falls to the ruler to fashion a rational music to control the eruptions of raw emotions. The purpose of the "institution of ceremonies and music" is not to "satisfy the desires of the appetite and of the ears and eyes; [it is] intended to teach the people to regulate their likes and dislikes and to bring them back to the normal course of humanity."[104] Consequently, "on occasions of great sorrow," people may have "their rules according to which they express grief. The manifestations, whether of grief or joy, are all bounded by the limits of these rules,"[105] so that "the strong phase showed no excess such as anger, and the weak phase showed no shrinking like that of pusillanimity."[106] The ideal form of expression is to have "joy without wantonness and sorrow without breakdown,"[107] a Confucian disposition famously defined as "mild and gentle, sincere and good" (*wen-jou tun-hou*).[108]

All of this was mapped onto the realm of calligraphy in the seventh century. Emperor T'ai-tsung's obsession with calligraphy was apparently an integral part of a larger campaign to revive Confucian culture. Wang Hsi-chih was installed as the paragon of calligraphy mainly because the formal aspects of the style associated with him were seen as the perfect embodiment of the aesthetic and moral qualities set forth in Confucian thought. The moralization of calligraphic forms remained half-implicit and largely untheorized, yet its inedible impact was felt in T'ai-tsung's time. A few decades after T'ai-tsung's death, Sun Kuo-t'ing, a former Administrative Supervisor in Wu prefecture, wrote a full-fledged Confucian explication of calligraphy. His *Treatise on Calligraphy* is an eloquent exposition of what must have by that time become accepted wisdom. Sun Kuo-t'ing saw calligraphy as a display of the human disposition. It is essential to understand, Sun said, that "when a gentleman establishes himself he is obliged to cultivate the fundamentals."[109] The "fundamentals" (*pen*), as defined by a courtier in T'ai-tsung's court, are the qualities of "Equilibrium and Harmony" (*chung-ho*),[110] a reference to the classical Confucian dictum from the *Book of Rites*: "When there are no stirrings of pleasure, anger, sorrow, or joy, we call it the State of Equilibrium. When those feelings have been stirred, and all in their due measure and degree, we call it the State of Harmony."[111] As a result, good calligraphy should capture the qualities of a gentleman through what Confucius describes as "a well-balanced admixture of native substance and acquired refinement,"[112] with Equilibrium and Harmony serving as the ultimate standard. Calligraphy indeed can "give shape to joy and sorrow," and this is best achieved when "writers dignify their calligraphy with elegant spirit and soften it with delicate moisture, animate it with dry strength, and blend it with relaxed refinement."[113] The appeal of Wang Hsi-chih's calligraphy, as it was reconstructed in the T'ang period, is precisely its embodiment of balanced moderation, its display of a "tranquil disposition" that is "neither extreme nor fierce," and its "unassertive and graceful appearance concealing a strong and solid inside."[114]

A large body of Wang Hsi-chih's calligraphic work, as recorded in T'ang-period catalogues, consists of letters expressing sorrow, grief, and anxiety in response to illness, social disturbances, separation from friends or family, or the death of family members and friends. Upon hearing sad news, Wang typically responded with these expressions: "the pain has reached [my] Five Viscera";[115] "[my] sadness and distress are hurting"; "[I] lost control of [myself] in the deep sorrow";[116] or "[I] put down the brush, drenched in tears."[117] A T'ang epistolary manual typically contains such formal expressions of sorrow as the following:

> Letter to grandchildren from a son bereft of his parents: Misfortune has descended on us unexpectedly. Your.... parents have passed away. Sadness and pain are piercing. We cannot control ourselves. Now life will be harder for your generation. Woe is me. What can I do? What can I do?[118]

To employ such expressions in ritual communication is one thing, but to render their discursive content into a calligraphic representation and regard it as a work of art is quite another. The latter elevates the epistolary expressions from real-life situations to the realm of symbolic representation; it calls attention to the stylized posturing of the calligraphic act itself, and, in so doing, betrays dispositions that either meet or fall short of the Confucian standard of "sorrow without self-injury"(*ai erh pu shang*). Furthermore, the meaning of such epistolary calligraphy is in the eye of later beholders. The Sung scholar Ou-yang Hsiu (1007–1072) succinctly articulates this situation:

> What is called a model-book compendium [*fa-t'ieh*] is nothing more than exchanges between family members and friends, such as messages of condolences, inquiries after one's health, or correspondences with those from whom one is separated. These are normally no more than a few lines. Initially, no special meaning was intended [in the calligraphic execution] yet the untrammeled brushwork and lingering moods are all [visible in] the unreserved wielding of the brush — now beautiful, now ugly — in a variety of gestural manners. Unfolding the scrolls or opening the letters, one feels the palpable presence [of the writer]. At first glance, one is almost startled and overwhelmed; the more one looks at them, the more infinitely variegated are their diverse moods and manners.... The later generations ... can imagine the personality of the author.[119]

Both the *Letter on the Disturbances* and the *Old Capital Letter* belong to this epistolary category. In its calligraphic style, the *Old Capital Letter* conveys a cadenced grace and an unhurried disposition that are at odds with the emotional anxiety expressed in the text. The outpouring of feeling is tamed and the shrill tone of wailing muted. The tempered calligraphic style conforms to the Confucian ideal of "sorrow without self-injury," while the discursive content falls short of this ideal. The discrepancy and the tension between the text and its calligraphic rendition emphasizes the stylistic mood of restraint: to mourn is all too human and to restrain from excessive mourning is Confucian. While the discursive content may betray an instinctual lapse in propriety in response to sorrow, the calligraphic representation exudes stability and control.

The *Old Capital Letter* bears indelible marks of modification and mediation, if not downright fabrication in a T'ang-period style. This is evident in the upright rectangular and full-bodied expansiveness of the characters "old capital" (*chiu ching*) and "to receive" (*feng*). The calligraphy thus demonstrates the Confucian ideal of emotional expression in a way that the *Letter on the Disturbances* does not.

The *Letter on the Disturbances* would not have squared well with seventh-century calligraphic taste. With the early-T'ang revival of Confucianism and the ideal of gentlemanly restraint, the use of an intentionally dramatic style of calligraphy in the context of mourning would probably have been perceived as alien and unruly. Since funerary memorial tablets had in the past invariably been written in formal standard script, in the early T'ang the discursive content of a memorial text would have been sufficient to

Figure 12 (left)
Ch'u Sui-liang (596–658). Detail from *Preface to the Sacred Teaching* (*San-tsang sheng-chiao hsü*), 653. Stele enshrined on the west side of the south gate of the Great Goose Pagoda, Sian. Ink rubbing, 198 x 85 cm. From Inoue Yasushi et al., *Shodō geijutsu* (Tokyo: Chūō Kōronsha, 1971), v. 3, pl. 122.

Figure 13 (right)
Stele, *Preface to the Sacred Teaching* (*San-tsang sheng-chiao hsü*), copied by Ch'u Sui-liang (596–658), 653. Great Goose Pagoda, Sian. Photo by Eugene Y. Wang.

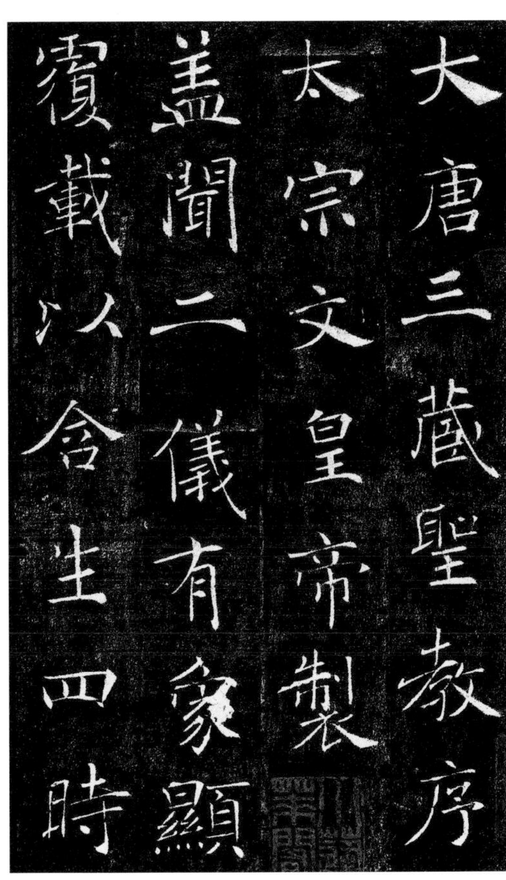

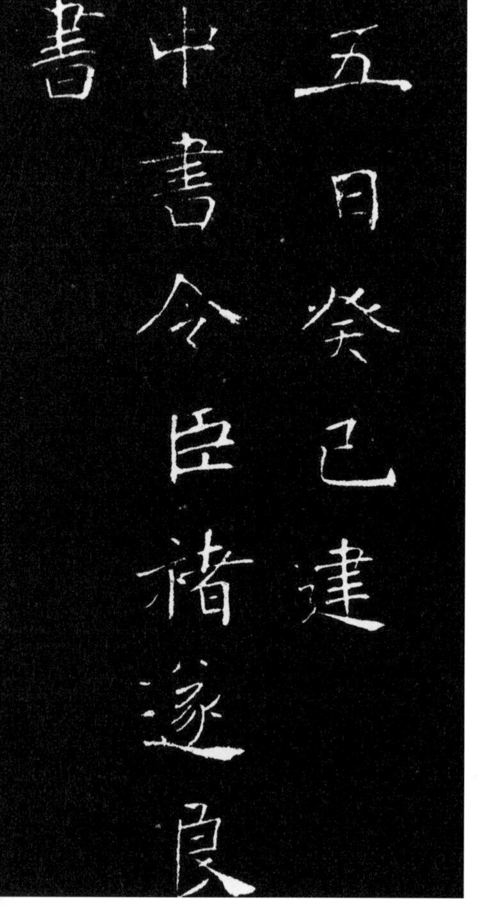

Figure 14
Ch'u Sui-liang (596–658). Detail from *Preface to the Sacred Teaching* (*San-tsang sheng-chiao hsü*), 653. Signed Secretariat Director (*Chung-shu ling*). Ink rubbing. From *Shosei meihin senshū* (Tokyo: Kabushiki kaisha marusha, 1988), v. 6, 64.

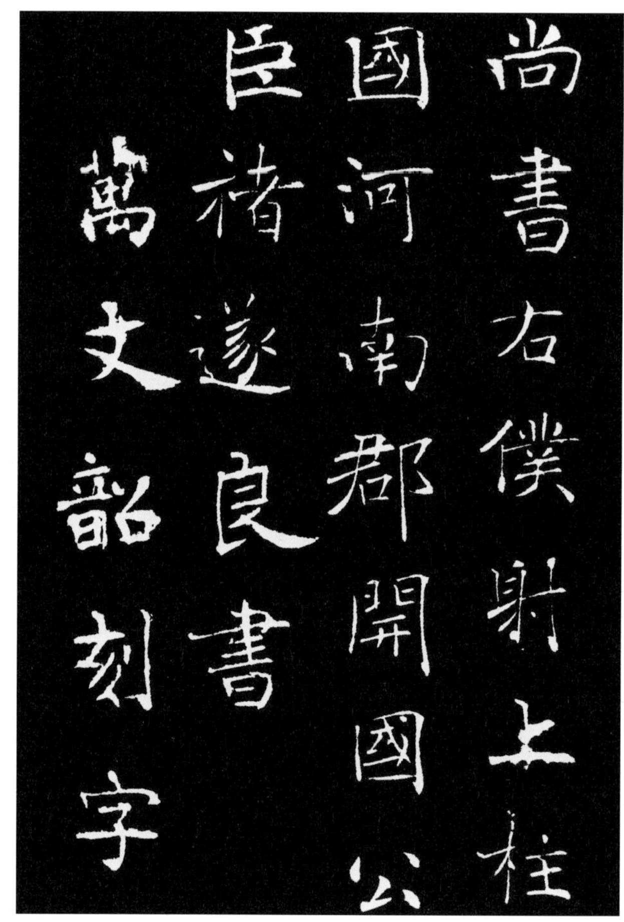

Figure 15
Ch'u Sui-liang (596–658). Detail from *Note on the Preface to the Sacred Teaching* (*San-tsang sheng-chiao hsü chi*), 653. Signed Vice Director of the Right Department of State Affairs (*Shang-shu yu-p'u-yeh*). Ink rubbing. From *Shosei meihin senshū* (Tokyo: Kabushiki kaisha marusha, 1988), v. 6, 112.

express mourning. In this period, one would have been hard pressed to read emotional overtones in the calligraphic form itself.

The experience of Ch'u Sui-liang, a key figure in shaping the T'ang calligraphic canon, says much about the mechanism of expressing mourning in calligraphy. Ch'u's celebrated calligraphic renditions of T'ai-tsung's *Preface to the Sacred Teaching* (fig. 12) and Kao-tsung's *Note on the Preface to the Sacred Teaching* (*San-tsang sheng-chiao hsü chi*; fig 15.), engraved on two stelae enshrined in Ch'ang-an's (modern Sian) Great Goose Pagoda (fig. 13), show him at his best. Chang Huai-kuan describes Chu's characters in feminine terms, such as "makeup and slender figures" and "fetching flavor," and compares them to delicate "female beauties and dames unable to bear [the weight of] silk."[120] This feminine characterization has dominated the perception of Ch'u's calligraphy ever since, and blinded viewers to other symbolic resonances latent in his calligraphy. Only later critics such as Wang Shih-chen and Yang Shou-ching voiced strong dissent from this view. Wang observed: "Critics see in Honan's [Ch'u Sui-liang] calligraphy delicate beauties and dames of the jade terrace unable to bear the weight of silk. The description pertains only to its resplendent manners. What people do not discern is that every single hook and right-slanting stroke carries with it a thousand-pound force."[121] If we take into account both of these different perceptions, we have a more balanced view of the tension in the calligraphic style of this work, which dimly hints at Ch'u's circumstances and the psychological strain that he faced at the time.

Ch'u transcribed the two emperors' stelae texts in 653, four years after T'ai-tsung's death. He was one of two ministers summoned to T'ai-tsung's deathbed to receive his testimony and was entrusted by him with overseeing state affairs after his death.[122] But the course of history did not accord with T'ai-tsung's wishes. His successor, Kao-tsung (r. 650–83), and, in particular, Kao-tsung's favored consort, Wu Tze-t'ien, saw Ch'u Sui-liang, the moralizing father figure, as a nagging and galling presence. In 651, two years after T'ai-tsung's death, Ch'u was relegated to the post of prefect of T'ung prefecture, the present-day area of T'ung-ch'uan, north of Sian.[123] The tension between Ch'u Sui-liang and the Kao-tsung/Wu Tze-t'ien regime came to a head on the occasion of Chu's transcription of the stelae texts for the Great Goose Pagoda. In 648 Prince Li Chih, the future Kao-tsung, commissioned, on the site of a Sui dynasty Buddhist monastery ruin, the construction of the Tz'u-en Temple in order to commemorate his deceased mother, Empress Wen-te (601–636).[124] In 652, the eminent monk Hsüan-tsang (596?–664), abbot of the temple, proposed to the throne that there be built a "stone stupa to install the Buddhist sutras [he had] brought from the Western Region" and to house stelae on which were to be inscribed texts composed by both T'ai-tsung and Kao-tsung. The request was granted.[125]

Figure 16
Ch'u Sui-liang (596–658). Detail from *Mourning T'ai-tsung* (*T'ai-tsung ai-ts'e*), 649. Ink rubbing. Tokyo National Museum. From Inoue Yasushi et al., *Shodo geijutsu* (Tokyo: Chūō Kōronsha, 1971), v. 3, 147.

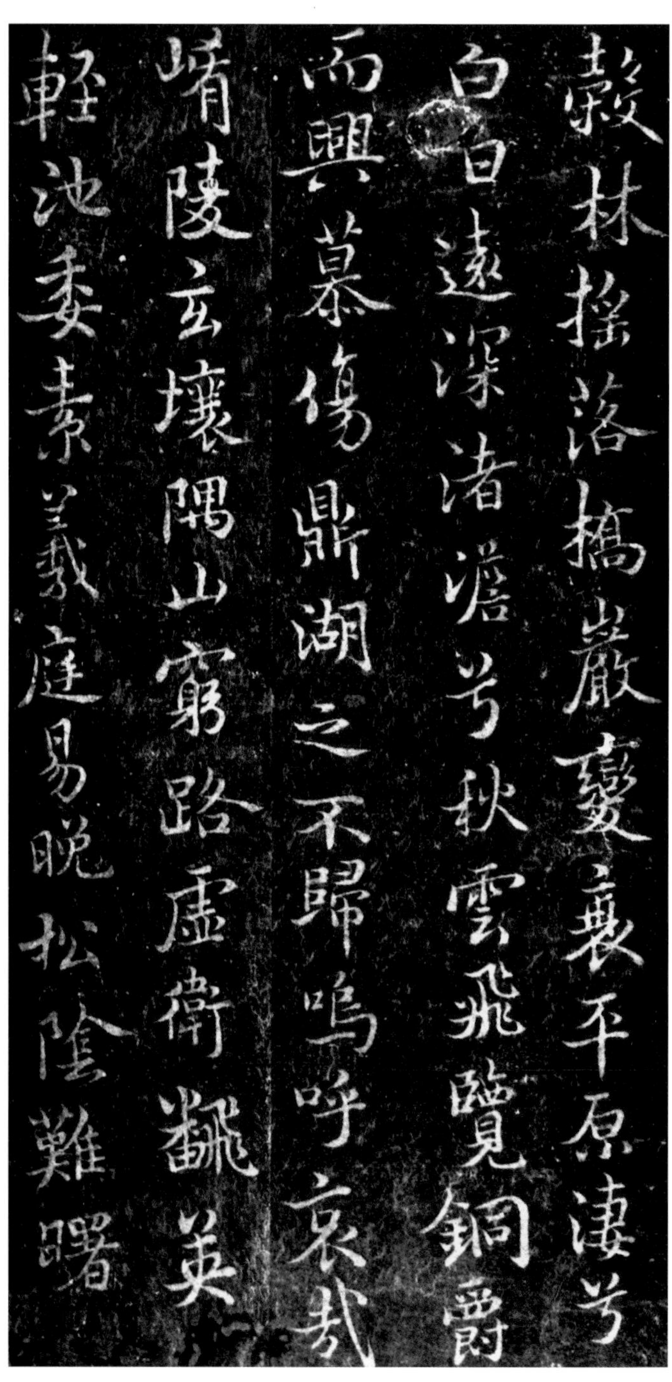

The prestigious honor of copying these texts as calligraphic monuments fell logically to Ch'u Sui-liang, whose eminence as both a consummate calligrapher and a revered statesman who bridged the old and new regimes was uncontested, despite his recent fall from grace. It seems certain that the Kao-tsung regime was reluctant to assign the job to Ch'u: none of the near-contemporary historical sources, except Hui-li's biography of Hsüan-tsang,[126] acknowledges Ch'u's authorship of the monumental calligraphic copies; instead, they describe the transcriptions as "a divine brush writing of its own accord" (*shen-pi tzu-hsieh* or *shen-han tzu-hsieh*).[127] This comes as no surprise since Li I-fu (d. 666), Drafter in the Imperial Secretariat (*Chung-shu she-jen*), who mediated between the court and the Tz'u-en Temple and coordinated the dedication of the stelae,[128] was a relentless slanderer of Ch'u Sui-liang.[129] Copying T'ai-tsung's and Kao-Tsung's texts must have been at the same time both a poignant and harrowing experience for Ch'u Sui-liang. Touching T'ai-tsung's text surely would have brought back fond memories of the past, and handling Kao-tsung's text would have intensified the humiliation of Chu's recent fall from high office and the apprehension concerning the present adverse circumstances he had to endure. At the close of his transcription of T'ai-tsung's text, Ch'u proudly signed his name and his former title, Secretariat Director (*Chung-shu ling*; fig. 14). Ch'u had been appointed to this position in 648, the same year in which T'ai-tsung composed his text. By signing this title, Ch'u was clearly harking back to and reliving the years that he had served under T'ai-tsung. In contrast, Ch'u signed his transcription of Kao-tsung's stele text with his current title, Vice Director of the Right Department of State Affairs (*Shang-shu yu-p'u-yeh*; fig. 15).[130] The implication of Ch'u's having signed different official titles on the same occasion is worth savoring. We are invited to speculate on Ch'u's state of mind: deep mourning for the late T'ai-tsung, who favored him, and a bitterness toward Kao-tsung and his consort, who spurned him. With hindsight we may read sentiment into Ch'u's calligraphy, which seems to display a tension between graciousness and stoicism (see fig. 12). We cannot but marvel at Ch'u's austere self-discipline, considering that he had to maintain a steady hand, however emotionally agitated he may have been.[131] But this is hindsight, and calligraphic style is ultimately impervious to such readings of the emotions and intentions of a calligrapher. Partly through Ch'u's influence, standard-script calligraphy had in the early T'ang become a stable medium that could *narrate* but not *dramatize* or *enact* varying degrees of joy and sorrow. Stability meant disciplinary rules, which were central to early-T'ang calligraphy and ultimately fulfilled the Confucian ideal that "manifestations, whether of grief or joy, are all bounded by the limits of these rules."[132]

Another calligraphic work allegedly by Ch'u Sui-liang that more openly mourns T'ai-tsung is the memorial text *Mourning T'ai-tsung* (*T'ai-tsung ai-ts'e*; fig. 16), written upon the emperor's death in 649.[133] Granted, the authenticity of this work is suspect, but it is another example from which we would be hard pressed to infer any emotions from the calligraphy alone.

Returning to Wang Hsi-chih's *Letter on the Disturbances*: Apart from the fact that it was relatively unknown until recent times, there is not sufficient contextual evidence to explain how this work escaped the taming that characterized the T'ang canonization of Wang. We can surmise that it is a relic from the tumultuous Eastern Chin period, three hundred years earlier than the T'ang. Surviving into the T'ang period, the *Letter on the Disturbances* seems to have been neglected as a major work by Wang Hsi-chih, partly because its forceful ruggedness and uninhibited quality did not mesh well with the tendency in the early T'ang to gentrify, civilize, and tame Wang Hsi-chih. Moreover, the notion of a calligraphic form enacting and dramatizing the extreme emotional expression of mourning, or any demonstration of feeling, lay outside the sensibilities and gentrified taste of the period. Even Yen Chen-ch'ing's (709–785) *Draft of the Eulogy for Nephew Chi-ming* (*Chi chih Chi-ming wen-kao*), the calligraphic epitome of the expression of mourning, had to wait until the Sung dynasty (960–1279) to find an appreciative audience.[134] In this regard, the *Letter on the Disturbances* was ahead of its time in comparison to the genteel sensibility of the *Orchid Pavilion*. That the *Letter on the Disturbances* is *not* the *Orchid Pavilion* is a reminder that the latter has blinded us to the possibility of an alternative reading of Wang Hsi-chih. Knowing the gentrifying ethos of the early T'ang in which Wang Hsi-chih was reconfigured, it becomes clear that the *Letter on the Disturbances* had to remain elsewhere as the eternal "Other Wang Hsi-chih," or it would have through generations of copying and reproduction been tamed and transformed into a stylistic twin of the gentrified *Old Capital Letter*.

In preparing this article, I have benefited from discussions with Professor Qianshen Bai of Boston University. Whatever idiosyncratic heresy there is, if any, remains mine.

1 Liu Pao-nan, ed., *Lun-yü cheng-i*, in *Chu-tzu chi-ch'eng* (hereafter CTCC), 8 vols. (Shanghai: Shang-hai: Shu-tien, 1986), v. 1, 7:125; translation based on D.C. Lau, *The Analects* (London: Penguin Books, 1979), 83.

2 Sun Kuo-t'ing, *Shu-p'u* (Treatise on calligraphy), in *Li-tai shu-fa lun-wen hsüan* (Shanghai: Shang-hai shu-hua ch'u-pan-she, 1992), 124.

3 Ibid., 129. Translation based, with modifications, on Chang Ch'ung-ho and Hans H. Frankel, *Two Chinese Treatises on Calligraphy* (New Haven and London: Yale University Press, 1995), 12.

4 For a succinct assessment of the historical significance of the *Orchid Pavilion*, see Lothar Ledderose, "Chinese Calligraphy: Its Aesthetic Dimension and Social Function," *Orientations* 17, no. 10 (October 1986), 39–40.

5 See Lothar Ledderose, *Mi Fu and the Classical Tradition of Chinese Calligraphy* (Princeton: Princeton University Press, 1979), 1–44; Amy McNair, "The Engraved Model-Letter Compendia of the Song Dynasty," *Journal of the American Oriental Society* 114, no. 2 (1994), 209–25; Amy McNair, "Engraved Calligraphy in China: Recension and Reception," *The Art Bulletin* 77, no. 1 (March 1995), 106–14.

6 Lothar Ledderose has long pointed out that the formation of the Wang tradition involved three factors: (1) the calligraphers who provided the model of notable aesthetic quality and stylistic novelty; (2) the critics who provided evaluations and descriptive terminology; and (3) the connoisseurs and historians who established a corpus of "authentic pieces." Lothar Ledderose, "Some Taoist Elements in the Calligraphy of the Six Dynasties," *T'oung Pao* 70 (1984), 253.

7 Two scrolls of calligraphy, the *Letter on the Disturbances* (*Sang-luan t'ieh*) and *Kung Shih-chung t'ieh*, both in ink on white hemp paper, are kept respectively at the Japanese Imperial Household and Maeda Ikutokukai, Tokyo. Each scroll consists of three unrelated letters Wang Hsi-chih wrote on different occasions. The first of these scrolls, known as the *Letter on the Disturbances*, consists of seventeen lines of text. The first eight lines constitute the text of the *Letter on the Disturbances*, the next five a fragment of another letter, and the last four a fragment of yet another letter. The calligraphy was produced through the method known as *hsiang-t'a* or *t'a-mo*, a process in which the outlines of the characters were traced from Wang Hsi-chih's original work and then meticulously inked in, resulting in a close copy. The scroll bears the stamp of the Japanese imperial seal of the Enryaku period (782–806), suggesting that it was in Emperor Shomu's collection in the Nara period (710–794). Emperor Shomu is said to have been particularly fond of the scroll and often placed it to the immediate right of his throne. Upon his death, the scroll was donated to the Todai-ji, in Nara, along with other imperial treasures. The calligraphy was thus brought to Japan sometime before the mid-T'ang period, probably by the monk Chien-chen (Ganjin, 688–763). It bears the signatures of Hsü Seng-ch'üan and Yao Huai-chen, two notable Liang dynasty (502–557) court copyists, which indicates that the T'ang copy was based on works that had been authenticated by Liang court connoisseurs. See Nakata Yūjirō, "So-ran-jo," in Inoue Yasushi et al., *Shodō geijutsu* (Art of calligraphy) (Tokyo:

Chūō Kōronsha, 1971), v. 1, 200–201; Nakata Yūjirō, ed., *Chinese Calligraphy*, trans. and adapted by Jeffrey Hunter (New York and Tokyo/Kyoto: Weatherhill/Tankosha, 1983), 168–69; Han Yü-t'ao, "A Study of Wang Hsi-chih's *Sang-luan t'ieh*" (in Chinese), *Chung-kuo shu-fa* 2 (1990), 18–20; Wang Yü-ch'ih, "The *Sang-luan t'ieh*: The Location of the 'Ancestral Tombs' and the Time of its Writing" (in Chinese), *Shu-fa yen-chiu* 47, no. 1 (1992), 81–87; Taniguchi Tetsuo and Sasaki Takeshi, *Rantei no jo ronsō yakuchū* (Translation and annotation of the Preface to the Orchid Pavilion) (Tokyo: Chūō Kōron Bijutsu Shuppan, 1993), 148–49.

8 Nakata Yūjirō, *Ō gishi o chūshin to suru hōjō no kenkyū* (A study of model letters related to Wang Hsi-chih) (Tokyo: Nigensha, 1970), 262, fig. 157; Liu T'ao and T'ang Yin-fang, *Chung-kuo shu-fa shih* (History of Chinese calligraphy) (Peking: Chung-yang mei-shu hsüeh-yüan, 1995), 64.

9 Nakata Yūjirō, *Chinese Calligraphy*, pl. 16. The translation is mine.

10 Fang Hsüan-ling, comp., *Chin shu* (Chin History) (Peking: Chung-hua shu-chü, 1974), 3:57.

11 Ibid., 33:991.

12 Ibid., 20:632–33.

13 Chao Ch'ao, *Han Wei Nan-Pei-ch'ao mu-chih hui-pien* (Compendium of the epitaphs of the Han, Wei, and Northern and Southern Dynasties) (Tien-chin: Ku-chi ch'u-pan-she, 1992), 6–8.

14 *Chin shu*, 31:957; Chao Ch'ao, *Han Wei Nan-Pei-ch'ao mu-chih hui-pien*, 10–11.

15 Chang Sheng-san, ed., *Chung-hua ti-ling* (Imperial tombs of China) (Cheng-chou: Chung-chou ku-chi ch'u-pan-she, 1997), 81.

16 *Chin shu*, 70:2611.

17 The damage of the imperial tombs by rain even before Liu Yao's desecration is recorded in Hsün Yüeh's (246–295) epitaph; see Chao Ch'ao, *Han Wei Nan-Pei-ch'ao mu-chih hui-pien*, 6.

18 *Chin shu*, 8:197–98.

19 Han Yü-t'ao, "A Study of Wang Hsi-chih's *Sang-luan t'ieh*," 81–87.

20 Yve-Alain Bois, "The Use Value of 'Formless'," in Yve-Alain Bois and Rosalind Krauss, *Formless: A User's Guide* (New York: Zone Books, 1997), 21.

21 *Hsüan-ho shu-p'u* in Lu Fu-sheng et al., eds., *Chung-kuo shu-hua ch'üan-shu* (hereafter CKSHCS), 11 vols. (Shanghai: Shang-hai shu-hua ch'u-pan-she, 1993), v. 2, 15:45.

22 *Pao-Chin-chai fa-t'ieh* (Model calligraphies from the Precious Chin Studio) (Shanghai: Shang-hai ku-chi shu-tien, 1961), v. 3, 2. The same compendium also contains a letter written by Wang Ts'ao-chih, Wang Hsi-chih's fifth son, expressing mourning over the same event (*Pao-Chin-chai fa-t'ieh*, v. 9, 5–6). What is noteworthy is that some of the characters appear strikingly identical to those in the *Old Capital Letter* allegedly by Wang Hsi-chih, hinting at the possibility that the two works are by the same hand, though whose hand we do not know. Both letters contain certain characters — notably *chiu-ching hsien-mu* (ancestral tombs at the old capital) — that are executed with the evenly spaced strokes and rectangular compositions characteristic of the T'ang period, instead of a compressed core radiating outward which is typical of the Chin period.

23 It consists of one scroll by Hsieh An, two scrolls by Wang Hsi-chih, one scroll by Wang Hsien-chih, and two paintings by Ku K'ai-chih and Tai Lu. See Mi Fu, *Shu-shih* (History of calligraphy), in CKSHCS, v. 1, 970a. See also Peter Sturman, *Mi Fu: Style and the Art of Calligraphy in Northern Song China* (New Haven: Yale University Press, 1997), 113.

24 Hsü Sen-yü, "A Study of the *P'ao-Chin-chai fa-t'ieh*" (in Chinese), *Wen-wu* 146, no. 12 (1962), 9–19; T'ang Lan, "Notes on the *Pao-Chin-chai fa-t'ieh*" (in Chinese), *Wen-wu* 149, no. 3 (1963), 30–33.

25 Ch'en I-tseng, *Han-lin yao-chüeh*, in CKSHCS, v. 2, 845b. Ch'en pronounced Ts'ao's compendium as "the lowest of all the model-book compendia."

26 Sun Kuo-t'ing, *Shu-p'u*, 128–29; translation in Ch'ung-ho Chang and Hans H. Frankel, *Two Chinese Treatises on Calligraphy*, 10–12.

27 That is, inferring the personality of the calligrapher from his calligraphy. Wang Shih-chen found Sun's rhetorical way of grafting the characterization of calligraphy onto its calligrapher flimsy. Commenting on the passage cited here, Wang wrote: "It was unlikely that Yu-chün [Wang Hsi-chih] had anticipated such intricacies and cunning [*chiao-k'uai*] when he wrote the calligraphy." Wang Shih-chen, *I-yüan chih-yen* (Remarks on arts over wine cups), in Ts'ui Erh-p'ing, ed., *Ming Ch'ing shu-fa lun-wen hsüan* (Selected calligraphic criticism by Ming and Ch'ing authors) (Shanghai: Shang-hai shu-tien, 1994), 163.

28 *Lan-t'ing lun-pien* (Debates over the "Preface to the Orchid Pavilion") (Peking: Wen-wu ch'u-pan-she, 1973), 37.

29 Ibid., part 2, 1–28.

30 Ibid., 37, 110.

31 See, for instance, Hua Rende, "Eastern Chin Epitaph Stones — With Some Notes to the 'Lan-t'ing Hsü' Debate," *Early Medieval China* 3 (1997), 30–72.

32 Ch'i Kung, "The Cult of the *Orchid Pavilion* Ought to be Broken," in *Lan-t'ing lun-pien*, 69.

33 Wang Pao, "Rhapsody on the Pan Pipes," in Hsiao T'ung, comp., *Wen-hsüan* (Shanghai: Shang-hai ku-chi ch'u-pan-she, 1986), v. 2, 17:786; David R. Knechtges, ed. and trans, *Wenxuan* or *Selections of Refined Literature* (Princeton: Princeton University Press, 1996), v. 3, p. 239.

34 "T'ang-jen shu-p'ing" (T'ang critics' commentary on calligraphy), in Chen Ssu, ed., *Shu-yüan ching-hua*, in CKSHCS, v. 2, p. 454a; Ma Tsung-huo, ed., *Shu-lin tsao-chien* (Peking: Wen-wu ch'u-pan-she, 1984), 6:53–54.

35 *Ch'un-hua-ko t'ieh* (T'ien-chin: T'ien-chin ku-chi ch'u-pan-she, 1996), 5:228; appendix 47.

36 Wei Shuo, "Pi-chen t'u," in *Li-tai shu-fa lun-wen hsüan*, 21–23. For a study of the treatise, see Richard M. Barnhart, "Wei Fu-jen's *Pi Chen T'u* and the Early Texts on Calligraphy," *Archives of the Chinese Art Society of America* 18 (1964), 3–25.

37 See Chang Yen-yüan, *Fa-shu yao-lu* (hereafter FSYL), in CKSHCS, v. 1, 32a–33a.

38 Ibid., v. 1, 32b.

39 Liu I-ch'ing, *Shih-shuo hsin-yü*, in CTCC, v. 4, 136.

40 *Chin shu*, 80:2093.

41 *Shih-shuo hsin-yü*, 25:215.

42 Liang Wu-ti, "Letter to T'ao Hung-ching," in FSYL 2:40b. It is also attributed to Hsiao Yen (464–549); see *Li-tai shu-fa lun-wen hsüan*, 80. Similar taxonomic descriptions appear in "Battle Formation of the Brush," see FSYL 1:32b.

43 *Li-tai shu-fa lun-wen hsüan*, 47.

44 Sun Kuo-t'ing, *Shu-p'u*, 130.

45 Ibid., 129.

46 Chang Huai-kuan, *Shu-i*, in FSYL 4:62b–63a.

47 Ibid., 4:63b.

48 Han Yü, "Song of the Stone Drum," in *Han Yü ch'üan-chi* (Complete works of Han Yü) (Shanghai: Shang-hai ku-chi ch'u-pan-she, 1997), 67.

49 Chang Huai-kuan, *Shu-tuan,* in FSYL 9:97a.

50 *Ch'un-hua-ko t'ieh* 5:228, appendix, 47.

51 The *Chiu T'ang shu* (Old T'ang history) is explicit about the emperor's resolve to change his image as ruler of the empire: "The Emperor pacified the world with his military prowess. Battling winds and braving rains he had little leisure for poetry and calligraphy. Now that he succeeded the throne, he sought out the loyalists and virtuous ... and in his leisure hours, paid attention to literature and history." Liu Hsü et al., eds., *Chiu T'ang shu,* 16 vols. (Peking: Chung-hua shu-chü, 1975), 73:2600.

52 Liu Su, *Ta T'ang hsin-yü* (Peking: Chung-hua shu-chü, 1984), 9:133.

53 Wu Ching, *Chen-kuan cheng-yao* (Shanghai: Shang-wu yin-shu-kuan, 1934), 1:26.

54 Ssu-ma Kuang, *Tzu-chih t'ung-chien* (Peking: Chung-hua shu-chü, 1956), 193:6085.

55 CTS 28:1044.

56 See the chapter on "Cultivation of Confucianism," in *Wu Ching Chen-kuan cheng-yao* 7:1–8.

57 *Tzu-chih t'ung-chien* 192:6054.

58 The text appears in Ou-yang Hsün, ed., *I-wen lei-chü* (Shanghai: Shang-hai ku-chi ch'u-pan-she, 1965), 22:407–408.

59 See Ssu-ma Ch'ien, *Shih chi* (Peking: Chung-hua shu-chü, 1962), 80:2427–2436.

60 Denis Twitchett, ed., *Cambridge History of China,* v. 3 (London and New York: Cambridge University Press, 1979), part I, 407–408.

61 *I-wen lei-chü* 22:4007–4008.

62 FSYL 3:58b.

63 For studies of early-T'ang calligraphy with special reference to these three calligraphers, see Yin Sun, "On Ou-yang Hsün" (in Chinese), *Shu-fa yen-chiu* 23, no. 1 (1986), 47–65; Yin Sun, "On Yü Shih-nan" (in Chinese), *Shu-fa yen-chiu* 24, no. 2 (1986), 12–23; Yin Sun, "On Ch'u Sui-liang" (in Chinese), *Shu-fa yen-chiu* 25, no. 3 (1986), 48–62; Stephen J. Goldberg, "Court Calligraphy of the Early T'ang Dynasty," *Artibus Asiae* 49, 3/4 (1988–89), 189–237; Chu Kuan-tien, *T'ang-tai shu-fa k'ao p'ing* (A study of Tang dynasty calligraphy) (Hang-chou: Che-chiang jen-min ch'u-pan-she, 1992), 1–29; Liu T'ao, "Three Great Masters of Calligraphy of the Early T'ang" (in Chinese), *Wen-shih chih-shih,* no. 1 (1996), 87–91. See also Amy McNair, "Public Values in Calligraphy and Orthography in the Tang Dynasty," *Monumenta Serica* 43 (1995), 263–78.

64 Li Ssu-chen, *Shu-hou-p'in,* in FSYL 3:53a; *Shu-lin tsao-chien* 8:118.

65 Chang Huai-kuan, *Shu-tuan,* in FSYL 8:93ab.

66 *T'ang-jen shu-p'ing,* in Chen Ssu, ed., *Shu-yüan ching-hua,* in CKSHCS, v. 2, 454; Ma Tsung-huo, ed., *Shu-lin tsao-chien* 8:118.

67 Chang Huai-kuan, *Shu-tuan,* in FSYL 8:93b.

68 *T'ang-jen shu-p'ing,* 454a.

69 Li Ssu-chen, *Shu-hou-p'in,* in FSYL 3:53a.

70 Chang Huai-kuan, *Shu-tuan,* in FSYL 8:93b.

71 Sun Kuo-t'ing, *Shu-p'u,* 129; translation based, with modifications, on Chang and Frankel, *Two Chinese Treatises on Calligraphy,* 12.

72 The critical wisdom that Yü's calligraphy "conceals the sinews and bones inside" and Ou-yang's calligraphy "flaunts an angular and showy outside" is frequently reiterated in traditional calligraphic commentary. See for instance, *Hsüan-ho shu-p'u* 8:26a; Liu Hsi-chai, *I-kai*, in *Li-tai shu-fa lun-wen hsüan*, 701.

73 Wang Po, *T'ang hui-yao* (Shanghai: Shang-hai ku-chi, 1991), 64:1317.

74 "T'ao Hung-ching's Letter to Liang Wu-ti," in FSYL 2:41b.

75 The biography of Ou-yang Hsün in CTS claims that "Ou-yang first started by modeling his calligraphy on Wang Hsi-chih." His works indicate otherwise. Chu Kuan-tien argues that the standard history presented Ou-yang Hsün in a more orthodox light because T'ai-tsung's denigration of Wang Hsien-chih had made stylistic identification with him unflattering. See Chu Kuan-tien, *T'ang-tai shu-fa k'ao p'ing*, 9.

76 The *T'ai-p'ing kuang-chi* cites an excerpt from *Kuo-shi i-chuan* that states in effect that Ou-yang once spent three days and nights beside a stele on which was engraved So Ching's calligraphy. Li Fang et al., eds., *T'ai-p'ing kuang-chi* (Peking: Chung-hua shu-chü, 1961), v. 5, 208:1592. See also Ou-yang Hsiu and Sung Ch'i, *Hsin T'ang shu* (New T'ang History) (hereafter HTS), 20 vols. (Peking: Chung-hua shu-chü, 1975), 198:5646. While this anecdotal report is to be taken with a grain of salt, it at least registers a medieval perception of the source of influence on Ou-yang Hsün's calligraphic style.

77 Among the memorial texts composed by Ou-yang are those for eminent generals and high-ranking officials. See Chu Kuan-tien, *T'ang-tai shu-fa k'ao p'ing*, 3.

78 Yao Ssu-lien, *Ch'en shu* (Peking: Chung-hua shu-chü, 1972), 5, 78; 9, 159–160.

79 His physical appearance was so repugnant that a court officer laughed at him during a solemn funeral ritual for Empress Wen-te. See HTS 223:6335.

80 Ou-yang Hsün, "Preface to *I-wen lei-chü*," in *I-wen lei-chü*, v. 1, 27.

81 *I-wen lei-chü*, 4:71. Kuo Mo-jo argues that Ou-yang Hsün, an erudite scholar, must have known all too well that the paragraph (which begins with "For in men's association with one another in their journey through life . . ." and ends with "what an agonizing thought!") is a textual corruption. Ou-yang Hsün must have used the need for brevity as an excuse to eliminate the version from his edited version. See *Lan-t'ing lun-pien*, 80–81.

82 Many critics in the past have noted this. See Mi Fu, *Shu-shih*, in CKSHCS, v. 1, 965a; *Hsüan-ho shu-p'u*, in CKSHCS, v. 2, 1, 7a; Chu Kuan-tien, *T'ang-tai shu-fa k'ao p'ing*, 13.

83 CTS 72:2565; FSYL 3:52a.

84 Sui Yang-ti observed that "Chih-yung has acquired Yu-chün's flesh and Chih-kuo has inherited his bones." Cited in *Li-tai shu-fa lun-wen hsüan*, 93; Chih-kuo made a similar remark; see Chu Kuan-tien, *T'ang-tai shu-fa k'ao p'ing*, 11. This perception endured well into the T'ang dynasty. Chang Huai-kuan remarked that Chih-yung only "acquired half of Yu-chün's flesh"; Chang Huai-kuan, *Shu-tuan*, in FSYL 8:94.

85 Chu Kuan-tien, *T'ang-tai shu-fa k'ao p'ing*, 11.

86 See, for instance, Yü Shih-nan, "Yüan-ko hsing," in Li Fang et al., eds., *Wen-yüan ying-hua* (Peking: Chung-hua shu-chü, 1966), v. 2, 211, 1045.

87 CTS 72:2582; HTS 102:3976–3977.

88 CTS 80:2729. Modern scholars have cast serious doubts about Chu Sui-liang's connoisseurship. See, for instance, *Lan-t'ing lun-pien*, 118–19.

89 CTS 80:2729–2739.

90 This analysis of the three early-T'ang calligraphers draws heavily upon Liu T'ao, "Three Great Masters of Calligraphy of the Early T'ang."

91 Chang Huai-kuan, *Shu-tuan*, in FSYL 8:93b.

92 FSYL 3:55a.

93 CTS 80:2736.

94 CTS 80:2733–2736.

95 FSYL 2:48b.

96 FSYL 2:40a.

97 Emperor T'ai-tsung is known to have believed that one could see in the mirror of the past the moral for the present. See, for instance, Li Shih-min [T'ai-tsung], "Preface to Imperial Models," in Tung Kao et al., eds., *Ch'üan T'ang wen* (Shanghai: Shang-hai ku-chi ch'u-pan-she, 1990), 10:47; CTS 71:2561.

98 *Chin shu* 80:2107–2108.

99 Liu Hsi-tsai, *I-kai*, in *Li-t'ai shu-fa lun-wen hsüan*, 694.

100 Mi Fu, for one, speculated that T'ai-tsung's denigration of Wang Hsien-chih resulted from his own failure to reach the height of Wang Hsi-chih. See Mi Fu, *Shu-shih*, in CKSHCS, v. 1, 965a.

101 *Ying-yin-pen nei-fu ts'ang Yu-chün mo-pao* (Facsimile of Wang Hsi-chih's calligraphy in the collection of the inner court), cited in *Lan-t'ing lun-pien*, 61.

102 James Legge, trans., *Li Chi, Book of Rites* (New York: University Books, 1967), v. 2, 93–94.

103 Ibid., v. 2, 107.

104 Ibid., v. 2, 96.

105 Ibid., v. 2, 107.

106 Ibid., v. 2, 108.

107 *Lun-yü cheng-i* (CTCC edition), 3, 62. Translation based, with modification, on D.C. Lau, *Confucius, The Analects*, p. 70.

108 Legge, *Li Chi*, v. 2, 255.

109 Sun Kuo-t'ing, *Shu-p'u*, 125; translation by Chang and Frankel, *Two Chinese Treatises on Calligraphy*, 4.

110 A courtier in T'ai-tsung's court defined the "fundamentals" as "moderation and harmony constitute the fundamentals." *Tzu-chih t'ung-chien* 192:6052.

111 Legge, *Li Chi*, v. 2, 300.

112 *Lun-yü cheng-i*, 7:125; translation based on D.C. Lau, *Confucius, The Analects*, 83. Sun Kuo-t'ing, *Shu-p'u*, 124.

113 Sun Kuo-t'ing, *Shu-p'u*, 126; translation based on Chang and Frankel, *Two Chinese Treatises on Calligraphy*, 6.

114 Sun Kuo-t'ing, *Shu-p'u*, 129; translation based, with modifications, on Chang and Frankel, *Two Chinese Treatises on Calligraphy*, 2, 94.

115 FSYL 10:103b.

116 FSYL 10:106b.

117 FSYL 10:115b.

118 Tu Yu-chin, *Hsin-ting shu-i ching*, in numbered Pelliot manuscripts from Tun-huang in the Bibliothèque Nationale, Paris, no. 3637.

119 Ou-yang Hsiu, "Colophon on the Epistolary Calligraphy of Wang Hsien-chih of Chin," in *Ou-yang wen-chung kung chi* (The complete works of Ou-yang Hsiu) (Shanghai: Shang-wu yin-shu-kuan, 1933), v. 3, 15:127.

120 Chang Huai-kuan, *Shu-tuan*, 93b.

121 Ma Tsung-huo, ed., *Shu-lin tsao-chien*, 8:125

122 CTS 80:2738

123 Ibid.

124 CTS 191:5109; Takakusu Junjirō and Watanabe Kaigyoku, eds., *Taishō shinshū Daizōkyō* (The Tripitaka in Chinese), 100 vols. (Tokyo: The Taishō Issai-kyō Kankōkai, 1922–34), 50:457b.

125 The historical sources are inconsistent about the dates of Hsüan-tsang's proposal and the dedication of the stelae. Tao Hsüan (596–667), the eminent monk of Ch'ang-an's Hsi-ming Temple, puts it in 651 in his *Hsü Kao-seng chuan* (Sequel to the biographies of eminent monks), T50:457b. Both Tao Hsüan and the *Chiu T'ang shu* record 656 as the year when the engraved stelae were sent to the temple (T50:457b; CTS 4:75), which was during the time that Ch'u Sui-liang had been relegated to Tan prefecture, in the present-day Ch'ang-sha area (CTS 80:2738). Yet according to Hsüan-tsang's student Hui-li, a monk at Tz'u-en Temple and author of *Ta-T'ang ta-tz'u-en-ssu San-tsang fa-shih chuan* (A biography of the Tripitaka master of the great Tz'u-en Monastery of the Great T'ang Dynasty), dated 688, the stelae dedication took place between 652 and 654; T50:260c. This tallies well with the date, "the fourth year of Yung-hui" (653), which Ch'u Sui-liang signed at the end of his calligraphic transcription of the stelae texts by T'ai-tsung and Kao-tsung. One possible explanation for the divergent dates given by different sources is that after Ch'u copied the texts, the stelae were held at the court for three years before they were sent to the Tz'u-en Temple in 656.

126 T50:260c.

127 T50:256a; T50:457c.

128 T50:457bc; T50:260c.

129 It was Li I-fu who accused Ch'u Sui-liang of plotting an insurgence against the throne after Ch'u's banishment from the capital; CTS 80:2739; HTS 105:4029.

130 Ch'u was given this title in the ninth month of 653; CTS 4:72.

131 Hsü Wu-wen argues that Ch'u transcribed the texts directly onto the stelae, while Chu Kuan-tien maintains that the tradition of writing calligraphy directly on a stele must have changed by that time, as T'ai-tsung's *Chin Temple Inscription* of 646 was transferred from its written form on paper to a stele engraving. Furthermore, Ch'u, given his high rank and self-conscious dignity, would have declined to stoop over a stele. See Hsü Wu-wen, "Tentative Notes on Ch'u Sui-liang" (in Chinese), *Shu-fa* 33, no. 6 (1983), 26–27, and Chu Kuan-tien, *T'ang-tai shu-fa k'ao-p'ing*, 26.

132 Legge, *Li Chi*, 107.

133 That Ch'u is the author of the text is fairly certain. See *Wen-yüan ching-hua*, v. 6, 835:4407–4408. The attribution of the calligraphy as it survives in the Sung rubbings handed down to us is still an open question. There is speculation that the calligraphy came from Mi Fu's hand, though this also remains equally unverifiable. See *Shosei meihin senshū* (Selected famous works by masters of calligraphy) (Tokyo: Kabushiki Kaisha Marusha, 1989), v. 6, 180–81.

134 See Amy McNair, *The Upright Brush: Yan Zhenqing's Calligraphy and Song Literati Politics* (Honolulu: University of Hawaii Press, 1998), 44–50.

Harold Mok
The Chinese University of Hong Kong

Seal and Clerical Scripts of the Sung Dynasty

Beginning in the Wei-Chin period (3rd–5th century), seal (*chuan-shu*) and clerical (*li-shu*) scripts were gradually replaced by standard (*k'ai-shu*), running (*hsing-shu*), and cursive (*ts'ao-shu*) scripts in daily use. By the T'ang dynasty (618–907), these two script forms were basically regarded as archaic and used only for special purposes. Nonetheless, some eighth-century seal-script masters, such as Li Yang-ping, Ch'ü Ling-wen, and Yüan Tzu, and some of their contemporary clerical-script masters, including Shih Wei-tse, Ts'ai Yu-lin, and Han Tse-mu, attained eminence. Seal- and clerical-script calligraphy was even less frequently practiced in the Sung dynasty (960–1279), a period in which the literati pursuit of artistic spontaneity and spiritual freedom engendered the development of running- and cursive-script calligraphy, as exemplified by works of the Four Great Sung Masters, Ts'ai Hsiang (1012–1067), Su Shih (1037–1101), Huang T'ing-chien (1045–1105), and Mi Fu (1052–1107). Because the works of these masters captivated the minds of later calligraphers and scholars, the seal- and clerical-scripts of the Sung have largely been neglected in modern scholarship, and, when they are mentioned, they are usually viewed in a negative light. However, Sung interest in and study of seal and clerical scripts are too important to be dismissed. Indeed, an examination of the importance of the two scripts during the period adds significantly to our understanding of the development of Sung calligraphy as a whole.

Epigraphy and the Literati's Interest in Antiquity

In the T'ang dynasty, calligraphy was one of the six disciplines (*liu-hsüeh*) in the imperial university. Students were required to learn ancient scripts, especially seal script, through the study of the *Stone Classic of the Hsi-p'ing Era* (*Hsi-p'ing shih-ching*), the *Philological Dictionary of Chinese* (*Shuo-wen chieh-tzu*), and the *Tzu-lin*. Such training was useful, since seal and clerical scripts were commonly employed in titles of stone stelae. Similar training was provided by the imperial academy in the Sung dynasty. According to the *History of the Sung Dynasty* (*Sung shih*), calligraphy students were required to practice both large- and small-seal scripts, in addition to standard and cursive script.[1] Elsewhere, it is also recorded that under the tutorship of Mi Yu-jen (1074–1151) and Hsü Ching (1091–1153), students in the calligraphy academy had to follow specific models for the different script forms: bronze inscriptions for large-seal script; Li Ssu (active 221–208 BC) for small-seal script; Ts'ai Yung (133–192) and Chung Yu (151–230) for clerical script; Ou-yang Hsün (557–641), Yü Shih-nan (558–638), Ch'u Sui-liang (596–658), and Hsüeh Chi (649–713) for standard script; and Wang Hsi-chih (303–361), Li Yung (678–747), Yen Chen-ch'ing (709–785), Liu Kung-ch'üan (778–865), and Hsü Hao (703–782) for cursive script.[2] The study of seal and clerical scripts was clearly an established tradition observed in the training of court calligraphers in the Sung period.

Outside the academy, Sung scholar-calligraphers acquired their knowledge of seal and clerical scripts in a different way. In addition to the *Shuo-wen*, a basic philological study known to most Sung scholars, they learned about ancient scripts through scholarly studies of epigraphy inspired by their interest in collecting art and appreciating antiquities. Sung studies of epigraphy are impressive in quality and quantity, as well as in scope and methodology.[3] Jades, bronzes, and stones were treated comprehensively in catalogues, researches, commentaries, and other writings, providing a valuable legacy of the history of Chinese epigraphic studies. As noted by the antiquarian Liu Ch'ang (1019–1068), there were three major objectives in Sung studies of epigraphy: to understand the system of rites, to rectify ancient scripts, and to record family histories.[4] Since the key to achieving these objectives was to glean every possible piece of information from the inscriptions, most Sung epigraphical writings are devoted to recording, copying, interpreting, and discussing inscriptions, all of which inevitably facilitated a better understanding of ancient script forms.[5] Sung scholars also appreciated bronze and stone inscriptions for their calligraphic beauty. For instance, Chao Ming-ch'eng (1081–1129) mentioned in the preface to his *Collection of Texts on Bronze and Stone* (*Chin-shih lu*) that, in addition to historical information, one could find in bronze and stone inscriptions both "good and bad literary style as well as delicate and awkward strokes."[6] Sung epigraphic studies were thus associated with calligraphy, and bronze and stone inscriptions became for Sung scholars a primary source in studying seal and clerical scripts. The close relationship between epigraphy, philology, and calligraphy is reflected in Wang Po's (1197–1274) critical comments on the contemporary trend in calligraphy:

> The inscriptions on bronze artifacts were rarely known to later dynasties, resulting in the decline of large-seal script and the "six forms" [*liu-shu*] of characters [in philology].... Modern students, not being able to trace the origin and return to antiquity, tend to resort to eccentricity for fame and prominence. Since some of the components [of characters] had already been marred at the hands of some "skillful" calligraphers, there was no way to check the frantic pursuit for weird beauty. This must be rectified in the future by means of the "six forms."[7]

Many experts on bronze and stone inscriptions like Ou-yang Hsiu (1007–1072), Huang Po-ssu (1079–1118), Chao Ming-ch'eng, and Tung Yu (active early 12th century) began their scholarly careers by studying their own rich collections of antique bronze and stone inscriptions. The interest in collecting and studying antiquities was widely shared by their contemporaries, many of whom became familiar with the ancient scripts without actually engaging in serious epigraphical scholarship. The number of collectors in the Sung dynasty was remarkably large, and their collections were often admired and appreciated. For example, Su I-chien's (957–995) collection of ancient calligraphic masterpieces was built upon by his descendants, and Mi Fu had several opportunities to view this splendid family collection after it was inherited in the late eleventh century by Su I-chien's great-grandsons Su Mi, Su Chi, and Su Hsieh.[8] Huang T'ing-chien was privileged to have seen Chai Ju-wen's (1067–1141) collection of ancient stele inscriptions and wrote colophons commenting on the collection.[9] Sun Chüeh (1028–1090), another great Sung antiquarian, built the Pavilion of Marvelous Ink (*Mo-miao-t'ing*) to house his collection of ink rubbings from Han and T'ang stelae. References to his collection are found in literary works by Tseng Kung (1019–1083) and Su Shih.[10] Numerous other writings, inscriptions, and colophons similarly document the intense interest in collecting and studying antiquities in the Sung period.

Despite this interest, seal and clerical scripts were not major script forms in Sung calligraphy. They were overshadowed by the calligraphic conventions inherited from the Wei-Chin period. The dominance of the Wei-Chin tradition, as represented by Chung Yu and especially Wang Hsi-chih, is reflected in numerous Sung compilations and studies of calligraphy from the Wei-Chin period. A good example is the *Model Calligraphy from the Imperial Archives of the Ch'un-hua Era* (*Ch'un-hua-ko t'ieh*), published in 992. It consists of ten volumes, five of which are devoted to the Two Wangs, Wang Hsi-chih and his son Wang Hsien-chih (344–388). The supremacy of the Wei-Chin tradition was further reinforced by the renditions of this imperial model-book anthology and by writings like Huang Po-ssu's *Fa-t'ieh k'an-wu*, Mi Fu's *Colophons on the Model Calligraphy from the Secret Archives* (*Pa Mi-ko fa-t'ieh*), and Ts'ao Shih-mien's (act. 1240–45) *Fa-t'ieh p'u-hsi*, which focused on the calligraphy of the Two Wangs. Wang Hsi-chih's *Preface to the Orchid Pavilion* (*Lan-t'ing hsü*) itself became the subject of special study as the many versions of the text produced in carvings and rubbings became increasingly controversial.[11] Annotations, discussions, and eulogies concerning this work were innumerable, the most comprehensive being Sang Shih-ch'ang's (early 13th century) *A Study of Preface to the Orchid Pavilion* (*Lan-t'ing k'ao*) and Yü Sung's (d. after 1204) *Sequel Study of Preface to the Orchid Pavilion* (*Lan-t'ing hsü-k'ao*).

Sung criticisms of calligraphy also attest to the exalted position of the Wei-Chin tradition as Wei-Chin calligraphic models of the period were often used as the standard for appraising calligraphy. In his comments on the calligraphy of Wang Chu (d. ca. 990), Yang Ning-shih (873–954), and Li Chien-chung (945–1013), Huang T'ing-chien states explicitly that "one should use the Two Wangs as the criteria."[12] The Wei-Chin tradition was even more vigorously upheld by Huang's contemporary Mi Fu, who wrote, "If one's cursive calligraphy does not partake of the character of the Chin writers, it is merely a work of the lowest grade."[13] It was mainly because of its departure from the Wei-Chin tradition that Mi belittled the T'ang calligraphy tradition.[14] In the Southern Sung (1127–1279), the Wei-Chin tradition was still venerated, as evidenced by Emperor Kao-tsung's (r. 1127–62) return to this classical style through Chih-yung (act. late 6th-early 7th century), Chiang K'uei's (1163–1203) respect for the "untrammeled spirit" of Wei-Chin calligraphy, and Chao Meng-chien's (1199–1264) ultimate pursuit of the "plain and free" style of Chin calligraphy as learned through T'ang examples.

The Spirit of Antiquity and Seal and Clerical Scripts in Sung Texts

The passion with which antique objects were collected and appreciated in the Sung dynasty and the veneration for the spirit of antiquity conveyed in ancient inscriptions were often cited in discussions of calligraphy. For example, Liu Cheng-fu (1062–1119) observed:

> When the characters look pretty, they are not archaic.... When the characters do not look pretty, they must be archaic.... Thus, looking at today's characters is like looking at brocades, and looking at characters from the past is like looking at *tsung* and *ting* [ancient bronze vessels].[15]

Liu's respect for archaism and contempt for formalism were shared by many of his contemporaries.

Sung interpretation of the seal- and clerical-script traditions—and the relationship of those traditions to antiquity—was determined by predominant artistic beliefs rather than epigraphical or philological evidence. Writings from the latter half of the Northern Sung illustrate how leading calligraphers viewed seal and clerical scripts as a means to attain an antique spirit. Ts'ai Hsiang, whose calligraphy Su Shih regarded as unsurpassed in his own time, related his own experience in learning calligraphy:

> The key to learning calligraphy lies in achieving the spirit. By copying the form one can only achieve formal likeness, not the spirit. This is what people who do not understand calligraphy do. I have seen the *Stone Drum Inscriptions* [*Shih-ku wen*] and loved it for its antique

quality.... It was when I got the inscription of the [bronze] *ting* tripod collected by Yüan-fu that I realized that in ancient seal script one could add to or reduce the [number of] strokes, or move the radicals to the left or right as one wished, and the style thus produced could be delicate or awkward. Since the Ch'in and Han dynasties, the ancient script has been fused into a single form as can be seen now. What a shame![16]

In Ts'ai's view, the inscriptions on antique objects were prized for their simplicity and naturalness, and it was this spirit of antiquity that a calligrapher should pursue. For this reason, Ts'ai praised Li Yang-ping for his ability to convey the "spirit of antiquity" in his "strong and bold" calligraphic style.[17]

Ts'ai Hsiang once remarked, "I would say that seal, clerical, and standard scripts as well as running and cursive scripts are all one and the same in their principles." By this he meant that the key to calligraphy is to search for the golden rule common to both ancient and modern calligraphy and thus uncover the antiquity hidden in ink and brush.[18] This view was shared by Su Shih, who wrote in a colophon to a work of calligraphy by Ts'ai Hsiang:

All things fit into one rule. Once this rule is grasped, all things can be done properly.... Nowadays, in calligraphy people who write seal script cannot write clerical, and people who write running script cannot write cursive. This is because they are still unable to grasp the rule.[19]

Su Shih, like Ts'ai Hsiang, believed that calligraphy should be learned without regard to the different script forms since all script forms could be mastered by understanding the central rule governing any single script form. Similarly, Huang T'ing-chien said, "The brush method of the *Stone Drum Inscriptions* is as magnificent as the *kuei* and *chang* [ancient jades] and cannot be faked by later people. Having fully examined this work, one can achieve the method of the standard, running, and cursive scripts." Huang also stated, "At one time I saw seal and clerical scripts of Han stone engravings and thereby largely achieved the method of standard script."[20] Based on the view that ancient and modern script forms follow one common rule, late Northern Sung masters believed that the attainment of the spirit of antiquity depended more on an understanding of this basic rule than on a familiarity with the formal characteristics of the different scripts.

On yet another occasion, Huang T'ing-chien remarked, "For ingenuity in modeling calligraphy on seal-script forms, one should follow their slanting, modulating, and irregular strokes. Focusing on their regularity and uniform thickness will only produce 'earth-worm brushstrokes' [and not archaic seal script]."[21] His view echoes that of Ts'ai Hsiang in its emphasis on the artlessness of ancient scripts. This artlessness is exactly what Mi Fu extolled in his criticism of calligraphy. For Mi Fu, the regularity produced by uniform character size was contrary to ancient methods:

> With the rise of clerical script, the ancient methods of great-seal script were destroyed. In the [small-] seal and large-seal scripts, the size of the character was determined by its form. Thus, from them one knows the myriad manners of nature. Alive and full of motion, round and complete, each is a self-contained image. With clerical script the forces of stretching and compressing began, and the methods of the three ancient dynasties were lost.[22]

Charmed by the artless simplicity of seal script, Mi Fu dismissed clerical script for being too far removed from antiquity. Since he believed "to compress the large characters and stretch the small characters are not the methods of antiquity," he criticized many of the standard-script masters, including Yen Chen-ch'ing. However, he praised Yen's *Letter on the Controversy over Seating Protocol* (*Cheng tso-wei t'ieh*), executed in running script, for having "a spirit of the large-seal script."[23]

Such Northern Sung views continued to be warmly embraced in the Southern Sung. This is evident in the following observations by Emperor Kao-tsung:

> In practicing calligraphy, which consists of the standard, running, cursive, clerical, and seal scripts, scholars very often are confined to either the seal and clerical or the standard, running, and cursive. They regard these [groups of] scripts to be different in nature and cannot break themselves free from the dots and dashes, so that the two groups of scripts fall into two separate domains. Once the variations embodied in them are understood, the five scripts are joined into one at the tip of the brush. The key to this lies in achieving the Tao.[24]

Owing to the belief that all scripts were based on the same principles, the achievement of the spirit of antiquity was not necessarily thought to be confined to the study of ancient scripts. In the eyes of Sung masters, seal and clerical scripts were valuable not because of their script form but because of their antique flavor which could be incorporated even in the modern scripts.

Masters of Seal and Clerical Scripts in the Northern Sung

During the first half of the Northern Sung when the T'ang and Five Dynasties (907–960) traditions of engraving calligraphy on stelae were still observed and the new artistic trends of the literati had not yet developed, there were many calligraphers who specialized in seal script. Among the early Northern Sung seal-script masters whose calligraphy can still be seen today, Hsü Hsüan (916–992) was the most famous. As a philologist, he was entrusted with the imperial project of revising the *Shuo-wen.* As a calligrapher, he was one of the three Sung seal-script masters recognized in the imperial calligraphy catalogue *Hsüan-ho shu-p'u.*[25] His calligraphy was also held in high regard outside the court. Even his handwritten letters were treasured by Sung scholars.[26] Unfortunately, Hsü's seal-script style cannot be clearly defined by his surviving works; his epitaph titles consist of only a few characters, and his best known calligraphy, *Stele of Mount I* (*I-shan pei*), is a copy of Li Ssu's work, dated 219 BC. Hsü's *Stele of Mount I* nonetheless displays relatively fine brushwork similar to the style of the T'ang calligrapher Li Yang-ping. His seal-script style can perhaps be better understood from this description by Shen Kua (1031–1095):

> When [Hsü Hsüan's work] is held against the sun, one can see that the ink is thicker at the center of each stroke, even at the turns and folds. This is because the brush tip remains upright without slanting, so that it is always at the center of the stroke. This is how the brush was employed.[27]

Kuo Chung-shu (ca. 910–977) was another Northern Sung master of seal script whose calligraphy was derived from his philological expertise. Kuo's scholarship in philological studies was remarkably broad, encompassing small-seal script, the more archaic large-seal script, and other ancient scripts. His competence in writing ancient script forms is evident in his *Yin-fu Classic* (*Yin-fu ching*), now in Pei-lin (Forest of Stelae), in Sian. The text is written in three different scripts, large seal, small seal, and clerical. Although well versed in ancient scripts, Kuo was mostly praised for his small-seal script. For example, Ou-yang Hsiu considered him a great master after Li Yang-ping.[28]

The monk Meng-ying (act. 965–999) also won his fame as a master of seal script. He was particularly interested in writing in a variety of seal-script styles, and was able to write as many as eighteen different forms of seal script on a single piece of wood.[29] Meng-ying's *Poems in Eighteen Scripts* (*Shih-pa t'i shih*), in Pei-lin, is probably the only surviving example of this type of composition. As seen in this work as well as other seal-script stelae in Pei-lin, the characters are slightly elongated and symmetrical in structure, a style recalling that of Li Ssu and Li Yang-ping.

Other seal-script calligraphers active in the first half of the Northern Sung are named in historical documents, but few examples of their calligraphy are extant. Wang Wen-ping (10th century) was mentioned frequently by Ou-yang Hsiu, who thought more highly of Wang's work than that of his contemporary Hsü Hsüan.[30] Another was Chü Chung-cheng (929–1002), a philologist who worked with Hsü Hsüan in revising the *Shuo-wen.*[31] Aside from the calligraphy in eight different scripts that he presented

Figure 1 (left)
Chang Yu-chih (1006–1062). Colophon to *Imperial Sedan Chair* (*Pu-nien t'u*), attribued to Yen Li-pen (600–674), mid-11th century. Palace Museum, Peking. From *Ku-kung po-wu-yüan ts'ang-hua-chi* (Peking: Jen-min mei-shu ch'u-pan-she, 1978), v. 1, 6 (text).

Figure 2 (right)
Detail from *Stone Classic of the Chia-yu Era* (*Chia-yu shih-ching*), 1041–61. Ink rubbing. From *Wen-wu*, no. 7 (1985), 64.

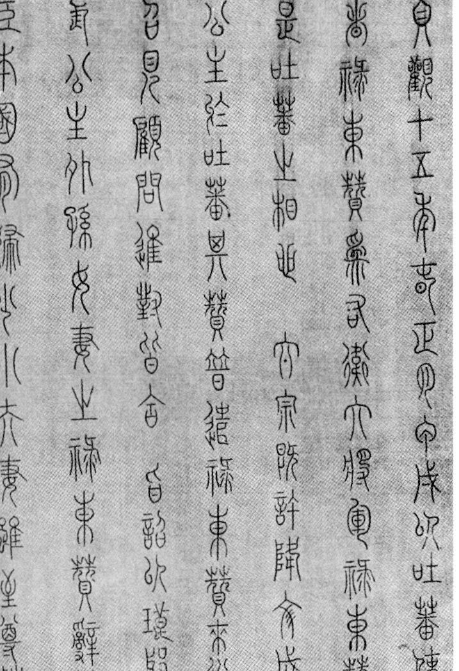

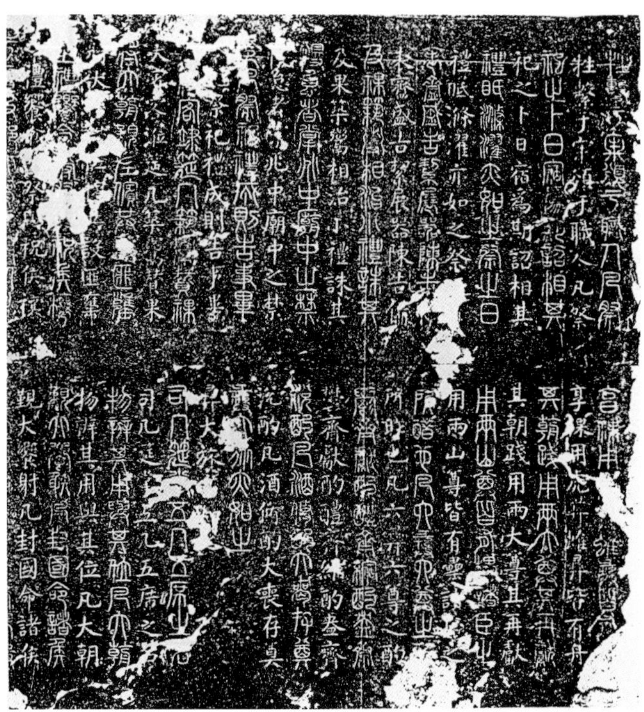

to the imperial court, his works include the *Classic of Filial Piety* (*Hsiao-ching*) engraved into stone in large- and small-seal script and writings executed in a form of clerical script known as *pa-fen*.[32] Less well-known figures in this group of seal-script calligraphers from the late tenth to the early eleventh century include Li Wu-huo, Cheng Wen-pao (953–1013), Ch'a Tao (955–1018), Kao Shen, Shen Ko, Ko T'uan, and Yin Hsi-ku.[33]

Seal-script calligraphers active in the second half of the Northern Sung include Chao T'ing (11th century), Shao Su (11th century), and Chang Yu-chih (1006–1062). Chao T'ing was praised by Mi Fu for his ability to demonstrate an antique spirit in seal script, while Shao Su was known for his "hairpin seal script" (*ch'a-ku chuan*), but none of their work survives.[34] Chang Yu-chih was one of the three famous seal-script masters mentioned in the *Hsüan-ho shu-p'u.* Well versed in philology, he participated in the writing of the *Stone Classic of the Chia-yu Era* (*Chia-yu shih-ching*). Critics regarded him as the greatest seal-script calligrapher after Li Ssu and Li Yang-ping.[35] His renown continued into the Southern Sung, and his seal-script calligraphy merited a detailed description by Ch'en Yu (*chin-shih* 1190):

> [Chang Yu-chih] once drew a square and a circle to represent a chessboard and a target [respectively], both in one single stroke. The strokes were perfect in their thickness, and their placement was precise. This is because Chang was skillful in the brush method. When the hand and the heart are at one unawares, perfect squares and circles can be drawn without effort.[36]

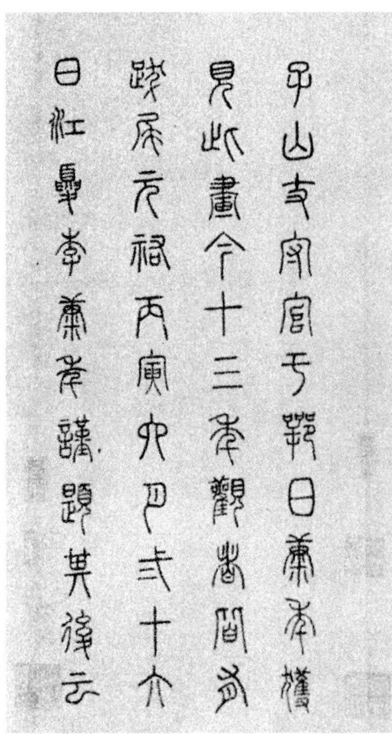

Figure 3
Li K'ang-nien (late 11th century). Colopon to *Imperial Sedan Chair* (*Pu-nien t'u*), attribued to Yen Li-pen (600–674), 1086. Palace Museum, Peking. From *Ku-kung po-wu-yüan ts'ang-hua-chi* (Peking: Jen-min mei-shu ch'u-pan-she, 1978), v. 1, 7.

As seen in his colophon to the painting *Pu-nien t'u* (fig. 1), attributed to Yen Li-pen (600–674), Chang's seal-script characters are elongated and well balanced with thin, rounded strokes, and the characters and columns are evenly spaced. His style is in the manner of Li Yang-ping, thus echoing the critic Chu Ch'ang-wen's (1039–1098) remark that Chang "won his fame from his *yü-chu* style."[37] Chang's colophon is stylistically related to the *Stone Classic of the Chia-yu Era* (fig. 2), which presumably represents the standard imperial style of seal-script calligraphy in the Northern Sung period. Another colophon to the *Pu-nien t'u* was written by Li K'ang-nien (late 11th century; fig. 3) in a seal-script style similar to that of Chang Yu-chih. Li's seal script was widely recognized by Northern Sung literati like Su Shih and Huang T'ing-chien. Su once praised Li for his "interests in antiquity, knowledge in various disciplines, and especially his mastery of small-seal script."[38] Huang T'ing-chien compared Li to Li Ssu and Li Yang-ping for "having attained enlightenment in the large- and [small-] seal scripts in his late years, so that the brush could be moved effortlessly and at will to produce straight woodlike strokes and curved ironlike strokes."[39]

In their studies of ancient script forms, Northern Sung calligraphers were less interested in clerical script than seal script, for two reasons: first, they thought clerical script was not as archaic as seal script; and, second, clerical script was less commonly used for stelae titles than seal script.[40] Many seal-script calligraphers, such as Kuo Chung-shu and Meng-ying, practiced clerical script but did not owe their fame to this style of writing.

There are only a few extant works in clerical script attributed to Northern Sung calligraphers. One of the most important of these works is the *Stele for the Spirit Road of Fan Chung-yen* (*Fan Chung-yen shen-tao pei*; fig. 4), in Loyang, Honan, which was carved in 1056.[41] The calligrapher was Wang Chu (997–1057), a philologist and court calligrapher who is recorded as being knowledgeable in seal and clerical studies. Chu Ch'ang-wen wrote favorably of him, saying that Wang "loved clerical script in his late years and particularly mastered the antique methods. Calligraphy students at that time came to model [their styles] on his, and clerical script was thus revived."[42] Wang's characters are slightly elongated and evenly structured with angular and straight brushstrokes. His style is close to the clerical script practiced in the T'ang period, and resembles the writing style of Shih Wei-tse. The title of the stele was executed by Emperor Jen-tsung (r. 1022–63) and the text composed by Ou-yang Hsiu to eulogize the great courtier Fan Chung-yen (989–1052). Since the stele was sponsored by the court, it may well reflect the official clerical style of the Northern Sung.

Among the small number of extant Northern Sung works in clerical script is Wu Li-li's (11th century) colophon to Fan Chung-yen's *Tao-fu tsan* (fig. 5). Wu's calligraphy is similar in style to Wang Chu's, although the

Figure 4 (left)
Wang Chu (997–1057). Section from *Stele for the Spirit Road of Fan Chung-yen* (*Fan Chung-yen shen-tao pei*), 1056. Ink rubbing. From *Shu-fa ts'ung-k'an* 2 (1996), 78.

Figure 5 (right)
Wu Li-li (11th century). Colophon to Fan Chung-yen's *Tao-fu tsan*, 11th century. Palace Museum, Peking. From *Ku-kung po-wu-yüan ts'ang li-tai fa-shu hsüan-chi* (Peking: Wen-wu ch'u-pan-she, 1980), v. 1, no. 7.

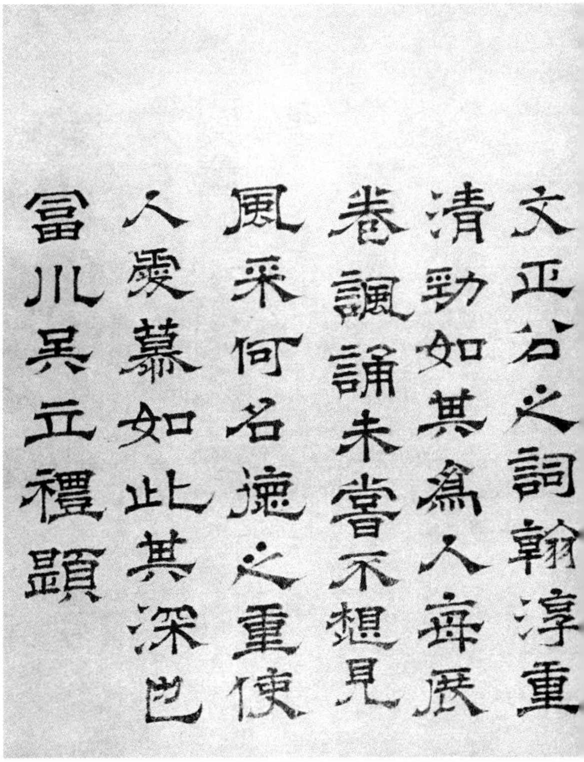

Figure 6 (left)
Ssu-ma Kuang (1019–1086). Section from *Epitaph for Wang Hsiang-kung* (*Wang Hsiang-kung mu-chih-ming*), 1084. Ink rubbing. From *Pei-ching t'u-shu-kuan ts'ang Chung-kuo li-tai shih-k'o t'a-pen hui-pien* (2nd ed; Cheng-chou: Chung-chou ku-chih, 1989), v. 39, 159.

Figure 7 (right)
Huang Po-ssu (1079–1118). Colophon to *Poem of the Orchid Pavilion* (*Lan-t'ing shih*), 1111. Palace Museum, Peking. From *Ku-kung po-wu-yüan ts'ang li-tai fa-shu hsüan-chi* (Peking: Wen-wu ch'u-pan-she, n.d.), v. 1, no. 2.

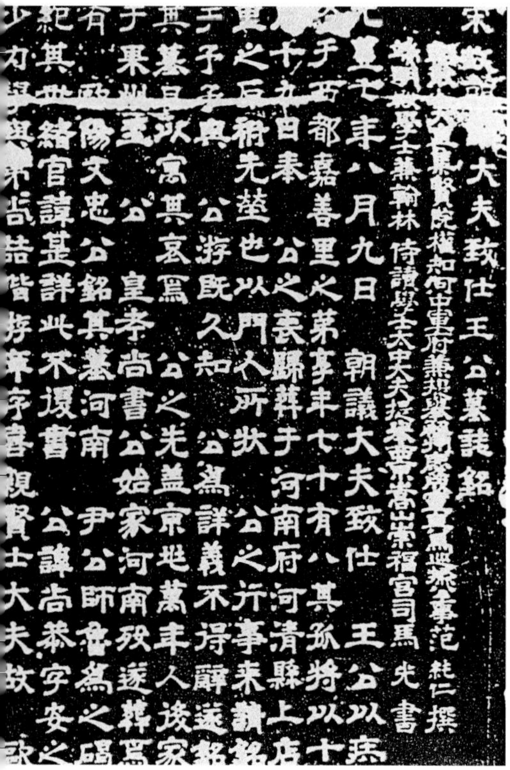

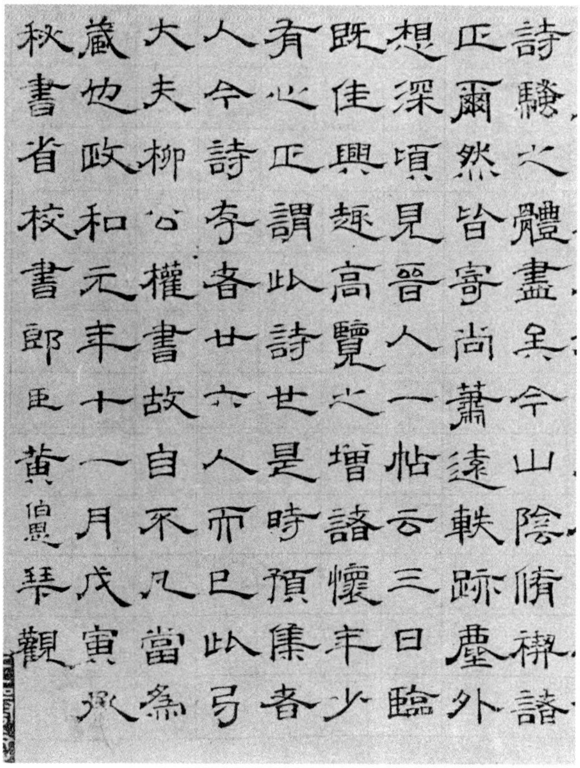

brushstrokes are more pointed and angular. Some of the characters are nearly identical to Wang's in structure. This relatively rigid style, which is also found in the calligraphy of Ssu-ma Kuang (1019–1086; fig. 6), can be regarded as typical of the Northern Sung. A markedly different style is found in Huang Po-ssu's (1079-1118) colophon to *Poem of the Orchid Pavilion* (*Lan-t'ing shih*), formerly attributed to Liu Kung-ch'üan (fig. 7).[43] The characters are elegantly structured with crisp brushstrokes that produce a strong archaic touch. Huang once said that when learning calligraphy, he studied the bronze inscriptions of the Hsia, Shang, and Chou dynasties and the stone inscriptions from the Ch'in to the Han and Wei dynasties.[44] His knowledge of stone and bronze inscriptions strongly influenced his clerical script and calligraphy.

Masters of Seal and Clerical Scripts in the Southern Sung

There are even fewer surviving specimens of seal- and clerical-script calligraphy from the Southern Sung. Again, some Southern Sung masters of seal script were also experts in philology, such as Hung Kua (1117–1184), who wrote *Clerical Characters: Explanations* (*Li shih*; 1167) and *Clerical Characters: Revised Supplement* (*Li hsü*; 1168), and Hsüeh Shang-kung (died after 1144), the author of *Model Inscriptions from Ritual Vessels throughout History* (*Li-tai chung-ting i-ch'ih k'uan-chih fa-t'ieh*; 1168). Among the masters of ancient script forms in the Southern Sung, Hsü Ching came first. Hsü served in the Hsüan-ho Academy of Calligraphy and gained fame for his seal-script style. When discussing calligraphy, Emperor Kao-tsung singled out Hsü for his writings in seal script.[45] In his comments on contemporary trends in calligraphy, Ch'en Yu (*chin-shih* 1190) gave credit to Hsü Ching as well as his contemporaries Tseng Ta-chung and Tseng Ch'i-nien for their seal script.[46] He described Hsü's seal-script characters as having a "slender waist and long legs" and reminiscent of antiquity.[47] Unfortunately, none of Hsü's writing in clerical script survives. *The Thousand Character Essay* (*Ch'ien-tzu wen*; fig. 8), bearing a spurious inscription by the early Northern Sung calligrapher Hsü Hsüan, is actually the work of an unidentified calligrapher active no later than the period of Emperor Hsiao-tsung (r. 1163–89).[48] The characters are smoothly and crisply executed, the brushstrokes have sharp endings, and the structure is deliberately archaic. The scroll perhaps reflects the seal-script style that was dominant in Hsü Ching's time. Another example of archaic-script calligraphy, *Sung Tz'u-Poems* (*Sung-jen tz'u*; fig. 9) by the lesser-known thirteenth-century calligrapher Ch'ang Shao, resembles *The Thousand Character Essay* in its delicate and crisp brushwork and generally meticulous style.

As for the clerical-script masters of the Southern Sung, Ch'en Yu mentioned the twelfth-century calligraphers Lü Sheng-chi, Huang Chu (1131–

Figure 8 (left)
Unidentified calligrapher. Section from *The Thousand Character Essay* (*Ch'ien-tzu wen*), 12th century. Heilongjiang Provincial Museum. From *Chung-kuo mei-shu ch'üan-chi, Shu-fa chuan-k'o pien* (Peking: Jen-min mei-shu ch'u-pan-she, 1986), v. 4, no. 1.

Figure 9 (right)
Ch'ang Shao (13th century). Section from *Sung Tz'u-Poems* (*Sung-jen tz'u*), 1227. National Palace Museum, Taipei. From *Chung-kuo mei-shu ch'üan-chi, Shu-fa chuan-k'o pien* (Peking: Jen-min mei-shu ch'u-pan-she, 1986), v. 4, 97.

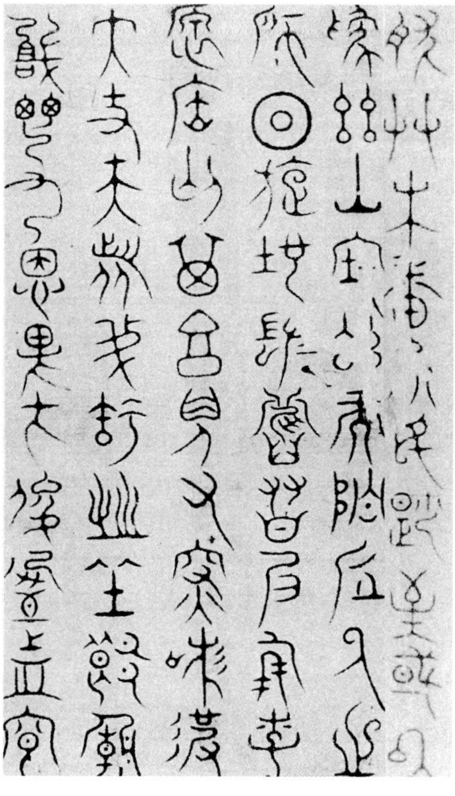

1199), Tu Chung-wei, and especially Yü Ssu-liang.[49] Yüan Mao is another calligrapher of the period who deserves mention. The sense of austerity in Yüan's clerical-script calligraphy, as seen in cliff carvings, recalls Han clerical script.[50] It is probably for this reason that Yüan was once regarded as the most accomplished clerical-script calligrapher in the Sung dynasty.[51]

Most of the Sung calligraphers who specialized in ancient scripts were expert philologists who based their calligraphy on their knowledge of philology rather than any theory of calligraphy. They were not interested in establishing new styles, but instead mainly followed the T'ang dynasty models. As a result, although seal and clerical scripts were practiced by a number of calligraphers in the Sung, the style was basically conservative.

The Literati's Use of Seal- and Clerical-Script Traditions

While the Sung dynasty produced many seal- and clerical-script masters and there was a widespread interest in studying and appreciating bronze and stone inscriptions, none of the leading Sung calligraphers earned their fame by practicing these scripts. Even Ou-yang Hsiu, whose passion for and expertise in bronze and stone inscriptions were second to none in the Northern Sung, made no mention of the two script types when he wrote about his own experience in learning calligraphy.[52] Those who were competent in seal and clerical scripts were in fact masters of many types of script. Li Chien-chung (945–1013), Su Shun-yüan (1006–1054), and Wen T'ung (1019–1079) all can be cited as examples, although no relevant works by them have survived.[53] Neither did seal and clerical scripts contribute to the esteem attained by the Four Great Masters of the Sung. In Ts'ai Hsiang's case, this was not because he was not interested in antiquity. He was in fact an ardent student of antiquity, and, driven by this passion, compiled fourteen volumes of Han stelae calligraphy.[54] According to the *Hsüan-ho shu-p'u*, Ts'ai, who was best known for his running script, was competent in a variety of script forms, including tadpole (*k'o-tou wen*), large and small seal, standard, clerical, flying-white (*fei-pai*), running, cursive, draft-cursive (*chang-ts'ao*), and wild-cursive.[55] Su Shih also mentioned Ts'ai's clerical script, but did not particularly praise it.[56] Su Shih's own calligraphy seems to have had nothing to do with seal or clerical script. There is no documentary evidence of his ability to write ancient scripts, and none of his surviving work is executed in any of these script forms. A master of both running and cursive scripts, Huang T'ing-chien modeled his running script on *Eulogy on Burying a Crane* (*I-ho ming*) and derived his cursive script mainly from that of the T'ang calligrapher Huai-su (ca. 735–ca. 799). Like Su Shih, Huang was not interested in writing either seal or clerical script. Mi Fu strove to adhere to the Chin tradition of the Two Wangs, but his early exposure to various masters of earlier periods led to the criticism that his writing was "a compendium of ancient characters."[57] According to the *Hsüan-ho shu-p'u*, Mi "basically followed [Wang] Hsi-chih in calligraphy, strove to emulate Li Po [701–762] in poetry, learned [large-]seal script from the *Shih-chou* [*p'ien*], modeled his clerical script on Shih I-kuan [2nd century], and, in his late years, achieved full spiritual freedom [in calligraphy]."[58] Mi Fu himself remarked that he started with the T'ang and Chin traditions and then traced them back to Han stelae, Chin stone engravings, bamboo slips, and bronze inscriptions.[59] From this, it is evident that he studied and practiced seal and clerical scripts. Mi's extant calligraphic works are either in running or in cursive script, but examples of his seal- and clerical-script calligraphy are included in *Model-Book Calligraphy by Mi Fu in the Shao-hsing Collection* (*Shao-hsing Mi-t'ieh*; figs. 10, 11). Both his seal- and clerical-script characters display a strong sense of movement and very often an unbalanced structure. His style appears to depart from that of the T'ang as well as that of most Sung seal- and clerical-script masters. This led later critics to declare that Mi Fu was unskilled in writing seal and clerical scripts.[60] Although Mi was probably not at his best in writing ancient scripts, his calligraphy in seal and clerical script is significant in that it reflects the extent to which individuality was emphasized by Sung literati in interpreting the two script forms.

In their discussions of calligraphy, Sung literati stressed the quality of artlessness and spontaneity in bronze and stone inscriptions and their belief that there was a basic principle that applied to all kinds of scripts. Hence, they did not confine themselves to writing in archaic script forms in their pursuit of antiquity. Instead, they sought to imbue their modern scripts with an antique spirit. Huang T'ing-chien's powerful and austere round brushwork, for example, was sometimes viewed as having the quality of seal-script strokes.[61] Mi Fu's manipulation of archaic-script brushwork in his own expressive calligraphy has already been pointed out by modern scholars.[62] The slightly slanting characters of his seal and clerical scripts produce a visual rhythm, as shown in figures 10 and 11, and may well reflect Mi's attempt to achieve the unstudied distinctiveness of archaic inscriptions.

The Sung literati's pursuit of an antique spirit is also revealed in the calligraphy of the scholar-artist Li Kung-lin (ca. 1041–1106). Li's transcription of the text of *The Classic of Filial Piety* (*Hsiao-ching*), for example, emulates Chung Yu and shows traces of clerical-script brush methods, culminating in a kind of austere beauty and a strong sense of simplicity (fig. 12).[63] Li Kung-lin was known as an antiquarian in literary circles of the second half of the Northern Sung, and he recorded what he had seen and collected in his *Catalog of Antiquities* (*K'ao-ku t'u*).[64] In modeling his writing on a Wei dynasty master, he exemplified his adherence to the antique tradition.

Figure 10 (left)
Mi Fu (1052–1107). Section in seal script from *Model-Book Calligraphy by Mi Fu in the Shao-hsing Collection* (*Shao-hsing Mi-t'ieh*), late 11th century. Ink rubbing. From *Chung-kuo shu-fa ch'üan-chi* (Peking: Jung-pao-chai, 1992), v. 38, 407.

Figure 11 (right)
Mi Fu (1052–1107). Section in clerical script from *Model-Book Calligraphy by Mi Fu in the Shao-hsing Collection* (*Shao-hsing Mi-t'ieh*), late 11th century. Ink rubbing. From *Chung-kuo shu-fa ch'üan-chi* (Peking: Jung-pao-chai, 1992), v. 38, 408.

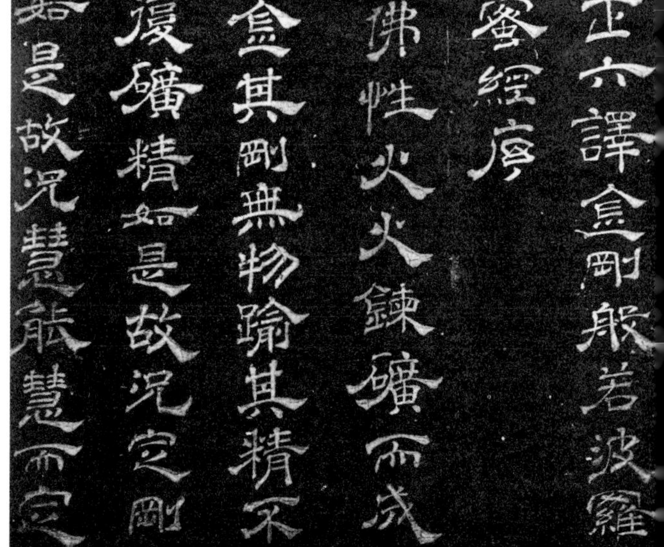

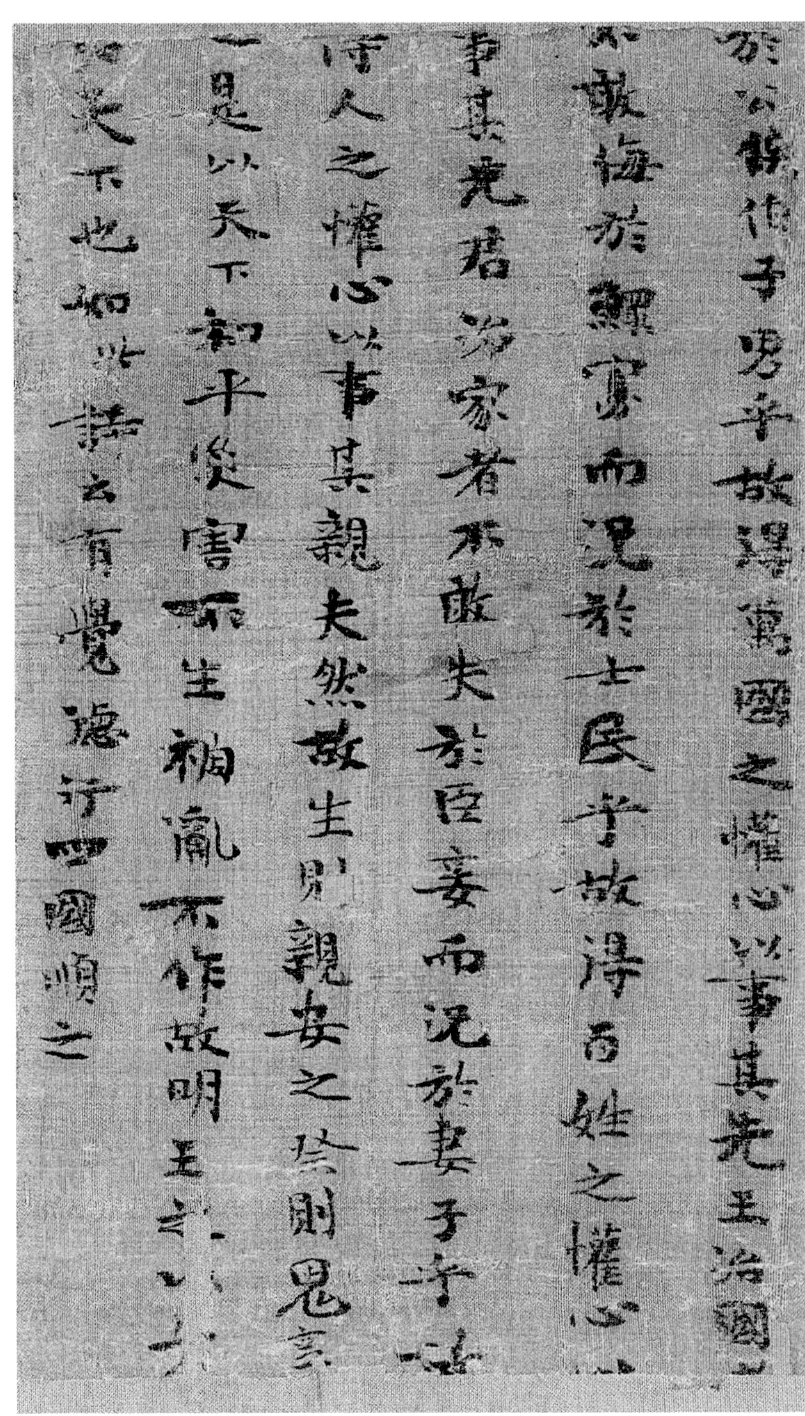

Figure 12
Li Kung-lin (ca. 1041–1106). Detail from *The Classic of Filial Piety*, ca. 1085. Handscroll, ink on silk, 21.9 x 475.5 cm. The Metropolitan Museum of Art, From the P.Y. and Kinmay W. Tang Family Collection, Partial and Promised Gift of the Oscar L. Tang Family.

Documentary evidence also shows that the trends in calligraphy at the time indeed caused seal- and clerical-script calligraphy to develop in new directions away from ancient forms. For instance, according to Su Shih's colophon to a work of calligraphy by Li Yüan-chih (11th century), "For decades Li Yüan-chih had painstakingly studied seal script. He knew well the form of the characters, achieved the spirit of antiquity, and used a pointed brush tip to write rapidly, paying no heed to any rules."[65] Such a manner of execution is a marked departure from the traditionally stern and regular forms of seal script. Wei Liao-weng's (1178–1237) seal-script calligraphy, which was described as "conveying a quality of naturalness without being bound by rules," can also be seen as an outcome of the enthusiasm for individuality.[66] Although none of Li Yüan-chih's and Wei Liao-weng's seal script has survived, the colophons written in clerical script by Yüan Shuo-yu (1140–1204) and Shih Tso (act. late 12th century) to Mi Yu-jen's painting *White Clouds over the Hsiao and Hsiang Rivers* (*Hsiao-Hsiang pai-yün t'u*; figs. 13, 14) may serve to illustrate the extent to which Sung calligraphers stressed individuality in interpreting ancient script forms. Yüan Shuo-yu was agile and delicate in manipulating his brush. Some of the strokes are extended outward for rhythmic effect, at the expense of stability. Shih Tso, on the other hand, was deliberate and subtle, and the structure of his characters is even and natural. Even though they do not rank among the renowned calligraphers of the Sung, both Yüan and Shih each have their own distinctive clerical-script style. The wide variety of styles is a notable feature of Sung clerical-script calligraphy as it was practiced under the influence of the pursuit of individuality. Another calligrapher of this period is Chao Meng-chien, who advocated the revival of T'ang and Chin traditions in calligraphy. He was fond of collecting bronze and stone inscriptions and must have had knowledge of ancient script forms.[67] With its crisp strokes and slight variations in structure, his clerical-script inscription on his *Poems of Myself* (*Tzu-shu shih*; fig. 15) is in a class of its own. The relationship between the pursuit of antiquity and individuality in calligraphy during the Southern Sung is summarized in these remarks by the scholar Ch'en Yu:

> Nowadays, people esteem Hsü Ching for his seal script, Yü Ssu-liang for his clerical script, and Chang Hsiao-hsiang [1132–1169] for his running-cursive script. Ignorant of its true meaning, people are attracted by the untrammeled charm of their calligraphy without knowing that their characters are all re-formed in style. It is nonetheless commendable to have a style of one's own even though the calligraphy does not conform fully to antiquity.[68]

* * *

Seal and clerical scripts were actively practiced in the Sung dynasty. However, there was no major stylistic breakthrough in these script forms because most of the practitioners were content to engage in the study of philology and were not concerned with establishing a sound theoretical basis for their calligraphy. Yet there were calligraphers who pursued an antique spirit by referring to archaic scripts for artistic individuality and expressiveness. Based on the concept that all scripts are one, Sung calligraphers borrowed from the ancient scripts or projected their own styles through these scripts. While this stimulated the development of seal- and clerical-script calligraphy, scant practice and lack of new interpretation left these two scripts in the shadow of running script, which was invigorated by many stylistic innovations. This trend continued until the Ch'ing dynasty (1644–1911) when the study of bronze and stone inscriptions met with renewed interest and the Model-book school (*t'ieh-hsüeh*) was enervated. With new standards for the practice and evaluation of the art of calligraphy firmly in place, seal-and clerical-script calligraphy were once again brought to the forefront.

Figure 13
Yüan Shuo-yu (1140–1204). Colophon to Mi Yu-jen's (1074–1151) *White Clouds over the Hsiao and Hsiang Rivers* (*Hsiao-Hsiang pai-yün t'u*), 1181. Shanghai Museum. From *Chung-kuo ku-tai shu-hua t'u-mu* (Peking: Wen-wu ch'u-pan-she, 1987), v. 2, 29.

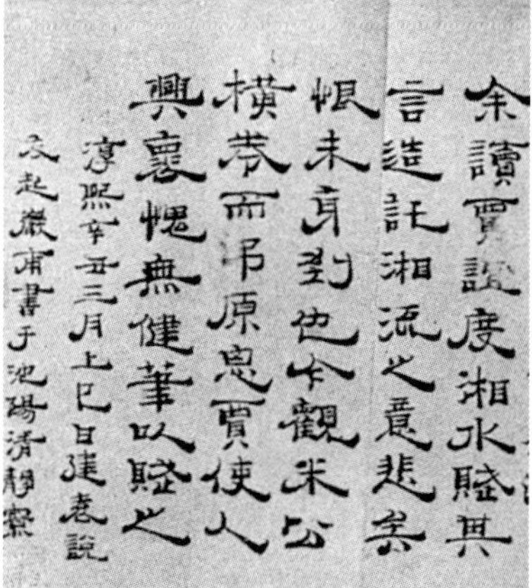

Figure 14
Shih Tso (act. late 12th century). Colophon to Mi Yu-jen's (1074–1151) *White Clouds over the Hsiao and Hsiang Rivers* (*Hsiao-Hsiang pai-yün t'u*), 1187. Shanghai Museum. From *Chung-kuo ku-tai shu-hua t'u-mu* (Peking: Wen-wu ch'u-pan-she, 1987), v. 2, 29.

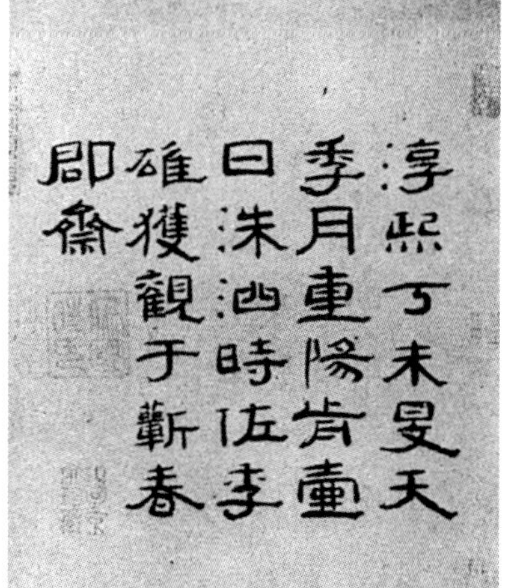

Figure 15
Chao Meng-chien (1199–1264). *Poems of Myself* (*Tzu-shu shih*). Palace Museum, Peking. From *Ku-kung po-wu-yüan ts'ang li-tai fa-shu hsüan-chi* (Peking: Wen-wu ch'u-pan-she, 1980), v. 3, no. 3.

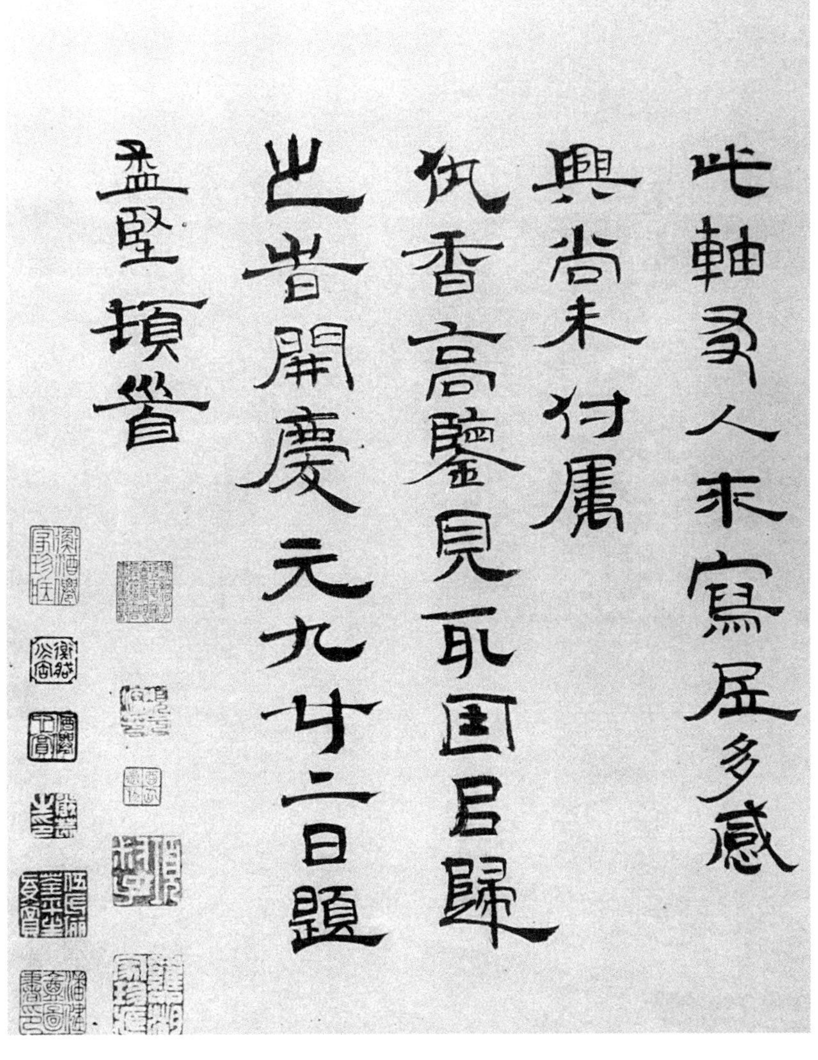

1 *Sung shih* (Taipei: Chung-hua shu-chü, 1972), *chüan* 157, *hsüan-chü* 3, 3688.

2 Li T'ao, *Hsü Tzu-chih t'ung-chien ch'ang-pien*, appendix, *chüan* 48.

3 For Sung writings on epigraphy, see Ch'en Chün-ch'eng, "Sung-tai chin-shih-hsüeh chu-shu k'ao" (Master's thesis, Taiwan National Political University, 1976).

4 Liu Ch'ang, "Hsien-Ch'in ku-tz'u chi," *Kung-shih chi* (*Ssu-k'u ch'üan-shu* ed., Shanghai: Shanghai ku-chi ch'u-pan-she, 1987), *chüan* 36, 15.

5 Some Sung scholars even viewed studies of bronze and stone as part of philological studies. Wang Ying-lin (1223–1296), for example, placed studies of bronze and stone under the category of philology. See Wang Yin-lin, *K'un-hsüeh chi-wen* (rpt. ed., Peking: Commercial Press, 1959), *chüan* 8.

6 Chao Ming-ch'eng, *Chin-shih lu* (annotated ed., Shanghai: Shang-hai shu-hua ch'u-pan-she, 1985), 1–2.

7 Wang Po, "Pa tzu-yün," *Lu-chai Wang Wen-hsien kung wen-chi* (rpt. ed., Taipei: Hsüeh-sheng shu-chü, 1970), *chüan* 12, 11a–12b.

8 Mi Fu, *Shu-shih*, in *Chung-kuo shu-hua ch'üan-shu* (Shanghai: Shang-hai shu-hua ch'u-pan-she, 1993), v. 1, 963-75.

9 Huang T'ing-chien, "Pa Chai Kung-shun so-ts'ang shih-k'o," *Shan-ku t'i-pa, chüan* 4, in *Chung-kuo shu-hua ch'üan-shu*, v. 1, 685–86.

10 Tseng Kung, "Chi Sun Shen-lao Hu-chou mo-miao-t'ing," in *Nan-feng hsien-sheng yüan-feng lei-kao* (rpt. ed., Taipei: Chung-hua shu-chü, 1966), *chüan* 7, 8a; Su Shih, "Sun Shen-lao ch'iu mo-miao-t'ing shih" and "Mo-miao-t'ing chi," *Su Tung-p'o ch'üan-chi* (Taipei: Shih-chieh shu-chü, 1969), *ch'ien-chi, chüan* 3, 70 and *chüan* 31, 382.

11 For a discussion of Sung studies of *Lan-t'ing hsü*, see Shui Lai-yu, "Sung-tai Lan-t'ing hsü te yen-chiu," in *Ch'üan-kuo ti-ssu-chieh shu-hsüeh t'ao-lun-hui lun-wen-chi*, Chung-kuo shu-fa-chia hsieh-hui, ed. (Chungking: Ch'ung-ch'ing ch'u-pan-she, 1993), 84–103.

12 Huang T'ing-chien, "Pa fa-t'ieh," *Shan-ku t'i-pa, chüan* 4, 682.

13 Mi Fu, "Lun ts'ao-shu," an ink work collected in the National Palace Museum, Taipei.

14 Mi Fu's criticism of T'ang calligraphy is best reflected in his *Hai-yüeh ming-yen*.

15 *P'ei-wen-chai shu-hua-p'u* (rpt. ed., Peking: Chung-kuo shu-tien, 1984), 976–77.

16 Shui Lai-yu, ed., *Ts'ai Hsiang shu-fa shih-liao chi* (Shanghai: Shang-hai shu-hua ch'u-pan she, 1983), 8.

17 Ibid.

18 Ibid.

19 Su Shih, "Pa Ts'ai Chün-mo fei-pai," *Tung-p'o t'i-pa, chüan* 4, in *Chung-kuo shu-hua ch'üan-shu*, v. 1, 628.

20 Huang T'ing-chien, "Pa Chai Kung-shun so-ts'ang shih-k'o" and "P'ing-shu," *Shan-ku t'i-pa, chüan* 4 and 7, 685 and 697.

21 Ch'en Yu, *Fu-hsüan yeh-lu*, in *Chung-kuo shu-hua ch'üan-shu*, v. 2, 648.

22 Mi Fu, *Hai-yüeh ming-yen*, in *Chung-kuo shu-hua ch'üan-shu*, v. 1, 977. The translation is based on Peter C. Sturman, *Mi Fu: Style and the Art of Calligraphy in Northern Song China* (New Haven and London: Yale University Press, 1997), 168.

23 Ibid., 976.

24 Emperor Kao-tsung, *Han-mo chih*, in *Chung-kuo shu-hua ch'üan-shu*, v. 2, 2.

25 *Hsüan-ho shu-p'u, chüan* 2, 11.

26 Tung Shih, *Huang-Sung shu-lu*, in *Chung-kuo shu-hua ch'üan-shu*, v. 2, 631.

27 Shen Kua, *Meng-hsi pi-t'an*, annotated version, 4th ed. (Hong Kong:

Chung-hua shu-chü, 1987), *chüan* 17, 172.

28 Ou-yang Hsiu, "Kuo Chung-shu Yin-fu ching," *Liu-i t'i-pa*, in *Chung-kuo shu-hua ch'üan-shu*, vol. 1, 572.

29 *Hsüan-ho shu-p'u*, *chüan* 2, 11.

30 Ou-yang Hsiu, "Hsü Hsüan Shuang-hsi-yüan chi," "Wang Wen-ping hsiao-chuan ch'ien-tzu-wen," and "Wang Wen-ping Tzu-yang shih-ch'ing ming," *Liu-i t'i-pa*, 571–72.

31 *Sung-shih*, *chüan* 441, *lieh-chüan* 200, 13049.

32 Chu Ch'ang-wen also regarded Chu highly, ranking his seal script in the "competent class." See *Hsü Shu-tuan*, *shang*, in *Li-tai shu-fa lun-wen hsüan* (Shanghai: Shang-hai shu-hua ch'u-pan-she, 1979), vol. 1, 348–49.

33 Chiang Shao-yü, *Sung-ch'ao shih-shih lei-yüan* (annotated ed., Shanghai: Shang-hai ku-chi ch'u-pan-she, 1981), *chüan* 50, 656, *chüan* 51, 671.

34 Mi Fu, *Shu-shih*, 975; Ch'en Yu, *Fu-hsüan yeh-lu*, 648.

35 *Hsüan-ho shu-p'u*, *chüan* 2, 11.

36 Ch'en Yu, *Fu-hsüan yeh-lu*, 648.

37 Chu Ch'ang-wen, *Hsü Shu-tuan*, *hsia*, 351.

38 Su Shih, "Pa Li K'ang-nien chuan Hsin-ching hou," *Tung-p'o t'i-pa*, *chüan* 4, 631.

39 Huang T'ing-chien, "Pa Li K'ang-nien chuan," *Shan-ku t'i-pa*, *chüan* 5, 692.

40 One example of the preference for seal script over clerical script is the *Stone Classics of the Chia-yu Era*, which was written in seal and standard scripts, but not in clerical script.

41 Li Hsien-ch'i and Kuo Yin-ch'iang, "Lo-yang hsin-huo mu-chih shu-fa i-shu kai-shu," *Shu-fa ts'ung-k'an* 6 (1996), 2-5, 77-78.

42 *Sung shih*, *chüan* 294, *lieh-chuan* 53, 9816. Chu Ch'ang-wen, *Hsü Shu-tuan*, *hsia*, 350.

43 The *Lan-t'ing shih* has recently been shown not to be written by Liu Kung-ch'üan. The authenticity of Huang Po-ssu's colophon has also been questioned. See *Chung-kuo shu-fa ch'üan-chi* (27): *Liu Kung-ch'üan* (Peking: Jung-pao-chai, 1993), 228-29. No other specimens by Huang are available for comparison.

44 Huang Po-ssu, "Pa Su-shih shu-hou," *Tung-kuan yu-lun*, in *Chung-kuo shu-hua ch'üan-shu*, vol. 1, 873.

45 Emperor Kao-tsung, *Han-mo chih*, 20.

46 Ch'en Yu, *Fu-hsüan yeh-lu*, 648.

47 Ibid.

48 *Chung-kuo mei-shu ch'üan-chi*, *Shu-fa chuan-k'o pien* (Shanghai: Shang-hai jen-min mei-shu ch'u-pan-she, 1986), v. 4, explanation, 1–2.

49 Ch'en Yu, *Fu-hsüan yeh-lu*, 648.

50 Shan-hsi Han-chung shih Pao-hsieh shih-k'o yen-chiu-hui and Shan-hsi Han-chung shih po-wu-kuan, eds., *Shih-men Han-Wei shih-san p'in* (Sian: Shan-hsi jen-min mei-shu ch'u-pan-she, 1988).

51 Ou-yang Fu, *Chi-ku ch'iu-chen* (Hong Kong: Hsiang-kang Chung-kuo shu-hua yen-chiu-hui, 1971), *cheng-pien*, *chüan* 10, 176.

52 Ou-yang Hsiu, "Hsüeh chen-ts'ao shu," *Shih-pi* in *Li-tai shu-fa lun-wen hsüan*, v. 1, 308.

53 *Hsüan-ho shu-pu*, *chüan* 12, 34; *Sung shih*, *chüan* 443, *lieh-chuan* 202, 13101.

54 Cheng Shao, *Yen-chi*, in *Li-tai shu-fa lun-wen hsüan*, v. 1, 308.

55 *Hsüan-ho shu-p'u*, *chüan* 12, 36.

56 Su Shih, "P'ing Yang-shih so-ts'ang Ou Ts'ai shu," *Tung-p'o t'i-pa*, *chüan* 4, 630.

57 Mi Fu, *Hai-yüeh ming-yen*, 976.

58 *Hsüan-ho shu-p'u*, *chüan* 12, 36.

59 Mi Fu, *Pao-Chin ying-kuang chi* (*Ts'ung-shu chi-ch'eng ch'u-pien* edition, Shanghai: Shang-hai Commercial Press, 1939), *chüan* 8, 66. For a full English translation, see Wen C. Fong et al., *Images of the*

Mind: Selections from the Edward L. Elliott Family and John B. Elliott Collections of Chinese Calligraphy and Painting at The Art Museum, Princeton University (Princeton: The Art Museum, Princeton University, 1984), 86.

60 See *Chung-kuo shu-fa ch'üan-shu (38): Mi Fu* (Peking: Jung-pao-chai, 1992), 524.

61 For example, K'ang Yu-wei (1858–1927) associated Huang T'ing-chien's brushwork with seal script. See K'ang Yu-wei, "Lun-shu chüeh-chü: 14," *Kuang I-chou shuang-chieh* (Taipei: Commercial Press, 1970), *chüan* 6.

62 See, for instance, Wen C. Fong et al., *Images of the Mind*, 91.

63 For a detailed discussion of this work, see Chu Hui-liang J., "The Calligraphy of Li Kung-lin in The Classic of Filial Piety," in *Li Kung-lin's Classic of Filial Piety*, Richard M. Barnhart, ed. (New York: The Metropolitan Museum of Art, 1993), 53–71.

64 Ts'ai T'ao, *T'ieh-wei shan ts'ung-t'an, chüan* 4, in *Sung-tai pi-chi hsiao-shuo* (Hopei: Ho-pei chiao-yü ch'u-pan-she, 1994), v. 18, 390.

65 Su Shih, "Pa Wen Yü-k'o mo-chu Li T'ung-shu chuan," *Tung-p'o t'i-pa, chüan* 5, 636.

66 Tung Shih, *Huang-Sung shu-lu*, 642.

67 Chou Mi, *Ch'i-tung yeh-yü* (rpt. ed., Taipei: Taiwan Commercial Press, 1979), *chüan* 19.

68 Ch'en Yu, *Fu-hsüan yeh-lu*, 648.

Peter C. Sturman

University of California, Santa Barbara

Wine and Cursive: The Limits of Individualism in Northern Sung China

Of the various topics that served as magnets for ideas that contributed to the development of literati values in the arts during the late Northern Sung period (960–1127), none perhaps is as rich as cursive calligraphy (*ts'ao-shu*). This is because in discussions among the prominent theoreticians and practitioners of calligraphy—notably Su Shih (1037–1101), Huang T'ing-chien (1045–1105), and Mi Fu (1052–1107/08)—we find subtle differences of opinion about both the practice of cursive calligraphy and the early masters of the script. These, in turn, point to deeper questions concerning creativity itself. This study begins with a review of the debate that took place in the last two decades of the eleventh century before focusing on one particular element in the mix and its relationship to the practice of calligraphy in Northern Sung China: alcohol. Wine may be universal in its attractions, addictions, and effects, but it is also specific as a cultural construct—the manner in which an individual culture mythicizes its qualities. As Northern Sung literati artists wrestled with the very nature of creativity—its sources of inspiration and expression—they found themselves face to face with a formidable tradition that brought together booze and brush.

The Discourse on Cursive

One camp in the cursive debate is represented by Mi Fu and his friend Hsüeh Shao-p'eng. Both men were prominent collectors of calligraphy, and as such were naturally drawn to genuine works by early writers, following the general principle that older was rarer and (at least in China) better. Their focus was firmly set on Chin dynasty (265–317) calligraphy, especially that of the Two Wangs, Wang Hsi-chih (303–361) and Wang Hsien-chih (344–388).[1] As the following "lesson" by Mi Fu demonstrates (fig. 1), the glories of Chin cursive calligraphy were established in distinct contrast to that of the T'ang dynasty (618–907), or more accurately, T'ang dynasty cursive calligraphy that followed the innovations of Chang Hsü (ca. 700–750):

> If one's cursive calligraphy does not partake of the character of Chin writers, it then becomes a work of the lowest category. Crazy Chang, that vulgar fellow, altered and confused the ancient methods, inciting the common masses [to rise up and follow his lead]. There were a few who comprehended. Huai-su [ca. 735–ca. 799] somewhat added *p'ing-*

Figure 1
Mi Fu (1052–1107/08). *The Sage of Cursive Calligraphy*, Northern Sung dynasty (960–1127), ca. 1097–99. Album leaf, ink on paper, 24.7 x 37 cm. National Palace Museum, Taipei.

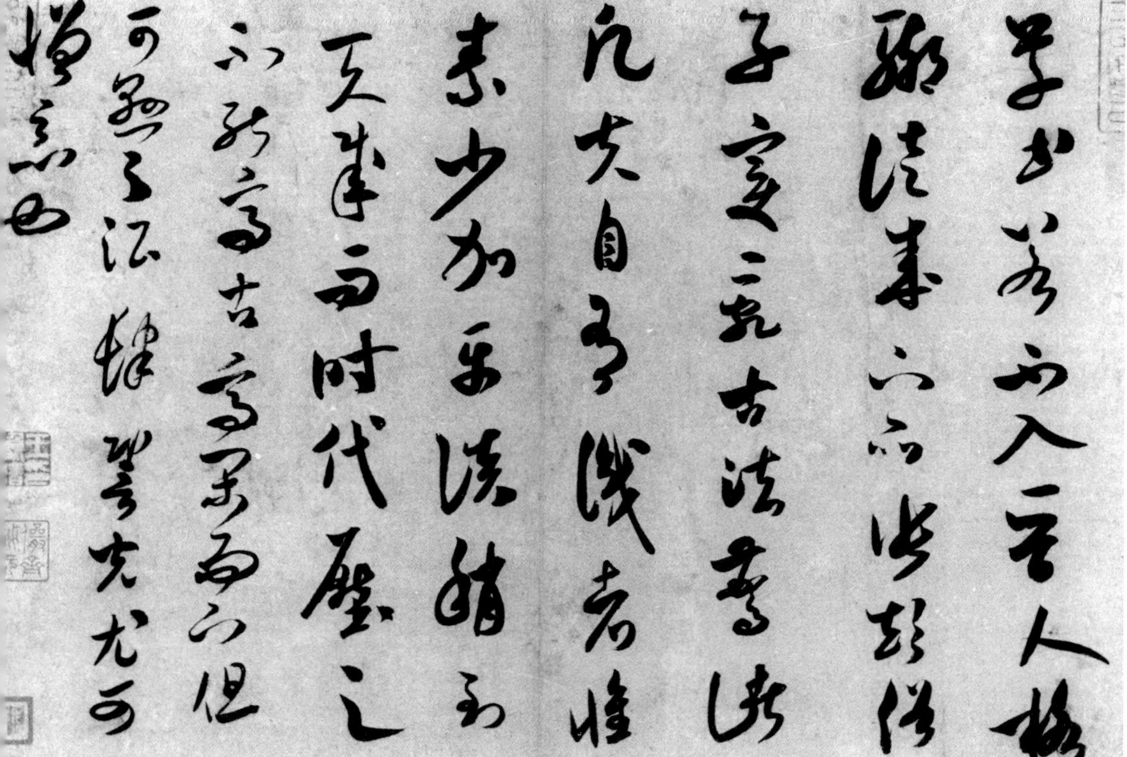

> *tan* [the even and light], and to a slight degree reached a level of naturalness. But the times were against him and he was unable to achieve "lofty antiquity." Kao-hsien [act. early 9th century] and those below him can be hung in wineshops. Pien-kuang is especially detestable.[2]

There are two fundamental movements recognized in the cursive-script tradition. The first occurred around the fourth century and the milieu of Wang Hsi-chih with the development of what was then called modern cursive (*chin-ts'ao*), so named to distinguish this new form of writing from the now archaic draft-cursive calligraphy practiced by earlier writers. The second movement took place in the eighth century and is credited almost exclusively to Chang Hsü. Chang's transformation of cursive calligraphy centered on the increase of both energy and speed to the writing, oftentimes exaggerating the characters to the point of near illegibility. T'ang dynasty tracing copies of cursive calligraphy attributed to Wang Hsi-chih today suggest that "modern cursive," when it first appeared, was richly varied, spontaneous to a degree, and far from predictable. Nonetheless, by the early T'ang, Wang's style of writing had been mandated as orthodox, resulting in a high degree of control, restraint, and decorum.[3] This made Chang Hsü's experimentation in "wild cursive" (*k'uang-ts'ao*) extraordinarily distinctive if not revolutionary.[4] Huai-su, Kao-hsien, and Pien-kuang were all Buddhist monks famous for the practice of Chang Hsü's manner of wild-cursive script.

The ideas Mi Fu expresses in *The Sage of Cursive Calligraphy*, as this writing is now titled, also appear in a poem Mi Fu sent to Hsüeh Shao-p'eng probably about the time this calligraphy was written. The poem was spurred by Hsüeh's declaration of having purchased a work by Wang Hsi-chih:

> Ou's strangeness and Ch'u's charm were not self-reliant,
> Able still to half leap back to the rules of ancient writers.
> Kung-ch'üan, ugly and weird, ancestor to horrid writing,
> From this time forward the ancient methods disappeared without a trace.
> Crazy Chang's crime, more or less the same as Liu's:
> He incited vulgar fellows to give rise to utter chaos.
> Huai-su, that southern cur, showed a little understanding;
> Diligently he chased after the "even and light," like a doctor who is blind.[5]

The theme is the degeneration of art over time, the falling away from a classical ideal that was largely personified by Wang Hsi-chih. The early T'ang dynasty calligraphers Ou-yang Hsün (557–641) and Ch'u Sui-liang (596–658), despite their strong stylistic differences, were both understood by Northern Sung critics as having developed out of the Chin tradition. With Liu Kung-ch'üan (778–865), active two centuries later, all ties to the past had come unstrung. Here, Mi Fu must be referring primarily to the *k'ai* (standard) script, for which all three of these T'ang calligraphers were famous. Liu Kung-ch'üan's writing was, by Mi Fu's standards, excessively mannered—an exaggeration of "bones and muscle."[6] The calligraphy of those who followed was even worse—"horrid writing," as Mi Fu calls it. Liu's counterpart in cursive calligraphy was Chang Hsü, whose exciting new form of writing was quickly imitated. In place of a distant but focused view of the Chin tradition there was the "utter chaos" of wild cursive. Huai-su earns qualified praise as a bit of an exception, but his search for the "even and light" is never fully realized, swept away by the popularity of this slick new manner of writing. Chang Hsü's share of blame actually extends beyond the cursive tradition. Elsewhere, Mi Fu makes it clear that Liu Kung-ch'üan's mannerisms were strongly influenced by the great T'ang dynasty statesman-calligrapher Yen Chen-ch'ing (709–785). And Yen, in turn, had been influenced by Chang Hsü, who, Mi Fu tells us, had taught Yen Chen-ch'ing to manipulate unnaturally the structures of his characters using "methods *not* of antiquity."[7]

Mi Fu's historical view of calligraphy's degeneration over time, culminating in the parallel "crimes" committed by Liu Kung-ch'üan and Chang Hsü, may not have been entirely his own. A poem by Su Shih originally inscribed for some unspecified cursive calligraphy by Wang Hsi-chih pronounces the same view of Chang Hsü's writing. The Ch'ing dynasty (1644–1912) editors of Su Shih's poetry place this verse in 1085, more than a decade earlier than Mi Fu's "The Sage of Cursive of Calligraphy":

> Crazy Chang and Drunken Su [Huai-su], those two hairless fellows,
> Chased shamelessly after the public fancy and called their calligraphy
> skillful.
> Even in their dreams they could not have laid eyes upon Wang
> [Hsi-chih] and Chung [Yu],
> Foolishly adorning themselves with powder and jewels to cheat the
> deaf and blind.
> Like a street trollop smearing herself with red and blue [makeup],
> [Performing] a bewitching song and seductive dance to dazzle the
> eyes of youngsters.
> The lady of the Hsieh clan adorned herself but lightly,
> Untrammeled, she naturally possessed the air of one who sits in the grove.
> Heaven's Gate, in the vast expanse, is startled by a bounding dragon,
> And the flying bird leaving the woods is swept away clean.
> In order to write cursive for you, Sir, picking up where they left off,
> You will have to wait for another day, when I am not quite so hurried.[8]

In Su Shih's poem, the two most prominent practitioners of wild-cursive calligraphy during the T'ang period, Chang Hsü and Huai-su, are contrasted with the two most notable figures in the calligraphy of the Three Kingdoms and the Chin, Wang Hsi-chih and Chung Yu (151–230). The former are likened to cheap sing-song girls, the latter to a fourth-century paragon of gentle feminine charm, Hsieh Tao-yün (Wang Hsi-chih's daughter-in-law).[9] The fanciful metaphors for cursive calligraphy toward the end of Su Shih's poem refer specifically to earlier critiques of Wang's and Chang's writing, with the former, again, coming out on top. Su Shih's last line is particularly curious. He turns around the well-known story of how the Han dynasty calligrapher Chang Chih often signed his hastily written notes with the apology, "Busy, busy, no time, cursively written." One of Su Shih's commentators states that this is because Su Shih chose to write this poem in either standard or running script (more likely the latter), but there is more to this reversal, as we will see at a later point in this article.

Su Shih's poem and Mi Fu's various writings establish one view of Chang Hsü and the cursive tradition — a negative perspective that laments the loss of Chin classical standards with the advent of wild-cursive writing. There was also current, however, a slightly different viewpoint, in which Chang Hsü is seen in a more positive light. The key proponent of this view was Huang T'ing-chien, though it is also evident in the following excerpt from a comment by Su Shih:

> The cursive calligraphy of Chang Ch'ang-shih [Chang Hsü] is drunken and naturally unrestrained. Dots and strokes are scattered about, yet the ideas are self-sufficient. This is what is called divine untrammeledness.

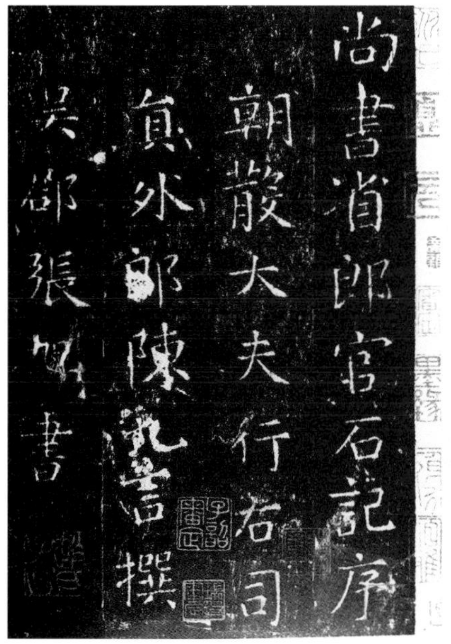

Figure 2
Chang Hsü (ca. 700–750). Detail of *Record of the Lang-kuan Stone*, T'ang dynasty (618–907), 741. Ink rubbing on paper. From *Chung-kuo mei-shu ch'üan-chi, Shu-fa chüan-k'o pien* (Peking: Jen-min mei-shu ch'u-pan-she, 1986), v. 3, 120.

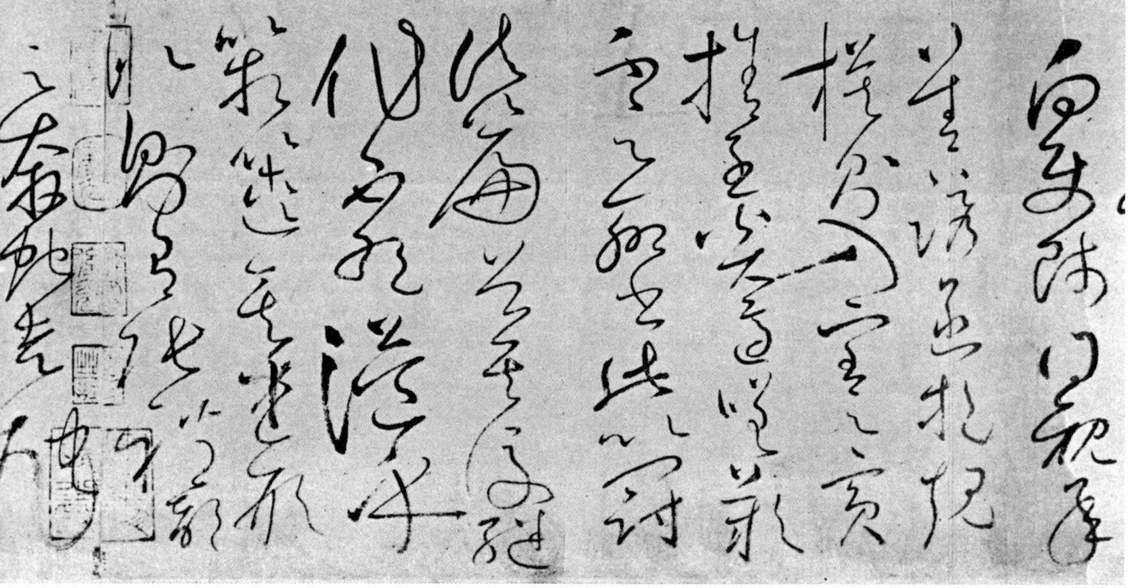

Figure 3
Huai-su (ca. 735–ca. 799). Detail of *Autobiographical Essay*, T'ang dynasty (618–907), 777. Handscroll, ink on paper, 28.2 x 755 cm. National Palace Museum, Taipei. From *Shoseki meihin sōkan* series, v. 27 (Tokyo: Nigensha, 1989), 3.

> Those who today are called excellent at cursive script oftentimes are incapable of writing the standard and running. This is a great absurdity. Standard calligraphy gives rise to the running, which in turn gives rise to the cursive. The standard script can be likened to standing, the running script to walking, and the cursive to running. There's never been anyone who could run without first learning how to stand and walk. Today in Ch'ang-an one still finds the standard-style calligraphy of Chang Hsü titled "Record of the Lang-kuan Stone Pillar." The characters are simple and distant, like the calligraphy of someone of the Chin or [Liu] Sung dynasties.[10]

Extant rubbings of the Chang Hsü calligraphy to which Su Shih refers, "Record of the Lang-kuan Stone" (fig. 2),[11] reveal generous, open structures in the character compositions — what Su Shih describes as simple and distant. This was an important characteristic of pre-T'ang calligraphy in the eyes of Northern Sung critics. Huang T'ing-chien went so far in his praise of this particular piece of writing as to call it peerless among all standard-script writing of the T'ang dynasty — a remarkable statement given the number of renowned *k'ai-shu* specialists active in the seventh and eighth centuries.[12] We quickly ascertain the importance of "Record of the Lang-kuan Stone." It validated Chang Hsü's unconventional cursive because it proved that Chang was steeped in rules and methods. One might carry further Su Shih's analogy of scripts to human motor skills by likening the wild cursive to a hop, skip, and jump. "Record of the Lang-kuan Stone" proved that Chang's gymnastics were no illusion.

This, however, was precisely the problem with those who followed Chang Hsü. Huang T'ing-chien described *The Thousand Character Essay* (*Ch'ien-tzu wen*) attributed to Chang Hsü as "strange and untrammeled," "thoroughly original," but ultimately fake. He goes on to say that there were many such fakes, all borrowing Chang's famous name: "Lord Chang's manner and character were off-beat and untrammeled, [but] each of the characters of his calligraphy entered rules and methods." Imitators, in contrast, often had no idea what they were even imitating. Huang T'ing-chien prided himself on his ability to spot such fakes after he himself "somewhat awakened" to the secrets of cursive calligraphy.[13]

In many ways, the retrospective view of the cursive tradition is unified among the late Northern Sung critics. Mi Fu, Su Shih, and Huang T'ing-chien, for example, all are in agreement that the cursive script, and wild cursive in particular, degenerated over time, and the strongest words of condemnation are always reserved for those who followed Chang Hsü. What differs is the perception of Chang Hsü himself. Mi Fu views him as "vulgar" ("one who confused and altered the ancient methods.") Huang

Figure 4
Huang T'ing-chien (1045–1105). Detail of *Sayings of a Ch'an Buddhist Monk* (*Chu-shang-tso*), Northern Sung dynasty (960–1127). Handscroll, ink on paper, 33 x 729.5 cm. Palace Museum, Peking. From *Chung-kuo mei-shu ch'üan-chi, Shu-fa chüan-k'o pien* (Peking: Jen-min mei-shu ch'u-pan-she, 1986), v. 4, 38.

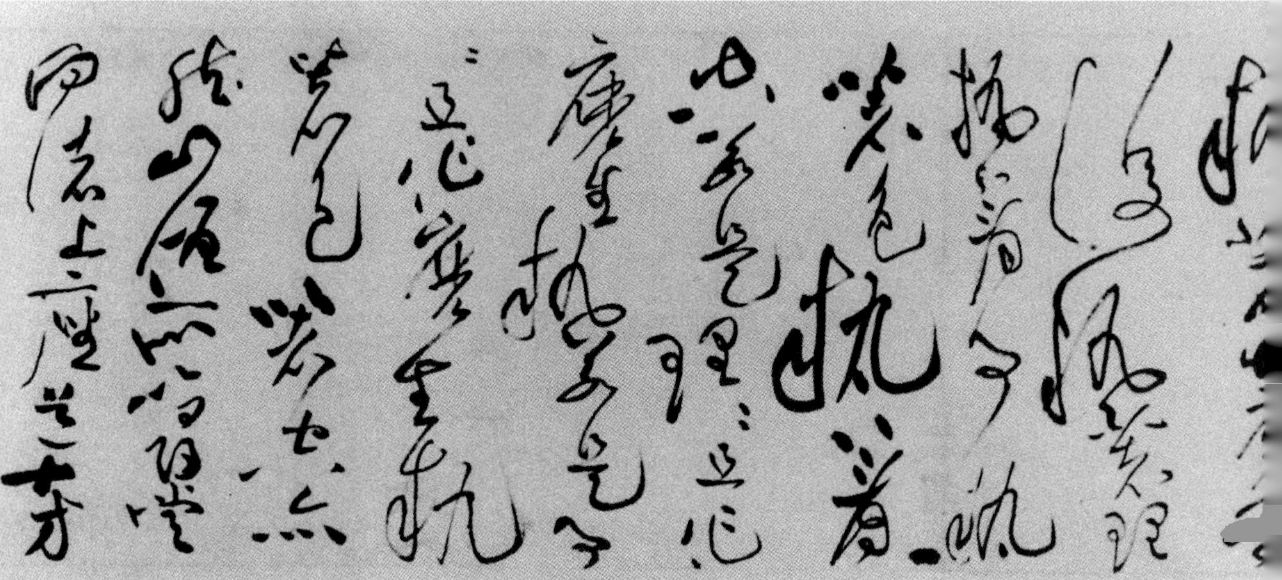

T'ing-chien, in contrast, saw the methods of the Two Wangs in Chang Hsü's genuine writing.[14] In another inscription, Huang even suggests that Chang Hsü's inspiration came from viewing the archaic seal-script writing found in the bronze vessels of great antiquity, and thus "the Sage of Cursive [Chang] held his own against the General of the Right [Wang Hsi-chih], father and son."[15] Far from confusing the ancient methods, Huang T'ing-chien promoted Chang Hsü as their enlightened master.

Wine and Calligraphy

If reliable examples of Chang Hsü's cursive calligraphy were extant one could accept Huang T'ing-chien's challenge to find the "rules and methods" in Chang's wild cursive, though one suspects it would be a highly interpretive exercise. With Huai-su, the visual record is slightly more promising, but problems exist here as well. The renowned *Autobiographical Essay* of 777 (fig. 3), despite its privileged status as one of the supreme representatives of the essence of Chinese art, is considered by some connoisseurs to be a copy of undetermined value.[16] Another piece of writing attributed to Huai-su, *Bitter Bamboo Shoots* (*K'u-sun t'ieh*), in the Shanghai Museum, may be more convincing as a genuine work from the monk's hand, but the writing is limited to only two lines and a handful of characters. In any case, the goal of this essay is not to analyze the fine balance between propriety and chaos that the Northern Sung critics may have read into these earlier masters' cursive writing, but to recognize the importance of this issue in the eleventh century and utilize it to understand developments in the cursive-script tradition.[17] The key figure is Huang T'ing-chien: the only true heir to Chang Hsü's innovations among the late Northern Sung individualists well represented today by extant writing (figs. 4, 5). First, however, it is instructive to take a closer look at exactly how Chang Hsü and his followers were perceived.

The inspiration for Chang Hsü's wild-cursive calligraphy is commonly attributed to two general sources: wine and phenomena of the physical world. The two are distinct from one another but not mutually exclusive. The latter, which include porters struggling on a road balancing heavy loads and the famed sword dance of Lady Kung-sun, ties into a longstanding tradition in calligraphy of recognizing the forces that enliven calligraphy as fundamentally the same as those found in nature. Although this connection was made for all forms of calligraphy, there is no question that the unbridled nature of the wild-cursive script made its link to physical phenomena particularly pronounced in viewers' eyes. Yet, it is wine that establishes the primary association with Chang Hsü and his art. The connection already is noted in the calligrapher's own time. One of Tu Fu's (712–770) more famous poems, "Song of the Eight Immortals of the Wine Cup," makes a direct connection between Chang's drinking and writing:

> Chang Hsü, three cups, and the art of the cursive sage is passed on,
> Doffing hat and revealing his head amidst kings and lieges,
> Wielded brush descends to paper like clouds and mist.[18]

We can supplement this with early descriptions of Chang Hsü amidst his cups, shouting and running about wildly, splashing the ink "so that endless transformations emerged, as if aided by a spirit." As a commentator to Tu Fu's poem notes, Chang's revealed head signaled extreme unrestraint. Perhaps Tu Fu is alluding to reports of Chang Hsü literally dipping his head in the ink to write with his hair as well as his brush. Regarding his writing after sobering, Chang himself reportedly subscribed to the "spirit possession" theory.[19]

As the "out of body" explanation for Chang Hsü's wild cursive talents reflects, a common theme in the tales told of the T'ang calligrapher's drunken writing is the effacement of Chang's self—his ego. Pickled to an effective state of un-self-consciousness (if not near-unconsciousness), the calligrapher becomes a medium for forces outside of his control. The writer is the tool, not the source, his brush a conduit for the mysteries of Creation. Huang T'ing-chien wrote, "Chang Hsü's cursive has its moments of transcendence, cut off from the dust. If one has the intention of trying to do this, there is no way to come close."[20] As many of us are aware, alcohol has a way of doing away with those bothersome "intentions," at least temporarily. However, there was more to Chang's drinking and writing than a bottle of Wu-liang-yeh and writing utensils. Chang Hsü was plugging into a longstanding tradition that recognized alcohol as a key component in the idealized lifestyle of the Taoist sage. The Seven Worthies of the Bamboo Grove were particularly known for their wine-imbibing "merry revelry," especially Juan Chi and Liu Ling (fig. 6). The former, who requested to become commandant of infantry only because it offered access to three hundred vats of wine stored in the commissary, was described as "a man beyond the realm of ordinary morality," one who "pays no homage to the rules of propriety" (exemplified by his drunken appearance while in mourning for his mother).[21] The latter, under the influence of wine, would often take off his clothes, "completely free and uninhibited." Only one literary composition by Liu Ling exists today, his "Hymn to the Virtue of Wine." In it, Liu establishes a direct correspondence between wine and the Tao with allusions to the Taoist classics *Tao-te ching* and *Chüang-tzu*. His Great Man knows no bounds:

> There is a Mr. Great Man,
> For whom Heaven and Earth is a single morn,
> And ten thousand epochs but a moment in time.
> Sun and moon are his gate and window,

Figure 5
Huang T'ing-chien (1045–1105). Detail of *Sayings of a Ch'an Buddhist Monk* (*Chu-shang-tso*), Northern Sung dynasty (960–1127). Handscroll, ink on paper, 33 x 729.5 cm. Palace Museum, Peking. From *Chung-kuo mei-shu ch'üan-chi, Shu-fa chüan-k'o pien* (Peking: Jen-min mei-shu ch'u-pan-she, 1986), v. 4, 39.

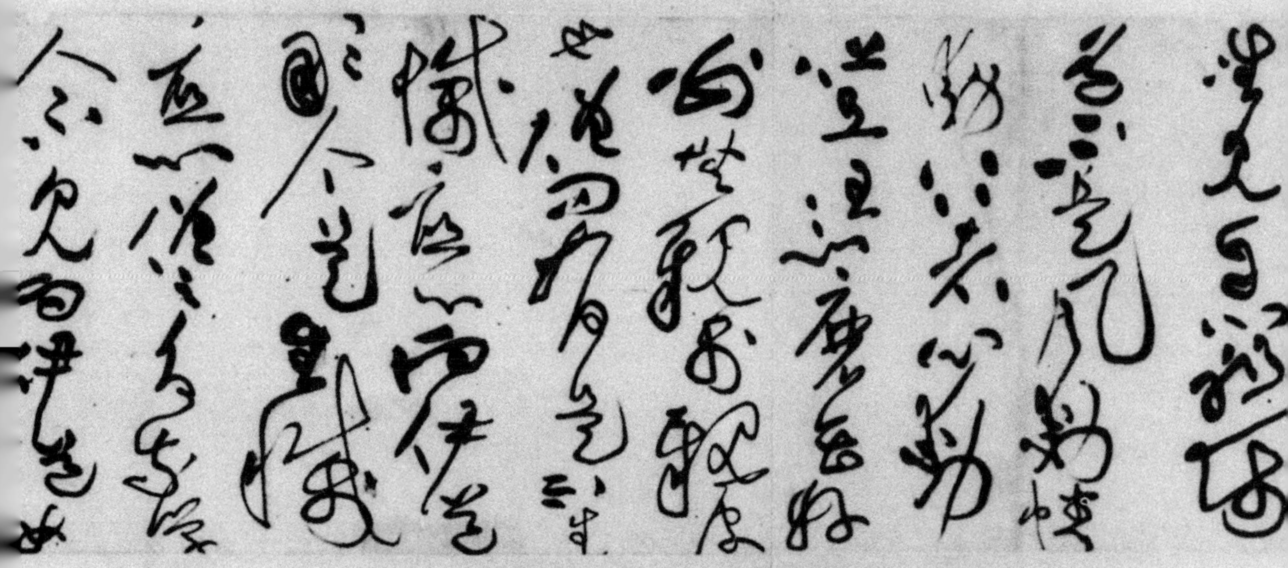

The Eight Tracts of Wilderness his courtyard and street.
He travels without cart tracks
And has no shelter for a dwelling.
Taking Heaven for his canopy
And Earth for his mat,
He lets his mind roam where it may.
Stationary, he grasps goblet and grips beaker,
Moving, he clutches tankard and hoists vat.
Only wine is his concern,
How could he know the rest?

The hymn continues with a confrontation between the great drinker and a prince and gentleman-official, whose array of arguments are met with absolute indifference and more drinking. This is an interesting variation on a common theme found in *Chüang-tzu*—the meeting of the Confucian good citizen, guardian of the rites, with the Taoist sage. The latter, of course, always emerges as superior. Liu Ling's hymn ends by praising intoxication—"No thoughts, no concerns, its bliss a harmonious joy.... Quietly listening, but the sound of thunder goes unheard. Looking carefully, yet the form of Mount T'ai goes unseen. Unaware of cold and hot cutting the flesh, nor the emotions of profit and desire."[22]

As Wolfgang Bauer documents, after the Seven Sages of the Bamboo Grove, the drunken official increasingly became an admired counterculture ideal, whose breaking of social taboos was "the expression of the freedom of genius." The new attitude is best expressed by a change in the description of lands of paradise, with the Taoist Eden of yore turning into the "Land of the Drunk" (*Tsui-hsiang*). The poet and philosopher Wang Chi (585–644) lovingly described this intoxicating realm. It had no shores, nor mountains or cliffs. Its climate was perfectly mild and constant, and the contrasts of light and dark, cold and heat, were unknown. It also possessed people of the highest intellect, who sound remarkably like ethereal immortals, "sipping wind, drinking dew, and abstaining from the Five Cereals." At the end, Wang Chi tells us that the way of life in the Land of the Drunk is like that of the ancient Taoist paradise *Hua-hsü*—"pure and calm."[23]

Judging from the stories told of Chang Hsü's behavior, it is self-evident that his writing of cursive calligraphy was pointedly associated with this popular Taoist tradition of superior man, wine, and paradise. He was its representative, communicating through his calligraphy some sense of the freedom that blessed this allegorical land. On the other hand, his writing was not at all characterized by the calm and even state that describes the Land of the Drunk, at least if late Northern Sung accounts are accurate. These report that Chang Hsü ran about crazily, hooting loudly as he let the

Figure 6 (left)
Liu Ling with his wine, one of the "Seven Sages of the Bamboo Grove," Six Dynasties period (222–589), 5th century. Rubbing of a detail of a multiple-brick tomb mural, Hsi-shan-ch'iao, Nanking. From *Chung-kuo mei-shu ch'üan-chi, Hui-hua pien* (Peking: Jen-min mei-shu ch'u-pan-she, 1986), v. 1, 144.

Figure 7 (right)
Unidentified artist. Detail of *Water Wheel at the Sluice Gate*, Northern Sung dynasty (960–1127), ca. 975–1000. Handscroll, ink and light color on silk. Shanghai Museum. From *I-yüan to-ying*, no. 2 (1978), 24.

Figure 8
Poems by Yü Hsin [513–581] and Hsieh Ling-yün [385–433], Northern Sung dynasty (960–1127), 11th century. First section of a handscroll, ink on "five-colored" paper, 29.1 x 195.2 cm. Liaoning Provincial Museum. From *Shoseki meihin sōkan* series, v. 168 (Tokyo: Nigensha, 1990), 3.

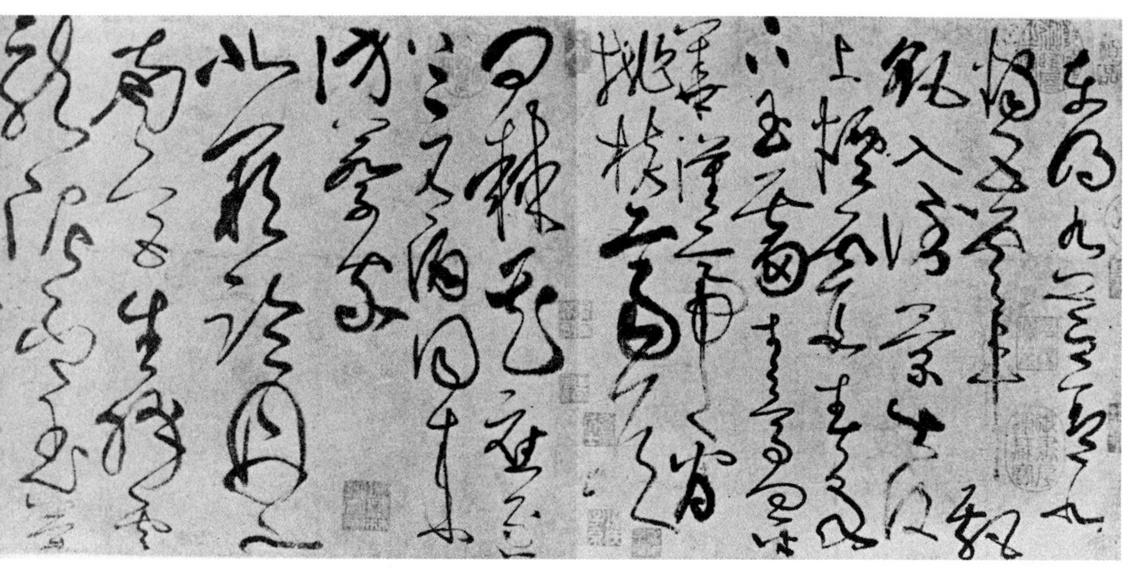

brush descend.[24] After Chang, the association of wine with wild cursive was further strengthened by Huai-su. A number of poems were written by contemporaries celebrating Huai-su's cursive script, some of which were cited by Huai-su himself in the self-promoting *Autobiographical Essay.* Wine, together with madness (*tien*), wildness (*k'uang*), naturalness (*chen*), and the assistance of "ghosts and spirits" are the main motifs of these poems.[25] However, an interesting problem emerges, as demonstrated in the first line of a short verse by Chu K'uei: "Resolved to be novel and unusual, no fixed rules."[26] Huai-su's intention to be wild is baldly stated, hinting that the whole enterprise is contrived. This sits uneasily next to the naturalness that is presumed to color Huai-su's drunken writing.

The popular association of wine and cursive calligraphy during the period of time that separated Chang Hsü and Huai-su from the late Northern Sung is indirectly referred to in Mi Fu's *The Sage of Cursive Calligraphy.* Among the "common masses" which rose in emulation of Chang Hsü's example, Huai-su, Kao-hsien, and Pien-kuang (all monks) were three of the better known wild-cursive writers. Dozens of others vied for the public's attention, and many, no doubt, utilized wine drinking as a part of their performance. Taverns and wineshops decorated their interiors with examples of cursive writing. Mi Fu alludes to this when he insults the wild cursive of Kao-hsien and Pien-kuang as fit to be hung in drinking establishments. Early Northern Sung paintings already reveal this. In the anonymous *Water Wheel at the Sluice Gate* (fig. 7), a hanging scroll of cursive calligraphy is just visible in the entranceway to a tavern. The sign on the outer lattice says "New Wine." Cursive writing also forms a backdrop for two men conversing in a rustic streamside wineshop in *A Solitary Temple amid Clearing Peaks*, attributed to Li Ch'eng (919–967), in the Nelson-Atkins Museum of Art. Such calligraphy was a perfect advertisement for the proprietor—drink our brew and enter the immortal's paradise.

Paradise and immortality are precisely the subject matter of what is certainly one of the finest of extant examples of early wild-cursive writing, *Poems by Yü Hsin [513–581] and Hsieh Ling-yün [385–433]* (figs. 8–10). This anonymous scroll of four transcribed verses, once attributed to Chang Hsü, probably dates to sometime in the early- or mid-eleventh century.[27] Elsewhere I have translated and discussed the first poem of the scroll, Yü Hsin's "The Taoist Master Strolls through the Empyrean"—a wildly imaginative wine-inspired romp through a mythical and magical landscape.[28] The calligraphy possesses a dynamic, electric charge in the tightly wound first seven columns, which is in perfect harmony with the vivid images of the text (fig. 8). The wild movement of the high-flying Master is also conveyed through an emphasis on directional characters, such as *tung* (east), *pei* (north), *nan* (south), *shang* (up), and *hsia* (down), strategically placed at the tops or bottoms of individual columns. The last lines of the poem speak of the search for Lantern Festival Wine.

The two poetic eulogies (*tsan*) of Hsieh Ling-yün present a more sedate picture of immortality. The second of these, the last of the four verses of the scroll, is titled "Beneath a Cliff at Mount Heng, I Meet an Old Man and Four or Five Youths" (fig. 9):

> Herb pickers of Mount Heng
> Have lost their way, provisions at an end.
> We rest, sitting beneath the cliff,
> Facing one another in mutual conversation.
> An old man and four or five youths,
> Could not part from this immortal reclusion.
> Writing such as theirs is not taught in this world.
> Their hearts must be sage and profound.[29]

The immortals of this poem are decidedly more recognizable—hermits who have forsaken the dusty marketplace for spiritual well-being in the mountains. There is little if any drama in this quiet eulogy, and while the writing remains highly dramatic in size and speed, its tenor once again matches the text. The writing here is much looser and flowing. The broadly spaced characters, in contrast to the first poem, are composed so that each poetic line fits into a column (five characters per column). This is maintained until the penultimate line of the verse, where a miswritten character forced a change in the easy-going pattern. No doubt it is for this and the very last line of verse that this particular poem was chosen in the first place. It cements the calligraphy's overall message: this extraordinary writing reflects a world of immortal transcendence.

Poems by Yü Hsin and Hsieh Ling-yün conveniently highlights both the nature of the wild-cursive tradition and its problems. We focus first on the fact that the highly energetic appearance of the writing is misleading. It initially appears contradictory that the wine paradise of Wang Chi's Land of the Drunk emphasizes a land of neither highs nor lows, yet the calligraphy it inspires aims for every possible motion and angle. The fact that Liu Ling similarly paints a picture of drunken bliss as a state of pure equanimity supports Wang Chi's Land of the Drunk as an accurate portrayal of the wine paradise. We must recognize that within the Chinese tradition, at least this particular tradition, drunkenness equals purity—the return to a more natural state of being. The dwellers of the Land of the Drunk are people of the highest intellect—not the bombed alkies one might first imagine. Alcohol, in other words, leads not to degeneration, but rather to transparency and self-effacement. This explains the stories of Chang Hsü's shamanic channeling. Wine obliterates the ego so that he becomes an empty vessel or

Figure 9
Poems by Yü Hsin [513–581] and Hsieh Ling-yün [385–433], Northern Sung dynasty (960–1127), 11th century. Last section of a handscroll, ink on "five-colored" paper, 29.1 x 195.2 cm. Liaoning Provincial Museum. From *Shoseki meihin sōkan* series, v. 168 (Tokyo: Nigensha, 1990), 4.

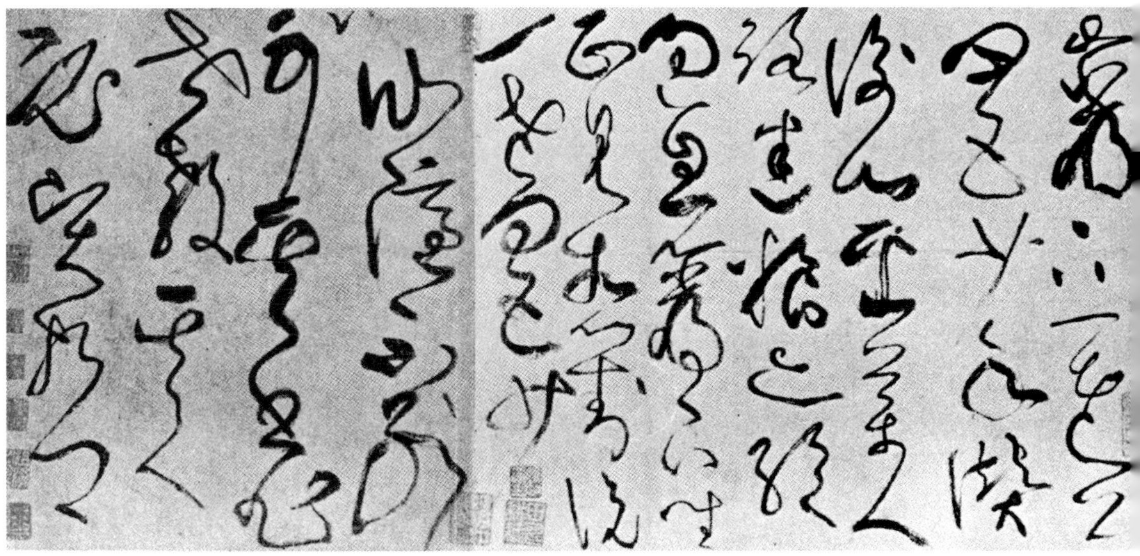

Figure 10
Poems by Yü Hsin [513–581] and Hsieh Ling-yün [385–433], Northern Sung dynasty (960–1127) 11th century. Detail of a handscroll, ink on "five-colored" paper, 29.1 x 195.2 cm. Liaoning Provincial Museum. From *Shoseki meihin sōkan* series, v. 168 (Tokyo: Nigensha, 1990), 12.

tool — that through which creation's powers can flow. Similarly, once wine is seen as a medium through which one is led to a higher state of spiritual understanding, Huai-su's curious position as a guzzling, scribbling mendicant begins to make sense. It is not a coincidence that the most eminent practitioners of the wild-cursive script following Chang Hsü were Buddhist monks.[30] Whether or not they partook of the bottle, they aspired to the same transcendental realm of absolute tranquility that characterizes the topography of the Land of the Drunk. An insightful exchange between Han Yü (768–824) and the wild-cursive calligrapher Kao-hsien highlights this. Han Yü wrote a preface for Kao-hsien in which he interpreted the wide-ranging forms of Chang Hsü's wild cursive as the direct expression of Chang's far-reaching emotions. In Han Yü's opinion it was therefore inappropriate that Kao-hsien, a Buddhist monk and one who by definition should wish to still the heart, also write in such a manner.[31] Two hundred fifty years later, Su Shih wrote a defense on Kao-hsien's behalf, remarking that Han Yü's interpretation of Chang Hsü's art was incorrect. "In quietude," Su Shih writes, "one comprehends the myriad movements. In emptiness one absorbs the ten thousand scenes."[32] In other words, the wild forms of Kao-hsien's calligraphy were but the reflection of the world's boundless phenomena as channeled through the "selfless" monk.

Judging from the comments of Mi Fu, Su Shih, and Huang T'ing-chien, one would expect that the problem of the wild-cursive tradition was largely a matter of excess: wildness for the sake of wildness. However, *Poems by Yü Hsin and Hsieh Ling-yün* suggests that the issue is decidedly more subtle than it sounds. *Poems* is not excessively wild, but it is calculated to appear so. The writing appears dramatic, but in fact, most of it is monotonous in tone — it just happens to be a sustained loud tone. Once one becomes accustomed to the magnitude and speed of the writing one notices that the characters are generally the same in size and dimension. The brushwork is largely unmodulated (in other words, flat) and the habits of brush unchanging. This is particularly evident where the calligrapher abbreviated with a simple zigzag movement (fig. 10). The beginning — more or less corresponding to the first poem by Yü Hsin (lines 1–10) — is more thoughtful, with a visually dynamic display of contraction and expansion, but this section too has a noticeably constrained feeling that is antithetical to the sentiments of freedom the poem seeks to convey. The calculated placement of directional words, as mentioned above, further reflects upon the forced quality of this beginning section. In summary, the calligrapher is open to the criticism of being too calculated and too pretentious in the places where he makes a genuine artistic effort, and too ordinary in the places where he simply lets it flow.

Cursive in an Era of Self-Consciousness

As the debate that circled about Chang Hsü and his influence demonstrates, the cursive script presented a particular set of difficulties to late Northern Sung writers. It remained a much-practiced script form, especially earlier in the Northern Sung with the popularity of Chou Yüeh (act. ca. 1021–48) and Su Shun-ch'in (1008–1048).[33] But as the retrospective view that recognized a general decline in calligraphy leading from the mid-T'ang into the Five Dynasties (907–960) and Sung periods became increasingly current in the third quarter of the eleventh century, it was hard to avoid the negative associations that had accrued to Chang Hsü's particular tradition of wild-cursive writing. One option was to excavate and adopt alternative traditions. This route, followed most notably by Mi Fu and Hsüeh Shao-p'eng, was highly exclusive, as it focused on genuine examples of pre-T'ang writing that were out of the purview of all but the most privileged collectors and connoisseurs. Mi Fu's *The Sage of Cursive Calligraphy* (fig. 1) is representative, commenting in both form and written content on the superiority of Chin dynasty calligraphy. Su Shih too had access to the great collections, but he adamantly refused to follow the route Mi Fu marks in *The Sage of Cursive Calligraphy.* Su's approach to cursive calligraphy was largely personal—familiar with past traditions but more concerned with individual expression. If there is a single theme in his various recorded comments, it is the emphasis on naturalness, or conversely, an absence of premeditation in one's writing. His "Critique of Cursive Calligraphy" makes this clear:

> If at first one does not have the idea to be good in one's calligraphy, then the writing will be good. Although cursive calligraphy matures upon the accumulation of learning, it nonetheless is essential that the writing emerge quickly. The ancients wrote: "Busy, busy, no time, cursively written." But these words are entirely wrong. If [one only writes this way] when "busy, busy, with no time," this means that when not hurried one is trying to write consciously, building upon one's learning. This is the ultimate of mistakes, and it helps to explain why Chou Yüeh's and Chung I's [cursive calligraphy] appear as they do. Although my calligraphy is not particularly good, it displays new ideas on its own, without copying the ancients. It is simply an inspired flash.[34]

Here Chou Yüeh and Chung I (another early Northern Sung cursive calligrapher of repute) are criticized not for the phony imitation of wildness that Su Shih, Mi Fu, and Huang T'ing-chien aimed at Chang Hsü's followers, but for just the opposite: not being enough like Chang Hsü. They are too concerned with being artful and consequently are unable to achieve the freedom that Su Shih here associates with speed in writing.

As they were for Chang Hsü, speed, naturalness, and wine are the paramount ingredients in Su Shih's formula for inspired cursive. With Su Shih, however, there exists a more detailed record of the mix of alcohol and art, and what we find is both interesting and curious.[35] Su Shih was very much a social drinker, but he was also a light drinker. He once wrote that among poor drinkers—those who could not hold their liquor—no one was beneath him, yet no one enjoyed drinking more than he, especially in gatherings.[36] In another passage, Su Shih describes his limitations:

> I drink extremely little, frequently gaining pleasure from just holding the goblet. Oftentimes I will suddenly fall asleep sitting. Those who see me think that I am drunk. But then I will awaken, so that people cannot tell whether I am drunk or sober.[37]

Huang T'ing-chien provides a view from the outside:

> By nature [Su Shih] liked wine, but he couldn't go four or five cups without getting thoroughly plastered. Without excusing himself, he would just keel right over, snoring away like rumbling thunder. In a short while he would then awaken, and his brush would descend like wind and rain. Even though he would just be fooling around, [his calligraphy] would all have the quality of genuineness. Truly, this is some kind of divine immortal. How could he be compared with today's scholars?[38]

Su Shih confirms the positive effects of wine on his cursive writing: "After getting drunk, I immediately write dozens of lines of cursive calligraphy, feeling that the essence of the wine erupts through my ten fingers."[39] Elsewhere Su Shih specifies that it is large-sized cursive calligraphy that he particularly excelled at under the influence of the bottle. He continues with the observation that, strange as it may seem, he also seemed to be quite good at writing small-sized standard script when under the influence of wine.[40] Actually, considering what we know of Su Shih's drinking habits perhaps it is not so strange. One or two shots and he seems to have passed out, but only briefly. It was enough alcohol to loosen him up, but not so much as to impair his motor skills, hence his success with the small-sized standard script, which demands great control. Interestingly, Su Shih was not entirely happy about his alcoholic triumphs with the brush:

> Chang Ch'ang-shih [Hsü] always needed to get drunk in order to write cursive calligraphy. Perhaps some consider this strange, but when sober Chang's naturalness [*t'ien-chen*] was not whole. This distinction of being drunk and sober is what kept Chang Hsü from entering the divine realm. I-shao [Wang Hsi-chih], for example, never had to rely upon wine. [Unfortunately], I too cannot avoid the fact [that wine improves my cursive].[41]

Figure 11
Su Shih (1037–1101). *Plum Blossoms*, Northern Sung dynasty (960–1127), 1079. Rubbing in *Hsi-lou Su-t'ieh*. From *Chung-kuo shu-fa ch'üan-chi* (Peking: Jung-pao-chai, 1991), v. 33, 128–29.

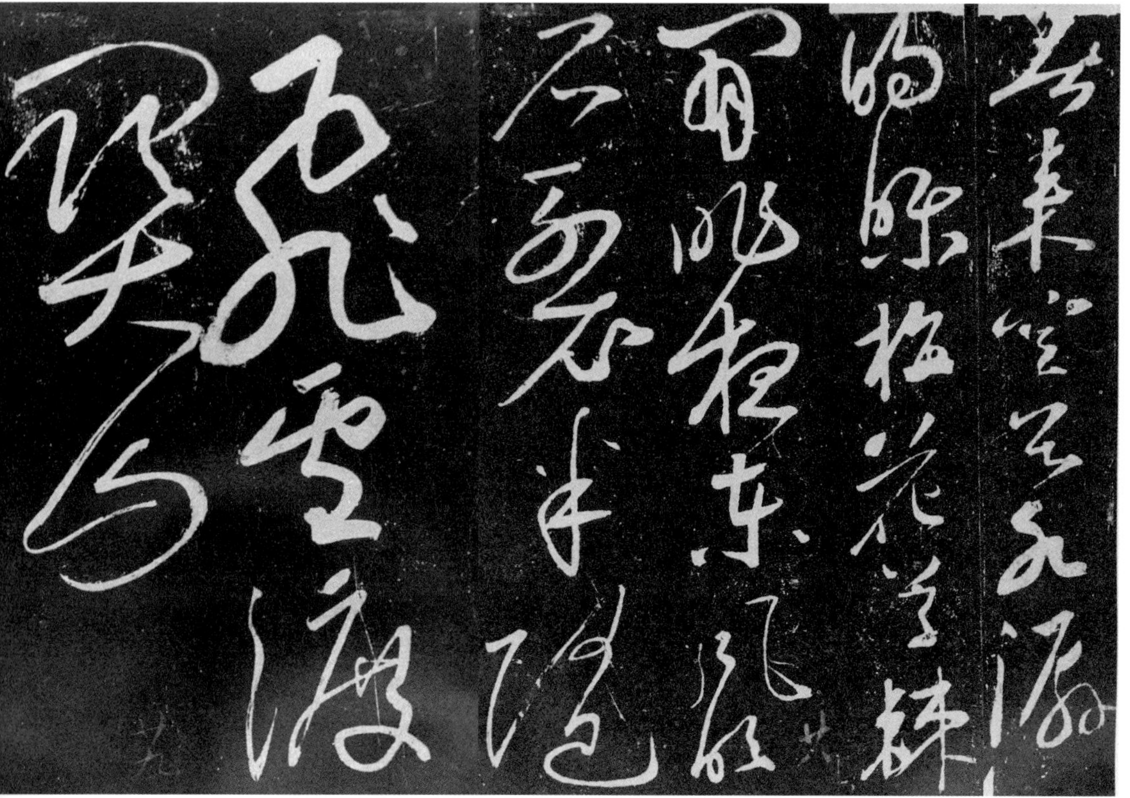

This passage reminds us of the late Northern Sung preoccupation with the paramount value of naturalness in expression. Wine, at its best, allows the attainment of naturalness, the effacement of the cognitive processes that muddy the realization of the Tao in brush and ink. But how much better, Su Shih suggests, if one can attain this rarefied state without the assistance of inebriation? One senses here an innate distrust and distaste of true alcoholic abandon, and with it an important departure from the tradition of wine and creativity as passed down from Chang Hsü. Certainly, as the guardians of the state, responsible literati like Su Shih could not afford to indulge in the kind of bacchanalian excesses that characterized the behavior and even official careers of such legends of the wine cup as Liu Ling and Juan Chi. Sober propriety is very much the tone of at least one early commentator of Su Shih's record of experiences with wine. Adding to Su Shih's admittance to gaining satisfaction from just drinking a minimal amount, Fei Kun (13th century) writes, "Although Tung-p'o [Su Shih] was not able to drink much, he deeply understood the marvels of wine. The men of Chin truly did not understand such pleasure. Sousing their heads and pickling their bodies, crazily keeling over and wildly losing their way, conversely, they became enchained [by their addiction]."[42]

Another important reason to suspect that Su Shih's experiences with wine and cursive calligraphy were something fundamentally different from those of Chang Hsü is the simple fact that practically no exuberant cursive calligraphy from the hand of Su Shih is extant today. In fact, the one piece of writing that might qualify is precisely the last thing one would expect (fig. 11). This is a short poem Su Shih wrote bewailing falling plum blossoms he encountered in the wilderness on his way to his first exile at Huang-chou in 1079, intending that his own pitiful situation be likened to that of the soon-to-be-sullied blossoms:

> Spring comes to the hidden valley, the stream gurgles along,
> Bright plum blossoms stand amid wild grasses and brambles.
> As the east wind howls all night, splitting boulders apart,
> Half the blossoms follow the flying snow across Barrier Mountain.[43]

This is Su Shih's highly self-conscious re-enforcement of the old adage spoken by Han Yü for the hard-luck poet Meng Chiao (751–814) that one sounds forth from a state of disequilibrium.[44] In graphic terms, it translates into the transformation of Su Shih's customary running style into wild-cursive script, as the poem reaches a growing crescendo of raw emotion. Wine, one presumes, had nothing to do with the writing of this calligraphy, but what is really surprising is how this equation of emotion and wild cursive contradicts what Su Shih wrote in defense of Kao-hsien's calligraphy.

No doubt, on occasion Su Shih wrote cursive calligraphy under the influence of alcohol, but perhaps it was in extremely casual and infrequent circumstances. The absence of any such writing today suggests that Su Shih did not favor the cursive script and that he rarely practiced it. In contrast, there are a number of attributions to Huang T'ing-chien, even though his total sum of extant writings is considerably less than that of Su Shih.[45] Huang T'ing-chien's status as a serious practitioner of wild-cursive calligraphy is also evident from his recorded comments on this script. In one he bemoans recent writers' loss of ancient methods in cursive, claiming that during the past several hundred years only three have understood the art: Chang Hsü, Huai-su, and himself.[46] This specific lineage of three cursive calligraphers bridging antiquity to the Northern Sung is reiterated in a number of Huang T'ing-chien's comments. He describes Chang Hsü and Huai-su in glowing terms, with Chang's calligraphy "marvelous with plump brushstrokes," and Huai-su's "marvelous with slender brushstrokes" (the former being the more difficult to attain).[47] Huang T'ing-chien then proudly establishes himself as one of the few true connoisseurs of this style of writing, having himself attained the secrets of cursive in his middle years. Huang credits his practice of cursive for his ability to spot Chang Hsü fakes.[48]

Significantly, although Huang T'ing-chien comments upon the wildness in Chang Hsü's cursive, he avoids the traditional association of Chang's calligraphy with wine. Huang describes Chang Hsü's manner and person as "crazed and untrammeled" (*tien-i*), and his calligraphy as "transcending boundaries, in a realm unsullied by dust."[49] But alcohol would seem to play an insignificant role in Chang's wild cursive for Huang T'ing-chien, who would prefer to see Chang's extraordinary writing as the fruit of the T'ang calligrapher's knowledge and understanding of the ways of antiquity combined with his untrammeled personality. As mentioned earlier, more than anything, Huang noted the "propriety" that underlies Chang Hsü's writing. This is a very distinctive view of the earlier calligrapher, one that no doubt reflects as much about Huang T'ing-chien's approach to writing cursive as it does about Chang Hsü.

Huang T'ing-chien may not have been much of a drinker, at least of alcohol. Considering the number of poems written on the subject of tea, it is possible that he preferred a pot of Lung-ching as part of his preparation for writing calligraphy. Tea, in any case, sounds more like the appropriate beverage for what Huang T'ing-chien describes as the preferred circumstances for writing cursive:

> In the *chia-shu* year of the Shao-sheng reign [1094], at Yellow Dragon Mountain, I suddenly awakened to the secrets of cursive calligraphy. I felt that my writing in the past had revealed too much of the tip of the brush. With a bright window and immaculate table, brush and ink of

excellent quality, I can write a thousand characters without tiring. But such an occasion is hard to come by.[50]

Huang T'ing-chien's ideal working environment is a model of reduction. With only the bare essentials, the artist can concentrate on the task at hand, free of outward distractions. Under such preferred circumstances, the calligrapher finds the stamina to write hundreds of characters. Yet, what this statement implies is that under normal circumstances the writing of cursive is fundamentally taxing. Huang's techniques for writing suggest the same. The fingers grasp the brush with extreme strength. One applies full energy to each stroke (*pi-chung yung-li*) in a process of "seizing and releasing" (*ch'in-tsung*) so that a sense of substantiality is conveyed in accordance with the ancients.[51] "The heart must be entirely focused; this is the essential path to 'entering the spirit.'"[52] These principles may be drawn from comments directed primarily at Huang T'ing-chien's standard and running writing, but it is precisely my argument that Huang is consciously amending the "running" cursive tradition by applying the foundation learned in these "standing" and "walking" scripts. The fact that he finds it desirable to rein in the brushtip, which would result in a more concentrated, slower pace of writing, further supports this idea. Huang T'ing-chien transforms a tradition of writing that had become synonymous with drunken, unfettered ease and public exhibitionism into an intensely meditative practice. The association with Ch'an is made by Huang himself: "In my use of the brush [referring to his older, inferior writing], I did not understand seizing and releasing, and hence there was no 'brush' in the characters. In each character there must be brush, just as there exists the 'eye' in Ch'an sayings. This is hard to explain to those who fail to comprehend deeply the teachings of the patriarchs."[53]

A number of excellent scrolls of Huang T'ing-chien's cursive calligraphy are extant, but certainly the most extraordinary—and the benchmark by which all others are measured—is *Sayings of a Ch'an Buddhist Monk* (*Chu-shang-tso*), in the Palace Museum, Peking (figs. 4, 5).[54] Huang T'ing-chien pronounces his own satisfaction with the calligraphy, stating in his trailing inscription that the writing was done "by a bright window on an immaculate table." The writing is a transcription of the dictums of Wen-i, the Five Dynasties founder of the Fa-yen sect. Appropriately, given its Buddhist content, since at least the seventeenth century *Sayings of a Ch'an Buddhist Monk* has been associated with the style of Huai-su.[55]

Huai-su's *Autobiographical Essay* (fig. 12) is characterized by a fluidly moving line of relatively even modulation. The narrowness of the calligrapher's brush and the nearly constant exposure of the brush tip add to the writing's sense of ease and speed. In places, particularly towards the end of the scroll, characters expand dramatically in size, but the calligraphy remains smooth and even. Huang T'ing-chien's writing (fig. 13) is also characterized by speed, and his characters also vary dramatically in size, but too much attention goes into the compositions of individual characters to allow for the fluidity of *Autobiographical Essay*. The complexity of the brushwork, which is magnificently varied, also demands a slower appreciation of the calligraphy. Huang emphasized the importance of generating tension in calligraphy; he claims to have finally learned how to make his "crooked and bent" strokes come together in a meaningful way after watching old boatmen pull on the oars and hawsers. The brush, he says, was finally able to catch up with his ideas.[56]

No doubt reflecting on the problem posed by the many eager followers of Chang Hsü's tradition of writing wild-cursive calligraphy, Huang T'ing-chien remarked that Chang's quality of transcendence was not something that could be consciously imitated. Inspiration has to come from within for the calligraphy to be natural. This meditative, inward orientation ultimately results in a strong bond between Huang T'ing-chien's cursive and his standard and running writing, as the artist reacts to what he knows as opposed to what he perceives. Introspection replaces outward channeling, and the myriad phenomena to be expressed in one's writing must now be found within. The great achievement of Huang T'ing-chien's cursive calligraphy, and *Sayings of a Ch'an Monk* in particular, is precisely this ability to convey images of an interior world every bit as compelling as what may exist outside of the artist. The complexity of his character compositions, the quirky, personal touches of construction and brushwork, the tensions generated between strokes and characters — what Huang T'ing-chien refers to as *yün*, resonance — all contribute to the creation of a richly pictorial tableau, a landscape of the mind.

Huang T'ing-chien, self-proclaimed heir to Chang Hsü's and Huai-su's tradition of drunken cursive, wrote cursive without the drink. Potent potables, of course, remain an enduring element in the Chinese artistic tradition, but an important transformation had now taken place. In medieval China drunkenness symbolized naturalness, the cleansing that allows the freedom to express and interpret the exterior world. The self-conscious efforts of the late Northern Sung individualist calligraphers to explore naturalness demanded a reassessment of wine's relationship to creativity. Their practice may not have debunked entirely the value of wine in art, but it did highlight the fact that as long as naturalness was a consciously determined goal in art, more often than not creativity's sources would be found within rather than from without. Huang T'ing-chien's cursive proves that such an inward turn was far from limiting, that the brush can move just as freely in the spaces projected by the mind.

Figure 12
Huai-su (ca. 735–ca. 799). Detail of *Autobiographical Essay*, T'ang dynasty (618–907), 777. Handscroll, ink on paper, 28.2 x 755 cm. National Palace Museum, Taipei. From *Shoseki meihin sōkan* series, v. 27 (Tokyo: Nigensha, 1989), 25.

Figure 13
Huang T'ing-chien (1045–1105), Detail of *Sayings of a Ch'an Buddhist Monk*, (*Chu-shang-tso*), Northern Sung dynasty (960–1127). Handscroll, ink on paper, 3 x 729.5 cm. Palace Museum, Peking. From *Chung-hua wu-ch'ien nien wen-wu chi-k'an, Fa-shu pien* (Taipei: Chung-kuo wu-ch'ien nien wen-wu chi-k'an pien-chi wei-yüan-hui, 1985) v. 2, 72.

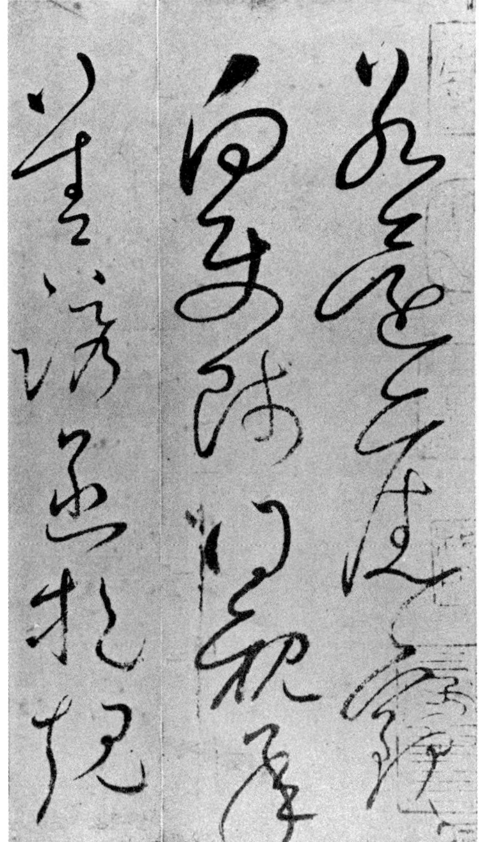

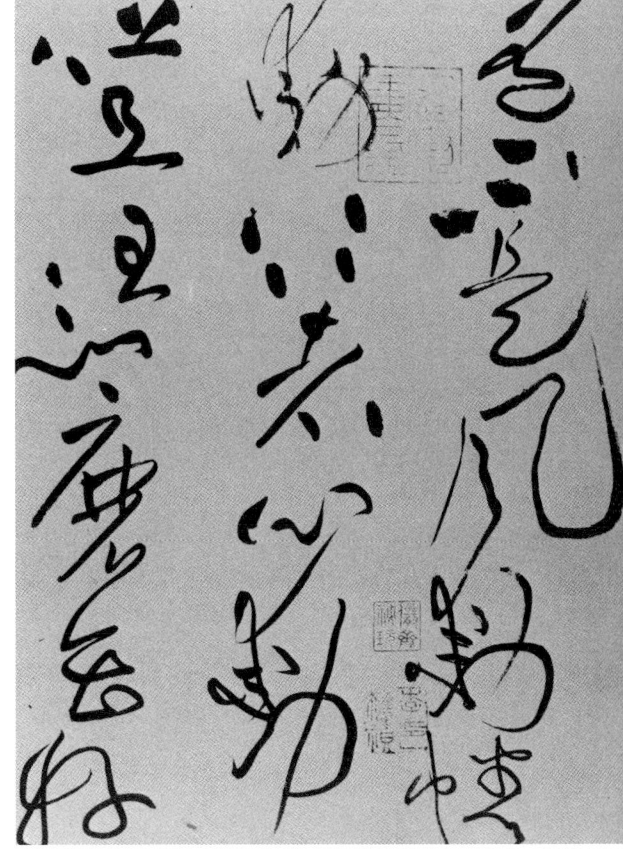

1 The classic study of Mi Fu and Chin calligraphy is Lothar Ledderose, *Mi Fu and the Classical Tradition of Chinese Calligraphy* (Princeton: Princeton University Press, 1979). For other aspects of Mi Fu as a calligrapher see my *Mi Fu: Style and the Art of Calligraphy in Northern Song China* (New Haven: Yale University Press, 1997). Relatively little is known of Hsüeh Shao-p'eng, and certainly less would be known if not for his close friendship with Mi Fu. Descended from a line of prominent officials, he was the son of Hsüeh Hsiang, and, according to T'ao Tsung-i, called himself a descendant of the "three phoenixes of Ho-tung" — Hsüeh Yüan-ching, Hsüeh Shou, and Hsüeh Te-yin — well-known figures of the early T'ang. T'ao Tsung-i, *Shu-shih hui-yao* (rpt. ed., Shanghai: Shang-hai shu-tien, 1984), *chüan* 6:18a.

2 This missive, which is titled "The Sage of Cursive Calligraphy" after Chang Hsü, is one of the "Nine Cursive Works" by Mi Fu (seven are extant). This set of writings, originally edited together during the Southern Sung, is divided between the Osaka Municipal Museum and the National Palace Museum, Taipei. Almost all of the "Nine Cursive Works" can be dated by their content to Mi Fu's period in Lien-shui (Shantung), ca. 1098–1100.

3 This is apparent in the cursive writing of the notable Wang Hsi-chih follower Sun Kuo-t'ing (648?–703?), whose famous *Shu-p'u* (Treatise on calligraphy) was written in 687.

4 See Nakata Yūjirō, "Tōdai no kakushinha no sho" (The calligraphy of the T'ang "revolutionary" school), in *Nakata Yūjirō chosakushū* (Tokyo: Nigensha, 1984), v. 3, 193–211.

5 Mi Fu, *Shu shih*, in Wang Shih-chen, ed., *Wang shih shu-hua-yüan* (Central Library manuscript copy, Taipei), 33b–34a. This is the first half of Mi Fu's poem.

6 On the general failure of excessive bones and muscle in calligraphy see Mi Fu, *Hai-yüeh ming-yen*, in Nakata Yūjirō, ed., *Chūgoku shoron taikei* (hereafter CST) (Tokyo: Nigensha, 1977–92), v. 4, 362.

7 Mi Fu, *Hai-yüeh ming-yen*, CST 4:360. Mi Fu specifically criticizes the squeezing of large characters small and small characters large. According to Yen Chen-ch'ing's attributed text *Chang Ch'ang-shih shih-erh i pi-fa chi*, CST 2:243, after serving as sheriff of Li-ch'üan in the 740s, he met and was influenced by Chang Hsü.

8 Su Shih, "T'i Wang I-shao t'ieh," *Su Shih shih-chi* (rpt. ed., Peking: Chung-hua shu-chü), *chüan* 25: 1342–43.

9 Hsieh Tao-yün was the daughter of Hsieh I (d. 358) and the wife of Wang Ning-chih, one of Wang Hsi-chih's sons. The pertinent anecdote concerning Hsieh Tao-yün is found in Liu I-ch'ing's *Shih-shuo hsin-yü*: "Hsieh Hsüan held his elder sister, Hsieh Tao-yün, in very high regard, while Chang Hsüan constantly sang the praises of his own younger sister, and wanted to match her against the other. A certain Chi Ni went to visit both the Chang and Hsieh families. When people asked him which family was superior and which inferior, he replied, 'Lady Wang's [Hsieh Tao-yün] spirit and feelings are relaxed and sunny; she certainly has the manner and style of [the Seven Worthies] beneath the [Bamboo] Grove.'" Translation by Richard Mather, *A New Account of Tales of the World* (Minneapolis: University of Minnesota Press, 1976), 355.

10 Su Shih, "Shu T'ang shih liu chia shu hou," *Su Shih wen-chi* (rpt. ed.; Peking: Chung-hua shu-chü, 1986), *chüan* 69:2206.

11 *Lang-kuan* is a general term for the official positions of *lang-chung* (director) and *yüan-wai-lang* (vice-director). The original stele commemorated the names of those who filled the sixty-one *lang-kuan* positions when Chang Hsü wrote the record in 741. See Kanda Kiichirō, ed., *Shodō zenshū*, n.s. (Tokyo: Heibonsha, 1954–61), v. 8, 100–103.

12 Huang T'ing-chien, "T'i Chiang-pen fa-t'ieh," *Shan-ku chi* (*Ssu-k'u ch'üan-shu* reprint ed., Shanghai: Shang-hai ku-chi, 1987), *chüan* 28: 10b–11a.

13 Huang T'ing-chien, "Pa Chai Kung-chüan so-ts'ang shih-k'o," *Shan-ku chi*, *chüan* 28:20a.

14 Huang T'ing-chien, "Pa Chou Tzu-fa t'ieh," *Shan-ku chi*, *chüan* 29:17b.

15 Huang T'ing-chien, "Pa wei Wang Sheng-tzu tso tzu," *Shan-ku t'i-pa*, CST 4:309.

16 Ch'i Kung, "Lun Huai-su Tzu-hsü t'ieh mo-chi pen" (Discussion on the ink version of Huai-su's *Autobiographical Essay*), *Wen-wu*, no. 12 (1983), 76–83.

17 For an attempt to determine why Huai-su's calligraphy occupied the curious position between propriety and wildness, *p'ing-tan*/naturalness and falseness, see my "The 'Thousand Character Essay' Attributed to Huai-su and the Tradition of Kuangcao Calligraphy," *Orientations* (April 1994), 38–46.

18 Tu Fu, "Yin-chung pa-hsien ko," *Tu shih hsiang-chu* (rpt. ed., Peking: Chung-hua, 1979), *chüan* 2:84.

19 For early descriptions of Chang Hsü and his cursive writing, see Chu Ch'ang-wen, *Hsü shu tuan*, CST 4:403–04, and *Hsüan-ho shu-p'u*, CST 6:147.

20 Huang T'ing-chien, "Pa Chang Ch'ang-shih ts'ao-shu," *Shan-ku t'i-pa*, CST 4:251.

21 A number of anecdotes are told in Liu I-ch'ing's *Shih-shuo hsin-yü*. See Mather, 375.

22 Liu Po-lun, "Chiu-te sung," in Hsiao T'ung, ed., *Wen hsüan* (rpt. ed., Taipei: Wen-chin ch'u-pan-she, 1987), *chüan* 47:2098–99.

23 Wolfgang Bauer, *China and the Search for Happiness*, trans. Michael Shaw (New York: The Seabury Press, 1976), 150–151.

24 Chu Ch'ang-wen, *Hsü shu tuan*, in CST 4:404; *Hsüan-ho shu-p'u*, in CST 6:147.

25 The poems were written by Wang Yung, Tou I, Lü Shou, Chu K'uei (the given name is sometimes read as the character Yao), Jen Hua, Tai Shu-lün, and Su Huan, all active in the Ta-li reign (766–79). See *Ch'üan T'ang shih* (rpt. ed., Shanghai: Shang-hai ku-chi, 1985), *chüan* 204: 483, *chüan* 255:643–44, *chüan* 261: 651, and *chüan* 273:685. Jen Hua's poem in particular emphasizes Huai-su's drinking (651).

26 Chu K'uei, "T'i Huai-su shang-jen ts'ao-shu," *Ch'üan T'ang shih*, *chüan* 204:483.

27 As senior Chinese scholars have pointed out, a changed character in one of the verses possibly reflects the avoidance of an early Northern Sung taboo character; this would suggest a date after 1012. Hsü Pang-ta, *Ku shu-hua wei-o k'ao-pien* (Changsha, 1984), 94–98, and Ch'i Kung, "Chiu t'i Chang Hsü ts'ao-shu ku-shih t'ieh pien" (Study of "Poems" in cursive calligraphy formerly attributed to Chang Hsü), in *Ch'i Kung ts'ung-kao* (Peking: Chung-hua shu-chü, 1981), 90–100. Since "Poems" is recorded (erroneously) in Sung Hui-tsung's *Hsüan-ho shu-p'u* under Hsieh

Ling-yün's name, we know that the calligrapher's identity was lost very early. *Hsüan-ho shu-p'u*, in CST, 6:99.

28 *Mi Fu: Style and the Art of Calligraphy*, 133–35. Yü Hsin's "The Taoist Master Strolls through the Empyrean" consists of ten verses. The second poem of this scroll is another from the series.

29 The poem's title is somewhat abbreviated in the calligraphy; I provide the full title. The calligraphy adopts a variant character in the last line: *jen*, "people," for *hsin*, "hearts." Hsieh Ling-yün, "Heng-shan yen-hsia chien i lao ssu-wu shao-nien tsan," *Hsieh K'ang-lo chi* (rpt. ed., Taipei: Shang-wu yin-shu-kuan, 1968), *chüan* 4:59.

30 Huai-su, Pien-kuang, Kao-hsien, Kuang-hsiu and Ya-hsi were coined the Five Calligrapher Monks of the T'ang by Mi Fu's friend Liu Ching. All have entries in Hui-tsung's *Hsüan-ho shu-p'u, chüan* 19. The wild cursive writing of yet another monk of the T'ang-Five Dynasties Period named Yen-hsiu (otherwise unknown) is preserved in a stele at Sian. See *Hsi-an pei-lin shu-fa i-shu* (Sian: Shan-hsi jen-min mei-shu ch'u-pan-she, 1988), 202–3.

31 Han Yü, "Sung Kao-hsien shang-jen hsü," *Wu-pai-chia chu Ch'ang-li wen-chi* (*Ssu-k'u ch'üan-shu* edition), *chüan* 21:3b–5a. See also Charles Hartman, *Han Yü and the Search for T'ang Unity* (Princeton: Princeton University Press, 1986), 222–23.

32 Su Shih, "Sung Ts'an-liao shih," *Su Shih shih-chi, chüan* 17:905–07. This poem is translated and discussed by Ronald Egan in "Ou-yang Hsiu and Su Shih on Calligraphy," *Harvard Journal of Asiatic Studies* 49, no. 2 (December 1989), 406–08.

33 During the Tien-sheng (1021–31) and Ch'ing-li (1041–48) reigns "emulators thronged in admiration" of Chou Yüeh, who was famous for his running and cursive scripts. Chu Ch'ang-wen, *Hsü shu tuan*, CST, 4:515. According to Ou-yang Hsiu, "Su Shun-ch'in excelled at cursive calligraphy, wielding the brush each time he was flush with wine. People competed in circulating his writings, which became even more highly treasured after his demotion and death." Ou-yang Hsiu, "Su Shih wen-chi hsü," in "Chü-shih chi" (2), *Ou-yang Hsiu ch'üan-chi* (rpt. ed., Hong Kong: Kuang-chih shu-chü, n.d.), *chüan* 2:122.

34 Su Shih, "P'ing ts'ao-shu," *Su Shih wen-chi, chüan* 69:2183.

35 We must learn to distrust some of the apocryphal descriptions of Su Shih as a wine-imbibing artist, as these often match longstanding cultural stereotypes, such as that of the meeting of famous artists who mutually inspire in a wine- and ink-splattering session. In one, Su Shih meets Mi Fu at Yung-ch'iu, where the latter served in office early in the 1090s. Mi Fu sets out a feast to entertain. A long table is arranged with superb brushes, fine ink, and three hundred sheets of paper. The wine flows, the calligraphy as well (two ink-grinding assistants hardly able to keep up), until finally the paper is finished. "Both men felt that their everyday writing could not compare." Liang T'ing-nan, ed., *Tung-p'o shih-lei* (rpt. ed., Kwangchow: Chi-nan ta-hsüeh ch'u-pan-she, 1992), 283. Of course, this is not to suggest that such stories are necessarily false. Mi Fu himself describes his first meeting with Su Shih in Huang-chou (1081), during which time Su Shih, flush with wine, demonstrated his painting of bamboo, withered tree, and strange rock. Mi Fu, *Hua*

shih, in Yü An-lan, *Hua-p'in ts'ung-shu* (Shanghai: Jen-min mei-shu ch'u-pan-she, 1982), 200.

36 Su Shih, "Shu Tung Kao-tzu chüan hou," cited from Liang T'ing-nan, ed., *Tung-p'o shih-lei*, 186.

37 Su Shih, "Ho Yüan-ming Yin-chiu shih hsü," cited from Liang T'ing-nan, ed., *Tung-p'o shih-lei*, 187.

38 Huang T'ing-chien, "T'i Tung-p'o tzu hou," *Shan-ku t'i-pa*, in CST 4:293.

39 Su Shih, "Pa ts'ao-shu hou," *Su Shih wen-chi, chüan* 69:2191.

40 Su Shih, "T'i tsui-ts'ao," *Su Shih wen-chi, chüan* 69:2184.

41 Su Shih, "Shu Chang Ch'ang-shih ts'ao-shu," *Su Shih wen-chi, chüan* 69:2178.

42 Fei Kun, "Liang-hsi man-chih," cited from Liang T'ing-nan, ed., *Tung-p'o shih-lei*, 187.

43 Translation by Ronald C. Egan, *Word, Image, and Deed in the Life of Su Shi* (Cambridge: Council on East Asian Studies, Harvard University, and the Harvard-Yenching Institute, 1994), 253–54.

44 Han Yü, "Sung Meng Tung-yeh hsü," *Wu-pai-chia chu Ch'ang-li wen-chi, chüan* 19:12a–14b. Hartman, *Han Yu*, 230ff.

45 Shen C.Y. Fu, "Huang T'ing-chien's Cursive Script and Its Influence," in Alfreda Murck and Wen C. Fong, ed., *Words and Images: Chinese Poetry, Painting, and Calligraphy* (New York and Princeton: The Metropolitan Museum of Art and Princeton University Press, 1991), 107–22.

46 Cited from Shen C.Y. Fu, "Huang T'ing-chien's Calligraphy and His *Scroll for Chang Ta-t'ung*: A Masterpiece Written in Exile" (Ph.D. diss., Princeton University, 1976), 50–51.

47 Huang T'ing-chien, "T'i Chiang-pen fa-t'ieh," *Shan-ku t'i-pa*, CST 4:239.

48 Huang T'ing-chien, "Pa Chai Kung-chüan so ts'ang shih-k'o," *Shan-ku t'i-pa*, CST 4:261.

49 Huang T'ing-chien, "Pa Chang Ch'ang-shih ts'ao-shu" and "Pa Chai Kung-chüan so ts'ang shih-k'o," *Shan-ku t'i-pa*, CST 4:251, 262.

50 Huang T'ing-chien, "Shu tzu-tso ts'ao hou," *Shan-ku t'i-pa*, CST 4:315.

51 These observations are drawn from a number of excerpts cited in Shen Fu's excellent discussion of Huang T'ing-chien's techniques and principles, "Huang T'ing-chien's Calligraphy and His *Scroll for Chang Ta-t'ung*," 105 and following.

52 Huang T'ing-chien, "Shu tseng Fu-chou Ch'en Chi-yüeh," *Shan-ku t'i-pa*, CST 4:318.

53 Huang T'ing-chien, "Tzu p'ing Yüan-yu chien tzu," *Shan-ku t'i-pa*, CST 4:316.

54 "Sayings of a Ch'an Buddhist Monk" has an inscription written in running script by Huang, in which he explains that the calligraphy was written for his friend Li Jen-tao. Shen Fu, in "Huang T'ing-chien's Cursive Script," uses this scroll as the standard for authenticating other attributions.

55 Chang Chou, *Ch'ing-ho shu-hua fang* (rpt. ed., Taipei: Hsüeh-hai ch'u-pan-she, 1975), *chia*, 11b.

56 This occurred during Huang T'ing-chien's residency at Jung-chou (Szechwan Province), 1098–1100. Cited from Shen Fu, "Huang T'ing-chien's Calligraphy," 49–50.

Uta Lauer
University of Heidelberg

The Strange, the New, and the Orthodox: Calligraphy of the Ch'an Monk Chung-feng Ming-pen (1262–1323)

This paper examines the calligraphy of the venerated Chinese Buddhist monk Chung-feng Ming-pen (1262–1323), the sources of his writing style—namely Buddhist sutras and the revival of draft-cursive (*chang-ts'ao* or *chi-chiu-chang*) script during the Yüan dynasty (1260–1368)—and the pivotal role of his works in the transmission of developments in Chinese calligraphy to Japan. Ming-pen's highly personal, idiosyncratic style defies categorization as simply Ch'an (Zen) calligraphy. In Japan, since the Kamakura period (1185–1333), the calligraphy of Zen Buddhist monks and nuns has been called *bokuseki* (ink traces).[1] In China, the equivalent term, *mo chi* (ink traces), had been applied earlier to the art of writing in general, and then in the Sung dynasty (960–1279) to the calligraphy of individualists in particular. The conventional distinction between *bokuseki* as the eccentric calligraphy of Zen clerics and *mo chi* as the orthodox calligraphy of the literati is misleading. In fact, there were numerous points of contact and mutual influences between the two stylistic categories. An analysis of Chung-feng Ming-pen's calligraphy demonstrates this strong interconnection.

Biography of Chung-feng Ming-pen

Chung-feng Ming-pen was born in Ch'ien-t'ang (modern Hangchow) in 1262, fourteen years before the fall of the Southern Sung capital to the Mongol rulers of the Yüan dynasty in early 1276.[2] He began school at the age of seven and received a Confucian education. Many of the books he was required to read, including the *Analects* (*Lun-yü*), were woodblock editions, most of which at the time were printed in characters modeled after the calligraphy of Su Shih (1037–1101). When he was fifteen years of age, Ming-pen began to observe the five precepts for Buddhist laymen[3] and recite sutras daily. Since they served to transmit faithfully the sacred words of the Buddha, sutras were written in legible small standard script. A particular feature of these early sutras is the teardrop-like ending of the *heng* (horizontal) and the *na* (diagonal to the lower right) brushstrokes. Chung-feng Ming-pen was inspired by his religious devotion to model his life on that of a Buddhist hermit. He often meditated in a solitary place in the mountains, and even burned off the small finger of his left hand. The missing finger became a distinctive trait depicted in portraits and sculptures of Ming-pen.

Ming-pen eventually became a disciple of Kao-feng Yüan-miao (1238–1295), abbot of Shih-tzu-yüan, a monastery on Mount T'ien-mu, about eighty kilometers west of Hangchow on the provincial border of modern Chekiang and Anhwei.[4] The mountain was noted for its cool summers, and since ancient times poets and officials had visited there and written poems celebrating the area's beauty.[5] The young Ming-pen probably would have seen original ink calligraphies by celebrities like Su Shih, who visited Mount T'ien-mu and composed a poem on the occasion. As is still customary today, famous visitors to the monastery were asked for a specimen of their handwriting, which was then stored in the temple library. In his first years on Mount T'ien-mu, Ming-pen studied diligently in the library. Apart from Buddhist texts, he also continued his studies of Confucian works and learned how to compose poetry. The monastery functioned as a cultural center. Visiting lay Buddhists made donations of land, money, or works of art to the temple, and the educated elite exchanged letters with the monks or came to the monastery where they engaged in learned discussions.

In 1288 Ming-pen was fully ordained as a Ch'an Buddhist monk. After the death of his teacher, in 1295, Ming-pen declined to succeed him as abbot and left the mountain monastery to take up the life of an itinerant monk. He spent time in Wu-men (modern Soochow, Kiangsu) and in Chien-k'ang (modern Nanking, Kiangsu). In the winter of 1298, he stayed at Mount Pien, where he built the first of a series of retreats which he called the Illusory Abode (Ch. *Huan-chu-an*; Jpn. *Genjū-an*). Ming-pen presumably met Chao Meng-fu (1254–1322) as early as 1299, the year in which Chao dedicated a sutra that he had copied to Ming-pen.[6] This date is five years earlier than the year, 1304, commonly given as the beginning of their friendship. Chao Meng-fu had an art collection that included many pieces of calligraphy. In order to determine the influence of previous calligraphers on his style, it would be helpful to know what works Ming-pen might have seen in the collection.

Ming-pen occasionally returned to Mount T'ien-mu, but he resolutely declined all offers to become abbot of that temple or other temples, including Ling-yin in Hangchow. From 1306 to 1308 he lived in Wu-sung, northeast of Shanghai. In 1306 Enkei Soyū (d. 1344), one of Ming-pen's first Japanese disciples, came to study Ch'an under his guidance for ten years. Ming-pen presented him with a portrait of himself, inscribed in his own hand, which is now preserved at Kōgen-ji temple, in Hyōgo prefecture.[7] By this time, Ming-pen had become well known and was much sought after by Buddhist monks and lay persons alike. In 1308 the crown prince (the future Yüan emperor Jen-tsung, r. 1311–20) bestowed on him the title "Ch'an Master of Dharma Wisdom" (*Fa-hui Ch'an-shih*). Not pleased with all the attention he was receiving, in the following year Chung-feng Ming-pen went to I-chen (west of modern Yangchow, Kiangsu) where he bought a houseboat. He later recorded his insights into life on the rivers and lakes of the area in a series of ten poems composed in seven-character meter.[8]

In 1310 Ming-pen again returned to Mount T'ien-mu where Muin Genkai (d. 1358) and another Japanese monk became his disciples. After his return to Japan, in 1326, Genkai built the Genjū-an subtemple at Nanzen-ji temple, in Kyoto.[9] Genkai was acquainted with Ming-pen's friend, the official, literatus, and calligrapher Feng Tzu-chen (1257–after 1327).[10] A poem by Feng dedicated to Genkai is in the Tokyo National Museum.[11] Feng Tzu-chen had been introduced to Ming-pen through Chao Meng-fu. At first, Feng looked down on the monk, but after Ming-pen had replied in rhyming verse to Feng's "Hundred Poems on the Plum Blossom" (*Mei-hua pai-yung*), they became fast friends. Interestingly, Ming-pen's responding poems not only contained verses on Buddhist themes but also covered a whole range of topics associated with plum blossoms,[12] including their allusions to beautiful palace ladies. This shows Ming-pen's extensive learning and creativity, his close ties with men of literature, and his knowledge of classical poetic themes. Although he attempted to lead the life of a recluse, he was very much a part of the learned and literary world of his time.

In 1311 Chung-feng Ming-pen returned to live on his houseboat. His followers soon discovered his whereabouts and paid him their respect by greeting him as the Old Buddha from the South (*Chiang-nan ku-fo*). This so embarrassed him that he took up his walking staff and left for Mount Liu-an, near the modern city of Liu-an, Anhwei province, where he built a hut and wrote another set of ten poems, this time recording his experience in dwelling in the mountains.[13] Although he often traveled and stayed in small retreats, Ming-pen should not be thought of as a hermit who lived in total seclusion. Most of the time he was probably accompanied by some of his disciples. It was for them and their small community that he wrote the monastic code "Pure Rules of Huan-chu" (*Huan-chu ch'ing-kuei*),[14] which was influential in Japanese monasteries. In 1318 Emperor Jen-tsung conferred another Buddhist title on Chung-feng Ming-pen and presented him with a robe woven in golden thread.[15] The emperor also elevated the status of the temple at Mount T'ien-mu, renaming it Shih-tzu cheng tsung Ch'an-ssu (Shih-tzu, Ch'an temple of the orthodox lineage), and ordered Chao Meng-fu to compose a text for a stele erected to commemorate the occasion.[16] A year later, the Korean king Ch'ungsŏn (r. 1308–13) came to Mount T'ien-mu to pay the famous monk his respect. King Ch'ungsŏn built a pavilion there for Ming-pen and donated a statue of the bodhisattva Kuan-yin; Ming-pen in return bestowed on Ch'ungsŏn a Buddhist sobriquet. Chung-feng Ming-pen died on 14 August 1323, at the age of sixty-one. Emperor Wen-tsung (r. 1328–32) posthumously honored him with a prestigious

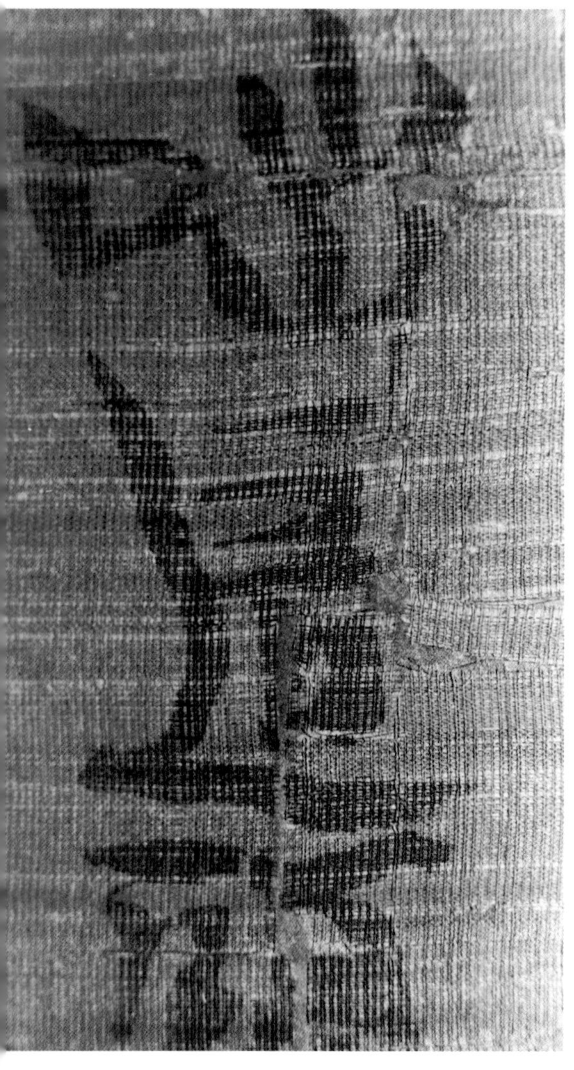

Figure 1
Unidentified artist (14th century). Detail from *Portrait of Chung-feng Ming-pen* (1262–1323), with inscription by Chung-feng Ming-pen, ca. 1310. Hanging scroll, ink and color on silk, 108 x 47.5 cm. Yabumoto Collection, Kobe.

Figure 2
Unidentified artist (14th century). *Portrait of Chung-feng Ming-pen* (1262–1323), with inscription by Chung-feng Ming-pen, ca. 1310. Hanging scroll, ink and color on silk, 108 x 47.5 cm. Yabumoto Collection, Kobe.

Buddhist title, as did Emperor Shun-ti (r. 1333–67), in 1334.[17] Six years after Chung-feng Ming-pen's death, the calligrapher Yü Chi (1272–ca. 1333) wrote an epitaph for a pagoda built at his gravesite.[18]

The Calligraphy of Chung-feng Ming-pen

Chung-feng Ming-pen's calligraphy appears eccentric and not clearly tied to any established tradition. In Japan, his work has generally been classified as *bokuseki*, or calligraphy by Ch'an monks. Such calligraphy was believed to express the devotee's state of enlightenment; consequently, it has traditionally escaped the scrutiny of critical stylistic analysis. However, Ch'an monks did not live in an artistic void. As noted earlier, there are close connections and mutual influences between idiosyncratic Ch'an calligraphy and orthodox literati calligraphy, specific examples of which are revealed in an examination of the works of Chung-feng Ming-pen.

A term often used to characterize Ming-pen's calligraphy (fig. 1) is "willow-leaf style" (Ch. *liu yeh t'i*; Jpn. *sasa no ha kaki*). The first person to describe Ming-pen's handwriting was the Ming dynasty (1368–1644) scholar Liu Chang. In his *Imperial History of Painting and Calligraphy* (*Huang ming shu-hua shih*), Liu comments: "Ming-pen wrote a type of willow-leaf [script]. Although he cannot be classified, he is a master of his own."

The term "willow leaf" refers to a type of small-seal script. It is a decorative script (*hsiang-hsing shu*) like bird script (*niao-shu*) or snake script (*she-shu*). The Sung dynasty scholar Chu Chang-wen (1039–1089) described the script as follows:

> Willow leaf seal script was practised by Wei Kuan [220–291]. For three generations, the Wei family worked hard at calligraphy and was particularly good at clerical script. They revived the old and learned the new ... [willow-leaf script] is like a type of shallot-leaf [*hsieh-yeh*] seal script, not straight, and the power of the brush is clear and strong. This cannot be studied.[19]

As indicated here, the willow-leaf style referred specifically to Wei Kuan's seal script, yet Chung-feng Ming-pen wrote almost exclusively in running script. Thus, when Liu Chang described Ming-pen's style as "willow-leaf," he was not referring to a particular script type but to Ming-pen's own innovative brush technique. Significantly, Chu Chang-wen delineates in his comments three qualities or characteristics that also apply to Ming-pen's willow-leaf style:

> 1. "Not straight." The lines and dots are always curved and bent. They have a pointed beginning, become wider in the middle and then narrow again at the end, thus forming a shape resembling that of a willow leaf.

2. “Strong and clear brushwork.” The movement of the brush is always clearly discernable. The characters are written so energetically that the curves sometimes produce a carvedlike effect.

3. “This cannot be studied.” The writing style is unorthodox and cannot be mastered through the traditional means of copying. It is highly individualistic and thus cannot be used as a model.

The observations on Chung-feng Ming-pen’s writing style by early writers must be weighed against actual examples of his calligraphy. For this purpose, I have chosen a portrait of the monk with an inscription in his own hand, now in the Yabumoto Collection, Kobe (figs. 1–3). The inscription (fig. 3) identifies the Japanese monk Ketsuzan Ryoi as the recipient of the portrait.[20] Ketsuzan was a disciple of Hakuun Egyō (1228–1297), the founder of the Rikkyoku-an subtemple of Tōfuku-ji, in Kyoto. Ketsuzan studied Ch’an Buddhism in China, but exactly when he arrived there or departed is unclear. Leaving aside the complex question of Ketsuzan’s dates,[21] I tentatively suggest that the portrait was painted late in Ming-pen’s life, probably around 1310. The inscription provides two clues that support this dating. Ming-pen says with humility that he feels unable to answer Ketsuzan’s quest for the dharma and the Ch’an way, and then states that he has lived on Mount T’ien-mu for thirty years and now “snow has gathered on the black turtle’s head.” From this it can be surmised that Ming-pen wrote the inscription in his late fifties when his hair had started to turn white. The seven lines of the inscription correspond to the second half of a text recorded in *chüan* 9 of Ming-pen’s *Comprehensive Record of Monk Chung-feng of Mount T’ien-mu* (*T’ien-mu Chung-feng ho-shang kuang lu*). A 1643 Japanese edition of the *Record* notes that this portrait, along with a portrait of Ketsuzan’s teacher Hakuun, was initially housed at Rikkyoku-an. Ming-pen’s portrait later went to the Akishinkō-ji temple, and in the Edo (1615–1867) period was acquired by a private collector, Ryoen (1704–1774), whose written comments on the portrait are still kept in the storage box with the painting. Eventually, the portrait went to the Seun-ji temple, in Yamanashi prefecture, and from there it entered the Yabumoto Collection.

The Yabumoto portrait of Ming-pen resembles a more well-known version in Kōgen-ji temple, Hyōgo prefecture,[22] which also shows the subject seated in a chair with his legs tucked beneath him and wearing the same brown robe opened down to his stomach. In the Yabumoto portrait, the legs of the chair and the stool have a similar cloud-shaped form. The monk’s shoes, placed on the stool before him, are painted two shades of blue. The cushion on which Ming-pen sits is light blue and has a floral pattern. In his right hand he holds a fly whisk (*hossu*); his left hand, depicted

Figure 3
Unidentified artist (14th century). Detail from *Portrait of Chung-feng Ming-pen* (1262–1323), with inscription by Chung-feng Ming-pen, ca. 1310. Hanging scroll, ink and color on silk, 108 x 47.5 cm. Yabumoto Collection, Kobe.

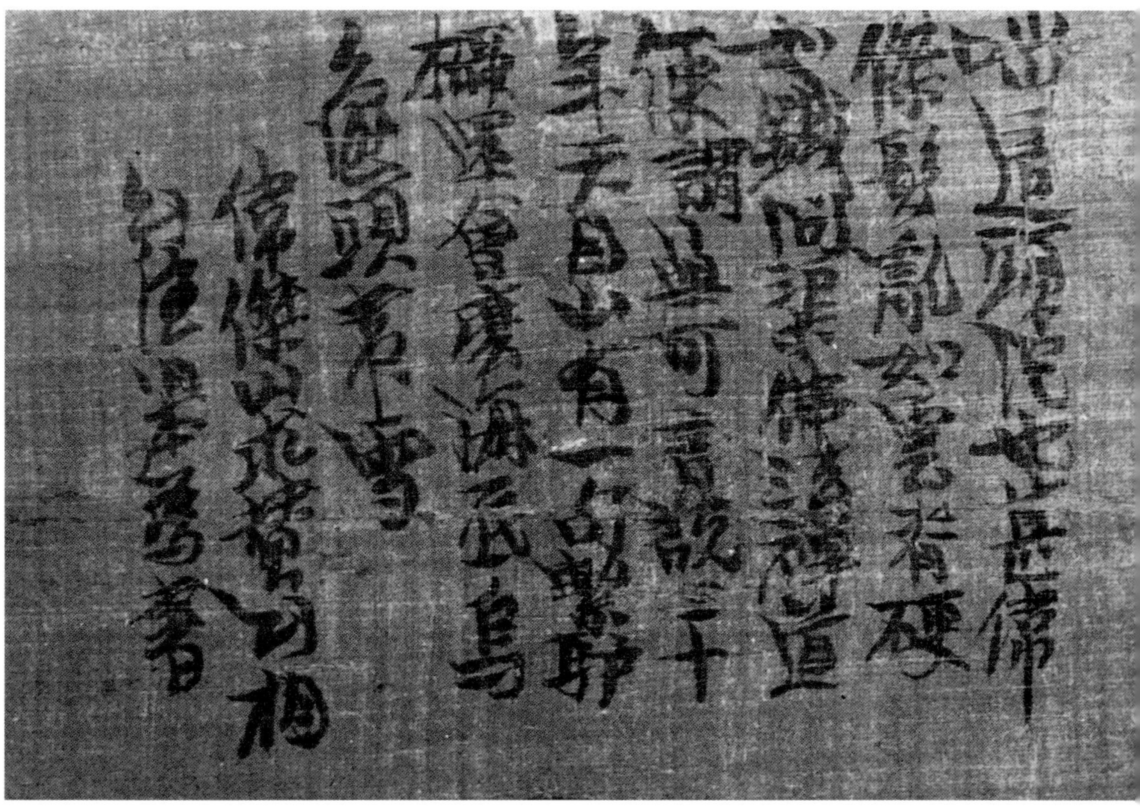

with the missing little finger, is turned palm-up and holds the hair of the fly whisk. His head is lowered slightly, revealing a double chin. It appears that he has not shaved for some time, as the hair on his chin has already grown into a thin beard. The hair on top of his head resembles a *ushnisha* (cranial bump), which suggests that it was the painter's intention to portray Ming-pen as a Buddha. The monk's eyes are half closed, creating an impression of self-contentment, again a possible reference to the Buddha. The deep wrinkles in his forehead show that Ming-pen is no longer a young man.

The inscription on the portrait, written in running script, consists of seven lines and a two-line dedication. It is signed Huan-chu Ming-pen. In the inscription, Ming-pen mentions the recipient, Ketsuzan Ryoi, twice, and includes a quotation from Yüan-wu's (1063–1135) *The Blue Cliff Record* (*Pi-yen lu*): "to tie the donkey to the pole" [*hsi lü chüeh*].[23]

A striking feature of Ming-pen's inscription is the pronounced arched tilt to the upper left that is seen in many of the left-hand components of the characters. The characters in the first column are all elongated in height, providing a dramatic and powerful opening to the inscription. The proportions of the characters are reminiscent of Ou-yang Hsün's (557–641) calligraphy. A pulsating rhythm is created through the alternation of thick heavy strokes with thin light ones, and the tight spacing between the columns makes the overall composition appear compact.

When we look at the shape of the individual strokes and dots, we realize how appropriate the description "willow-leaf style" is to Ming-pen's calligraphy. The pointed beginning, the swelling middle section, and the rounded ending of the brushstrokes indeed resemble the shape of a willow leaf. Ming-pen's calligraphy has a rustic, simple quality, and an unstudied spontaneity that makes an immediate impact on the viewer. For example, the enlarged "mouth" (*k'ou*) radical and the pronounced energy of the first character, *to*, visually capture the meaning of this word, "to cry out," or "to exclaim 'oh'!" Chung-feng Ming-pen's highly idiosyncratic style may strike us as odd or strange. However, closer analysis reveals that the sources of his style can be traced back to the orthodox tradition.

Sources of Chung-feng Ming-pen's Calligraphic Style

When the Sung calligrapher Mi Fu (1052–1107) described his own training in the art of writing, he said:

> Then I was attracted to the tight composition of Liu Kung-ch'üan [778–865], so I started to study his *Diamond Sutra*. After a while, I realized that Liu had derived his style from Ou-yang Hsün, so I studied Ou-yang, but before long my writing looked like printed blocks or the sliding beads on the abacus.[24]

In this passage, "printed blocks" and "sliding beads" refer to the round, teardrop-like endings of strokes in early sutras (fig. 4). Indeed, the earliest printed versions of sutras were modeled after Ou-yang Hsün's handwriting. As a monk, Chung-feng Ming-pen almost certainly read and copied many such sutras, and it should come as no surprise that this influenced his own handwriting. Even Mi Fu could not escape this influence and eventually abandoned his copying of sutras because he found the result undesirable. Ming-pen, by contrast, incorporated the teardrop-shaped endings of certain strokes into his own personal style of writing.

Other stylistic peculiarities in Ming-pen's calligraphy, such as the slightly compressed characters, the wavelike movement of the horizontal strokes, and the emphasis on the lower right diagonal strokes, do not derive from Buddhist sutras but from the revival of draft-cursive script during the Yüan dynasty. While Chung-feng Ming-pen wrote almost exclusively in running script, he incorporated draft cursive in his calligraphy.

Draft cursive, a type of script that developed from clerical script during the Eastern Han (25–220) period, had long fallen out of popular use. None of the Four Great Masters of the Sung—Ts'ai Hsiang (1012–1067), Su Shih (1037–1101), Huang T'ing-chien (1045–1105), or Mi Fu (1052–1107)—practiced this script. The only exception was the Sung emperor Kao-tsung (r. 1127–62), who transcribed the Confucian Classics in draft-cursive script. What prompted Yüan calligraphers to revive this ancient script form? Before addressing this question, let us review the sequence of events as they unfolded in the Yüan period. Chao Meng-fu, a descendant of the Sung imperial family, was one of the first to practice the draft-cursive script. Several works by him in this script still exist today, including three transcriptions of the *Model Essay on Draft Cursive* (*Chi-chiu-chang*), written entirely in draft cursive, and *The Thousand Character Essay* (*Ch'ien-tzu wen*), dated 1320, written in six different script types (fig. 5). The *Model Essay on Draft Cursive* was composed by Shih Yu of the Western Han (206 BC–AD 9). Written in rhymes in seven-character meter, the text is divided by subject matter and contains information on family and given names, clothes, food and drink, and objects of everyday use. A transcription of the essay by Chao Meng-fu, dated 1303, survives as an original ink manuscript in the collection of the National Palace Museum, Taipei;[25] a Ch'ing dynasty (1644–1911) version based on this work is included in the *Model Calligraphies from the Hall of the Three Rarities* (*San-hsi-t'ang fa-t'ieh*).[26] However, the 1303 manuscript is problematic.[27] It bears a colophon by Yü Ho (1307–1382) in which he records that he viewed the scroll with Chou Mi (1232–1308) and Hsien-yü Shu (1257–1302) in his studio. The colophon is dated 1291, which, if correct, would predate both the writer, Yü Ho, and the work of art to which it is appended. Despite questions about the history of this work, it should be

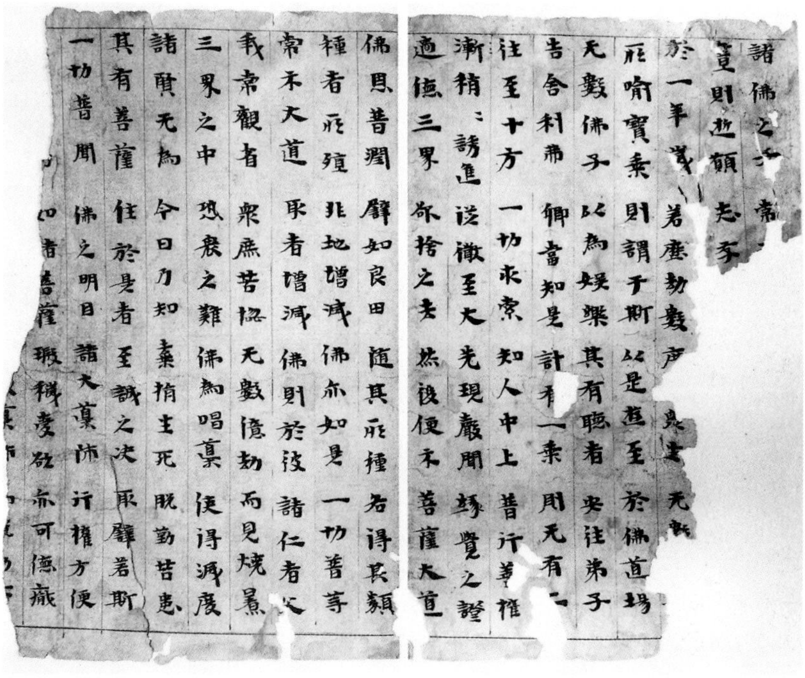

Figure 4
Fragment of *Sutra* (*Cheng-fa hua ching*), 400. Handscroll, ink on paper, 25.2 x 30.4 cm. Museum of Indian Art, Berlin SMPK.

considered among the several surviving examples that illustrate Chao Meng-fu's keen interest in reviving the draft-cursive script. Other extant transcriptions by Chao of the *Model Essay on Draft Cursive* include a 1309 version in the Liaoning Provincial Museum (fig. 6) and an undated version in the Shanghai Museum.[28] Chao's 1320 transcription of the *Thousand Character Essay* in six scripts, with draft cursive as the fourth script, serves as yet another example.

Chao Meng-fu was not the only Yüan calligrapher who practiced draft-cursive script. Teng Wen-yüan (1258–1328) also copied the *Model Essay on Draft Cursive* (fig. 7), in 1299, and Yü Ho's interest in draft cursive led him to copy Chang Chih's (d. 192) *Letter of the Ninth Day of the Eighth Month* (*Pa yüeh chiu ji t'ieh*) from the *Model Calligraphies from the Imperial Archives of the Ch'un-hua Era* (*Ch'un-hua-ko t'ieh*). K'ang-li Nao-nao's (1295–1345) familiarity with draft cursive is evident in his running script. K'ang-li, who was from northwestern China, was an official at the Mongol Yüan court and the first in the Yüan period to specialize in draft-cursive script. One of his best works in this script is the *Ancient Times of Li Po* (*Li Po ku-feng*),[29] preserved in the Tokyo National Museum. The characters have a carvedlike quality and display an energetic rhythm created by an almost tangible elasticity and the contrast of thick and thin strokes. Another calligrapher whose works show the strong influence of draft cursive is Yang Wei-chen (1296–1370). His *Drinking with My Wife under the First Full Moon*

Figure 5
Chao Meng-fu (1254–1322). Detail from *The Thousand Character Essay* (*Ch'ien-tzu wen*), in six scripts, 1320. Handscroll, ink on paper, 23 x 1448 cm. Palace Museum, Peking.

Figure 6 (left)
Chao Meng-fu (1254–1322). Detail from *Model Essay on Draft Cursive* (*Chi-chiu-chang*), 1309. Handscroll, ink on paper, 24.7 x 278.4 cm. Liaoning Provincial Museum.

Figure 7 (right)
Teng Wen-yüan (1258–1328). Detail from *Model Essay on Draft Cursive* (*Chi-chiu-chang*), 1299. Handscroll, ink on paper, 23.3 x 398.7 cm. Palace Museum, Peking.

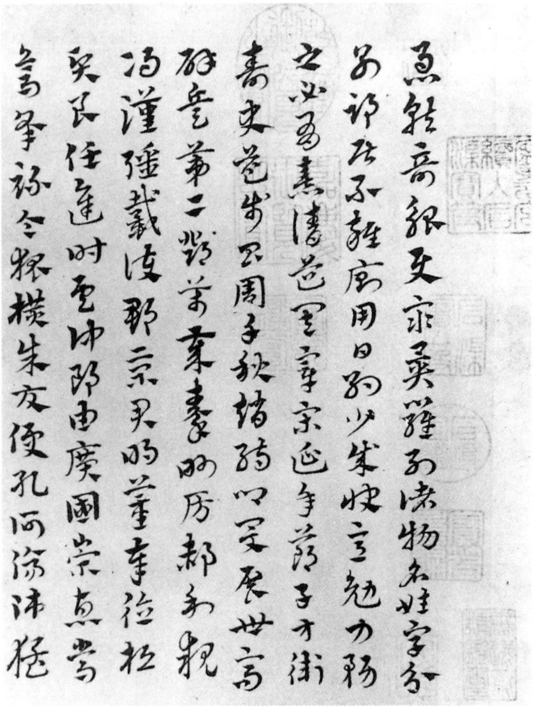

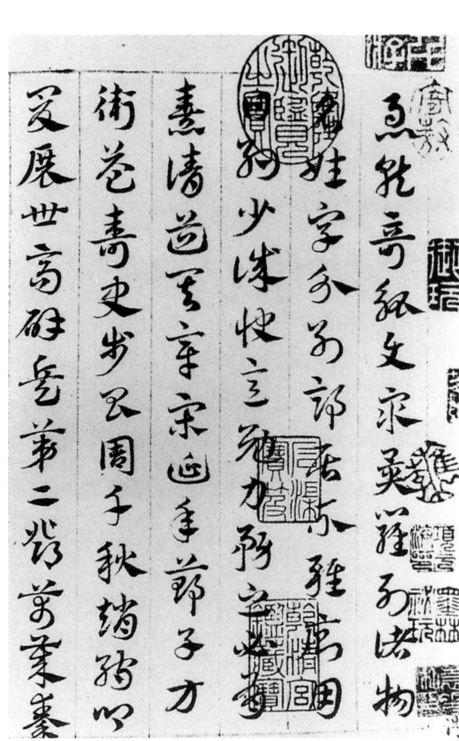

(*Yüan hsi yü fu yin*)[30] is written in running script but with draft-cursive methods.

These early Yüan calligraphers chose to revive draft cursive for two reasons. Within the context of the "return to the past" (*fu-ku*) movement, they wanted to go back to the roots of their art. Draft cursive was an early form of cursive script and thus had an aura of authenticity about it as the prevalent type of cursive script during the time of the Two Wangs, Wang Hsi-chih (303–361) and his son Wang Hsien-chih (344–388). Yüan calligraphers copied early models of the draft-cursive style by Wei Kuan, So Ching (239–303), and Chung Yu (151–230). Cursive script had always been associated with a certain anti-government attitude. Most of the above-mentioned calligraphers collaborated with the Mongols, so their practice of draft cursive may have been intended as a kind of personal refuge or inner withdrawal, the implications of which the Mongols failed to grasp. It is probably not a coincidence that the *Model Essay on Draft Cursive* and *The Thousand Character Essay* were the preferred texts, since they dealt with Chinese culture and values and could be understood as an implied criticism of the Mongols, whose nomadic tradition had nothing comparable to offer.

Calligraphers soon recognized the potential of the draft-cursive brush method, which in turn led to the development of running script written with draft-cursive methods. Later calligraphers such as Yang Wei-chen, Jao Chieh (act. ca. 1300–1367), and Sung K'o (1327–1387) were free to explore fully the artistic potential of this new combined script form. In his *Eulogy for Chung-feng Ming-pen* (*Chung-feng Huan-chu hsiang chieh*; fig. 8), dated 1365, Jao Chieh not only borrowed stylistically from Ming-pen by using willow-leaf strokes, but also incorporated draft-cursive methods in his running script. This new script type reached its zenith in the art of the early Ming calligrapher Sung K'o, who in 1370 copied the *Model Essay on Draft Cursive* (figs. 9a, 9b) in a pure form of draft cursive. In the same year he transcribed twenty-eight poems by T'ao Ch'ien (365–427) in *T'ao Ch'ien's Poems, and Bamboo and Rocks* (*T'ao Yüan-ming shih, Chu-shih hsiao-ching*), now in the John B. Elliott Collection, The Art Museum, Princeton University.[31] The poems are written in various scripts; the third section with nine poems is written in draft cursive. With Sung K'o, the revival of the draft-cursive script that began in the early Yüan period reached its climax. Some Sung-chiang school calligraphers continued to practice draft cursive in the manner of Sung K'o, but the use of this style eventually lost its appeal and died out.

The developments discussed above form the cultural context in which Chung-feng Ming-pen developed his calligraphic style. An active participant in the literati life and culture of his time, Ming-pen exchanged letters with the foremost figures in literati circles and had access to their art

Figure 8
Jao Chieh (act. ca. 1300–1367). *Eulogy for Chung-feng Ming-pen* (*Chung-feng Huan-chu hsiang chieh*), 1365. Handscroll, ink on paper, 26.3 x 109.1 cm. National Palace Museum, Taipei.

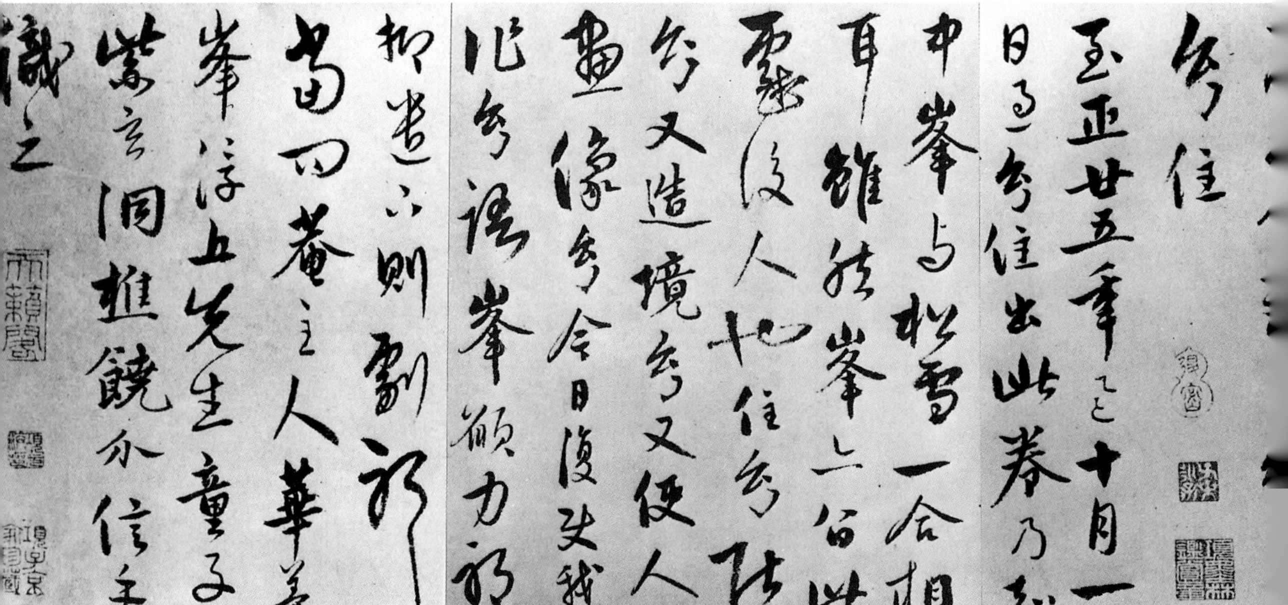

collections. His colophons recorded in the Ch'ing dynasty imperial painting and calligraphy catalogue, *Shih-ch'ü pao-chi*, attest to his pivotal role in the cultural milieu of the Yüan period. Chung-feng Ming-pen absorbed the orthodox calligraphic trends established and followed by the literati and transformed them into a highly personal style.

The Influence of Chung-feng Ming-pen's Style on Japanese Calligraphy

As a famous religious teacher, Chung-feng Ming-pen attracted a wide following. Lay people and monks from such distant places as Vietnam, Korea, and Japan came to visit him or to study Ch'an Buddhism under his guidance. He even received donations from Japanese feudal lords; in a letter addressed to Lord Ōtomo Sadamune (d. 1333), now in the Seikadō Foundation (fig. 10), Ming-pen thanked his patron for a contribution of gold sent to him by messenger. Japanese monks who had become disciples of Chung-feng Ming-pen returned to Japan with portraits of their teacher inscribed in his own hand, sermons and letters, and sobriquets that had been bestowed on them by the monk. These works were often copied and distributed to temples of the same lineage, namely the Genjū (Ch. *Huan-chu*) sect. Woodblock prints of Chung-feng Ming-pen's calligraphy were produced in an effort to copy faithfully the characteristics of his writing. One such print, a portrait with Ming-pen's inscription at the top, survives today at Shōjyū-ji temple, Ibaragi prefecture.[32]

The calligraphic works and portraits of Chung-feng Ming-pen that were taken to Japan were used there in religious ceremonies. From Kyūshū

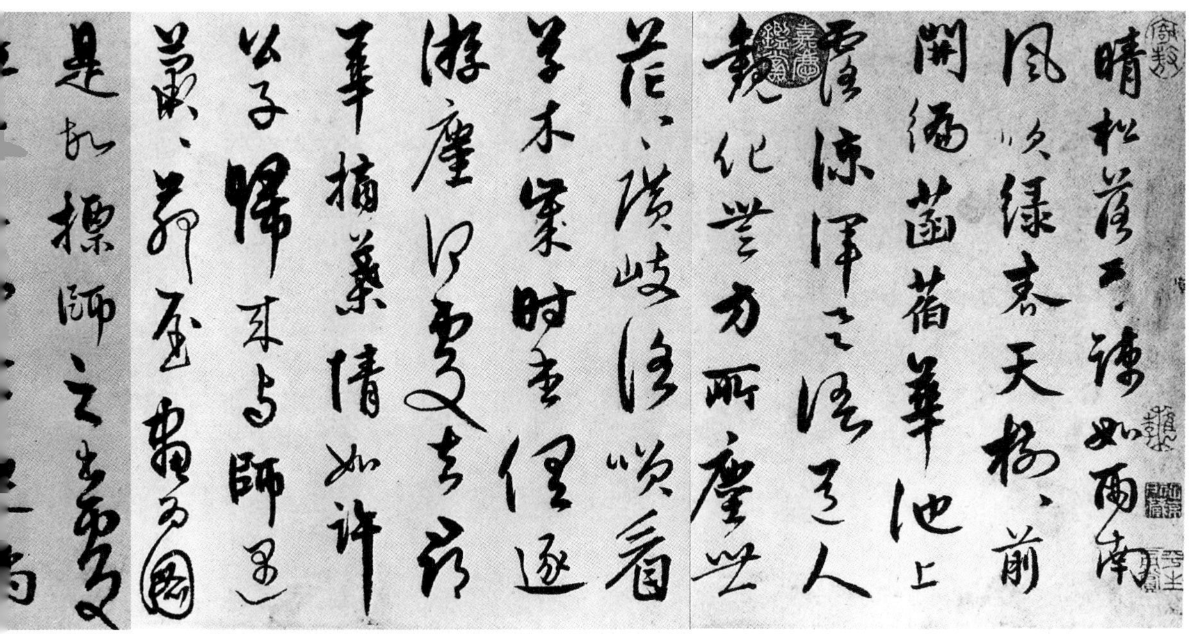

Figure 9a (right)
Sung K'o (1327–1387). First section from *Model Essay on Draft Cursive* (*Chi-chiu-chang*), 1370. Handscroll, ink on paper, 20.4 x 342.8 cm. Palace Museum, Peking.

Figure 9b (left)
Sung K'o (1327–1387). Last section from *Model Essay on Draft Cursive* (*Chi-chiu-chang*), 1370. Handscroll, ink on paper, 20.4 x 342.8 cm. Palace Museum, Peking.

Figure 10 (facing page)
Chung-feng Ming-pen (1262–1323). *Letter to Lord Ōtomo Sadamune*. Hanging scroll, ink on paper, 44.7 x 64.2 cm. Seikadō Foundation, Tokyo. Important Cultural Property.

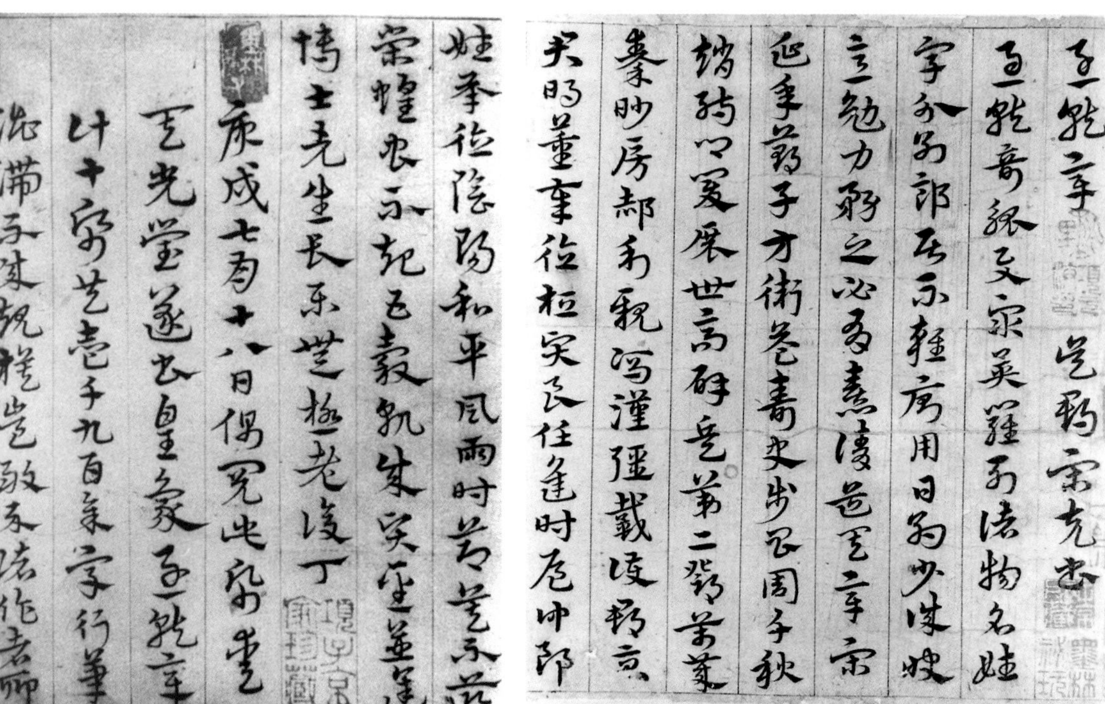

in the south to Yamanashi prefecture in the north, many temples of the Genjū lineage treasured works by this revered Chinese monk. Those temples that did not possess an original work by Ming-pen had copies made. Statues based on painted portraits of the monk were carved, a fine example of which is in Seun-ji temple, Yamanashi prefecture.[33] It was commissioned by Gyōkai Honjō (d. 1352), a Japanese monk who had been Ming-pen's disciple in China from 1317 to 1326. Gyōkai founded Seun-ji temple in 1348 and asked two monks, Injun and Inkō, to make a statue of Ming-pen which they completed in 1353, a year after Gyōkai's death. This lifelike statue, with inlaid crystal eyes, was produced with the joined-wood technique.

Chung-feng Ming-pen's works did not disappear in the flickering candlelight of temples, nor were they solely employed in religious ceremonies. His calligraphies, even the ordinary letters with no religious content, were mounted as hanging scrolls and hung in the *tokonoma* alcove during tea ceremonies or poetry meetings. Learned monks and the educated Japanese elite had a keen interest in Chinese culture. The calligraphy of eminent Chinese monks, such as Chung-feng Ming-pen, played a central role in transmitting this culture to Japan and served as a vital cultural link between Japan and China in the early fourteenth century, a period in which contact between the two countries was restricted. The Japanese monks who had braved the dangers of sea travel to go to China brought back the materials that were so eagerly emulated by the rising warrior class. The calli-

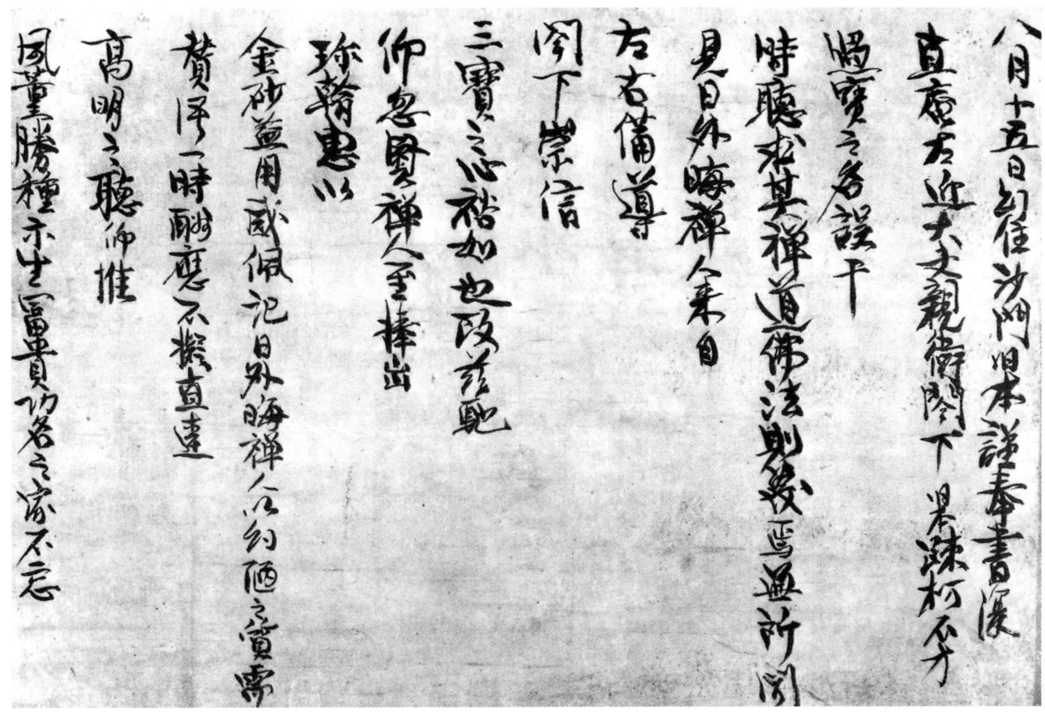

graphy of Chinese priests, which in its rustic, simple, and expressive style appealed to the aesthetic ideals of the Japanese, served as their models.

In China, Chung-feng Ming-pen's calligraphy was considered strange, rough, and unsophisticated. It did not suit the taste of the literati, and was cherished only for its content, not for its artistic style. Nevertheless, Ming-pen was a central figure in early Yüan cultural life and played an active part in elite circles. He knew the foremost representatives of literati culture, had access to their art collections, and occasionally was asked to provide inscriptions or colophons to paintings and calligraphies. In his own writing, Ming-pen absorbed the contemporary developments in literati calligraphy by writing running script with draft-cursive methods, but he turned this combination of script forms into his own unmistakable style. In Japan, against the background of the tea ceremony and poetry writing, the function of his works changed. His calligraphy was no longer treasured primarily for its content, but for its form and style. His handwriting, along with that of other venerated Chinese Ch'an masters, came to epitomize Chinese culture. Chung-feng Ming-pen's calligraphy permeated Japanese literati calligraphy and helped to shape a new orthodoxy. What began as the strange contained the seeds of the new and finally blossomed into the maturity of the orthodox.

1 For a discussion of the term *bokuseki*, see Nakata Yūjirō, ed., *Chinese Calligraphy* (New York: Weatherhill/Tankosha, 1983), 137.

2 Wang Te-i et al., "Yüan-jen chuan-chi ts'ai-liao so-yin" (Index to biographical material of Yüan figures) (Taipei: Hsin wen-feng ch'u-pan kung-ssu, 1977), 2148–49, contains 23 entries on where to find material on Chung-feng Ming-pen. The most important source is the *T'ien-mu Chung-feng ho-shang kuang-lu* (Comprehensive record of Monk Chung-feng of Mount T'ien-mu) in 30 *chüan*; hereafter cited as *Record*. This record was compiled by Chung-feng Ming-pen's disciple Pei-t'ing Tzu-chi. In 1334 it was presented to the Yüan emperor Shun-ti (r. 1333–68), who ordered it included in the *Ta tsang ching*. Unfortunately, the temple where the woodblocks were cut burnt down. Some years later, in 1387, the record was recut and published on the Buddha's birthday.

Biographical data is contained in *chüan* 18 *hsia*, a short autobiography written by Chung-feng Ming-pen on his sixtieth birthday; *chüan* 30, biographies by (1) Ming-pen's disciple Tz'u Shun — the most comprehensive but very anecdotal; (2) the well-known scholar and calligrapher Yü Chi (1272–ca. 1333) — the text of the inscription for Ming-pen's tomb pagoda; and (3) an official named Sung Pen — the text of an inscription for a stele.

A tabulatory biography appears in Ide Seinosuke, "Portraits of Chung-feng Ming-pen with Autograph Inscription," *Bijutsu Kenkyū* (*The Journal of Art Studies*) 343 (February 1989), 36. A summary English account of Ming-pen's life can be found in Yü Chün-fang, "Chung-feng Ming-pen and Ch'an Buddhism in the Yüan," in Hok-lam Chan and William Th. de Bary, eds., *Yüan Thought, Chinese Thought and Religion under the Mongols*, (New York: Columbia University Press, 1982), 422–30. Interestingly, the *Yüan shi* (History of the Yüan) does not mention Ming-pen even though he received several imperial honors.

3 Slay not, steal not, lust not, drink no intoxicants, eat no meat.

4 Hsi T'ien-mu shan chih pien tsuan wei-yüan-hui, comp., *Hsi T'ien-mu shan chih* (Hangchow: Che-chiang jen-min ch'u-pan-she, 1991); this is a modern edition based on earlier local gazetteers from the Ming and Ch'ing period.

5 Collected in Ku P'eng-jung and T'u Shu-hsün, *T'ien-mu shan shih hsüan* (Hangchow: Che-chiang shih ying ch'u-pan-she, 1989) and Fang-li Shao-ch'en, *Ming jen yü T'ien-mu shan* (Ling-an: Che-chiang hsin-wen ch'u-pan-she, 1991).

6 This opinion is based on the date (fourth day of the fourth month of 1304) of the first of a set of six letters by Chao Meng-fu to Chung-feng Ming-pen, which are now in the Seikadō Collection, Tokyo. See The Seikadō Foundation, ed., *Seikadō Art Treasures* (Tokyo: The Seikadō Foundation, 1992), fig. 99.

7 Hanging scroll, ink and color on silk, 122 x 54.7 cm; the portrait belongs to the Kōgen-ji but is on loan to the Osaka Municipal Museum. Discussed by Ide Seinosuke, "Portraits of Chung-feng Ming-pen with autograph inscription," 102, and Nakagawa Kenichi, "Chūhō Myōhon zo ni zuite," *Chūgoku hoshō gaido* 49 (Gen Chō Mōfu, Tokyo, 1989), 17–23.

8 "Ch'uan-chu shih shou" (Ten poems [composed while] living on a boat), *Record*, *chüan* 29.

9 The portrait of Chung-feng Ming-

pen at Senbutsu-ji (hanging scroll, ink and color on silk, 125.2 x 51.9 cm), now on loan to the Kyoto National Museum, was originally housed in the library at Genjū-an. It is possible that this portrait was brought to Japan by Genkai. Unfortunately, the inscription on the portrait is so badly damaged that it is impossible to read the recipient's name. See Jan Fontein and Money L. Hickman, *Zen Painting and Calligraphy* (Boston: Museum of Fine Arts, Boston, 1970), fig. 15; Helmut Brinker and Hiroshi Kanazawa, *Zen Meister der Meditation in Bildern und Schriften* (Zürich: Museum Rietberg, 1993), fig. 25.

10 On Feng Tzu-chen, see Wang I, *Hai-li chi chi-tsun* (Ch'ang-sha: Yüeh-lu shu ch'u-pan-she, 1990).

11 Hanging scroll, ink on paper, 32.7 x 102.4 cm; published in the catalogue of the special exhibition for the 120th anniversary of the Tokyo National Museum, *Nihon to Tōyu no bi* (Tokyo, 1992), fig. 336.

12 See Hans Frankel, "The Plum Tree in Chinese Poetry," *Asiatische Studien* 6 (1952), 88–115.

13 "Shan-chu shih shou" (Ten poems [composed while] living in the mountains), *Record, chüan* 29.

14 See Yü Chün-fang, "Ming-pen, Creator of a Monastic Code," in "Chung-feng Ming-pen and Ch'an Buddhism in the Yüan," 448–56.

15 The title that the emperor conferred on the monk was Ch'an Master of the Perfect Splendor and Profound Wisdom of the Buddha's Compassion (*Fu tzu yüan chao kuang hui Ch'an shih*).

Such a robe still exists at the Nara National Museum. It came from Seun-ji temple, Yamanashi prefecture, which was founded by Ming-pen's disciple Gyōkai Honjō. Honjō stayed in China from 1317 to 1326. In addition to the robe, he also brought back to Japan his master's whisk, which is still kept at Seun-ji. The robe bears an inscription in ink, dated 1572, which identifies it as belonging to Ming-pen.

16 The stele no longer exists, but the text has been preserved in *Hsi T'ien-mu ts'u shan chi, chüan* 4, stele section.

17 Wen-tsung conferred on him the title Ch'an Master Chih Chüeh (*Chih chüeh Ch'an shih*), and Shun-ti the title State Teacher P'u ying (*P'u ying kuo-shih*).

18 "Che-chüeh ch'an-shih t'a-ming," *Record, chüan* 30.

19 Chu Chang-wen, *Mo-ch'ih pien* (Ink Pond compilation), *chüan* 1.

20 Published in *Ide* (1989), 102–4; *Nihon no bukkyō kizuita hitobito, sono shōzo to shō* (Nara, 1981), 181, no. 179.

21 I will discuss this issue in detail in my forthcoming dissertation.

22 Hanging scroll, ink and color on silk, 122 x 54.7 cm. The portrait is on loan to the Osaka Municipal Museum.

23 The Liang emperor Wu-ti asked the question, "What is the highest meaning of the holy truth?" Yüan-wu K'o-ch'in, remarking on this question, exclaims: "What a donkey's pole!" In his excellent German translation, Wilhelm Gundert explains that as a donkey can be tied to a pole so can the diffident spirit to theorems and dogmatic formula. In all the transcriptions of Chung-feng Ming-pen's inscription on the Yabumoto portrait, the character *lü* (donkey) is misread and hence impossible to translate. I identified the character *lü* and the source of the quote, *The Blue Cliff Record.*

24 Translation by Wen C. Fong, in Marilyn Wong Fu, "Calligraphy and Painting: Some Sung and Post-Sung

Parallels in North and South — A Re-assessment of the Southern Tradition'" (New York, 1985), 18–19.

25 Handscroll, ink on paper; 22 leaves, each measuring 14.4 x 14.2 cm.

26 It appears in section 18 of the publication.

27 See Chang Kuang-pin, "Pan Chao Meng-fu shu Chi-chiu-chang t'se wei Yü Ho ling-pen," in his *Yüan-ch'ao shu-hua-shih yen-chiu lun-chi* (Taipei: National Palace Museum, Taipei, 1979), 89–112.

28 See *Chung-kuo li-tai shu-fa chan-lan* (Shanghai: Shanghai Museum, 1973), 22–23.

29 Ink on paper, 35 x 63.8 cm.

30 Album leaf, ink on paper, 28.7 x 56.8 cm.

31 Handscroll, ink on paper, 25.9 x 627.9 cm, dated 1370. This work is now considered to be a later close copy or tracing copy of an original by Sung K'o. For a discussion of copies and questions of authenticity, see Hsiao Yen-i, "Sung K'o *T'ao shih ping hua chu shih hsiao ching* liang pen pien-wei," *Ku-kung po-wu-yüan yüan-k'an*, no. 1 (1985), 48–52.

32 It measures 64.4 x 25.6 cm.

33 See *Nihon no Bijutsu* 8, no. 123; and Helmut Brinker and Hiroshi Kanazawa, *Zen Meister der Meditation in Bildern und Schriften*, 236–37.

Shih Shou-ch'ien

Academia Sinica

Calligraphy as Gift: Wen Cheng-ming's (1470–1559) Calligraphy and the Formation of Soochow Literati Culture

Apart from being a form of art, Chinese calligraphy is an act of writing. This is because it conveys specific meanings or sentiments. In this regard, the expression of meaning is an essential part of a work of calligraphy, while the shape or form this expression of meaning is given is secondary. In other words, calligraphy must be a "meaningful writing." Only after this requirement is fulfilled can the aesthetic form of what is expressed be considered. Seen from this perspective, almost all great classical examples of Chinese calligraphy, from ancient oracle-bone and bronze inscriptions to stone rubbings, are "meaningful writings." It is this reality that underlies calligraphic theories that define calligraphy as an "image of the mind." To cite one example, in his famous *Preface Dedicated to Kao-hsien* (*Sung Kao-hsien shang-jen hsü*), Han Yü (768–824) describes the cursive-script calligraphy of Chang Hsü (ca. 700–750). The emotions of happiness, anger, sorrow, and sadness, says Han Yü, "move the heart, and find their expression in his [Chang Hsü] cursive script," and contemplation of the landscape, the sun and moon, and all "changing phenomena between heaven and earth, the joyful as well as the fearful, are expressed in his writing."[1] Such ideas are clearly based upon the concept of calligraphy as primarily an act of writing, in which the expression of meaning is at the core of its making.

The process of expressing meaning in a work of calligraphy is not complete with the creation of the work by the calligrapher, but extends to the intended audience as the recipient of the message. The nature and the size of this audience have a direct bearing upon the calligrapher's writing. Calligraphy for a publicly displayed stele inscription conveys a public message to an unlimited number of people with whom the writer has no personal relationship. Letters between friends, in contrast, carry private messages that are meant for a limited number of readers with whom the writer shares a personal relationship. Somewhere in between these two extremes are writings intended for joint appreciation by both the public and the private audience. There exists a large number of such writings, most of which are calligraphic transcriptions of literary compositions. Numerous writings of this kind appear after the Sung dynasty (960–1279), and may be said to represent the mainstream of the history of later Chinese calligraphy.

Writings that encompass private as well as public dimensions tend to engage the writer and his audience in a process of "gift giving." When a work of calligraphy takes the form of a gift, it is invested with certain social and cultural connotations. Gift giving not only engenders a particular pattern of exchange within a social network, but also requires that the recipient recompense the gift giver. This results in an effective system that shapes relationships between members of a particular social group. Since the socio-cultural value of the gift is difficult to quantify — even in cases where the recipient offers money as reimbursement — the relationship established by the exchange of gifts cannot easily be dissolved.[2] The unique and irreproducible character of a work of calligraphy only enhances its social value when exchanged as a gift, deepening the bond between the calligrapher as giver and his audience as recipient. The use of a distinctly personal calligraphic style reinforces the work's uniqueness, which in turn further intensifies the social value of the gift. This not only accounts for the high status accorded the art of calligraphy in Chinese society, but has also stimulated the rise to prominence of personal styles in the history of Chinese calligraphy. The topic of this paper, Wen Cheng-ming's (1470–1559) calligraphies of the poems he composed in Peking, is one of the most remarkable examples of calligraphy-as-gift in Chinese history.

Wen Cheng-ming's Peking Poems

Aside from being an outstanding painter, Wen Cheng-ming was throughout his life a dedicated calligrapher. Living to the advanced age of ninety, he left behind a considerable number of writings, most of which were created to be used as gifts. These writings-as-gifts were not always executed for a particular occasion; sometimes they were written in advance and later presented to his friends as gifts when the need arose.[3] From this, it is evident that the relationship between Wen Cheng-ming and his audience was not necessarily always a close one. This may also explain another idiosyncrasy in Wen's calligraphic activities, namely that he transcribed the same text more than once. In fact, Wen Cheng-ming's gift-writings that survive today mainly fall into two categories: transcriptions of *The Thousand Character Essay* (*Ch'ien-tzu wen*) and calligraphies of the poems he composed during his stay in Peking. *The Thousand Character Essay*, which served as a model-book for the learning of calligraphy, had been transcribed by numerous calligraphers over the centuries, and its textual content had little specific meaning to any of its writers. Although Wen Cheng-ming produced an astonishingly large number of transcriptions of this text — as many as one thousand, according to some sources[4] — it seems unlikely that he attached any particular significance to its textual content. In contrast, his Peking poems are highly personal in content, and his repeated transcriptions of the poems — outranking in number the transcriptions of his other compositions — deserves special attention.

Wen Cheng-ming stayed in Peking only a few years, from 1523 to 1526, but the relatively short time he spent in the capital would play a crucial role in his life. Before going to Peking, he had become a prominent member of the Soochow literati society. He harbored grand political ideals, but was unsuccessful in at least ten attempts to pass the provincial examinations. It was not until political reforms were introduced in 1523, at the beginning of the Chia-ching reign (1522–66), that he received the exceptional recommendation to the post of Editorial Assistant (*Tai-chao*) in the Hanlin Academy (*Han-lin yüan*) in Peking. Though the position was only that of a second-class official of the ninth rank, this office allowed him to work at the Hanlin Academy, the most highly respected institution among the literati class, and to associate with prominent Academy officials. The appointment must have been a great honor for Wen Cheng-ming. After the years of frustration following his repeated failures in the provincial examinations, his appointment to the Hanlin Academy must have been emotionally gratifying, especially in light of the despair he would soon experience upon his departure from Peking under adverse circumstances.[5] Evidence of Wen's state of mind during his stay in Peking is most clearly recorded in his Peking poems.

The poems, collected in Wen Cheng-ming's *Collected Writings of Wen Cheng-ming* (*Fu-t'ien chi*), may be divided into four distinct groups. The first group consists of poems that relate his feelings and impressions while at the Hanlin Academy. The second group of poems describes the grand court ceremonies in which he took part, and the third depicts the scenic areas of the Forbidden City that he was privileged to see. Nostalgic poems about his home in Soochow comprise the fourth group of the Peking poems. Of these categories, the first three became the primary material for Wen Cheng-ming's later calligraphic writings.

A verse from his "Morning Audience at the Heavenly Endowment Hall" (*Feng-t'ien-tien tsao-ch'ao*) is a typical example of the first group of poems:

> The moon moves to the Blue Dragon constellation,
>   casting the shadow of imperial palaces to the West;
> Surrounding the Chien-chang Hall,
>   clouds are dispersing and starlight is dim.
> Jade flutes compete with each other,
>   creating fabulous music of the heavenly phoenix;
> Colored fans are laid out in balanced symmetry,
>   their pheasant feathers orderly arranged.
> The old [I] gratefully join those arranged in a row,
>   approaching the palace stairs;
> Shamed and ridiculous I feel,
>   my humble name is found on the Golden Horse Gate.

When the sun is high, I return to the Hanlin office,
and receive the imperial edicts;
With the fragrance of ceremonial incense in my sleeves,
I break open the emperor's vermilion seal paste.[6]

In this description of the gathering of officials at the palace in the early morning hours for the court audience, Wen Cheng-ming conveys his feelings of reverence and awe at being present at such a grand and solemn occasion.

The second category of Wen Cheng-ming's Peking poems, describing palace ceremonies, is represented by his "Awaiting the Emperor's Return from the Southern Suburbs" (*Kung-hou ta-chia huan tzu nan-ch'ao*):

The bell on the Imperial Lord's returning chariot calms the singing
of myriad larks;
Purplish clouds, gathering above, shelter the powerful essence.
Chariots and armor glitter like brilliant constellations.
On banners preceding the emperor's chariot, sun and moon shine
brightly.
For ten miles the spring wind heralds the approach of the imperial
procession;
All quarters are in harmony with the music of sage emperors.
In my old age I have the chance
to view personally the glory of this imperial procession;
And wish to take the "Ssu wen" ode [in the *Book of Poetry*]
as my example in praise of this peaceful reign.[7]

"Southern Suburbs" refers to the yearly sacrifice to Heaven by the emperor at the time of the winter solstice, which was held in the southern outskirts of the capital. Upon completion of this state ceremony—a reaffirmation of the emperor's link with Heaven, Earth, and the imperial ancestors—the entire court would await the return of the imperial procession to the palace in symbolic acceptance of the emperor's renewed Mandate from Heaven. Wen's ornate lyrics describe the grandeur of the imperial procession, imbuing this sacred occasion with a sense of universal harmony and participation. Once again one can detect in the poem Wen Cheng-ming's excitement at being a privileged observer and participant.

"Ten Poems on the Western Garden" (*Hsi-yüan shih shih shou*), composed by Wen in the spring of 1525 on the occasion of his visit to the Western Garden with his Hanlin colleagues, exemplifies the third category of the Peking poems. One of these, "Lake T'ai-yeh," reads:

The water's expanse, the vast pond merging with heaven;
Ten *li* of lotus, a smooth embroidered cloud.

I have heard that Emperor Chao of the Han dynasty wrote a
yüeh-fu song on the Yellow Crane that flew over Lake T'ai-yeh,
and have seen how the stone whale in Lake K'un-ming of Han Wu-ti's
palace stirred his fins at the blowing of the autumn wind.
The Jade Rainbow Bridge arches across the blue sky;
Silver mountains rise from the world through mist.
Now I know the realm through which the phoenix chariot passes,
where wild geese hover peacefully in the sky above and are
never startled.[8]

Lake T'ai-yeh, like other scenic spots in the Western Garden, refers to sites mentioned in Han dynasty literature and at the same time alludes to the realm of the supernatural. While Wen frequently refers to the supernatural, his lyrics also reveal his sense of awe and good fortune at being able to see this extraordinary scenery in person and to experience the difference between "paradise" and the "ordinary world."

Such special experiences as his visit to the Western Garden constitute a theme that runs through each of the first three categories of Wen Cheng-ming's Peking poems. Wen's personal presence at the occasions he describes figures prominently in the poems, and serves not only to reinforce the realism of the poetic description, but also to intensify the awareness that Wen Cheng-ming's lot was different from that of the ordinary scholar. After his return home to Soochow, Wen often transcribed these Peking poems, mostly for the purpose of conveying to his readers the honor of having been present at such special occasions in the capital, an experience that few of the educated elite of his time were privileged to share. The content of these poems sets off in even higher contrast his decision to take leave from office, and reinforces his image as a recluse disinterested in the pursuit of an official career.

Calligraphic Writings of the Peking Poems

According to Chou Tao-chen's compilation of Wen Cheng-ming's poetic works, *Wen Cheng-ming chi*, 1,721 of Wen's poems survive today. Although the Peking poems account for only a small part of this total, they served as the text for many of Wen's calligraphic writings. At least sixty-five of his works of calligraphy preserved today are transcriptions of his Peking poems. The original number must have been much larger. Such a high rate of repeated transcriptions is rare in the history of Chinese calligraphy. The dates of their execution range from 1526, when Wen was still in Peking, to 1558, the year before his death. The year 1537 marks a watershed in the production of these writings. After this date, examples of calligraphic transcriptions of his Peking poems can be found in every year, a fact that

Figure 1
Wen Cheng-ming (1470–1559). *Poems*, 1531. Two sections of a handscroll, ink on paper, 27.5 x 217.2 cm. Ex. coll. Lo Chih-hsi Collection. From *Lun-hsien ta-lu Ming-chia shu-fa* (San-ch'ung City, Taipei County: Shih-hsin ch'u-pan-she), pl. 10.

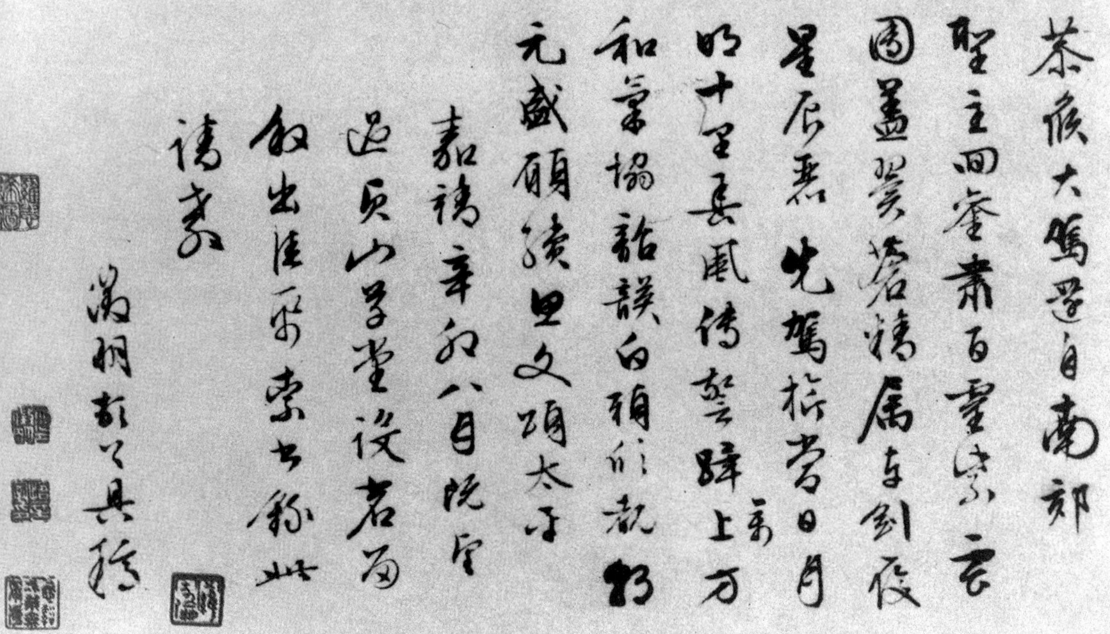

underscores the important role these transcriptions must have played in Wen Cheng-ming's later years.

The earliest of Wen's calligraphic writings of the Peking poems is *Morning Audience Poems in Running Script*, executed in the summer of 1526 and now in the collection of the Chi-lin Provincial Museum.[9] This handscroll, written for a National University student named Yu-ch'ing, contains transcriptions of fourteen poems from the first and second categories of the Peking poems, including "Morning Audience at the Heavenly Endowment Hall" and "Awaiting the Emperor's Return from the Southern Suburbs." Wen wrote these calligraphies while he was still at the Hanlin Academy, not long after he composed the poems. The Chi-lin scroll is clearly an early version of the original poetic compositions, as the transcriptions differ from the version of the poems recorded in Wen's collected writings. Apart from some differences in their titles, as many as eight of the fourteen poems are noticeably different in the wording of the verses.

Although the identity of Yu-ch'ing, the recipient of the scroll, remains unknown, Wen Cheng-ming's later letters indicate that the same person was appointed to a minor provincial post after his graduation from the National University, and Wen appears to have been in contact with him after his return home to Soochow.[10] While information on their relationship is scanty, it seems that Yu-ch'ing may have been a literatus from the Soochow area and that his visit to Wen Cheng-ming in the summer of 1526 in Peking was an expression of his admiration for Wen's position at the Hanlin Aca-

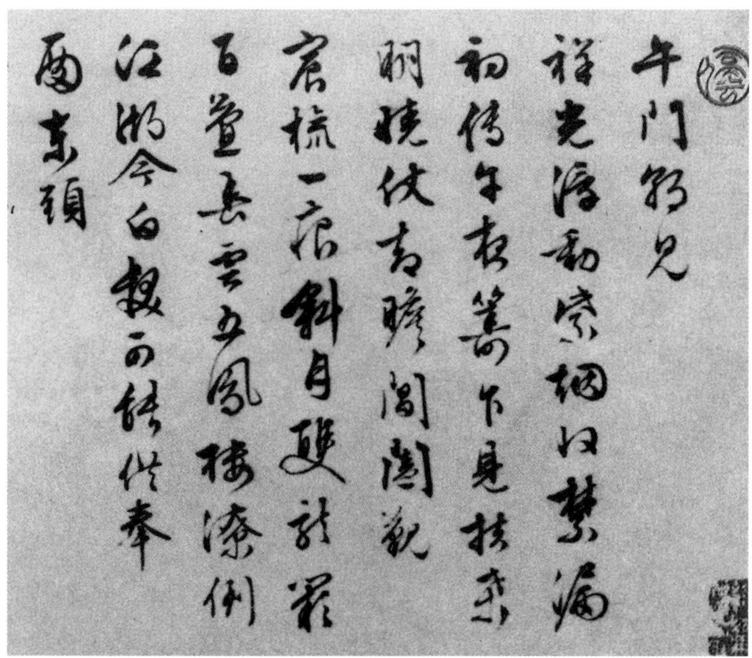

demy. The Chi-lin scroll, probably written and presented as a gift to Yu-ch'ing on the occasion of his visit, displays Wen's literary talent and gives an account of his recent experiences at court, which was probably one of the main topics of conversation during Yu-ch'ing's visit.

The Chi-lin scroll reflects characteristics of Wen Cheng-ming's early calligraphy. The characters are elegant and elongated in shape, and the brushstrokes remain sharp, with no traces of the intense modulations in brush movement seen in his later works. By 1531, his calligraphy already shows a fundamental change in style. A handscroll from that year (fig. 1), formerly in the collection of Lo Chih-hsi, contains eight poems written in running-cursive (*hsing-ts'ao*) script. The titles and phrasing of "Morning Audience at the Wu Gate" as well as "Awaiting the Emperor's Return from the Southern Suburbs" differ from that in the Chi-lin scroll and are identical to the version in his collected writings. This clearly indicates that Wen Cheng-ming continued to work on his Peking poems even after he returned home and that the 1531 version represents more or less what would become the final version of the poems. The Lo scroll also shows new developments in Wen's calligraphic style. The characters are squarer in shape and there is more modulation in the thickness of the brushstrokes, which creates a greater internal tension and balance in the structure of the characters. These characteristics become even more pronounced in the handscroll *Poem in Running Script in Response to a Gift Bestowed*, written three years later, in 1534, and now in the Kiangsi Provincial Museum.

The 1531 handscroll was executed in the Thatched Hall of the Pure Mountain (*Chen-shan ts'ao-t'ang*). According to Wen's inscription at the end of the scroll, the work was written at a tea party where the host "offered a fine piece of paper in request of writing" and Wen responded in appreciation of the host's hospitality. The Thatched Hall of the Pure Mountain was the residence of Lu Ts'an (1494–1551), an old acquaintance of Wen Cheng-ming's in Peking. At that time, Lu was pursuing advanced studies as a Bachelor at the Hanlin Academy in preparation for civil office. After his appointment to office, Lu Ts'an became renowned for being daring and straight- forward in his criticism, a trait that caused him to offend powerful officials. It was not long before he was banned from court and eventually returned home.[11] The poems Wen Cheng-ming transcribed for Lu Ts'an on the day of the gathering undoubtedly elicited recollections of their days at court.

In the 1530s Wen Cheng-ming apparently did not mind sharing his experiences at court with others. In fact, he actively engaged in the rewriting of his Peking poems. Apart from old acquaintances like Lu Ts'an, Wen also transcribed these poems for a number of other people. That a large percentage of these recipients remain unidentified suggests that Wen shared a less intimate relationship with them. Besides the Kiangsi Museum hand-

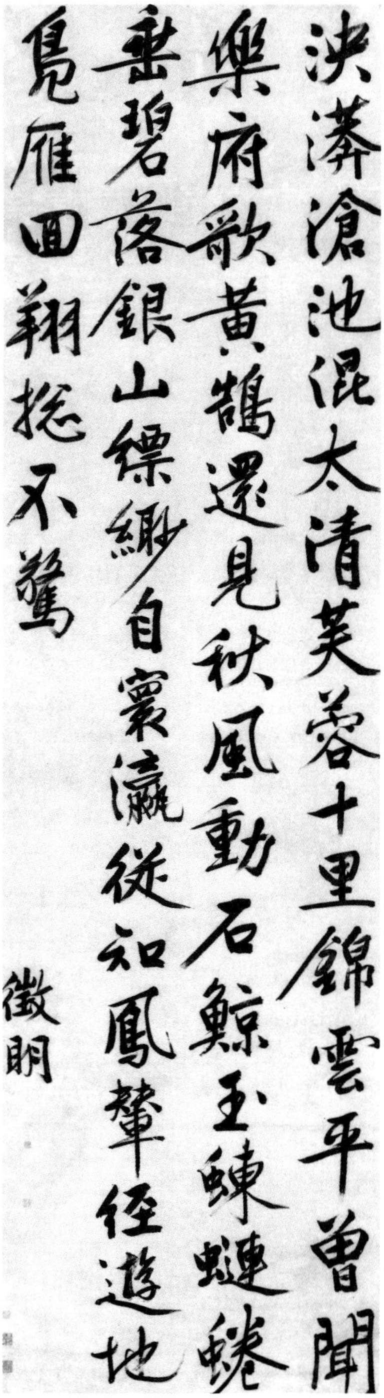

Figure 2
Wen Cheng-ming (1470–1559). *Lake T'ai-yeh.* Hanging scroll, ink on paper, 343.5 x 122.5 cm. The Art Museum, Princeton University, bequest of John B. Elliott.

Figure 3
Wen Cheng-ming (1470–1559). *Awaiting the Emperor's Return from the Southern Suburbs* (*Kung-hou ta-chia huan tzu nan-ch'ao*). Hanging scroll, ink on paper, 345.4 x 99.7 cm. The Metropolitan Museum of Art, Anonymous Gift, 1950. From Nakata Yūjirō and Shen Fu, eds., *Ōbei shūzō Chūgoku hōsho meisekishū*, Ming-Ch'ing vol. 1 (Tokyo: Chūō Kōronsha, 1983), pl. 72.

Figure 4
Wen Cheng-ming (1470–1559). *Morning Audience at the Heavenly Endowment Hall* (*Feng-t'ien-tien tsao-ch'ao*). Hanging scroll, ink on paper, 343.8 x 99.5 cm. National Palace Museum, Taipei. *From Ku-kung li-tai fa-shu ch'üan-chi* (Taipei: National Palace Museum, Taipei 1979), v. 30, pl. 45.

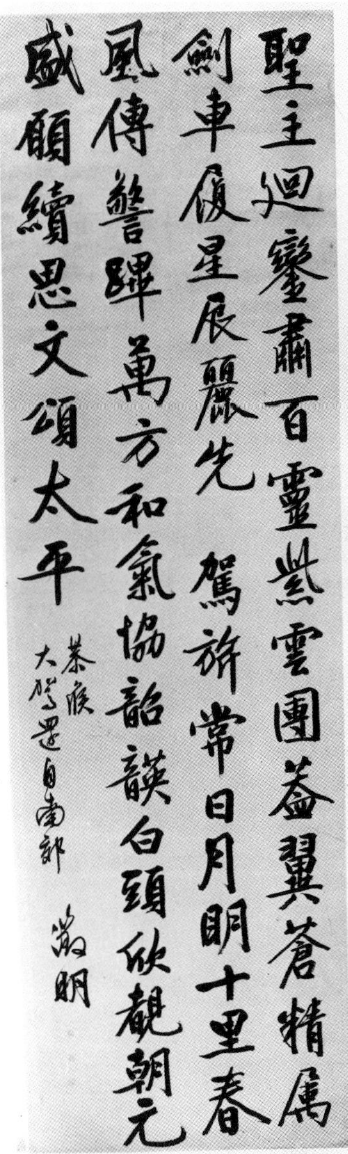

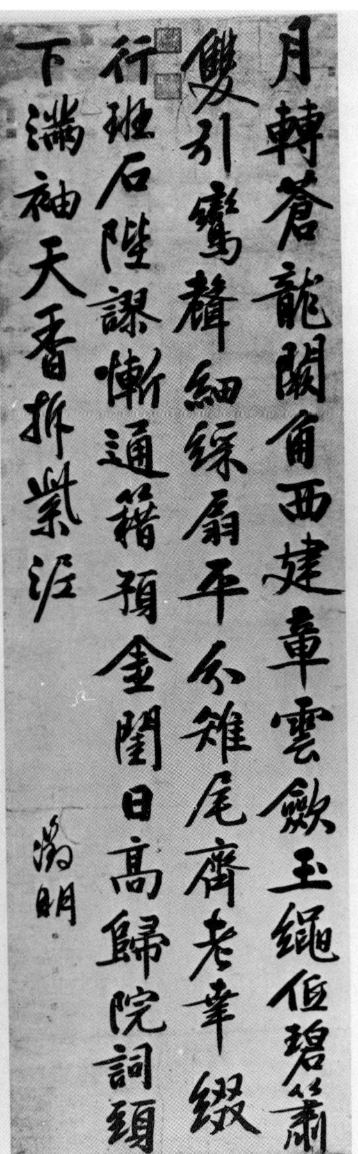

scroll mentioned above, many works of this type preserved today are in the format of large hanging scrolls. For example, *Lake T'ai-yeh* (fig. 2), in the John B. Elliott Collection, The Art Museum, Princeton University, *Awaiting the Emperor's Return from the Southern Suburbs* (fig. 3), in the collection of The Metropolitan Museum of Art, *Morning Audience at the Heavenly Endowment Hall* (fig. 4), in the National Palace Museum, Taipei, and *Longevity Embroidery Bestowed by the Emperor* (*Ssu ch'ang-ming ts'ai-lü*)[12] are all hanging scrolls over 350 cm in height. Although they all are of high quality, none of these works names the recipient. While scholarly opinion has tended to date these scrolls to Wen Cheng-ming's Peking period, close observation of their calligraphic styles calls for a reassessment. The running-cursive script of the inscription to the Metropolitan scroll as well as that of the text in the *Longevity Embroidery* scroll is similar in style to that of the Lo Chih-hsi and Kiangsi scrolls, which suggests the 1530s as a more appropriate date for these scrolls. While most of these large-format scrolls are written in the more formal running-standard script, the brushwork and character structure still display delicate modulation, which would have perfectly suited the grand halls where such huge calligraphy scrolls would have been hung. In his large-format works, Wen Cheng-ming seems to be proudly stating his court experiences to the viewer. Such works served not only to symbolize the importance of the halls, but also to confirm the moral identity and social status of the owners of the scrolls.

The *Lake T'ai-yeh* scroll in the Elliott Collection is probably one of the earliest of Wen Cheng-ming's many extant calligraphic transcriptions of his "Ten Poems on the Western Garden." In the 1540s Wen appears to have transcribed these poems with increasing frequency. A 1546 album of the *Ten Poems* (fig. 5) in the collection of the Nanking Municipal Museum dates from this period. The album contains the full set of poems written in running-cursive script. Each of the ten poems concerns different scenery in the imperial garden, and the wording of the transcription is nearly identical to the version in his collected writings. Although the original poems are not extant, the recorded postscript mentions that the poems were composed in the spring of 1525 when Wen was just about to return home.[13] It therefore seems likely that the calligraphic style of the original would have been close to that of the 1526 *Morning Audience Poems* in the Chi-lin Provincial Museum. In comparison, the Nanking album displays noticeable changes in Wen's calligraphic style. The brush is manipulated to create variations in tip pressure, and rhythmic movement is created in the spatial relationships within characters and the overall composition, in the variations of character size, and in the alternation between running and cursive script forms. While the characters are not entirely interconnected, the subtle alternation in their inclination toward left and right causes the whole com-

Figure 5
Wen Cheng-ming (1470–1559). *Ten Poems on the Western Garden* (*Hsi-yüan shih shih shou*), 1546. Album, ink on paper, 24 x 14 cm. Nanking Municipal Museum. From *Shu-fa ts'ung-kan* 28 (1991), 11–24.

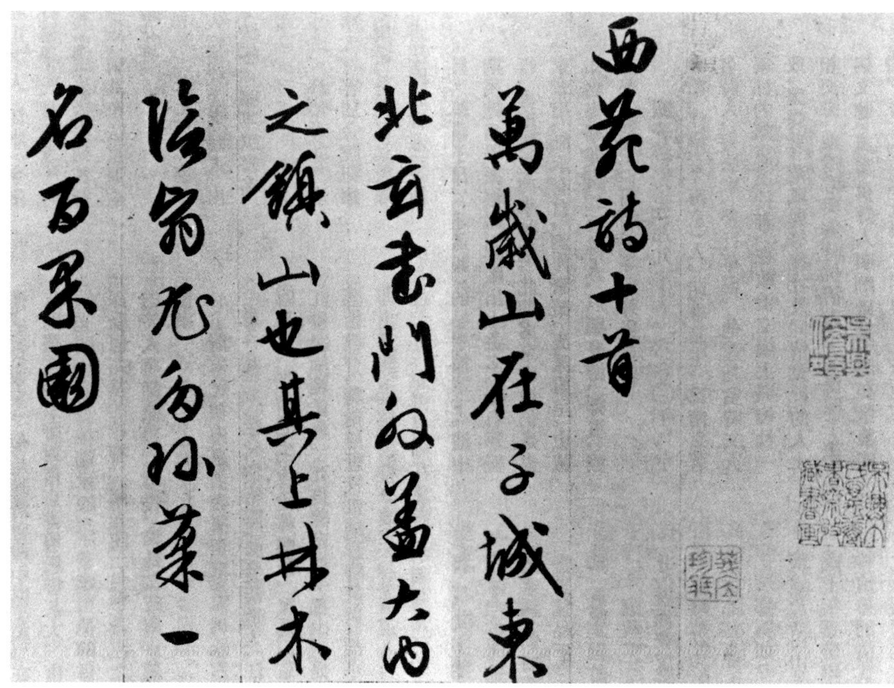

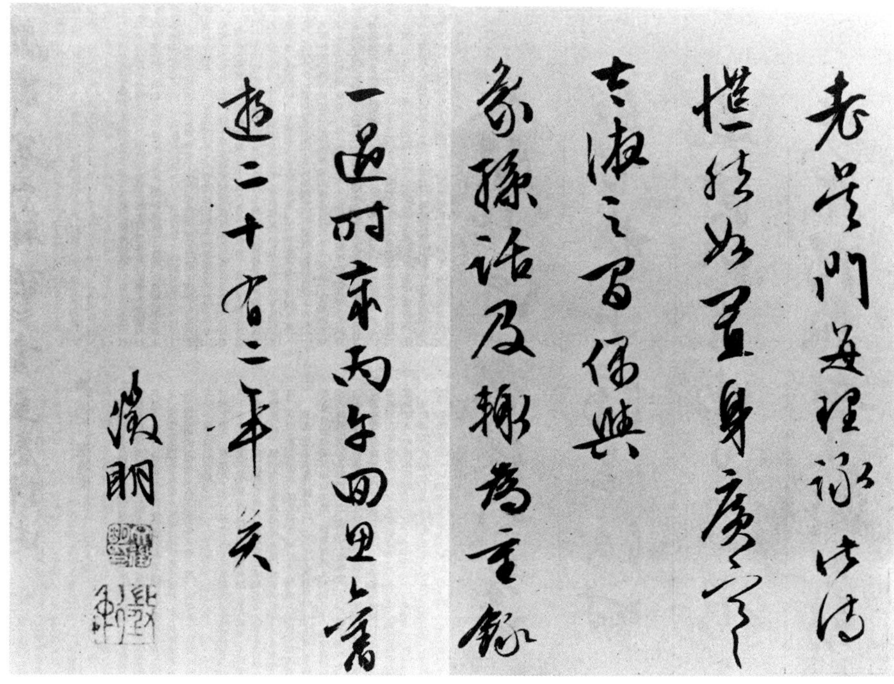

position to be drawn together in one movement. These are precisely the stylistic characteristics of Wen's mature calligraphy, the natural grace of which derives from both the Wang Hsi-chih (303–361) tradition and the expressionism of the Northern Sung (960–1127) masters. The imagery pervading the set of Western Garden poems is that of "magical palaces and magnificent mansions, rising up to the heavens," of which "the common man cannot even catch a glimpse." At the same time, these verses express the happiness and elation that Wen Cheng-ming felt in having the chance to visit these places. In this sense, the Nanking album may be said to be a true image of the author's mind.

Wen Cheng-ming composed his poems on the Western Garden with the intention that they would serve as a souvenir of his days in the capital. These memories were also meant to be shared with his friends back home, who in reading the poems would "find themselves as if present amidst the Moon Palace and Lake T'ai-yeh."[14] This was precisely the case with the Nanking album. In his colophon to the album, Wen repeats this phrase in reference to the impression of being present once again in the magical realm of the Western Garden that he had visited some twenty-two years earlier. The recipient of the album—and the person sharing these memories with him—was Lu Chih-ch'iu of T'ai-ts'ang, Kiangsu. The grandson of the famous official Lu Jung (1436–1494), Lu Chih-ch'iu was born into a prominent family and from an early age was a gifted literary talent. Although he harbored high political ideals, Lu never had the chance to put these ideals into practice. In his official career, he did not advance beyond the position of district school instructor. The pain and frustration that this must have caused him is reflected in his own words: "created from the material that heroes are made of, I was assigned to be no more than a poor scholar."[15] Lu Chih-ch'iu's experience in being unable to put his ideals into practice is somewhat similar to that of Wen Cheng-ming's. Although his words reveal a tone of arrogance that cannot be found in Wen's character, Lu undoubtedly would have admired Wen's account of his visit to the palace gardens. The fact that Wen Cheng-ming transcribed these poems especially for Lu Chih-ch'iu indicates that the album was intended not only to record Wen's personal, even dreamlike, memories of these glorious moments, but also to console his friend for his unrealized ambitions.

In the last stage of his calligraphic career, Wen Cheng-ming continued to transcribe his Western Garden poems, but his late work also reveals a deepened sense of his own place in history. By this time the recognized leader of the Chiang-nan literary circle, Wen Cheng-ming had also earned widespread esteem for his achievements in calligraphy. The fact that Wen regarded himself the successor to Chu Yün-ming (1461–1527) reflects his aspiration to attain a position of importance in the history of calligraphy.

Figure 6
Wen Cheng-ming (1470–1559). *Transcription of the Classic of the Yellow Court* (*Huang-t'ing ching*). Rubbing from *Model Calligraphies from the Hall of Lingering Clouds* (*T'ing-yün-kuan fa-t'ieh*), v. 12.

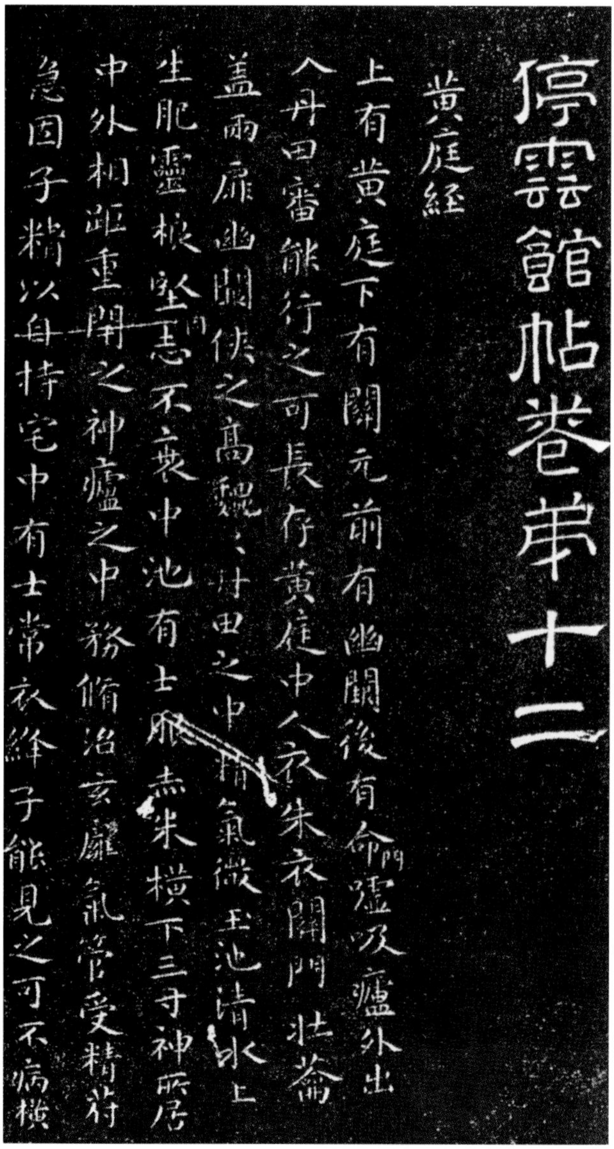

In 1537 he began the preparatory work for his *Model Calligraphies from the Hall of Lingering Clouds* (*T'ing-yün-kuan fa-t'ieh*), which was completed posthumously in 1560. Following Hua Hsia's (b. ca. 1498) *Model Calligraphies of the Studio of True Appreciation* (*Chen-shang-chai t'ieh*) of 1522, Wen's compilation of ink rubbings of calligraphic writings throughout the ages was an undertaking of considerable importance. The project, which totaled twelve volumes (nine volumes more than Hua Hsia's compilation) and to which he devoted the last twenty-three years of his life, was clearly one that Wen Cheng-ming took great pains to accomplish. The first volume of *Model Calligraphies from the Hall of Lingering Clouds* is dedicated to Wang Hsi-chih's *Classic of the Yellow Court* (*Huang-t'ing ching*). The next ten volumes cover the most important calligraphers from the T'ang (618–907), Sung (960–1279), Yüan (1260–1368), and Ming (1368–1644) dynasties, and the eleventh is dedicated to four works by the Ming calligrapher Chu Yün-ming. This compilation clearly represented Wen's personal vision of the history of Chinese calligraphy. The final volume is devoted to three of Wen's own writings, *Transcription of the Classic of the Yellow Court* (fig. 6), his *Poem on Dwelling in the Mountains*, and his *Ten Poems on the Western Garden* (fig. 7). A clear sense of purpose is reflected in his choice of works for this volume, especially in his selection of his transcription of Wang Hsi-chih's *Classic of the Yellow Court* to parallel the subject of the first volume of the compilation. One must bear in mind that Wen Cheng-ming was especially proficient in writing small-sized standard script and was in fact praised as the greatest calligrapher of this script since the beginning of the Ming dynasty. Moreover, his ability to continue writing this small script well into his eighties, without loss of eyesight, is close to legendary. Wen Cheng-ming's selection of his *Transcription of the Classic of the Yellow Court* to represent his achievements in calligraphy testifies to the fact that it was as an interpreter and a follower of the Wang Hsi-chih tradition that he wished to be recognized in the history of Chinese calligraphy.

Although Wen Cheng-ming excelled in small-sized standard script, he probably preferred writing running-cursive script. Among the large number of his writings in this script form that have come down to us, works such as the previously mentioned *Morning Audience Poems* as well as Su Shih's (1037–1101) "Ode to the Red Cliff" (*Ch'ih-pi fu*) are examples of texts that he transcribed repeatedly.[16] Again, Wen's decision to include in the last volume of his *Model Calligraphies from the Hall of Lingering Clouds* a 1552 version of his Western Garden poems illustrates the importance he attached to the writing of this set of poems.[17] Although the ink-rubbing version is very close to the Nanking version he wrote six years earlier, there is now a pronounced stress on the variations in the use of the sides of the brush tip. This reveals Wen's ambition to invigorate the running-cursive

Figure 7
Wen Cheng-ming (1470–1559). *Ten Poems on the Western Garden* (*Hsi-yüan shih shih shou*). Rubbing from *Model Calligraphies from the Hall of Lingering Clouds* (*T'ing-yün-kuan fa-t'ieh*), v. 12.

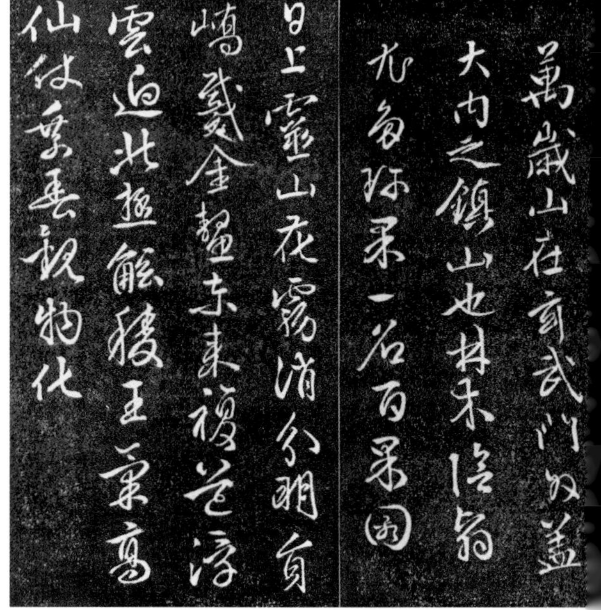

tradition derived from Chih Yung (ca. 514–604) and Ch'u Sui-liang's (596–658) *Preface to the Sacred Teaching* (*Sheng-chiao hsü*) with the style of the Northern Sung calligraphers Su Shih, Huang T'ing-chien (1045–1105), and Mi Fu (1052–1107). In this new interpretation of the Wang Hsi-chih tradition, Wen Cheng-ming endeavors to combine the natural elegance of the Wang style with the unaffected quality of the Northern Sung masters. It is essentially this achievement that he saw as his main accomplishment and contribution to the history of calligraphy.

Wen Cheng-ming's decision to include the *Ten Poems of the Western Garden* in his *Model Calligraphies from the Hall of Lingering Clouds* was not made solely on stylistic grounds. The content of the poems was also particularly important to the creation of the self-image to which Wen aspired. The unaffected elegance that he sought to achieve in his personal style of calligraphy helped to reinforce this image. Seen from this perspective, both written text and calligraphic style worked together to impart a particular "image of the mind" to the viewer.

Gift-Giver and Recipient

Wen Cheng-ming's transcription of his Peking poems unquestionably had dimensions of meaning that were known to him alone, yet these works were not written just for himself. They were also meant to be presented as gifts. Through this process of gift exchange, these writings transmitted a certain image of the author that prompted various responses, depending on the status of the recipient. These exchange relationships, in which an intimate bond was formed between both parties involved in the exchange, played an active role in the creation of the literati society in the Chiang-nan region.

Apart from relatives and students, Wen Cheng-ming's transcriptions of the Peking poems were presented to close acquaintances, such as Lu Ts'an, the recipient of the 1531 handscroll discussed earlier. These friends generally were men of high literary and scholarly accomplishment. Some had held official positions at court, but all had returned home after having encountered the frustrations of political life. Lu Ts'an is an example. Having enjoyed in his early years the support of the leader of the Chiang-nan literary community, Wang Ao (1450–1524), Lu gained a reputation for his boldness, which led him to criticize such powerful ministers as Chang Ts'ung (1475–1539) and Kuei O (act. 1511–30). Although this won him sympathy in political circles, he could not escape banishment from court. In this context, Wen Cheng-ming's gift of calligraphy of his Peking poems to Lu Ts'an can be seen from a new perspective. At first glance, the poems appear to be no more than a description of Wen's experiences at court and to serve as recollections for both him and his friend, since they shared similar memories of the past. From these recollections, however, inevitably followed memories of frustration, and these must have been unbearably painful for both men to look back upon. When Lu Ts'an received Wen's gift, the memories of these hardships must have been part of the exchange. On the other hand, looking beyond the similarities between Wen's and Lu's court experiences, there are important differences. Although Wen Cheng-ming had lost faith in politics, his return home, unlike Lu Ts'an's, had been a voluntary decision. Lu undoubtedly admired Wen Cheng-ming's being able to walk away unharmed from a perilous situation. This, in turn, must have deepened Lu's sense of self-pity for his own misfortune in having been forced to endure the humiliation of banishment, while accentuating Wen Cheng-ming's image as a recluse freed from the cares of political office. Thus was established an intimate tie between gift-giver and recipient.

It is easy to understand Lu Ts'an's response. At the root of the banishment and humiliation of these gifted people lay their inability to recognize the nature of politics and their lack of courage to retreat at a suitable moment. Wen Cheng-ming's ability to discern the perils in the political arena, even before they were made manifest, and resolutely request to leave office naturally earned him the admiration and respect of others who had faced similar situations. When Lu Ts'an composed his "Preface to Longevity" on the occasion of Wen Cheng-ming's eightieth birthday, in 1549, he noted that Wen Cheng-ming had been "promoted by recommendation to the Bureau of Dynastic History at the Hanlin Academy, but since he would not yield to influential officials, he requested leave from office and returned home. The world holds his moral integrity in high esteem, and it is a pity it was not given to him to succeed even once in the official examinations."[18] Another friend of Wen Cheng-ming's, Huang-fu Fang (1503–1582), expressed similar ideas in a composition he wrote in honor of Wen's ninetieth birthday.[19] In several of his poems, Huang-fu repeatedly praised Wen's lofty image: "soon weary with life at court, he took leave of the capital, and yet indulges in landscape to which he entrusts his lofty emotions."[20] In fact, Huang-fu Fang had had experiences similar to those of Lu Ts'an. He, too, showed literary talent at an early age and passed the *chin-shih* examination, at the age of twenty-seven. But not long after his appointment to civil office, he offended influential officials and was subsequently jailed and repeatedly demoted until his retirement from a post in far-off Yün-nan province.[21]

Quite a few literati experienced similar misfortune, and even though they may have never met Wen Cheng-ming in person, they identified with him as a role model and actively sought to obtain his calligraphic writings. Shen Lien (1507–1557) is one example. After earning his *chih-shih* degree in 1538, Shen was appointed to several provincial posts. A critical attack on Prime Minister Yen Sung (1480–1565) and his son, however, caused him to suffer public flogging, removal from office in 1541, and banishment to distant Pao-an prefecture, in Shansi. In 1557 Shen was falsely accused of plotting a rebellion, for which he received the death penalty.[22] During his years of banishment, Shen Lien had sent Wen Cheng-ming a request for his calligraphy, wishing to feel the spirit of Wen's "refined talents, of his lofty and pure integrity, his retirement to the countryside, his growth in esteem with old age."[23] Although Shen Lien never regretted his attack on Yen Sung, he could not but be deeply saddened by his inability to realize his ideals as a loyal official. At heart Shen desired to follow Wen Cheng-ming's example and live in reclusion like T'ao Yüan-ming (372–427). Unable to do so, it was in Wen's calligraphic writings that Shen sought solace with a kindred spirit.

Predicaments in government office were apparently a common source of frustration for many in the official class during the Ming dynasty. Such troubles were not necessarily brought about by harsh punishment such as the incarceration or flogging that Huang-fu Fang and Shen Lien had undergone. Even ordinary setbacks in career promotion commonly led to frustration. Such circumstances were the result of the ongoing struggles between political factions at court since the mid-Ming period, and reflected the psychological inability of officialdom to adjust its lofty ideals to political realities. Frustrated officials naturally sought to obtain Wen Cheng-ming's works of calligraphy as gifts. Wang Shih-chen (1526–1590) provides an interesting case. Obtaining his *chin-shih* degree in 1547, at the young age of twenty-two, Wang had an early start in his official career. But only six years later, in 1553, in his "Short Poem on Self-Ridicule," Wang vents his frustration at being stuck in a low-ranking position in the Ministry of Justice, unable to advance as fast as he wished: "Five years a junior secretary, I feel stranded and have no chance of promotion." He even hints at retiring from office: "I address a letter to the Director of Personnel Administration, in which I ask to retire."[24] In that year while traveling through the Chiang-nan region on official business, Wang Shih-chen encountered local upheavals caused by pirate attacks. When he subsequently escorted his mother to safety in Soochow, he had the chance to meet Wen Cheng-ming, who presented him with several works of painting and calligraphy. One of the works he received was a calligraphy of fourteen poems, the *Morning Audience Poems.*[25] At the time, Wang Shih-chen was not experiencing any particular difficulties in his career and did not harbor serious thoughts of resignation. When he met Wen Cheng-ming, however, Wang acknowledged his admiration for a life in reclusion, which Wen symbolized. Upon receiving the *Morning Audience Poems*, Wang seemed to respond by assuring Wen Cheng-ming that he was not at all infatuated with life as a government official.

Most of the recipients of Wen Cheng-ming's Peking poems, however, were not officials but members of a new social group in the Chiang-nan area who had recently risen to the upper echelons of Ming society. Although generally quite wealthy, members of this group held officialdom in high esteem. They not only made every effort to associate with the official class, but also tried to procure positions in civil office, if not for themselves, then for their sons. A few who had literary talent secured official title through the civil examinations and subsequent admission to the civil service. But the vast majority were obliged to buy their way into the National University in order to advance in social class. From the mid-fifteenth to the end of the sixteenth century, these so-called Students by Purchase (*li-chien*) grew in number; according to some sources, they eventually accounted for seventy percent of the seats in the two National Universities.[26] A considerable number of the recipients of Wen Cheng-ming's calligraphic writings are referred to as National University student (*t'ai-hsüeh*), Literary scholar (*wen-hsüeh*), or Cultivated scholar (*mao-hsüeh*), but there is no mention of their names in historical sources such as collected writings or local gazetteers. Wen's friends possibly included members of this new social group. Both Yu-ch'ing and Lu Chih-ch'iu, mentioned above, were National University students who may have had this kind of social background.

Among the few letters by Wen Cheng-ming that survive today, some mention calligraphies presented as gifts to friends who were National University students. For example, Wen once wrote two handscrolls of mixed compositions, one large hanging scroll, and four large and small hanging scrolls for a student named Hsin-ch'iu. (By nature a careful and polite man, in this instance Wen could not help complaining about the trouble this large request caused him.[27]) The famous collector Hsiang Yüan-pien (1525–1590) is yet another example of this type of recipient.[28] It is clear that Hsiang Yüan-pien had originally procured a title for himself as National University student following his financial success in business. Yet Hsiang would end up making less use of his acquired status as a Student by Purchase, possibly because the title had greatly diminished in social value by the end of the sixteenth century. A letter from Wen Cheng-ming in the collection of the Kwangtung Provincial Museum addressed to National University Cultivated Talent Mo-lin (Hsiang Yüan-pien) mentions a *Letter from the North Mountain* as well as two damask silk hanging scrolls that Wen wrote for his friend.[29] Though the works mentioned in the letter may well be lost, we may still form an impression about what the hanging scrolls were like from the large number of extant seventeenth-century writings on damask silk. Wen's scrolls must have resembled such huge hanging scrolls as those in the Elliott collection—Wang To's (1592–1652) *Calligraphy after Wang Hsi-chih* or Fu Shan's (1607–1684/85) *Poem on the Heavenly Emperor*—and must have been hung in a grand hall in Hsiang's residence. In 1547 Hsiang requested Ch'iu Ying (d. 1552) to paint at his residence. In response, Ch'iu painted his

Conversation in the Shade of Wu-t'ung Trees and *Passing the Summer Day beneath Banana Palms*, both in the National Palace Museum, Taipei. These huge paintings, measuring up to 280 cm in height, were probably ordered especially for display in the main hall of Hsiang's residence.[30] The large hanging scroll Wen Cheng-ming wrote for Hsin-ch'iu also may have belonged to this same category of writings. This is not surprising considering the luxurious lifestyle enjoyed by most National University students.

The effect these refined gentlemen desired to produce by adorning their mansions with Wen Cheng-ming's calligraphy is perhaps best expressed in Hu Ying-ling's (act. second half of the 16th century) comments about a Morning Audience poem by Wen: "grandeur and magnificence come together in refined harmony with the content of this inscription."[31] Such an effect was engendered not only by the specific calligraphic style that Wen created for his large-format works, but also by the symbolic presence of Wen Cheng-ming's image in his attached colophon. In the eyes of the recipient, Wen's colophon represented his presence as the "drafter at the heavenly court"[32] who revealed to his audience grand visions of the Forbidden City. As such, the hall in which the calligraphy hung was transformed into a domain of lofty refinement and the host and his guests transported to the courtly palaces, allowing them to cleanse themselves of any feelings of social inferiority.

Regardless of family background or lifestyle, the identification with literati values by this new social group of which these National University students were part was an acquired *noblesse oblige*. Those who belonged to this new class, therefore, may be regarded as members of the literati society, but members at its periphery who, as such, played a crucial role in its expansion. When we look at the relationship formed by the exchange of gifts between Wen Cheng-ming and members of this group we see the process of the transmission of literati values, which surpassed the limits originally imposed by boundaries of class. Through this process new members were attracted to the literati culture, and its values exerted an ever widening influence. At the same time, this new class reciprocated by making available its vast material resources to support the continued existence of the literati culture and to assure the uninterrupted creation of products that embodied its values. The growing influence of Wen Cheng-ming's image as recluse as well as the influence of the Chiang-nan literati milieu that centered on Wen Cheng-ming depended to a large extent on this interactive relationship. This phenomenon became more apparent in Wen's later years when his closest young friend was Chang Hsien-i (act. ca. 1573), a descendant of a wealthy family from Hua-t'ing, Kiangsu. Although Chang was not untalented, all he secured for himself was a title as National University student while continuing to live a life of affluence in the Chiang-nan

Figure 8
Mi Fu (1052–1107). Detail of *Poem Written in a Boat on the Wu River*, ca. 1100. Handscroll, ink on paper, 31.3 x 559.8 cm. The Metropolitan Museum of Art, Gift of John M. Crawford, Jr., in honor of Professor Wen Fong, 1984. From Wen C. Fong, *Beyond Representation: Chinese Painting and Calligraphy, 8th–14th Century* (New York: The Metropolitan Museum of Art, 1992), pl. 19.

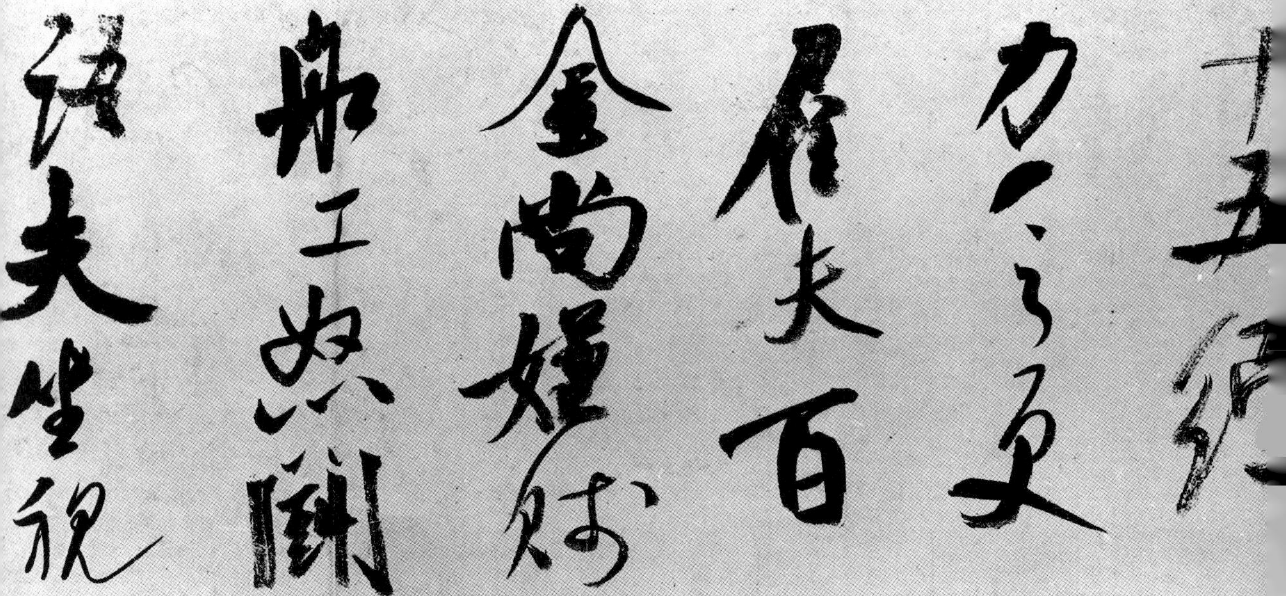

region. Still, he held Wen Cheng-ming and the literati values that Wen stood for in highest esteem and was an enthusiastic patron. In this capacity, Chang became the recipient of a large number of writings by Wen Cheng-ming,[33] an invaluable asset that would later play a role in his attaining a position of leadership in the Chiang-nan literati society.[34]

A Historical Perspective

Wen Cheng-ming's gift calligraphies of his Peking poems were not only stylistic and verbal evocations of Wen's emotions, but the embodiment of his character. As gifts, they served as the exchange of material goods between giver and recipient, yet they also entailed the communication of and response to Wen's image as a lofty recluse. Although such exchange relationships evoked widespread sympathy among the Chiang-nan literati, each exchange was in itself an individual activity, as the emotions that were committed to paper in text and in calligraphy were drawn from very personal experiences. In this regard, these calligraphies as gifts may be regarded as "lyrical" rather than "commemorative."

The "lyrical" mode of the gift calligraphy can be traced back to the Northern Sung dynasty, especially to Mi Fu, who may be considered its true founder. The difference between "commemorative" and "lyrical" modes of writing is not limited to works of calligraphy as gifts, but is closely linked to their form and content. A gift calligraphy that adopts the "commemorative" mode is obliged to be open and public in its content, and its stylistic presentation also demands a certain degree of technical virtuosity. Legend

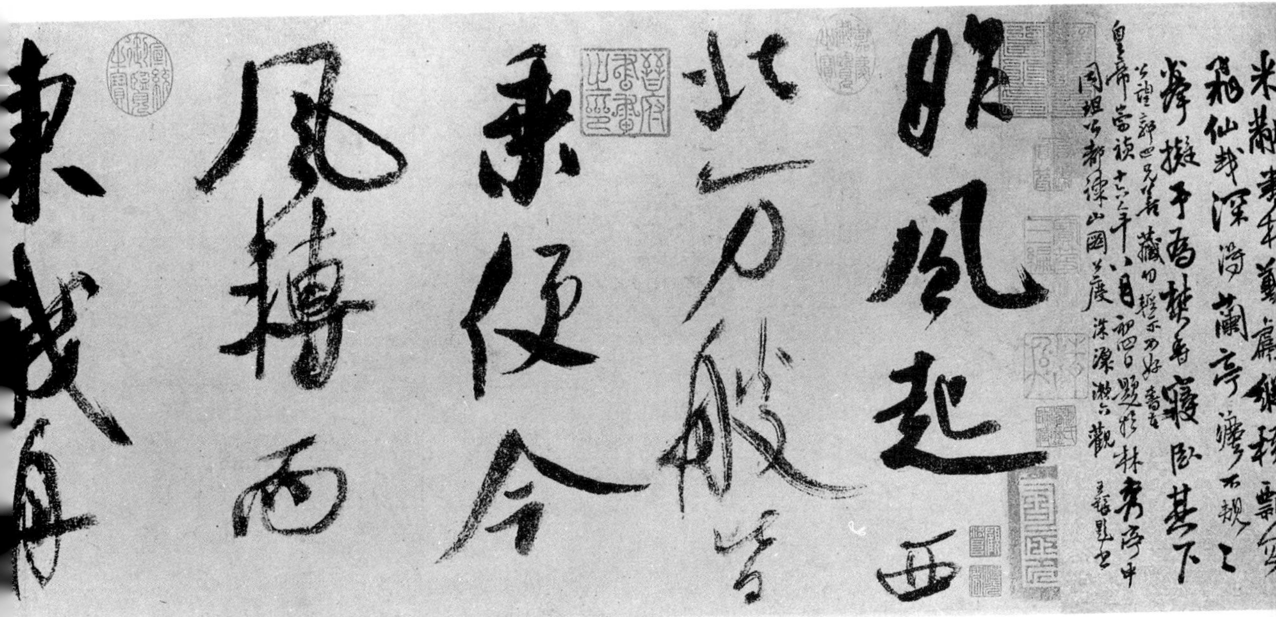

has it that Wang Hsi-chih wrote his "Classic of the Yellow Court" for a Taoist priest in exchange for a goose. Wen's transcription of this work may therefore be regarded as a typical gift calligraphy in the "commemorative" mode. Ink rubbings of this work allow us to envision the exquisite small-sized standard script of the original. In contrast, the "lyrical" mode is private in nature. In its style, it seeks to break away from convention and express naturally the individuality of its author. The earliest example of a conscious attempt at a calligraphy as gift is Mi Fu's *Poem Written on a Boat on the Wu River* (*Wu-chiang chou-chung shih*; fig. 8), written about 1100 for Chu Pang-yen, in the Metropolitan Museum. Mi Fu writes in a highly personal style a poem on his impressions of a boat trip on the Wu River. There is no grand "commemorative" statement in the poem, which is merely a record of his keen observations. The calligraphic style also shows countless instances of his personal touch in the brushwork. Mi's use of the brush, as in his private letter *Hasty Reply before Guests* (fig. 9), causes the brush tip to touch the paper surface from an infinite variety of angles in free and spontaneous movements. In this "lyrical" gift, there is no longer a need for the calligrapher to conceal his own individuality, which now clearly manifests itself in the traces of the brush and in the poetic text.

In comparison to Mi Fu's writings, Wen Cheng-ming's gift writings of his Peking poems go one step further in defining the "lyrical" mode, and perhaps even take this mode of calligraphic expression to its limits. The text of the Peking poems is an intimate expression of personal emotions, and with each transcription of the poems Wen reviewed and reexamined the experiences of his life, in which honor, sorrow, and self-affirmation went hand-in-hand. His calligraphic style became a symbolic expression of his self-image as he departed from the precise skill of his small-sized standard script and committed his ideal of a reclusive life in retirement to the natural brush movements of a strictly personal style.

The personal lyricism of Wen Cheng-ming's gift calligraphies of his Peking poems allowed the sympathetic recipient to identify with his ideal of reclusion. As a result, these writings became a vehicle for the communication of shared values within the social network of the Chiang-nan literati. That his calligraphy was able to produce this effect was clearly a result of the collective feelings of political frustration among many members of this literati society. Such feelings, however, did not continue to dominate the cultural atmosphere of Chiang-nan for very long. Within fifty years after Wen Cheng-ming's death, the traditional Confucian goal of serving the state had been replaced by the image of an independent mountain-dwelling recluse. This became the new focus of literati attention. In their eyes, politics and government service had become mundane concerns. They now considered themselves to be the successors to a great cultural tra-

Figure 9
Mi Fu (1052–1107). *Hasty Reply before Guests.* Letter mounted as an album leaf, ink on paper, 31.7 x 39.7 cm. The Art Museum, Princeton University, bequest of John B. Elliott.

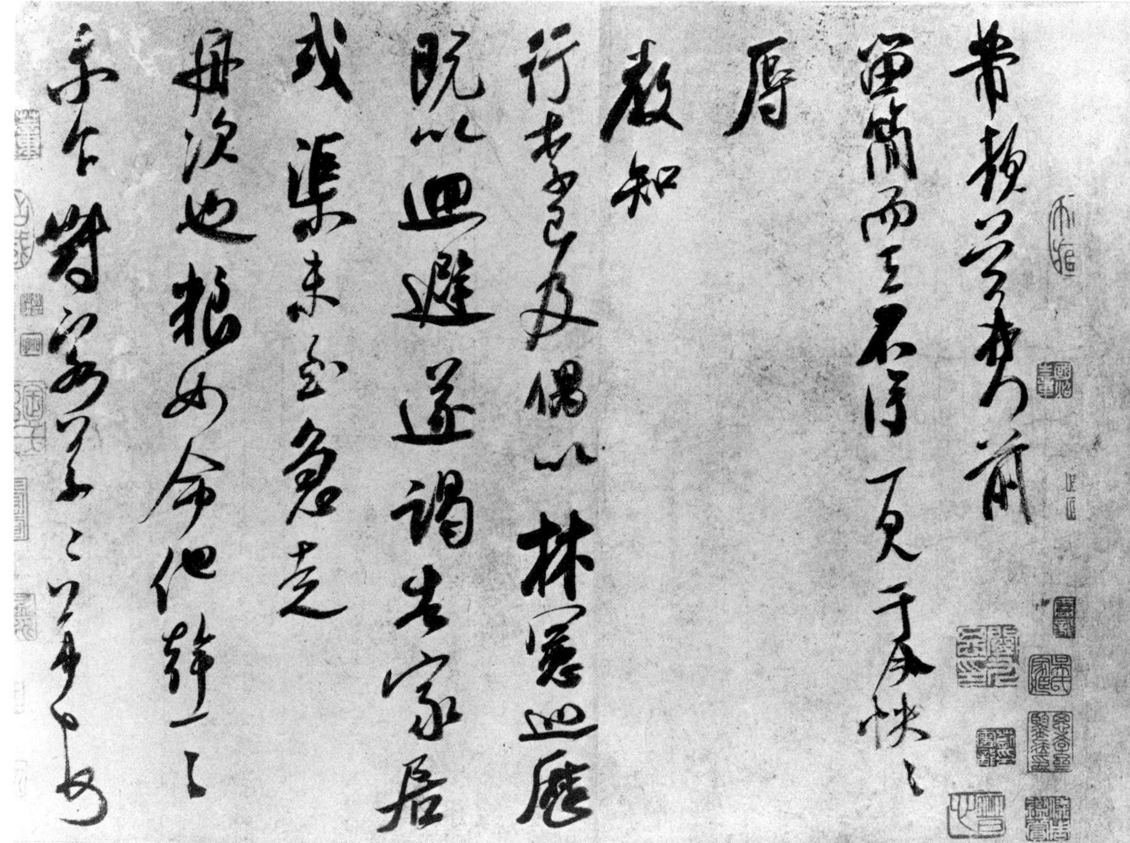

Figure 10
Tung Ch'i-ch'ang (1555–1636). *Nineteen Archaic Poems in the Style of Great Calligraphers*, 1610. Album. From Hironobu Kohara, *Tung Ch'i-ch'ang: The Man and His Work* (Tokyo: Nigensha Publishing Co., Ltd., 1981), pl. 46.

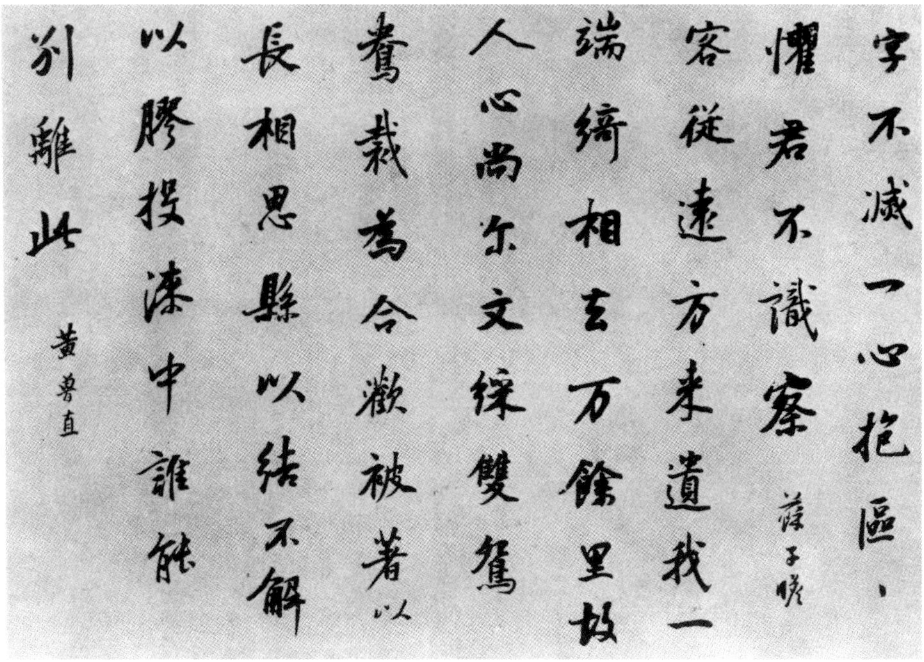

dition, and they sought to synthesize this tradition in order to give birth to a new creative vitality. Under these circumstances, the calligraphy-as-gift that functioned as a medium of communication within the literati society would in time generate new forms of interchange.

Of this new class of literati at the end of the sixteenth and the beginning of the seventeenth centuries, Tung Ch'i-ch'ang (1555–1636) was possibly one of the most prolific writers of gift calligraphies. While his calligraphic style was inspired by the tradition of Wang Hsi-chih and his son, Tung sought to create an innovative style in order to carry out his "great synthesis" of the Chinese calligraphic tradition.[35] He devoted much of his life to the writing of calligraphy and viewed politics as nothing more than a stepping-stone. Aside from being a common form of social courtesy, his many gift calligraphies were also an effective medium for the propagation of his artistic theories. For example, his album *Nineteen Archaic Poems in the Style of Great Calligraphers* (fig. 10) is a calligraphic performance of the style he created by emulating past masters. But the meaning of his writings is not conveyed in the text of these poems. The main concern of the album is how to synthesize seventeen different styles of past masters—from Huang Hsiang (ca. 220–ca. 279), Chung Yu (151–230), and Wang Hsi-chih to Su Shih, Huang T'ing-chien, and Mi Fu—in a new stylistic interpretation. In comparison to Wen Cheng-ming's writings of his Peking poems, one may point to an absence of personal emotion in Tung Ch'i-ch'ang's writing. What he actually accomplished—and what he aimed to

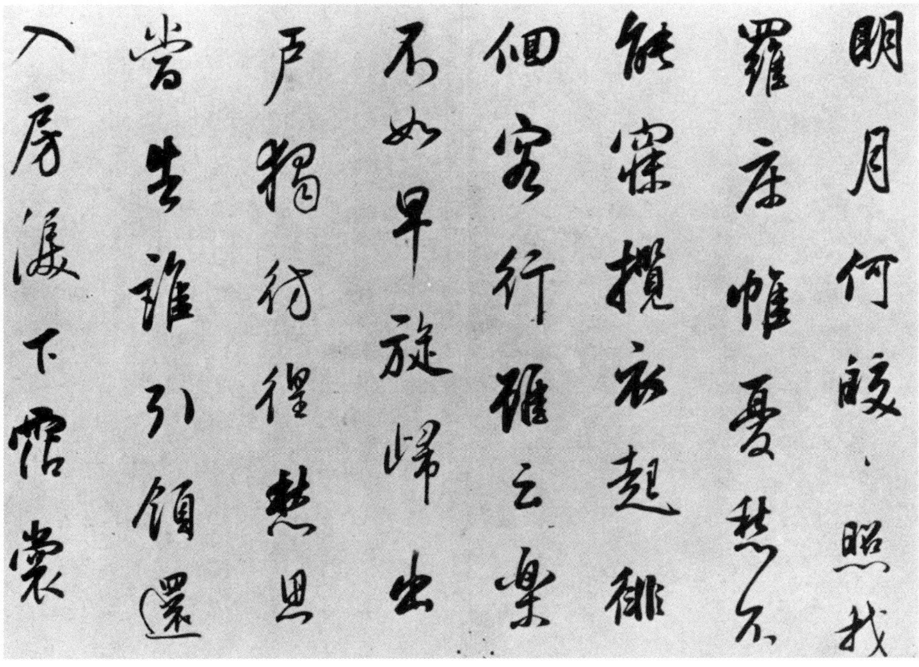

impart to the recipient of his album — is a rewriting of the entire tradition of calligraphy.

After completing his *Nineteen Archaic Poems in the Style of Great Calligraphers*, Tung presented the album to his friend Fang Chi-k'ang as a gift. On that occasion, Fang had showed him his own tracing of the *Preface to the Sacred Teaching* by Ch'u Sui-liang, which earned him Tung Ch'i-ch'ang's praise for his interpretation of Chin and T'ang dynasty masters. Tung then presented Fang with the album, requesting from his friend an appraisal of his writing and demanding that Fang reciprocate with a transcription of the *Nineteen Archaic Poems* in the same calligraphic style as his *Preface to the Sacred Teaching*. The art-historical value of "archaism" revealed through this exchange is entirely different from the lyricism that Wen Cheng-ming infused into his gift calligraphies. In the late Ming period, the network of gift exchange within the literati society would therefore become manifestly different in nature.

1 Wei Chung-chü, ed., *Wu-pai-chia chu Ch'ang-li wen-chi* (*Wen-yüan-ko ssu-k'u ch'üan-shu* edition, Taipei: Commercial Press, 1983) 21:3–5.

2 Marcel Mauss, *The Gift: The Form and Reason for Exchange in Archaic Societies*, trans. by W.D. Halls (New York and London: W.W. Norton, 1990). In Chinese society there exists a parallel concept of "social courtesy by reciprocity," see Lien-sheng Yang, "The Concept of 'Pao' as a Basis for Social Relations in China," in John K. Fairbank, ed., *Chinese Thought and Institutions* (Chicago and London: The University of Chicago Press, 1957), 291–309.

3 Chou Tao-chen, ed., *Wen Cheng-ming chi* (Shanghai: Shang-hai ku-chi ch'u-pan-she, 1987), 1451.

4 According to Chou Tao-chen's *Wen Cheng-ming shu-hua chien-piao* (Peking: Jen-min mei-shu ch'u-pan-she, 1985), extant and recorded versions of Wen Cheng-ming's transcription of *The Thousand Character Essay* total more than forty-two.

5 For a discussion of this period in Wen Cheng-ming's career, see Shih Shou-ch'ien, "Chia-ching hsin-cheng yü Wen Cheng-ming hua-feng chih chuan-pien," in *Style and Transformation* (Taipei: Yün-ch'en wen-hua, 1996), 261–97.

6 *Wen Cheng-ming chi*, 291.

7 Ibid., 293. Translation based on Richard Edwards, *The Art of Wen Cheng-ming, 1470–1559* (Ann Arbor: The University of Michigan Museum of Art, 1976), 94.

8 *Wen Cheng-ming chi*, 300. Translation based on Richard Edwards, *The Art of Wen Cheng-ming*, 95.

9 Published in Group for the Authentication of Ancient Works of Chinese Painting and Calligraphy, ed., *Illustrated Catalogue of Selected Works of Ancient Chinese Painting and Calligraphy*, v. 16 (Peking: The Cultural Relics Publishing House, 1997), 105, no. Chi 1-032.

10 *Wen Cheng-ming chi*, 1455.

11 Chiao Hung, *Kuo-ch'ao hsien-cheng lu* (*Ming-tai chuan-chi ts'ung-k'an*

edition, Taipei: Ming-wen shu-chü, 1991) 80:103.

12 Published in *Kaikodo Journal*, Spring, 1996, pl. 9.

13 *Wen Cheng-ming chi*, 304.

14 Ibid.

15 Ch'ien Ch'ien-i, *Lieh-ch'ao shih-chi hsiao-chuan* (*Ming-tai chuan-chi ts'ung-k'an* edition), 515–16.

16 For Wen Cheng-ming's transcription of Su Shih's "Ode to the Red Cliff," see Nakata Yūjirō and Shen Fu, eds., *Ōbei shūzō Chūgoku hōsho meisekishū*, Ming-Ch'ing vol. 1 (Tokyo: Chūō Kōronsha, 1983), v. 1, 174.

17 Although the last volume of *Model Calligraphies from the Hall of Lingering Clouds* was not printed until 1560, the year after Wen Cheng-ming's death, in a calligraphy written for Shen Lü dated 1554, Wen mentions that a printed version of the last volume was already in circulation. It is evident that before his death Wen had planned to include these works in the compilation. See Chou Tao-chen, ed., *Wen Cheng-ming shu-hua chien-piao*, 146.

18 Lu Ts'an, *Lu Tzu-yü chi* (*Wen-yüan-ko ssu-k'u ch'üan-shu* edition), 1:22.

19 Huang-fu Fang, *Huang-fu Ssu-hsün chi* (*Wen-yüan-ko ssu-k'u ch'üan-shu* edition), 46:9.

20 Ibid., 27: 3.

21 Shih Shou-ch'ien, "The Landscape Painting of Frustrated Literati: The Wen Cheng-ming Style in the Sixteenth Century," in Willard J. Peterson et al., eds., *The Power of Culture: Studies in Chinese History* (Hong Kong: The Chinese University Press, 1994), 235.

22 Shen Lien, *Ch'ing-hsia chi* (*Wen-yüan-ko ssu-k'u ch'üan-shu* edition), 12:1–9.

23 Ibid., 10:12.

24 Cheng Ming-hua, *Wang Shih-chen nien-p'u* (Shanghai: Fu-tan University Press, 1993), 78, 83–84.

25 Wang Shih-chen, *Yen-chou ssu-pu kao* (*Wen-yüan-ko ssu-k'u ch'üan-shu* edition), 131:20.

26 Lin Li-yüeh, *Ming-tai te kuo-tzu-chien-sheng* (Taipei: Tung-wu University Press, 1978), 101.

27 *Wen Cheng-ming chi*, 1478.

28 Although Tung Ch'i-ch'ang avoids mentioning in his epitaph that Hsiang was a National University student, Wang Hsien-chieh refers to him as "University student Hsiang" in his *Inscriptions of the Forest of Paintings* (*Hui-lin t'i-shih*). Hsü Ch'in also notes in his *Record of Ming Painting* (*Ming-hua lu*) that Hsiang "had initially been a National University student." Wang Hsien-chieh, *Hui-lin t'i-shih* (*Ming-tai chuan-chi ts'ung-k'an* edition) 12:61; Hsü Ch'in, *Ming-hua lu* (*Hua-shih ts'ung-shu* edition, Taipei: Wen-shih-che ch'u-pan-she, 1974), 4:51.

29 *Illustrated Catalogue of Selected Works of Ancient Chinese Painting and Calligraphy*, v. 13, 53, no. Yüeh 1–0061.

30 *Ku-kung shu-hua t'u-lu* (Taipei: National Palace Museum, Taipei, 1991), 269–72.

31 Hu Ying-ling, *Shao-shih shan-fang chi* (*Wen-yüan-ko ssu-k'u ch'üan-shu* edition), 108:10.

32 Chu P'u, *Hsi-ts'un shih-chi* (*Wen-yüan-ko ssu-k'u ch'üan-shu* edition), 2:11.

33 Wang Shih-chen, *Yen-chou ssu-pu kao*, 129:15.

34 For a biography of Chang Hsien-i, see Ch'ien Ch'ien-i, *Lieh-ch'ao shih-chi hsiao-chuan*, 452–53.

35 See Xu Bangda, "Tung Ch'i-ch'ang's Calligraphy," in Wai-kam Ho, ed., and Judith G. Smith, coord. ed., *The Century of Tung Ch'i-ch'ang 1555–1636* (Kansas City, Mo.: The Nelson-Atkins Museum of Art, 1992), 105–32.

Note: Alphabetization of this glossary is word by word, with hyphens counting as blank spaces. Apostrophes and other diacritical marks are ignored in the alphabetization.

ai erh pu shang 哀而不傷
Akishinkō-ji 安芸真光寺
An Shih-kao 安世高

bokuseki 墨蹟

ch'a-ku chuan 釵股篆
Cha Tao 查道 (955–1018)
Chai Ju-wen 翟汝文 (1067–1141)
Ch'an 禪
chang 璋
Ch'ang-an 長安
chang-ch'eng shu 章程書
Chang Cheng mu-chih 張整墓誌
Ch'ang Chi-fan mu-chih 常季繁墓誌
Chang Chieh-tsu 張杰祖
Chang Chih 張芝 (d. 192)
Chang Heng 張衡 (78–138)
Chang Hsiao-hsiang 張孝祥 (1132–1169)
Chang Hsien-i 張獻翼 (act. ca. 1573)
Chang Hsü 張旭 (ca. 700–750)
Chang Hsüan 張玄
Chang Hsüan mu-chih 張玄墓誌
Chang Huai-kuan 張懷瓘 (act. ca. 714–760)
Chang Meng-lung pei 張猛龍碑
Ch'ang Po-fu 常伯夫 (act. ca. 5th century)
Ch'ang Shao 常杓 (13th century)
Chang-shui 漳水
Ch'ang-sun huang-hou 長孫皇后
Chang T'ing-hsiang 張廷相
chang-ts'ao 章草
Chang Ts'ung 張璁 (1475–1539)
Chang Yü-chao 張裕釗 (1823–1894)
Chang Yu-chih 章友直 (1006–1062)
Chao 趙 (state; 304–329)
Chao Chih-ch'ien 趙之謙 (1829–1884)
Chao I 趙壹
Chao Meng-chien 趙孟堅 (1199–1264)
Chao Meng-fu 趙孟頫 (1254–1322)
Chao Ming-ch'eng 趙明誠 (1081–1129)
Chao T'ing 趙霆 (11th century)
Chao Wan-li 趙萬里
Che-chüeh Ch'an-shih t'a-ming 智覺禪師塔銘
chen 真
Ch'en Ch'ang 陳暢 (act. ca. 4th century)
Ch'en I-tseng 陳繹曾 (1286–1345)
chen Ju 真儒
chen kao 貞誥
Chen-kuan 貞觀 (reign period; 859–877)
Ch'en-liu 陳留
Chen-shan ts'ao-t'ang 貞山草堂
Chen-shang-chai t'ieh 真賞齋帖
ch'en wei 讖緯
Ch'en Yu 陳槱 (*chin-shih* 1190)
cheng 正
Ch'eng-p'ing 承平 (reign period; 931–938)
Cheng-shih 正始 (reign period; 504–508)
Cheng Tao-chao 鄭道昭 (d. 515)
Ch'eng-ti 成帝 (Han emperor; r. 32–7 B.C.)
Cheng tso-wei t'ieh 爭坐位帖
Cheng Wen-pao 鄭文寶 (953–1013)
ch'i 氣

Ch'i 齊
Chi chih Chi-ming wen-kao 祭姪季明文稿
Chi-chiu-chang 急就章
Ch'i-fa-ssu pei 啓法寺碑
Chi-ku lu pa-wei 集古錄跋尾
Chi Ni 濟尼
Chia-ching 嘉靖 (Ming emperor; r. 1522–66)
chia-ku-wen 甲骨文
Chia Shih-chün pei 賈使君碑
Chia Ssu-po pei 賈思伯碑
Chia-yu shih-ching 嘉祐石經
Chiang K'uei 姜夔 (1163–1203)
Chiang-ling 江陵
Chiang-nan 江南
Chiang-nan ku-fo 江南古佛
Chiang Shih 江式
Chiang-su 江蘇
chiao-k'uai 狡獪
Chien-chen 鑒真 (Jpn. Ganjin)
Chien-k'ang 建康
Ch'ien-lung 乾隆 (Ch'ing emperor; r. 1736–95)
Ch'ien Ta-hsin 錢大昕 (1728–1804)
Ch'ien-t'ang 錢塘
Ch'ien-tzu wen 千字文
Ch'ien-yen-t'ang chin-shih wen pa-wei 潛研堂金石文跋尾
Chih Ch'ien 支讖
Ch'ih-shih ching 持世經
Chih-yung 智永 (ca. 514–604)
Chin 晉
chin-shih ch'i 金石氣
Chin-shih hsüeh 金石學
Chin-shih lu 金石錄
Ch'in-shih-huang 秦始皇 (Ch'in emperor; r. 221–205 B.C.)
Chin-shih ts'ui-pien 金石萃編
Chin-shih wen-tzu chi 金石文字記
Chin-shih yao-li 金石要例
Chin shu 晉書
chin-ts'ao 今草
ch'in-tsung 禽縱
Chin-tz'u ming 晉祠銘
Ch'ing 清 (dynasty; 1644–1912)
Ching-chou wen-tzu chih kuan-chih 荆州文字之官志
Ch'ing-ho 清河
ch'ing i 清義
chiu ching 舊京
Chiu-ching t'ieh 舊京帖
Ch'iu-mu Ling-liang fu-jen yu-ch'ih tsao-hsiang-chi 丘穆陵亮夫人尉遲造像記
Ch'iu Ying 仇英 (d. 1552)
ch'o 輟
Chou 周
chou 籒
Chou Mi 周密 (1232–1308)
Chou shu 周書
Chou Tao-chen 周道振
Chou Yüeh 周越 (act. ca. 1021–48)
Chu Ch'ang-wen 朱長文 (1039–1089)
Chü Chung-cheng 句中正 (929–1002)
Ch'ü-fu 曲阜
Chu I-chang 朱義章
Chu K'uei 朱逵
Ch'ü Ling-wen 瞿令問 (8th century)
Chu Mu 朱穆
Chu Pang-yen 朱邦彥
Ch'u Sui-liang 褚遂良 (596–658)
Chu Yün-ming 祝允明 (1461–1527)
Ch'uan-chü shih-shou 船居十首
chuan-shu 篆書
chuang-shih 壯士
Chuang-tzu 莊子
Ch'un-hua-ko t'ieh 淳化閣帖
chün-tzu 君子
Chung-chou chin-shih chi 中州金石記
Chung-feng Huan-chu hsiang chieh 中峰幻住像偈
Chung-feng Ming-pen 中峰明本 (1262–1323)
chung-ho 中和
Chung I 仲翼
Chung-shu-ling 中書令
Chung-shu shih-lang 中書侍郎
Ch'ung-yang ling 崇陽陵
Chung Yu 鍾繇 (151–230)

en 恩
Enkei Soyū 遠溪祖雄 (d. 1344)
Erh Wang 二王
Erh ya 爾雅

Fa-hui Ch'an-shih 法慧禪師
fa-t'ieh 法帖

Fa-t'ieh p'u-hsi 法帖譜系
Fan Chung-yen 范仲淹 (989–1052)
Fan Chung-yen shen-tao pei 范仲淹神道碑
Fang Chi-k'ang 方季康
Fang yen 方言
Fei Kun 費袞 (13th century)
fei-pai 飛白
feng 奉
Feng, empress dowager 馮太后
Feng Ch'eng-su 馮承素
Feng Hsi 馮熙 (act. ca. 5th century)
feng-shan 封禪
Feng Shen-yü tsao-hsiang-chi 馮神育造像記
Feng Tzu-chen 馮子振 (1257– post 1327)
fu 賦
Fu Hsi 伏羲
fu-ku 復古
Fu-t'ien chi 甫田集

Genjū 幻住
Gyōkai Honjō 業海本淨

Hai-yüeh ming-yen 海岳名言
Hakuun Egyō 白雲慧曉 (1228–1297)
Han-lin yüan 翰林院
Han Hsien-tsung mu-chih 韓顯宗墓誌
Han Wei Nan-pei-ch'ao mu-chih chi-shih 漢魏南北朝墓誌集釋
Han Yü 韓愈 (768–824)
Han Yü-t'ao 韓玉濤
heng 横
Heng-ti 桓帝 (Han emperor; r. 146–167)
Ho-tung 河東
Honan 河南
Hopei 河北
hossu 拂子
Hou-chi 后稷
Hou Wei Shen-kuei tsao-pei-hsiang chi 後魏神龜造碑像記
Hsi-chih mu-chih 奚智墓誌
hsi lü chüeh 繫驢橛
Hsi-p'ing shih-ching 熹平石經
Hsia-hou Hsüan 夏侯玄 (209–254)
hsiang 象
hsiang-hsing shu 象形書
hsiang-t'a 響拓
Hsiang Yüan-pien 項元汴 (1525–1590)
Hsiao ching 孝經
Hsiao-Hsiang pai-yün t'u 瀟湘白雲圖
Hsiao Hsien-ching 蕭顯慶
hsiao hsüeh 小學
Hsiao-tsung 孝宗 (Sung emperor; r. 1163–1189)
Hsiao Tzu-yün 蕭子雲
Hsiao-wen 孝文帝 (Northern Wei emperor; r. 471–99)
Hsiao-wu 孝武帝 (Northern Wei emperor; r. 531–33)
Hsieh Ling-yün 謝靈運 (385–433)
Hsieh Tao-yün 謝道韞
hsieh-yeh 薤葉
Hsien-pei 鮮卑
Hsien-tsu p'in Hou-ku shih mu-chih 顯祖嬪侯骨氏墓誌
Hsien-yü Shu 鮮于樞 (1257–1302)
hsin 心
hsin Wei t'i 新魏體
Hsing-feng-lou t'ieh 星鳳樓帖
hsing-shu 行書
hsing-ya shu 行押書
hsiu wen 修文
Hsü Ch'in 徐沁
Hsü Ching 徐兢 (1091–1153)
Hsü Hao 徐浩 (703–782)
Hsü Hsüan 徐鉉 (916–992)
Hsü Seng-ch'üan 徐僧權
Hsü Shen 許慎
Hsüan-ho shu-p'u 宣和書譜
Hsüan-tsang 玄奘 (596?–664)
Hsüeh Hsiang 薛向
Hsüeh Shang-kung 薛尚功
Hsüeh Shao-p'eng 薛紹彭
Hsüeh Shou 薛收
Hsüeh Te-yin 薛德音
Hsüeh Yüan-ching 薛元敬
Hsün-tzu 荀子
Hsün Yüeh 荀岳 (246–295)
Hu Ying-lin 胡應麟 (act. 2nd half of the 16th century)
Hua-t'ing 華亭
Hua-yen ching 華嚴經

Huai-ho 淮河
Huai-su 懷素 (ca. 735–ca. 799)
Huai-yang 淮陽
Huan-chu-an 幻住庵 (Jpn. Genjū)
Huan-chu ch'ing-kuei 幻住清規
Huang-chou 黄州
Huang Chu 黄銖 (1131–1199)
Huang-fu Fang 皇甫汸 (1503–1582)
Huang-fu Tan pei 皇甫誕碑
Huang Hsiang 皇象 (ca. 220–ca. 279)
Huang ming shu-hua shih 皇明書畫史
Huang Po-ssu 黄伯思 (1079–1118)
Huang-ti nan-hsün chih sung 皇帝南巡之頌
Huang-ti san-lin p'i-yung pei 皇帝三臨辟雍碑
Huang-ti tung-hsün chih pei 皇帝東巡之碑
Huang T'ing-chien 黄庭堅 (1045–1105)
Huang-t'ing ching 黄庭經
Huang Tsung-hsi 黄宗羲 (1610–1695)
hui 會
Hui 惠王 (King, state of Yen)
Hui-ch'eng 慧成
Hui-lin t'i-shih 繪林題識
Hung Kua 洪适 (1117–1184)
Hung-tu-men hsüeh 鴻都門學
Hung-wen-kuan 弘文館

i 逸
I-chen 儀真
I ching 易經
I-ch'üeh fo-k'an ming 伊闕佛龕銘
I-fu tsao-hsiang-chi 一弗造像記
I-ho ming 瘞鶴銘
i ku keng ch'eng 以骨骾稱
I-lang 議郎
I-men hsien-sheng chi 義門先生集
I-mu t'ieh 姨母帖
I-shan pei 嶧山碑
I-shih Fa-tsung teng wu-shih-ssu jen tsao-hsiang-chi 邑師法宗等五十四人造像記
I-wen lei-chü 藝文類聚

Jao Chieh 饒介 (act. ca. 1300–1367)
jen 人
jen 仁
Jen An 任安
Jen Hua 任華
Jen-tsung 仁宗 (Sung emperor; r. 1022–63)
Ju 儒
ju shen 入神
Juan Chi 阮籍
Juan Yüan 阮元 (1764–1849)

k'ai-shu 楷書
K'ang-hsi 康熙 (Ch'ing emperor; r. 1662–1722)
K'ang-li Nao-nao 康里巎巎 (1295–1345)
K'ang Yu-wei 康有為 (1858–1927)
Kao Cheng-ch'en 高正臣
Kao Ch'ing pei 高慶碑
Kao-feng Yüan-miao 高峰原妙 (1238–1295)
Kao-hsien 高閑
Kao Huan 高歡
Kao Shen 高紳
Kao Shu, Hsieh Po-tu sa-erh jen teng tsao-hsiang-chi 高樹、解伯都卅二人等造像記
Kao-tsung 高宗 (Sung emperor; r. 1127–62)
Kao-tsung 高宗 (T'ang emperor; r. 650–83)
Kao-tsung ch'ung hua Chao shih mu-chih 高宗充華趙氏墓誌
Kao-tsung p'in Keng shih mu-chih 高宗嬪耿氏墓誌
Karakhoja 高昌
Ketsuzan Ryoi 傑山了偉
King Ch'ungson 忠宣王 (r. 1308–1313)
Ko T'uan 葛湍
k'o-tou wen 蝌蚪文
Kōgen-ji 高源寺 (Hyōgo-ken)
Koguryō 高麗
kou 鉤
K'ou Chen mu-chih 寇臻墓誌
K'ou Ch'ien 寇謙
K'ou P'ing mu-chih 寇憑墓誌
K'ou Yen mu-chih 寇演墓誌
ku 孤
ku-ch'i 骨氣
Ku-chin chih p'ien-chi 古今之篇籍

Ku-chin shu-p'ing 古今書評
K'u-sun t'ieh 苦筍帖
Ku T'ing-lin hsien-sheng i-shu shih-chung 顧亭林先生遺書十種
ku-wen 古文
Ku-yang tung 古陽洞
Ku Yen-wu 顧炎武 (1613–1682)
Kuan-hsiu 貫休
k'uang 狂
Kuang-chou 廣州
Kuang-ch'uan Wang tsu-mu t'ai-fei Hou wei wang-fu Ho-lan Han tsao-hsiang-chi 廣川王祖母太妃侯為亡夫賀蘭汗造像記
Kuang-ch'uan Wang tsu-mu t'ai-fei Hou tsao-hsiang-chi 廣川王祖母太妃侯造像記
Kuang i-chou shuang-chi 廣藝舟雙楫
Kuang-lu ta-fu 光祿大夫
k'uang-ts'ao 狂草
Kucha 庫車
kuei 圭
kuei-jen 貴人
Kuei-ming Hou 歸命侯 (Wu emperor; r. 264–84)
Kuei O 桂萼 (act. 1511–30)
kung shu niao chuan 工書鳥篆
Kung-sun, Lady 公孫大娘
K'ung-tzu miao-t'ang pei 孔子廟堂碑
K'ung Wen tzu 孔文子
Kuo Chung-shu 郭忠恕 (ca. 910–977)
Kuo Mo-jo 郭沫若

Lan-t'ing hsü 蘭亭序
Lan-t'ing hsü-k'ao 蘭亭續考
Lan-t'ing k'ao 蘭亭考
Lan-t'ing shih 蘭亭詩
lang-chung 郎中
lang-kuan 郎官
Lang-yeh 琅琊
Lei-pien 類編
li 隸
Li Ch'eng 李成 (919–967)
Li chi (*Book of Rites*) 禮記
li-chien 例監
Li Chien-chung 李建中 (945–1013)
Li Chih 李治
Li Ching-hsi 黎景熙
Li hsü 隸續
Li I-fu 李義府 (d. 666)
Li Jui-ch'ing 李瑞清 (1867–1920)
Li K'ang-nien 李康年 (late 11th century)
Li Kung-lin 李公麟 (ca. 1041–1106)
Li Po ku feng 李白古風
Li Po 李白 (701–762)
Li shih 隸釋
li-shu 隸書
Li Ssu 李斯 (act. 221–208 B.C.)
Li Ssu-chen 李嗣真 (d. 696)
Li T'ai 李泰
Li-tai chung-ting i-ch'i k'uan-shih fa-t'ieh 歷代鍾鼎彝器款識法帖
Li Wen-t'ien 李文田 (1834–1895)
Li Wu-huo 李無惑 (11th century)
Li Yang-ping 李陽冰 (act. 759–780?)
Li Yüan-chih 李元直 (11th century)
Li Yung 李邕 (678–747)
Liang Ku 梁鵠 (act. ca. late 2nd–early 3rd century)
Liang Wu-ti 梁武帝
lieh wen 烈文
Lin-su-yüan fa-t'ieh 鄰蘇園法帖
Ling-yün-t'ai 凌雲臺
Liu An 劉安
Liu Chang 劉璋
Liu Ch'ang 劉敞 (1019–1068)
Liu-ch'ao hsieh-ching-t'i 六朝寫經體
Liu Cheng-fu 劉正夫 (1062–1119)
Liu Ching 劉涇
Liu Hsi-tsai 劉熙載
Liu Hsiang 劉向
Liu Hsin 劉歆
liu-hsüeh 六學
liu-i 六義
Liu I-ch'ing 劉義慶 (403–444)
Liu Kung-ch'üan 柳公權 (778–865)
Liu Ling 劉靈
Liu Mu 劉睦
Liu shih 柳氏
liu-shu 六書
Liu Tai 劉岱 (d. 487)
Liu Yao 劉曜 (d. 329)
liu-yeh t'i 柳葉體
Liu Yüan 劉瑗
Lo-chou 洛州
Lo shui 洛水
Loyang 洛陽

Lü Ch'ao 呂超 (d. 489)
Lu Chia 陸賈
Lu Chih-ch'iu 陸之裘
Lu I-chen 魯一貞
Lu Jung 陸容 (1436–1494)
Lu Miao 盧邈
Lu Po-yüan 盧伯源
Lü Pu-wei 呂不韋
Lu Shen 盧諶 (284–350)
Lü Sheng-chi 呂勝己 (12th century)
Lu Shou 魯收
Lu Ts'an 陸粲 (1494–1551)
Lu Yen 盧偃
Lun heng 論衡
Lun Wei pei t'i 論魏碑體
Lun-yü 論語
Lung-men erh-shih p'in 龍門二十品
Lung-men shih-k'u 龍門石窟
Lung-ts'ang-ssu pei 龍藏寺碑
Luo Chih-hsi 羅志希

Ma-ming-ssu Ken fa-shih pei 馬鳴寺根法師碑
Mang-shan 邙山
mao-hsüeh 茂學
mei 媚
mei-ch'ü 媚趣
Mei-hua pai-yung 梅花百詠
mei o 美惡
Meng Chiao 孟郊 (751–814)
Meng fa-shih pei 孟法師碑
Meng Kuang-ta 孟廣達
Meng Ta 孟達
Meng-ying 夢英 (act. 965–999)
Mi Fu 米芾 (1052–1107)
Mi Yu-jen 米友仁 (1074–1151)
Ming-ti 明帝 (Sung emperor; r. 465–71)
Ming-hua lu 明畫錄
ming-shih shu 銘石書
mo 末
mo chi 墨跡
Mo-ch'ih pien 墨池編
Mo-kao k'u 莫高窟
Mo Yu-chih 莫友芝 (1811–1871)
mu 墓
mu-chih-ming 墓誌銘
Mu Liang mu-chih 穆亮墓誌
Muin Genkai 無隱元晦 (d. 1358)

na 捺
Nan Ch'i shu 南齊書
Nan Pei shu-p'ai lun 南北書派論
Nanking 南京
Nanzen-ji 南禪寺
neng ts'ao shu 能草書
niao-shu 鳥書

Ōtomo Sadamune 大友貞宗 (d. 1333)
Ou-yang Hsiu 歐陽修 (1007–1072)
Ou-yang Hsün 歐陽詢 (557–641)

pa-fen shu 八分書
Pa Mi-ko fa-t'ieh 跋秘閣法帖
pa wang chih luan 八王之亂 (291–305)
Pa-yüeh chiu-jih t'ieh 八月九日帖
Pan Ku 班固
Pan Piao 班彪 (32–92)
Pao-Chin-chai fa-t'ieh 寶晉齋法帖
Pao Shih-ch'en 包世臣 (1775–1855)
Pei pei Nan t'ieh lun 北碑南帖論
Pei-t'ing tz'u-chi 北庭慈寂
Pei Wei 北魏 (386–534)
pei wen 碑文
pen 本
peng 崩
Pi-chen t'u 筆陣圖
Pi-ch'iu Hui-ch'eng tsao-hsiang-chi 比丘慧成造像記
Pi-ch'iu Hui-kan tsao-hsiang-chi 比丘惠感造像記
Pi-ch'iu Tao-chiang tsao-hsiang-chi 比丘道匠造像記
pi-chung yung-li 筆中用力
pi-mo 筆墨
Pi-yen lu 碧巖錄
Pi Yüan 畢沅 (1730–1797)
p'ieh 撇
pien 變
Pien shan 弁山
p'in 貧
P'ing-ch'eng 平城
p'ing-tan 平淡
po 博
po-hsüeh 博學
po-shih 博士
pu chi pu li 不激不厲
Pu-nien t'u pa 步輦圖跋

Rikkyoku'an 栗棘庵
Ryoen 了延 (1704–1774)

San-hsi t'ang fa-t'ieh 三希堂法帖
san-kung 三公
Sang-luan t'ieh 喪亂帖
Sang Shih-ch'ang 桑世昌 (early 13th century)
Seun-ji 棲雲寺
Sha Meng-hai 沙孟海
Shan-chü shih-shou 山居十首
shan o 善惡
Shan-shan 鄯善
Shan shih shu 善史書
shang 上
shang-shu-lang 尚書郎
Shang-shu-yu-p'u-yeh 尚書右僕射
Shansi 山西
Shantung 山東
Shao-hsing Mi-t'ieh 紹興米帖
shao-jun 韶潤
Shao Su 邵餗 (11th century)
she-shu 蛇書
shen 神
shen-han tzu-hsieh 神翰自寫
Shen Ko 申革
Shen Kua 沈括 (1031–1095)
Shen Lien 沈鍊 (1507–1557)
Shen-nung 神農
shen-pi tzu-hsieh 神筆自寫
Shen Yin-mo 沈尹默
Sheng-chiao hsü 聖教序
Sheng-chiao hsü chi 三藏聖教序記
Shensi 陝西
shih 士
Shih chi 史記
Shih-chou p'ien 史籀篇
Shih-ch'ü pao-chi 石渠寶笈
Shih I-kuan 師宜官 (act. ca. late 2nd–early 3rd century)
shih ken chung ch'ien 始艮終乾
Shih-ku wen 石鼓文
Shih-men ming 石門銘
Shih-pa t'i shih 十八體詩
Shih-ping kung tsao-hsiang-chi 始平公造像記
Shih-shuo hsin-yü 世說新語
Shih Tso 時佐 (act. late 12th century)
Shih Wei-tse 史惟則 (act. ca. 742–ca. 756)
Shih yen chih 詩言志
Shih Yu 史游
Shōjyu-ji 正宗寺
Shou-t'ang chin-shih pa 授堂金石跋
shu 書
Shu-hou-p'in 書後品
Shu-i 書議
Shu-p'in 書品
Shu-p'u 書譜
Shu-tuan 書斷
Shun 舜
Shuo-wen chieh-tzu 說文解字
Sinkiang 新疆
So Ching 索靖 (239–303)
Ssu-ma Ch'ien 司馬遷
Ssu-ma Chin-lung 司馬金龍 (d. 484)
Ssu-ma Hsiang-ju 司馬相如
Ssu-ma Jui 司馬睿
Ssu-ma Kuang 司馬光 (1019–1086)
Ssu-ma Yüeh 司馬悅 (462–508)
Ssu-shih-erh-chang ching 四十二章經
Su Chi 蘇激 (late 11th century)
Su-chou 蘇州
Su Hsieh 蘇澥 (late 11th century)
Su Huan 蘇渙
Su I-chien 蘇易簡 (957–995)
su Ju 俗儒
Su Mi 蘇泌 (late 11th century)
Su Shih 蘇軾 (1037–1101)
Su Shun-ch'in 蘇舜欽 (1008–1048)
Su Shun-yüan 蘇舜元 (1006–1054)
Su T'ang-ch'ing 蘇唐卿
Sui 隋
Sun Ch'iu-sheng, Liu Ch'i-tsu erh-pai jen teng tsao-hsiang-chi 孫秋生、劉起祖二百人等造像記
Sun Chüeh 孫覺 (1028–1090)
Sun Kuo-t'ing 孫過庭 (648?–703?)
Sung Chung 宋忠
Sung-jen tz'u 宋人詞
Sung Kao-hsien shang-jen hsü 送高閑上人序
Sung-kao-ling-miao pei 嵩高靈廟碑
Sung K'o 宋克 (1327–1387)
Sung Pen 宋本
Sung-shan 嵩山

t'a-mo 搨模
Ta-tai Hua-yüeh miao pei 大代華岳廟碑
Ta-t'ung 大同
t'ai-hsüeh 太學
T'ai-pao 太保
T'ai-shan 泰山
Tai Shu-lun 戴叔倫
T'ai-tsung 太宗 (T'ang emperor; r. 626–49)
T'ai-tsung ai-ts'e 太宗哀冊
T'ai-wu 太武帝 (Northern Wei emperor; r. 424–52)
T'ai-wu ti tung-hsün pei 太武帝東巡碑
T'ai-yüan 太原
Tan-yang chün 丹陽郡
T'ao Ch'ien 陶潛 (365–427)
Tao-fu tsan 道服贊
T'ao Hung-ching 陶弘景 (452–536)
Tao-kuang 道光 (Ch'ing emperor; r. 1821–50)
Tao-te ching 道德經
T'ao Yüan-ming 陶淵明 (365–427)
Teng Shih-ju 鄧石如 (1743–1805)
Teng Wen-yüan 鄧文原 (1258–1328)
t'i-pang 題榜
Tiao Pi-kan wen 弔比干文
t'ieh hsüeh 帖學
tien 典
tien 顛
tien 癲
t'ien-chen 天真
tien chi 典籍
T'ien-fa shen-ch'en pei 天發神讖碑
T'ien-mu Chung-feng ho-shang kuang-lu 天目中峰和尚廣錄
T'ien-mu shan 天目山
T'ien-shui 天水
ting 鼎
T'ing-yün-kuan fa-t'ieh 停雲館法帖
T'o-pa 拓跋
Tōfuku-ji 東福寺
Tou Chi 竇冀
Tou Chien-te 竇建德 (573–621)
Ts'ai Hsiang 蔡襄 (1012–1067, *chin-shih* degree 1030)
Ts'ai ku-lai neng-shu jen-ming 采古來能書人名
Ts'ai Yu-lin 蔡有鄰 (8th century)
Ts'ai Yung 蔡邕 (133–192)
tsan 贊
Ts'ang Chieh 倉頡
Ts'ao Chih-ko 曹之格 (act. ca. 1265–74)
Ts'ao Ch'üan pei 曹全碑
tsao-hsiang chi 造像記
Ts'ao Shih-mien 曹士冕 (act. 1240–45)
ts'ao-shu 草書
Tseng Ch'i-nien 曾耆年 (12th century)
Tseng Hsi 曾熙 (1861–1930)
Tseng Kung 曾鞏 (1019–1083)
Tseng Ta-chung 曾大中 (12th century)
Tso Fen 左棻 (d. 300)
Tso ts'ao-shu ch'ih-tu 作草書尺牘
Tsou Yen 鄒衍
Ts'ui Ch'ien 崔潛
Ts'ui Ching-yung mu-chih 崔敬邕墓誌
Ts'ui Hao 崔浩 (d. 450)
Ts'ui Hung 崔宏 (Hsüan-po 崔玄伯; d. 418)
Ts'ui Yüeh 崔悅
ts'ung 琮
t'u 圖
Tu Chung-wei 杜仲微 (12th century)
Tu Fu 杜甫 (712–770)
t'u shu 圖書
Tun-huang 敦煌
tung 東
t'ung 痛
Tung Ch'i-ch'ang 董其昌 (1555–1636)
T'ung-chih 同治 (Ch'ing emperor; r. 1862–74)
Tung Chung-shu 董仲舒
Tung-fang Shuo 東方朔
Tung Yu 董逌 (early 12th century)
tzu 字
tz'u 辭
Tzu-shu shih 自書詩
Tz'u Shun 此順

wai ch'i 外戚
Wang Ao 王鏊 (1450–1524)
Wang Ch'ang 王昶 (1724–1806)
Wang Cheng 王正
Wang Chi 王績 (585–644)
Wang Chu 王著 (d. ca. 990)

Wang Chu 王洙 (997–1057)
Wang Ch'ung 王充
Wang Fu 王符
Wang Hsi-chih 王羲之 (303–361)
Wang Hsiang 王祥 (d. 265)
Wang Hsien-chieh 王顯節
Wang Hsien-chih 王獻之 (344–388)
Wang Kuei 王珪
Wang Lan 王覽 (206–278)
Wang Mang 王莽
Wang Ning-chih 王寧之
Wang Pao 王褒
Wang Po 王柏 (1197–1274)
Wang Shih-chen 王世貞 (1526–1590)
Wang Ts'an 王粲 (177–217)
Wang Wen-ping 王文秉 (10th century)
Wang Ying-lin 王應麟
Wang Yung 王邕
Wei 魏
Wei Cheng 魏徵
Wei fu-jen 衛夫人 (272–349)
Wei Kuan 衛瓘 (220–291)
Wei Liao-weng 魏了翁 (1178–1237)
Wei Ling-ts'ang, Hsüeh Fa-shao tsao-hsiang-chi 魏靈藏、薛法紹造像記
Wei pei t'i 魏碑體
Wei shu 魏書
wen 文
wen chang 文章
Wen Cheng-ming 文徵明 (1470–1559)
Wen Cheng-ming chi 文徵明集
Wen-ch'üan ming 溫泉銘
wen-hsüeh 文學
Wen-i 文益
wen-jen 文人
wen-jou tun-hou 溫柔敦厚
Wen-te 文德 (T'ang empress; 601–636)
Wen-ti 文帝 (Wei emperor; r. 220–26)
wen ts'ai 文采
Wen-tsung 文宗 (Yüan emperor; r. 1328–23)
Wen T'ung 文同 (1019–1079)
wen tzu 文字
wen wu 文武
Wu 吳
wu 武
Wu 梁武帝 (Liang emperor; r. 502–49)
Wu I 武億 (1745–1799)
Wu Li-li 吳立禮 (11th century)
Wu-men 吳門
Wu-ti 武帝 (Chin emperor; r. 265–89)
Wu Tze-t'ien 武則天 (T'ang empress; r. 684–704)

Yang Hsin 羊欣 (370–442)
Yang Hsiung 揚雄
Yang Ning-shih 楊凝式 (873–954)
Yang Shou-ching 楊守敬 (1839–1915)
Yang Ta-yen tsao-hsiang-chi 楊大眼造像記
Yang Wei-chen 楊維楨 (1296–1370)
Yao 堯
Yao Huai-chen 姚懷珍
Yao Po-to tsao-hsiang-pei 姚伯多造像碑
Yeh 鄴
yen 言
Yen Chen-ch'ing 顏真卿 (709–785)
Yen-hsiu 彥修
Yen Li-pen 閻立本 (600–674)
Yen-shih 偃師
Yen Shih-ku 顏師古
Yen Sung 嚴嵩 (1480–1565)
Yen-t'a Sheng-chiao hsü 雁塔聖教序
Yi shui 伊水
Yin-fu ching 陰符經
Yin Hsi-ku 尹熙古
Ying Shao 應劭
Yü Chi 虞集 (1272– ca. 1333)
Yü Chien-wu 庾肩吾
Yu-ch'ing 右卿
yü-chu 玉箸
Yü Ho 虞龢 (act. ca. 465–471)
Yü Ho 俞和 (1307–1382)
Yü Hsin 庾信 (513–581)
yu-i 有益
Yü Shih-nan 虞世南 (558–638)
Yü Ssu-liang 虞似良
Yü Sung 俞松
Yü Tzu-shan chi 庾子山集
Yü-wen T'ai 宇文泰
Yü-yen-lou shu-fa 玉燕樓書法
yü-yü 郁郁
yüan 願
Yüan Ang 袁昂

Yüan Chen 元楨 (447–496)
Yüan Chen mu-chih 元楨墓誌
Yüan Ch'eng chi Li Shih mu-chih 元澄妃李氏墓誌
Yüan Chien mu-chih 元鑒墓誌
Yüan Chien mu-chih 元簡墓誌
Yüan Ch'üan mu-chih 元詮墓誌
yüan hsi yü fu yin 元夕與婦飲
Yüan Hsü mu-chih 元緒墓誌
Yüan Mao 袁袤 (12th century)
Yüan Pin mu-chih 元彬墓誌
Yüan Shih-ho mu-chih 元始和墓誌
Yüan Shuo-yu 袁說友 (1140–1204)
Yüan Ssu 元思 (468–507)
Yüan Ting mu-chih 元定墓誌
Yüan Tzu 袁滋 (act. ca. 785–813)
yüan-wai-lang 員外郎
Yüan-wu K'o-ch'in 圜悟克勤
Yüan Yen mu-chih 元偃墓誌
Yüan Yü mu-chih 元羽墓誌
yüeh-fu 樂府
Yüeh I lun 樂毅論
yün 韻
Yün-kang shih-k'u 雲岡石窟
Yün-nan 雲南
Yung-cheng 雍正 (Ch'ing emperor; r. 1723–35)
Yün-yang po Cheng Ch'ang-yu tsao-hsiang-chi 雲陽伯鄭長猷造像記

Speakers

Hua Rende
Curator of Special Research Collections
Suzhou University Library

Uta Lauer
Assistant Professor
Heidelberg University

Huiwen Lu
Doctoral Candidate
Department of Art and Archaeology,
Princeton University

Harold Mok
Associate Professor
Department of Fine Arts,
The Chinese University of Hong Kong

Michael Nylan
Professor
Departments of History & Political Sciences and East Asian Studies,
Bryn Mawr College

Shih Shou-ch'ien
Research Fellow
Institute of History and Philology,
Academia Sinica, Taiwan;
Professor
Graduate Institute of Art History,
National Taiwan University

Peter C. Sturman
Associate Professor
Department of the History of Art and Architecture,
University of California, Santa Barbara

Eugene Y. Wang
Assistant Professor
Department of History of Art and Architecture,
Harvard University

Chair

Robert E. Harrist, Jr.
Associate Professor
Department of Art History and Archaeology,
Columbia University